From Java to C#

D1761332

From Java to C#

A Developer's Guide

Heng Ngee Mok

ADDISON-WESLEY

An imprint of **Pearson Education**

London • Boston • Indianapolis • New York • Mexico City • Toronto • Sydney • Tokyo • Singapore
Hong Kong • Cape Town • New Delhi • Madrid • Paris • Amsterdam • Munich • Milan • Stockholm

WITHDRAWN

BIRKBECK
LIBRARY
COLLEGE

PEARSON EDUCATION LIMITED

Head Office:
Edinburgh Gate
Harlow CM20 2JE
Tel: +44 (0)1279 623623
Fax: +44 (0)1279 431059

London Office:
128 Long Acre
London WC2E 9AN
Tel: +44 (0)20 7447 2000
Fax: +44 (0)20 7447 2170
Website: www.it-minds.com
        www.awprofessional.com

First published in Great Britain in 2003

© Pearson Education Ltd 2003

The right of Heng Ngee Mok to be identified as the Author of this Work has been asserted by him in accordance with the Copyright, Designs and Patents Act 1988.

ISBN 0-321-13622-5

British Library Cataloguing in Publication Data
A CIP catalogue record for this book can be obtained from the British Library

Library of Congress Cataloging-in-Publication Data
Mok, Heng Ngee.
   From Java to C#: a developer's guide / Heng Ngee Mok.
      p. cm.
   Includes bibliographical references and index.
   ISBN 0-321-13622-5 (pbk. : alk. paper)
    1. Java (Computer program language) 2. C# (Computer program language) I. Title.

   QA76.73.J38 M645 2003
   005.13'3--dc21

2002034461

All rights reserved; no part of this publication may be reproduced, stored in a retrieval system, or transmitted in any form or by any means, electronic, mechanical, photocopying, recording, or otherwise without either the prior written permission of the Publishers or a licence permitting restricted copying in the United Kingdom issued by the Copyright Licensing Agency Ltd, 90 Tottenham Court Road, London W1P 4LP. This book may not be lent, resold, hired out or otherwise disposed of by way of trade in any form of binding or cover other than that in which it is published, without the prior consent of the Publishers.

10 9 8 7 6 5 4 3 2 1

Typeset by Mathematical Composition Setters Ltd, Salisbury, Wiltshire.

Printed and bound in Great Britain by Biddles Ltd of Guildford and King's Lynn.

The Publishers' policy is to use paper manufactured from sustainable forests.

Dedication

This book goes to my ever-caring Mum, and my darling Siew Leng.

Not forgetting our dear 'fighting hamsters' who accompanied me through the night while I was hacking away at the computer: Hammok, Hammie, Hamzel, and the late Hammy.

Contents

About the author

Heng Ngee Mok is an experienced developer who has been involved in numerous large-scale software enterprise projects based on J2EE. Besides development work, Heng Ngee holds ad hoc training classes for Java and J2EE technology. He lectures regularly at Nanyang Polytechnic's School of IT, a tertiary institution in Singapore.

Heng Ngee writes frequently for *Computer Times*, a weekly local IT newspaper and has been invited to speak at Microsoft's Developer Festival and the official launch of Visual Studio .NET in Singapore. He was awarded Most Valuable Professional status by Microsoft Asia at the first Asia MVP Summit held at Shanghai.

As well as being a Sun Certified Programmer for Java 2, a Sun Certified Web Component Developer for J2EE, and a Microsoft Certified Systems Engineer, Heng Ngee holds a first degree in computer engineering, and is completing his thesis for his postgraduate degree in communications software and networks.

Heng Ngee lives in cosmopolitan and equatorial (read "warm and humid") Singapore. He enjoys nature trekking, lazing in bed with a good book, tinkering with the latest technical toys (he can't cultivate this habit to the fullest because of a meagre income), and poking his nose into foreign cultures on backpacking trips. Contact him at mok@ieee.org both to offer comments about this book, or if you intend to visit his country on a shoestring budget.

Preface

My first real contact with .NET started late in 2001. Since March 2000, I have been hosting a fortnightly Java-related column sponsored by Sun Microsystems (Singapore) in the *Computer Times*. A friend from Microsoft Singapore approached me and handed me a CD containing the beta version of VS .NET so that I could take a look at it and 'maybe write something interesting' if I so desired.

Of course by that time I had already heard of this new infrastructure from Microsoft. Microsoft had been marketing .NET aggressively for ages, and I had once written a relatively superficial introduction to the C# language. At that time, details were sketchy at best and there wasn't even a prototype C# compiler then.

And so I got my hands dirty with VS .NET Beta 2. After getting an understanding of what .NET is all about, I decided to pick up one of the several languages that support it. Naturally C# became my choice. In fact, my personal opinion is that anyone really interested in developing using .NET has only three choices: C#, VB .NET, and J#. In theory you can develop .NET applications using any of the twenty or so '.NET-enabled' languages (including modified versions of Eiffel and even COBOL). Nevertheless you can forget about all except those that came bundled with VS .NET and are supported by Microsoft. I suppose your project manager will not be very pleased if you submit your (albeit working) .NET module in COBOL codes.

Of the three, I chose C#. This is a powerful object-oriented language with its roots in C++ and Java. (Officially, C# has been touted as the offspring of C and C++ only. Despite the fact that Java isn't mentioned once in the C# Language Specification and other Microsoft literature, it is quite evident that the makers of C# had indeed studied and 'inherited' some features from Java.) With C#, you can do anything that can possibly be done within the .NET CLR. VB .NET is a significant improvement over VB 6 with the addition of real object-oriented features such as class inheritance and polymorphic method invocation. Nevertheless, there are tasks which a C# program can do that are beyond the reach of a VB .NET program. C# allows the developer to write *unsafe codes*. You can't do that with VB .NET or J#. The creators of .NET had written huge chunks of the .NET BCLs using C# itself. To me, C# means lots of power, while VB .NET is Microsoft's way of allowing VB 6 developers to migrate to .NET with as little pain as possible. J#, on the other hand, reeks of Visual J++'s failure.

Learning a new programming language from scratch can be an awesome task. Imagine learning a whole new development platform or multi-tiered infrastructure! Nevertheless, it should be noted that most parallel (or competing) technologies are based on similar computer science concepts, and it will be much easier to learn, say, a new object-oriented programming language once you have a good foundation in another object-oriented programming language (assuming you really understand the fundamental concepts behind object-oriented technology).

During my experimentation with .NET Beta, I realized that learning the CLR is easy if you already know what a JVM is. Similarly, picking up ASP .NET is easier if you have done JSP programming before.

As I was learning about .NET, I couldn't help but compare the differences between C# and Java, ASP .NET and JSP, the CLR and the JVM, .NET and the J2EE framework. I am an experienced Java developer and trainer, and as I was reading through books and documentation, I couldn't help noticing that C# and Java are syntactically very similar. I could have skipped a significant portion of the text – if only I knew which sections to skip.

I didn't want to read about how to use the `switch/case` keywords in C# again because I already knew that from my Java knowledge. All I wanted to know was that in C#, `switch` can take in not only numeric types but strings too. That's the difference, and that's all that I needed to know if I wanted to use the `switch/case` keywords in a C# program. I had to read a whole paragraph just to understand one small point. If only there was a book which highlighted just the differences between C# and Java!

Later that year, Microsoft invited me to a public forum and lecture during the Microsoft's Developers' Festival. While I was preparing my talk, entitled '.NET for Java Developers', I made a list highlighting the differences – syntactical and otherwise – between C# and Java. Eventually I decided to turn it into a book (which you are reading now).

The objective is to enable the reader to use current knowledge and experience in Java and J2EE to pick up C# and .NET concepts as quickly as possible. Instead of repeating what I think an average Java developer should already know, I will highlight the *differences* between Java and C#. This book will not explain what an exception is all over again – I shall zoom straight in to how C# treats exceptions differently from Java.

As such, this book assumes a working knowledge of the Java programming language, familiarity with the Java syntax, and experience with basic coding concepts such as exception handling and object-oriented programming.

I have tried to present each section using clear simple examples[1] that are short and to the point. Each section is meant to be quite independent of others, and where such dependent knowledge is required to understand a particular point, I state so. I have assumed that it is your responsibility to integrate all the knowledge gained in the separate sections to make use of the language's features in a complex complementary way. My code examples will avoid doing that for clarity purposes.

In order not to clutter up the real meat of each section, I have placed my personal observations, comments, and URLs where you can obtain more relevant information in footnotes.

I hope you find learning about C# and .NET as enriching an experience as mine.

H.N. Mok (mok@ieee.org)
July 2002

---

1. Have you ever seen tutorial examples which require you to have extensive knowledge of another topic? Such examples really irritate me. I don't like to read long pieces of code just to understand a simple principle, and that's why I have tried to keep my code examples short yet comprehensive.

Introduction

Targeted audience

This book is meant for Java developers who want to learn the C# language as quickly as possible. Basic familiarity with the Java language syntax and semantics, and an academic foundation in object-oriented programming are assumed. (Don't worry, you don't have to be an expert! And you don't need to read this book with a Java reference companion.)

Software prerequisites

In order to try out the C# codes in this book, you will need a copy of .NET SDK[2] or VS .NET from Microsoft. The .NET SDK and .NET Framework will be installed when you install VS .NET. If you are not using VS .NET, you may want to get a color-coded text editor instead of using Notepad for coding purposes.

What this book covers

The fundamental concepts of how .NET works are covered in Part 1. The rest of the book focuses on the C# language itself, with relevant comparisons between C# and the Java programming language.

What is covered:

● fundamental .NET concepts, especially those pertaining to how C# works;

● C# syntax and semantics;

● important .NET BCLs used for multi-threading, file I/O, reflection operations, and some useful collection classes.

What is not covered:

● use of other .NET BCLs;

● use of C# for web services, web forms (ASP .NET), graphics (GDI+), COM inter-operability, database access (ADO .NET);

● other .NET issues such as .NET security and remoting.

2. Can be downloaded from http://msdn.microsoft.com/netframework.

Typographic conventions used

Typeface	Meaning	Example
AaBbCc123	Names of commands, files, and directories	Edit the file `Test.cs`
	interfaces, classes, methods, and variables	Invoke the method `doSomething`
	programming language keywords	Create an instance of the `Human` class
AaBcCc123	Book titles, new words or terms, or words to be emphasized	You *must* invoke this method before instantiating the class

Codes

At the time of writing, a fully working implementation of C# in VS .NET has just been released. The C# codes shown in this book have been compiled and tested using the command line C# compiler (`csc.exe`) of the first final release version of VS .NET.

Errata discoveries

Being a realistic technologist, I expect errors – typos and even the technical variety – in my book. It would help if you can send me an e-mail so that I can make the necessary corrections in future reprints. Useful and constructive comments will be acknowledged in future editions. Expensive chocolate, fine wines, and generous praise are also welcome. You can find the latest erratum list at www.mokhengngee.per.sg/book.

Trademarks

".NET", "Visual Studio .NET", "Visual C# .NET", "Visual Basic .NET" are trademarks of Microsoft Corporation. "Java" is a trademark of Sun Microsystems.

Structure of the book

This book is divided into seven major parts.

Part 1: Introducing .NET and C#

This part gives a brief overview of what .NET and C# are all about without going into the specifics. There is a brief explanation of .NET technologies, and a good conceptual foundation is provided about how .NET applications work. You write your first `Hello World` in Part 1.

Part 2: Classes, methods, and other OO stuff

This part discusses how C# handles classes, namespaces, methods, constructors, and variables. Object-oriented related issues are covered here.

Part 3: Types, operators, and flow control

The language semantics and syntax of C# are almost identical with Java's. This part is written such that you can skim through it relatively quickly to appreciate the differences.

Part 4: Core topics

Topics covered in this part include arrays, event handling, exception handling, reflection, multi-threading, the collection classes, and file I/O. These are major topics which often warrant a *huge* separate chapter in other C# books. This book does not go through the basic ideas but does emphasize how to perform these operations in C#. The chapters in this part assume prior knowledge about exceptions, reflection, and multi-threading.

Part 5: Convenience features

Convenience features[3] are C# features which are good to have but not essential. Basically they help increase programmer productivity by providing shortcuts for the normal ways of doing things. Topics covered include C# properties, indexes, operator overloading, and user-defined conversions. These will all be new topics to a Java developer. Convenience features do not increase the power of a language, but just make it more convenient for a good programmer to use it. Like a double-edged sword, convenience features steepen the learning curve significantly, but give the programmer more elegant ways to accomplish tasks.

Part 6: C#-specific features

This part describes features found in C# which have no equivalents in Java. Topics include C# preprocessor directives, attributes, structures, enums, and unsafe coding. Care has been taken to write this part clearly, so that it is simple to understand yet comprehensive.

Part 7: Appendices

There are six appendices. Here you will find the full list of C# keywords, and their closest equivalents in Java. I have also included C# coding conventions (a good

---

3. I think I am the originator of the term 'convenience features'. I haven't read any literature using that term for C# properties, indexes, and the like.

starting point even before coding commences), a useful summary on how to write XML documentation (which resembles the Javadoc comments) and a short write-up on .NET assemblies. The many (necessary) abbreviations are also defined here – as opposed to the missable first-time definitions sometimes given in the text.

Acknowledgments

I would like to show my appreciation to the following friends. Without their assistance, encouragement, and influence this book would never have materialized. They are (in no particular order):

- Viki Williams, Senior Acquisitions Editor for Addison-Wesley (and avid English football fan) for all your patience and assistance.

- The editorial team and anonymous reviewers working hard at Addison-Wesley for picking out all those bugs and errors which I had (intentionally and unintentionally) embedded in the original manuscript.

- Grace, Hellen and Badi of *Computer Times*, Special Projects Team at Singapore Press Holdings. Writing for you guys opened up new worlds. And Jenny, thanks for introducing me to technical journalism.

- K.C. at Microsoft Singapore for getting me involved with the whole .NET thing, and introducing me to Microsoft's culture.

- Dr Ng Wee Keong, my academic mentor during my days at Nanyang Technological University

- Yixing, Jianhao, Fuzan, Zongrong, and the rest of the NPCC guys. My former classmates Bruce, Robert, Wanwen, Meili, and the late Zhenqiang. It has been more than a decade of friendship!

- Kelvin (aka Cilin), Mathematics whiz and Windows 2000 expert. I would not have got that distinction for that Math paper if not for your coaching (you didn't think I would remember that, did you?).

- My former colleagues at National Computer Systems where I started toying with Java. Huey Min for answering all those weird questions on Java (despite 'being permanently busy') during the years I was mastering that language; Yam Khoon, Chee Ying, Ben, Ghim Howe, Charles, Yong Kwan, Sufen, Otneil, Boon, Amanda, and our PM Ah Hock – thanks for providing me with a good learning environment; Joyce, Bee Ling, Jianwei, and Jiansong – thanks for going through the four-month long IT project management lesson.

- My other family members staying under the same roof who have to tolerate my vampirish life style.

Introducing .NET and C#

Introduction

The chapters in this part are:

- Chapter 1: Introducing .NET
- Chapter 2: Introducing C#
- Chapter 3: JUMP to .NET and J#
- Chapter 4: Hello C#!

This part serves as an introduction to the rest of the book. Though it is possible not to mention anything about .NET in a book about C# (C# is a standard in its own right), I would suggest at least a rudimentary understanding of Microsoft's grand .NET plan. Knowing what .NET is all about and the role that C# plays in it gives a good 'big picture' view and an appreciation of why C# has been designed in certain ways.

Chapters 1 and 2 give a whirlwind introduction to the world of .NET, including some other .NET-related technologies, without going into details. Important concepts such as how CLR works are covered in Chapter 1. I have also taken the liberty of including some personal opinions about the C# language in Chapter 2.

J# is briefly introduced in Chapter 3. Although this book is about C#, it will be useful to be at least acquainted with J#, especially since you have a Java background.

Part 1 ends with the all important "Hello World" program. If this is the first time you have met this new language, I highly recommend going through the Hello World exercise before continuing with the other parts of this book.

chapter 1

Introducing .NET

The creation of C# is part of the .NET initiative, and a brief introduction about .NET here seems timely.[1] It is important to get a rudimentary understanding of what .NET is, and the related technologies, in order to know how C# fits into the big picture. Understanding how CLR works is also important if you want to write a C# program.

1.1 Evolution: from COM to .NET

I am going to start by telling the story of how .NET came into being. Skip this section if you don't like history lessons.

1.1.1 The pioneers: COM, MTS and DCOM

Two significant Microsoft inventions to dominate the enterprise arena were MTS and COM technologies in the mid 90s.

If you are unsure of COM, you can just treat a COM module as a piece of software which has been written so that it is self-sufficient (properly encapsulated) and can be used by other classes without them knowing how the COM object is implemented internally. If this description reminds you of Javabeans, you are correct. A COM object is Microsoft's version of Javabeans. They are software components that can be bought off-the-shelf and integrated into your own applications. Talk about COM, and you might hear phrases such as 'reuse through interfaces' and 'component-based development'.

---

1. I had initially wanted to put this whole section in an appendix since the focus of this book is on the C# language rather than .NET. Nevertheless, it really is necessary to know at least a bit about .NET. Have you ever met someone who claims to be a Java developer but doesn't know that Java's platform independence is achieved via the JVM? In the same way, a C# developer should understand how language independence (and probably platform independence in the future) is achieved via the .NET CLR.

In theory, it doesn't matter which language is used to write COM components – those written in Visual C++ can be used in the same way in Visual Basic codes and vice versa because COM interfaces[2] are used for communication.

MTS is a middle-tier (or middleware) server which takes care of issues like transactions and security. MTS is like an EJB container in J2EE terminology, but not as complex. MTS is a layer built on top of COM and DCOM. It provides plumbing services in very much the same way as your EJB container provides them to the enterprise beans living within.

Like enterprise beans, COM components live in the MTS, which also provides them with services such as transaction, connection pooling, security, thread pooling, synchronization, and an administrative user interface.

DCOM is a remote invocation protocol from Microsoft. Like Java's RMI, DCOM's usage has been limited due to its platform bias.

1.1.2   Distributed interNetwork Architecture

Then came what Microsoft's marketing team coined as Distributed interNetwork Architecture. DNA is built with Windows 2000 as the backend server operating system working together with other Microsoft servers, such as Exchange 5.5/2000, SQL Server 7/2000, Site Server (or the newer Commerce Server 2000), SNA Server (or the newer Host Integration Server 2000), and others. Besides emphasizing *n*-tiered architecting (separation of presentation, business logic, and data services), DNA also saw the merger of COM and MTS into what is known as COM+.

COM+ improves over COM and MTS through new features such as role-based security (at method level), object pooling (as opposed to thread pooling of MTS), queued components (to work with MSMQ) and COM+ events. COM+ events are services which provide a mechanism for COM components to publish or subscribe to events.

That's all old stuff today.

Originally named COM+ 2.0, .NET blew COM and COM+ away with an entirely new framework, new programming languages, new code libraries, and new ideas. Although it is still possible for .NET components to communicate with COM components and vice versa,[3] it seems that technologies like COM, DCOM and COM+ will be labeled 'legacy' in the near future.

---

2. Not to be confused with 'interfaces' as used in Java or C#, COM interfaces are more like the IDL files of CORBA. It describes the public methods of a COM component, so that external codes are able to invoke them.
3. .NET treats COM components as legacy pieces of code. You can still use COM components in .NET applications by using a wrapper. COM components can also communicate with .NET codes via a wrapper. COM interoperation (or how to make legacy COM codes work with .NET codes) is an important topic in most C# and .NET books, but has been excluded in this one.

1.2 What exactly is .NET?

.NET is a general term which encompasses a variety of technologies and products.[4] .NET also contains technologies to reach out to the Internet via web services – a very hot topic today with a very bright future in distributed computing.

In Microsoft's own words, Microsoft .NET is "Microsoft's XML Web services platform." Using this definition for .NET is as good as calling J2EE "Sun's web application platform."

.NET is much more than that and, depending on your role in your software organization, your view of .NET may not be the same. To a system administrator, .NET means rolling out and deploying the new range of Windows .NET Server and the .NET Enterprise Servers. To an end user, .NET means a convenient single sign-in on the Internet via .NET My Passport, and .NET My Services.

So, what is .NET about for the developer?

To a developer (who this book is for), .NET signifies a new programming paradigm, new programming languages to master, and a new runtime engine. A web application developer will concentrate on ASP.NET and XML web services, while a desktop application developer will be writing Windows forms. A pocket PC developer will be mastering the .NET Compact Framework and the VS .NET extensions for writing constrained applications.

Picture a runtime platform which sits on top of the Windows operating system. This runtime platform supports the execution of applications by providing a basic infrastructure such as automatic memory management, security checking, and type checking. This runtime platform includes a wide selection of BCLs which the applications running within can invoke. One nice thing about these applications is that they can be written in any language. Another nice thing is that the applications can be of any type, not just common desktop applications which show a spreadsheet or word processor, but also web applications, servers providing web services, database clients – in fact almost anything that a program can do. That's the picture of the .NET world for the developer.

In essence, .NET encompasses two major components as far as the developer is concerned:

- A new runtime environment for new .NET applications to run within. Some use the term 'framework' to describe this runtime environment.

- A set of BCLs which .NET applications use. A BCL not only enables .NET applications to reach out to the Windows API, but is also a rich set of classes with lots of useful functionality.

I shall briefly describe each aspect of .NET.

---

4. For the general 'official definition' (which includes lots of marketing), check out www.microsoft.com/net/defined.

1.3 Multiple .NET programming languages and VS.NET

.NET is about multiple programming languages. VS .NET, the new version after Visual Studio 6.0, is a good tool for writing .NET applications and components. VS .NET comes with a few programming languages that are supported by Microsoft: C# .NET, VB .NET, Visual C++ .NET, JScript .NET and the last (surprising) inclusion, J# .NET.[5] Other vendors and educational institutions are independently developing other languages, or adapting current ones, to target the .NET platform. At the time of writing, there are about 30 such languages ready or in the process of being developed.[6]

The idea is to have a huge heterogeneous base of .NET developers writing .NET codes in their preferred language. It doesn't matter if a module is written in C# or J#, or managed C++, they all behave similarly when running on the .NET runtime.

This is very unlike Java's strategy. As shown in Table 1.1, Java insisted on having only one programming language (namely Java itself) and the ability for the codes to be run on multiple operating systems. .NET speaks about having the possibility of writing code in a theoretically infinite number of languages, but running them on a single operating system (Windows).[7,8]

TABLE 1.1 The two platforms emphasize different things

Java	.NET
One language (Java)	Multiple languages (C#, J#, managed C++, VB .NET, etc)
Many platforms (operating systems)	One platform (Windows)

5. The announcement of J# was an eleventh-hour surprise. When VS .NET was announced, apparently there hadn't been any plans to include a successor for the defunct Visual J++. (In fact, the first final release of VS .NET does not include J#. The final version of J# was recently released in July '02.) Visual J++ was prevented from evolving further after Microsoft lost a court case involving the illegal extension of the Java programming language. Sun alleged that Microsoft had violated the Java license agreement, and had attempted to kill off Java's platform independence. I believe the decision to include a Visual J++ successor in VS .NET is an attempt to provide another transition path for the huge number of Java developers out there when they move over to .NET development.
6. More well-known examples of .NET languages include Eiffel, COBOL, Fortran, Perl and Component Pascal. The rest are mostly obscure unheard-of languages used only for specific academic purposes. For a list of official "language partners", check out http://msdn.microsoft.com/vstudio/partners/language/default.asp.
7. Is it possible for .NET applications to run on operating systems other than Windows? See section 1.10 for a discussion.
8. Some may argue that the Java platform can be multi-language too. A good example is the Jython language which is an adaptation of Python so that the source codes compile to Java byte codes. Nevertheless, I would still consider the Java platform a single-language solution. How many developers use Jython instead of Java? In fact, most have not even heard of Jython.

As far as Microsoft is concerned, the ability to write .NET code on C#, J# and VB .NET is an essential move to provide a smooth transition for current C++, J++, and VB 6 developers to move over to .NET.[9]

The multi-language nature of .NET is generally seen as an advantage. It gives developers more choice. The idea is that if you are already a VB 6 developer, move on to VB .NET instead of C#. Despite having to learn some new stuff,[10] at least you are more at home with the comfort of the familiar VB syntax.

Another point I would like to make is the true language interoperability nature of .NET languages – something I really like.

True language interoperability[11] means that:

● You can write two separate classes – one in J# and the other in C#.

● These two classes can work with each other as if they have been written in the same language – the J# class can invoke a method in the C# class and vice versa.

● Better still, you can actually *inherit* one of the classes from the other despite them being written in different languages!

VS .NET is a true *integrated* development environment that enables you to open J# files, C# files, and VB .NET files all within the same work space. It has a debugger which actually steps through the codes written in different .NET languages during a trace, so that you can see exactly which line of which class is being stepped through regardless of the language that class has been written in.

How is this support for multiple languages achieved? The secret lies in MSIL and the .NET CLR. See Table 1.2.

TABLE 1.2 Parallel components between the Java/J2EE solution and the .NET solution

Java	.NET
Java source codes	.NET language source codes
Java byte codes	MSIL
JVM/JRE	.NET CLR/.NET runtime

9. Try breaking the news that Microsoft will no longer be supporting VB for .NET, and that all VB 6 developers will have to learn a new programming language (with a weird name called C#) closely related to the dreaded C/C++. There would be a global software revolt with current VB developers dumping Microsoft altogether. There are *so* many VB developers out there now and Microsoft somehow has to protect their intellectual skill set!

10. There's a great deal of difference between VB 6 and VB .NET due to the inclusion of true OO support (which is absent in VB 6) such as polymorphic method invocation and class inheritance. There are other new features such as multi-threading support. I suppose there is a wider gap between VB 6 and VB .NET compared to C++ and C#, or even Java and C#. I have read articles on how VB 6 developers are commenting that VB .NET is a whole new language itself. Well, at least the syntax is familiar to VB 6 developers.

11. The closest COM ever got to language interoperability is that you can write a COM component in VB 6 and call its methods from a C++ class, and vice versa. All this is achieved via a language-independent COM interface. There is no way you can do anything more than that using COM. .NET brought new meaning to language interoperability never seen before.

1.4 Intermediate language

How does Java achieve platform independence? Java source codes are compiled into byte codes (which are stored in .class files) by the Java compiler. Byte codes are portable because when they are executed, they are interpreted on-the-fly by the JVM for that specific platform. The JVM – for say the Macintosh operating system – understands both byte codes and how to translate them into native Macintosh machine codes that the Mac operating system understands. Similarly, the JVM for the Windows operating system knows how to translate byte codes into native machine codes for the Windows operating system.

The idea is suspiciously similar for .NET (see Figure 1.1). .NET source codes (whether written in J#, C# or any other .NET language) are compiled by a language-specific compiler into MSIL (or Common Intermediate Language-CIL) – these are both commonly abbreviated to IL. IL is .NET's equivalent to Java byte codes. IL codes are then distributed as .NET assembly files to the client where they are executed.

On the client which has the .NET runtime installed, the IL code executes within CLR. The CLR[12] works very much like JVM or JRE. It provides a virtual environment in which the IL codes 'bathe'.

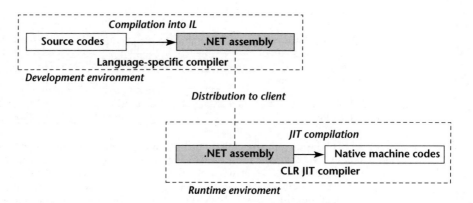

FIGURE 1.1 Language-specific source codes are precompiled into IL codes which are language-neutral, then distributed in assembly files. On the client machine, IL codes are then JIT-compiled into native machine codes when executed within the CLR.

12. The CLR is also commonly know as the '.NET runtime'. These two terms are synonymous.

1.5 The .NET Common Language Runtime

The CLR provides several basic runtime services:

- *Class loading.* A class loader loads the assembly into memory.

- *Assembly integrity check.* In addition to IL codes, each .NET assembly[13] contains a manifest. The manifest contains a hash code of the assembly contents. A check is made to see if the assembly contents have been altered based on this hash code. The CLR refuses to run assemblies that have been altered. This is an additional layer of protection to prevent malicious and illegal alteration of assemblies after distribution.

  This feature is not found in Java. The only way one can prove that a piece of Java byte code (such as an applet) hasn't been tampered with is to sign it with a digital signature. Verification is performed using the corresponding public keys of the signer.

- *Security checking.* .NET allows role-based security and code-based security. When dealing with role-based security, the application is limited to security restrictions placed on the Windows account which the process is using to run the application. With code-based security, certain security policies are laid out for a particular .NET application so that it cannot do more than it is supposed to do. The .NET application fails to run if the CLR determines that it has violated the security policy set out for this application.

- *Memory type safety checking.* .NET codes are considered to be memory type safe if they ever only access memory in a way that the CLR can control. Hence a memory type safe application will never attempt to read or write to a memory address that does not belong to it. Java developers should be familiar with this concept, since Java is also a memory safe language.

- *JIT compilation.* After passing the security and integrity checks, IL codes are compiled on-the-fly into native machine codes which the underlying operating system (Windows) can understand. The JIT compiler[14] works in very much the same way as most standard Java JIT compilers do.

  Instead of compiling everything into native machine code first, the JIT compiler only compiles methods when they are first invoked. The compiled codes are then cached so that the next time the same method is invoked, the native codes for that method in the cache are executed directly.

13. In short, a .NET assembly consists of individual software components placed together in a logical group. An assembly can consist of a single class or multiple classes. Assemblies are basically IL codes compiled from any .NET language. Refer to Appendix F for a more detailed explanation.
14. A JIT compiler is also known as a JITer in .NET literature.

Generally, JIT compilation yields superior runtime performance compared to the compile-everything-once-then-start-running strategy for most programs.

● *Garbage collection (automatic memory management)*. An important component of the CLR is the garbage collector. Like JVM's, the CLR garbage collector runs as a background thread and periodically sweeps through memory to detect and collect unreferenced objects. In .NET, you no longer have to manually deallocate memory for unwanted objects,[15] the CLR does it for you.

One difference between Java's garbage collector and the CLR's is that for the latter, it is possible to programmatically *force* a garbage collection sweep to occur. Calling `System.gc()` or `Runtime.gc()` in Java does not guarantee that a garbage collection sweep occurs. The invocation simply informs the Java garbage collector that the Java program *would like* to perform a garbage collection. According to the JVM specification, the Java garbage collector has absolute discretion as to whether it wants to perform a collection sweep or not.

For the CLR, calling `System.GC.Collect()` will force a collection sweep. Hence, although we can say that both garbage collection mechanisms are non-deterministic,[16] there is a bit more control over the process in .NET than in Java.

Another way to look at the CLR is as a 'buffer layer' between the Win32 API[17] and your IL codes (see Figure 1.2). Instead of directly calling these Win32 API functions, .NET applications use classes and methods of the .NET BCL (this will be introduced in section 1.7.3) to invoke operating system services.

There are differences between how Java runs byte codes on a JVM compared to how .NET runs IL codes in the CLR.

Java is fundamentally an interpreted language.[18,19] An interpreted language relies on a runtime interpreter which deciphers the codes (in Java's case, byte codes) for the local operating system during execution. Interpreted languages generally

---

15. For those with a C/C++ background: C# no longer needs you to `delete` objects in the destructor. So one trump card that Java has been holding over C++ has been annulled in C# – automatic garbage collection can help prevent some of those sneaky memory leaks. Be cautious here though – like Java, if you keep creating new objects and keep them referenced, you can still get an `OutOfMemoryError`. Only objects that are no longer referenced are garbage collected.

16. Meaning that our programs cannot determine when the next garbage collection sweep will occur.

17. The Win32 API is a set of functions provided by Microsoft for accessing operating system services. Because the Windows source codes are kept secret, Windows application developers can only interact with the Windows operating system through this set of API functions.

18. Other interpreted languages include BASIC, LISP, and SmallTalk. C and C++ are compiled languages.

19. There are (expensive) tools called native compilers which can convert all the byte codes into native machine-specific codes. Such precompiled codes do not need a JVM during execution, and generally perform better (depending on how good the native compiler is), but are no longer portable. Examples of such tools include Jove (www.instantiations.com), TowerJ (www.towerj.com), and Excelsior JET (www.excelsior-usa.com).

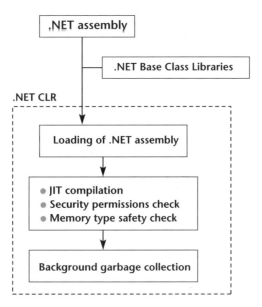

FIGURE 1.2   Services provided by the CLR are similar to those provided by the JVM.

perform worse than compiled languages because interpretation can be an expensive process. Every time a method is invoked, the interpretation process kicks in regardless of how many times the same method has been invoked. In the case of compiled languages, the source codes are all compiled into native machine codes. During runtime, the machine codes are executed directly – there isn't an additional layer of runtime interpretation by a runtime engine.

IL differs from Java here. IL is not interpreted but compiled on-the-fly into native machine codes by the .NET runtime. When a particular method coded in IL is invoked, the JIT compiler kicks in, converts the method from IL into native machine codes, and stores them in a cache. The next time the same method is invoked, the native codes from the cache are retrieved instead.

In performance, .NET on-the-fly compilation does have an advantage over *traditional* Java on-the-fly interpretation. However, it must be noted that most *modern* JVMs are implemented with a JIT compiler too (although this is not required). Most Java runtime engines today adopt the same JIT compilation model that .NET is running on.[20] Some JIT-based JVMs even allow you to turn the JIT feature on or off.

Theoretically, IL can be decompiled back into easy-to-understand source codes of

20. A good example of a very efficient Java JIT compiler is Sun's Hotspot Java technology engine incorporated into JRE 1.3 and beyond. Besides on-the-fly JIT compilation of byte codes into native codes, Hotspot uses heuristics to determine which parts of a program need to be optimized for better performance. This adaptive optimization is achieved mainly via code inlining.

any language[21] in very much the same way Java byte codes can be reversed back into Java source codes using a Java decompiler tool.

1.6 Competing in parallel with Java technologies

For developers, the picture of .NET represents one that competes directly with Java and J2EE technologies. Although most of the computer science concepts behind

Table 1.3 High-level comparison of parallel technologies in J2EE and .NET.

	Java/J2EE	.NET
General		
Language	Java	VB .NET, C#, C++, J# and many other third-party languages
Platforms	Windows, Solaris/Unix/Linux, Macintosh	Windows only (possibly Linux and FreeBSD in the near future)
Web/application server	A large variety to choose from: Tomcat (servlet/JSP), JBoss (EJB), Weblogic Application Server, Oracle Application Server, Borland Enteprise Server, Silverstream Server, HP Bluestone, JRun Application Server, IBM Websphere, Sun ONE Server (formerly iPlanet Application Server), etc.	Microsoft IIS, Windows 2000, Windows .NET Server
IDE/tools	A large variety to choose from: Forte, JBuilder, Netbeans, JCreator, Kawa, Visual Café, Visual Age, etc.	Microsoft VS .NET
Technologies		
Presentation tier technology	Servlets and JSP	ASP .NET
Business tier technology	EJB	.NET managed components
Technology for cell phones and PDAs	J2ME	.NET compact framework
Significant distribution protocols	Java RMI (RMI-IIOP or RMI-JRMP), CORBA IIOP (using Java IDL), SOAP (for web services)	DCOM, SOAP (for web services)
API classes		
Database access API	JDBC	ADO .NET
Messaging API	JMS	MSMQ
Web services API	Java Web Service Developer's Pack (includes JAXP)	Part of the .NET BCL

21. No such tool exists at the time of writing, but I am pretty sure such tools will surface soon.

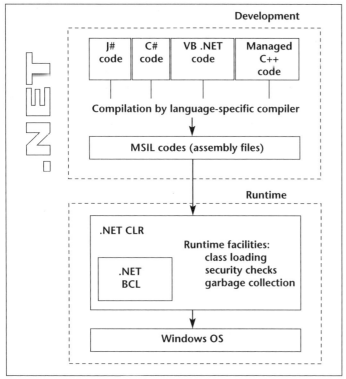

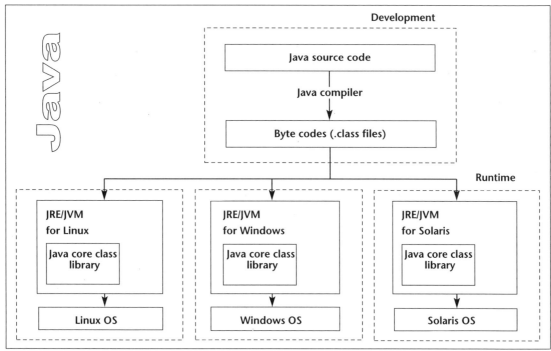

FIGURE 1.3 Comparing .NET and Java.

these two paradigms are similar, in most cases they represent two completely different ways of doing the same thing.[22]

Table 1.3 shows the parallelism and directly competing products/methodologies between .NET and J2EE. A detailed discussion is, unfortunately, beyond the scope of this book. Figure 1.3 shows the comparison in block diagram form. Finally, Figure 1.4 gives a schematic view of the parallelism.

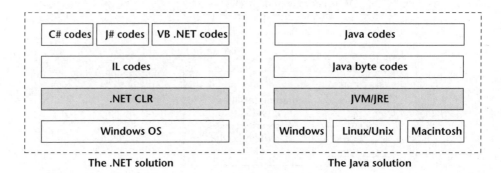

FIGURE 1.4   A simplified schematic showing parallel comparison of how .NET and Java work – .NET focuses on language independence, while Java's game is platform independence.

1.7 Common language infrastructure

You have seen that .NET supports multiple languages because the source codes of these languages are eventually compiled into IL codes. This has a serious implication – there must be a common minimum standard which all these .NET languages need to follow. There are certain rules that all must adhere to (or else they will never be able to be converted into the universal IL code). This set of rules is the Common Language Specification (CLS).

The Common Type System (CTS) (which will be elaborated on later) and the CLS form a major part of the Common Language Infrastructure (CLI) specification.[23,24]

22. I have read several white papers on the Internet attempting to compare J2EE with .NET. Unfortunately, no matter how unbiased the parties are trying to be towards the two technologies, a trained eye can often tell the prejudices 'encoded' between the lines. I have yet to see a really neutral and fair comparison released by an impartial third party such as an academic institution or standards body. If you try to use such comparisons, take them with a pinch of salt. It will be difficult for someone familiar with only one of the technologies to fully appreciate the facts and separate them from the red herrings.
23. The CLI is ECMA-335 (blue cover). You can download it free of charge in pdf/postscript format at www.ecma.ch/ecma1/STAND/ecma-335.htm.

1.7.1 The Common Language Specification

It is important that .NET objects – regardless of whether they are written in .NET COBOL or C# – should only expose (i.e. make protected or public) features that are common to all other .NET languages which they interoperate with. The CLS is the set of common language features that must be adhered to if you want to develop a new programming language targeted at .NET.

It is possible for a language to extend the feature set specified in the CLS with additional language features. But exposure of these extended features for interfacing with external classes may spell trouble for interoperation. If you want to write components that can interoperate seamlessly with other .NET components (which may be written in any other .NET language), ensure that you use only CLS-compliant features of your language.

Examples of some clauses in the CLS are:

- global static fields and methods of a class are prohibited;
- only the following data types are CLS-compliant – Byte, Int16, Int32, Int64, Single, Double, Boolean, Char, Decimal, IntPtr and String;
- methods are allowed to be overloaded based on the number and types of their parameters only;
- operator overloading is *not* CLS-complaint;
- pointer types and function pointer types are *not* CLS-compliant;
- for two identifiers to be distinct, they must differ by more than just their case.

A good example to illustrate non CLS-compliance is the case sensitivity of identifiers. Some CLS-compliant .NET languages can be case sensitive (such as C#, or J#) while others do not differentiate between an upper case 'A' and a lower case 'a' (such as VB .NET). For the latter group of languages, the variable name apple is not distinguishable from APPLE, nor aPPlE. Using a case sensitive language such as C#, you can easily declare two distinct variables APPLE and apple within the same scope and make the program work. This is because C# has a feature set bigger than that specified in the CLS – in particular, the feature of case sensitivity.

Nevertheless, a class written in this manner may not interoperate with another class written in VB .NET for, as far as VB is concerned, the variables APPLE and apple within the same scope are identical.

Here is another example. Most (not all) of the types in the .NET BCL are

---

24. Microsoft has released a set of source codes for the CLI standards. Called the Shared Source CLI Implementation, it is freely downloadable and the licence permits you to modify and redistribute the source codes. The Shared Source CLI Implementation is not the 'real' source codes of commercial release standard, but it will interest inquisitive developers (who really have time on their hands), educational institutions, and software companies interested in porting .NET to another platform. Get it from http://msdn.microsoft.com /library/default.asp?url=/library/en-us/Dndotnet/html/mssharsourcecli.asp?frame=true

CLS-compliant. An example of a non-CLS compliant type is the unsigned integer.[25] C# supports unsigned integers via the uint keyword. However, the CLS does not support unsigned types. Again, if you want to ensure that your C# codes are CLS-compliant, your public methods should not return unsigned variables even though the language provides such a feature. It is all right if you use uint *local* variables or private class members because they will not be visible outside the method or class. However, public or protected members in a non-private class are 'exposed' and hence should follow CLS rules if you want your codes to be CLS-compliant.

To ensure that your classes do work with other classes written in other .NET languages, it may be worth spending some time taking a look at the CLS.[26]

According to Microsoft, "the CLS was designed to be large enough to include the language constructs that are commonly needed by developers, yet small enough that most languages are able to support it."

1.7.2   The common type specification

I mentioned earlier that the CLI also includes the CTS (see Figure 1.5).

Communication infrastructures which support interactivity between components on heterogeneous systems usually need a common set of types shared by all the different systems.[27] Similarly, in order for .NET to be cross-language, there is a set of common shared types used by all .NET languages.

The CTS defines how types are declared, used and managed during runtime. It performs the following roles:

● enables cross-language integration and type safety;

● defines rules that .NET languages must follow to ensure that objects written in different languages can interoperate.

25. There is no such thing as an unsigned integer in Java (although if you have a background in C/C++, you would definitely have heard of the unsigned keyword). All Java numeric variables support signed storage, so that for a 32-bit signed integer (the Java int) one bit is always reserved for the sign bit, leaving only 31 to store the actual value. There is no way to 'save' on that bit even if you are sure this int variable will never be used to store negative values. Unsigned integers are integers that have been declared so that they can be used only to store positive values. That leaves a 32-bit integer all 32 bits for storing the numeric value, thus effectively doubling the *positive* range of values it can store compared to a signed 32-bit integer. In C/C++, unsigned integers are declared using the unsigned keyword. In C#, there is no such keyword.

26. See http://msdn.microsoft.com/library/default.asp?url=/library/en-us/cpguide/html/cpcon writingcls-compliantcode.asp for some useful information on writing CLS-compliant codes.

27. A good example is CORBA. CORBA has a set of common IDL (language-neutral) types and a mapping table for each language that supports CORBA. This mapping table defines the language's type to its corresponding IDL type. (for example, Java's java.lang.String maps to IDL type string, and Java's byte maps to IDL type octet.) This enables different CORBA-enabled languages to pass objects of IDL types to one another without affecting the way the object is typed within the language itself.

Like Java, .NET languages are strongly typed.[28] According to the CTS, all types can be broadly categorized into two groups – value types and reference types. Like value types in Java, value types in .NET are types that store a value. Similarly, reference types are types that store the memory address of an object. It is possible to have two reference types referring to the same object stored at a shared memory location.

Adherence to both the CTS and CLS ensures that codes written in any .NET language interoperates with codes written in any other .NET language.

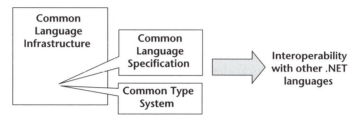

FIGURE 1.5   Both the CLS and CTS are part of the CLI specification.

1.7.3   The base class libraries

What you can do with a language will be severely limited if it doesn't come with a rich set of ready-made classes that you can just use. Like Java's core API classes, .NET comes with a set of .NET BCLs.[29]

However, unlike Java's core classes, which avoid any platform-specific features (and hence provides platform independence at the expense of not being able to utilize platform-specific features[30]), .NET's BCL contains powerful classes for your codes to interact with Windows-specific features. For example, a .NET program can use classes in the .NET BCL to read from or write to the Windows registry.[31] The .NET BCLs in turn interact with the underlying Win32 APIs to perform their jobs.

The BCL includes APIs that cover almost every aspect of development:[32]

● Windows GUI, controls, frames

28. In the quest for strong typing, VB .NET has got rid of the `variant` type of VB 6.
29. For Visual C++ programmers, you can roughly equate the BCL to MFC. But the BCL is much richer and much more powerful. There isn't much you can do with MFC besides the 'common stuff' such as drawing forms.
30. In Java, the only way you can write code which utilizes OS-specific features is via JNI. JNI bridges native codes (perhaps written in natively-compiled C/C++) to platform independent Java codes. This is a significant trade-off to maintain Java's platform independence.
31. As such, it becomes impossible to port 100% of the .NET framework to other operating systems – another reason why most would still classify .NET as a 'Windows-only thing'. Refer to section 1.10 for porting discussions.
32. This book does not describe the BCL in detail, although Chapters 16–19 introduce some useful classes.

- Networking
- Web browsing
- File system access
- Windows registry access
- Web forms (ASP .NET)
- COM interoperability
- Database access (ADO .NET).

A large portion of the BCL has been written in C# itself.

Instead of calling the Win32 API functions[33] directly, .NET applications use methods of classes in the BCL, (see Figure 1.6). While traditional windows programs access the operating system directly by calling the Win32 API. Visual C++ developers have the luxury of using a set of API classes called MFC which made programming Windows applications so much easier. The MFC abstracts low level details such as the creation of a Windows frame or button. Unfortunately, one common grouse of C++ programmers is that the MFC is not comprehensive enough – programmers still have to make direct calls to the Win32 API for less commonly used functionalities absent in the MFC. .NET applications access the operating system's functions via the BCL and never directly, because they execute within the .NET CLR.

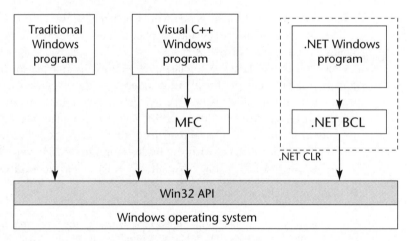

FIGURE 1.6   Invoking Windows functionality in different ways.

33. Notice that I used the term 'functions' instead of 'methods'. The Win32 API has been written in non-object-oriented C. Most of the Win32 functions take in C pointers and references, and programming directly to the Win32 API can be difficult for programmers inexperienced (or careless) with pointers.

1.8   Other .NET-related technologies

It is only fair to mention other important .NET technologies, such as ASP .NET, and web services. However, beyond the brief introduction here, these topics are out of the scope of this book.

1.8.1   ASP .NET

You must have heard of Active Server Pages.[34] ASP is a popular HTML template scripting technology for generating dynamic web pages. Java's equivalent of ASP is Sun's JSP technology.

ASP .NET[35] has been improved significantly over the previous version which supported only scripting languages. In ASP .NET, you can write ASP forms in a .NET language of your choice. As well as a more robust and cleaner architecture, ASP .NET is supposed to perform better and be more maintainable. I am expecting many new web applications to be written in ASP .NET because it really is a great improvement over ASP 3.0.

1.8.2   XML web services

.NET supports the creation of web services using VS .NET.[36] You can expose methods in your classes as web services easily, post them to a UDDI server, and consume web services offered by compatible servers. Most of the mundane tasks (creation of WSDL files, creation of SOAP packets, etc.) are automated by VS .NET and the developer is left to concentrate on the business logic codes.

1.8.3   .NET enterprise servers

You might have heard of them – SQL Server 2000, Commerce Server 2000, Exchange Server 2000, BizTalk Server 2000, Host Integration Server 2000, and others. These server tools from Microsoft are often mentioned together when .NET is being discussed. Each .NET enterprise server is a member of Microsoft's enterprise server family, and each has a specific part to play on the .NET football field.

Be aware that these so-called .NET enterprise servers do *not* yet run on .NET technology (notice that most of them have been released in year 2000, while .NET was

---

34. ASP was one of Microsoft's earliest answers to boring static HTML pages, and the first credible web technology to replace CGI. The last version of ASP before ASP .NET is 3.0.

35. ASP .NET was formerly called 'ASP+'. You can still find references to 'ASP+' in older literature.

36. The exposure of EJB or Servlet methods by Java servers has yet to be standardized, and although different Java tools (such as Forte for Java, Enterprise Edition, JBuilder 7 and BEA Weblogic Workshop) can be used to provide web services, they do so in their own proprietary manner. The forthcoming J2EE 1.4 specification will cover web services.

only finalized and released in 2002). I suppose they have been called .NET enterprise servers because they are still relevant today, and someone from marketing had a final say. For example, Commerce Server 2000 (which works together with Microsoft IIS to host a customizable commercial-quality e-commerce website) runs on ASP 3.0 rather than ASP .NET.[37]

So much for confusing names.

1.8.4   Windows .NET Server[38]

The Windows .NET server[39] will be the successor of the Windows 2000 server family. Built on the foundation of Windows 2000, Windows .NET server comes in four editions:

- Windows .NET *Web Server* – a lightweight dedicated server for hosting web applications and XML web services written in ASP .NET.

- Windows .NET *Standard Server* – a business-level server which supports the 'norms' of server operations such as file and printer sharing, etc.

- Windows .NET *Enterprise Server* – with features such as 4-node clustering and support for eight CPUs.

- Windows .NET *Datacenter Server* – for mission-critical applications.

Naturally, this new operating system integrates with other Microsoft technologies including .NET Passport, Microsoft Active Directory, and COM+ component architecture with XML web services through the .NET framework. It also provides native support for SOAP-based XML message parsing in MSMQ.

1.8.5   .NET My Services[40]

Formerly codenamed HailStorm, .NET My Services is a set of user-oriented XML web services provided and administered by Microsoft. A user of My Services is authenti-

---

37. At the time of writing, the only .NET enterprise server which really integrates with .NET technology is Commerce Server 2002. This is the successor to Commerce Server 2000 and was released in April 2002 and has 'native support' for the .NET platform. The suite works with the .NET framework and you can create Commerce Server applications from within VS .NET. Following Commerce Server 2002, I believe the other .NET enterprise servers will be 'converted' one at at time, to work with the .NET framework in future releases.
38. Check out the official website at www.microsoft.com/windows.netserver
39. The Windows .NET Server is currently in beta 3 at the time of writing. Hence, the information presented here is volatile.
40. Check out the official website at www.microsoft.com/myservices. At the time of writing, .NET Alerts 1.0 is already live. Other web services in the family are scheduled to be released late 2002. From the .NET Alert website, public users can sign in (via their .NET passport account) and opt to receive notifications from a list of third party providers. Notifications can be in the form of a pop-up window (if you are online and running Microsoft Messenger), or an SMS message on your cell phone.

cated via .NET Passport, which also stores your personal information. Through My Services the user can share information with any trusted third party, which may also provide its own web services. Relevant information stored at a central repository can be passed around and utilized without requiring the user to re-enter such information.

The initial set of .NET My Services includes:

- .NET Profile (your personal particulars);
- .NET Contacts (address book);
- .NET Alerts (alert message subscription);
- .NET Calendar (personal time management);
- .NET Wallet (stores receipts, payment information, and transaction records);
- .NET Inbox (stores e-mail, voice mail).

Third party developers can create SOAP-aware applications and portable devices that consume .NET My Services. These applications can also expose their own functionalities as web services which are compatible with .NET My Services.

1.8.6 .NET Passport[41]

.NET Passport is Microsoft's solution for an internet-based single sign-in (SSI).[42] Launched in 1999, it is a suite of web-based services that involves keeping a user's identity and encrypted credit card information at a central server. The merchant signs up with Microsoft and links its site to Passport (for a fee). When users wish to make an online purchase, they identify themselves by logging in using this Passport account. They do not need to key in personal particulars (shipping address, credit card information etc) all over again when they need to make a purchase because that information is already linked to their Passport account.

1.8.7 .NET Compact Framework

Java has J2ME for constrained devices; .NET has the Compact Framework. While the .NET Framework is suitable for desktop PCs, the .NET CF is a subset of the .NET framework meant for smaller 'smart' devices (personal digital assistants (PDA) running the Pocket PC operating system, TV set-top boxes, intelligent cell phones, etc).

41. Check out the official websites at www.microsoft.com/myservices/passport, and www.passport.com
42. In late 2001, Sun Microsystems, together with other vendors, formed an initiative which is similar to .NET Passport. Named the Liberty Alliance, this group aims to provide similar SSI services for users of the internet. The Liberty Alliance group has been 'attacking' Passport for recent security breaches (there had been a few incidences in 2001) and the monopolistic nature of Passport (largely controlled by Microsoft alone).

A Smart Device Extension (SDE) for VS .NET is an IDE extension for writing, debugging, and deploying applications for .NET CF. The SDE includes the .NET CF, additional device-specific functionality for Visual C# .NET and VB .NET, remote device debugging capabilities, and device emulators.

1.8.8   Visual Studio .NET

Efficient software development must be accompanied by an efficient development tool. For writing .NET codes, nothing comes close to VS .NET (naturally). Unlike Java's 'open market' for Java IDEs, VS .NET seems to be the only choice for writing .NET applications.

Learning how to write, compile, and run a C# program in VS .NET takes only 15 minutes. But there are several other useful tools and wizards provided in this IDE that will take a couple of days to be totally familiar with. VS .NET is beyond the scope of this book – the code examples can be all compiled using the command line .NET SDK.

VS .NET comes in four editions:

● Enterprise Architect
● Enterprise Developer
● Professional
● Academic.

VS .NET installs on Windows NT 4.0 Workstation/Server, 2000 Professional/Server, and Windows XP Professional only. A 60-day trial of VS .NET Professional is also available from Microsoft.[43]

1.9   Unsafe codes and real time programs

.NET literature uses the term 'unsafe code' to refer to code which involves pointer operations.[44] Only certain .NET languages, including C# and Visual C++ .NET, support unsafe coding.[45]

Using pointer operations, you can perform some tweaking to optimize your codes. A good example is implementing your array 'object' on the stack (like Java, arrays are objects in the various .NET languages). If you write safe codes, all array objects that you instantiate will be created on the heap. On the other hand, you can implement your own array storage structure *on the stack* using pointer operations. If you are careful about it, the result is a very efficient and fast array structure. You can read and write directly to memory locations using pointer operations – they offer you lots of flexibility and power.

43. Order it online from http://msdn.microsoft.com/vstudio/productinfo/trial.asp
44. C/C++ programmers will be familiar with pointers (and the bugs they often bring). As for Java programmers, pointers (or, more accurately, pointer variables) are just variables which contain the memory addresses of another variable.
45. In C#, unsafe codes must be used within code blocks marked with the `unsafe` keyword.

Nevertheless, pointer operations come with their own set of problems – it is very easy to write code involving pointers that can result in extremely difficult-to-find logical bugs (that's one reason why pointers are passed off in Java).

On the other hand, safe codes are relatively easier to write and debug. Safe codes are also type-safe. For example, it is impossible to refer to an index of an array that is out of bounds.

Going by .NET's definition of 'unsafe codes', since Java does not allow direct memory manipulation via pointer operations, it is a totally 'safe' language.

Java is facing a huge problem in the real time industry because the JVM is more a liability than an asset when it comes to real time issues. Performance has always been an important factor in the real time world, and real time engineers don't like the idea of not being able to control the JVM. In most cases, Java's apparently random non-deterministic garbage collection mechanism simply throws Java out as a potential language for writing real time applications.[46]

When you want to write to memory mapped devices in Java, there is no choice except to turn to JNI. Every respectable Java programmer knows the disadvantages of using JNI – not only do you need another C/C++ programmer in your team to code the native codes, there are also performance overheads.

With C#'s unsafe coding capability, you can write C# codes that use pointers and access memory locations directly. Such C# codes may directly communicate with the underlying Win32 API functions which take in pointers as parameters, and write directly to memory mapped devices.

It is unlikely that the real time industry will rush out to embrace C# because of its ability to write unsafe codes. In fact, *real* real time projects with very strict performance limitations avoid object-oriented (OO) languages altogether (even C++).[47] C and assembly would still be the reigning languages of the real time world.

Nevertheless, the ability to read/write directly to memory is a breakthrough – something useful that you can't do in pure Java.

1.10 Porting .NET to other operating systems

One common question is whether it is possible to port .NET to other non-Windows operating systems.[48] In theory, it is possible to write a .NET CLR for, say, a Linux

46. Nevertheless, work is being done on adapting Java for use in real time applications. Sun has published a Real Time Specification for Java. The J-Consortium (www.j-consortium.org), an independent organization, has also come up with their own real time specifications for Java.
47. OO features such as class inheritance and polymorphic method invocation carry pricey overheads.
48. There have been reports about Microsoft funding the development of .NET on non-Windows operating systems. Corel Corp (in which Microsoft has a US$135 million investment) will be building an implementation of .NET programming tools that allows developers to build XML web services based on .NET for FreeBSD. A project codenamed Rotor, which is currently running at Microsoft, is dedicated at porting .NET to a non-Windows platform.

machine.[49] This .NET CLR understands and provides a runtime environment for IL codes, in very much the same way that a JVM can be written for each operating system.

There are already projects under development to do just this,[50] but it is my belief that .NET will remain a Windows-*dominant* technology. The CLR just wasn't designed for operating system portability, unlike the JVM. While the JVM is centered around the idea of operating system portability, .NET is about multiple languages and a single-vendor solution.

49. Of course, Windows-specific codes such as reading or writing to the Windows registry will not be truly portable. Either some clever tweaking has to be done, or developers writing portable .NET codes must avoid such operating system-specific functionalities.
50. Project Mono (www.go-mono.com) by Ximian(www.ximian.com) aims to create an open source implementation of the .NET development framework. Mono includes a C# compiler, a runtime for the CLI, and a set of class libraries.

chapter 2

Introducing C#

C#[1] is *probably* the most important of all .NET languages. A large portion of BCL is written using C# itself. I have to stress that it is not the *only* viable language for writing .NET codes – VB .NET has a large following too – but it is obvious that C# does have a significant role to play in Microsoft's .NET plan.

Unlike Java, which is not a standardized language,[2] C# has been submitted to ECMA[3] by Intel, IBM, and Microsoft for standardization and future evolution.

The C# Language Specification stated the objectives and features of C#:

- a simple, *modern*, *general purpose*, *object-oriented* programming language;
- provides support for software engineering principles such as strong type checking, array bounds checking, detection of attempts to use uninitialized variables, and automatic garbage collection;
- for use in developing software components suitable for deployment in distributed environments;
- supports internationalization;
- suitable for writing applications for both hosted and embedded systems, ranging

---

1. Strictly speaking, there is a difference between C# and Visual C#.NET. They are very much like how C++ and Visual C++ are related. C# is a language standardized by ECMA and which has originated from Microsoft as a language to write .NET code. Visual C#.NET refers to the whole development environment in VS .NET. This book does not try to differentiate between the two terms – 'C#' and 'C#.NET' are used interchangeably.
2. Java is currently self-regulated by the JCP initiated by Sun. JCP involves setting up expert groups from members of the industry to make recommendations and propose new specifications. Such specifications resemble real industrial standards, except for the fact that they are not maintained by a neutral international standards body. The Java Language Specification, J2EE and other Java-related specifications are 'specifications', not real 'standards'. Sun twice submitted Java to ECMA for standardization, but had – on both occasions – withdrawn the submission.
3. ECMA (www.ecma.ch) is the standards body which regulates JavaScript too. The C# language specification is ECMA-334 (blue cover). You can download it freely in pdf/Postscript format at www.ecma.ch/ecma1/STAND/ecma-334.htm

from the very large that use sophisticated operating systems, down to the very small having dedicated functions.

Although primarily targeted at the .NET platform, C# can be adapted for many other purposes. It doesn't matter if you are writing a web application, a program that runs on your Windows desktop, or a minimalized version for use on a PDA – C# is suitable for either.

VB .NET is very much more powerful than VB 6 after real OO features and support for multi-threading are (finally) added in. However, there are things which can be done in C# which cannot be done in VB .NET – notably the writing of unsafe codes.

As mentioned in the previous chapter, C# has features that are not part of CLS. Such 'extended features' include operator overloading and unsigned types. It should be noted that although C# has been created to write code for the .NET runtime, the language itself can be quite independent of .NET.[4]

2.1 Potent combo of Java and C++

When I first started learning C#, I was mildly surprised at how much the C# team 'copied' from the Java programming language. Microsoft defined C# as "a modern object-orientated language that enables programmers to quickly build a wide range of applications for the new Microsoft .NET platform". It was added that C# was "derived from C and C++". It has never been mentioned in any official Microsoft literature (not even the C# Language Specification) that certain features in C# have been developed after considerable study of the Java language, though this fact is immediately obvious to anyone who knows a bit of Java and C++.

Many of us will agree that Java is an improved version of C++. Java got rid of several unpleasant C++ features such as multiple inheritance, the goto keyword, and added a host of nice features such as a common class ancestry for all Java classes and Java interfaces (in place of multiple inheritance).

C# can also be viewed as an improved version of Java. Like Java, C# supports only single inheritance, uses interfaces, and all objects have a common ancestral class (C#'s System.Object).

Despite the similarities between C# and Java, to say that C# has been totally modeled on Java alone is not fair[5]. There are also several C++ 'legacies': such as the destructor, preprocessor directives, enum keyword, structures, and operator over-

---

4. Despite the apparent 'decoupling' between C# and .NET, my personal opinion is that in order for C# to succeed, it has to 'ride on' the widespread deployment of .NET. C# will never become popular if .NET does not.
5. Java is, after all, a language that has its roots in C++ (and SmallTalk). Hence, some would argue that it is not wrong to state that C# is a direct descendent of C/C++ alone, although I believe some credit has to be accorded to the founders of the Java language. Java has proved the viability of some OO language features not found in C++ (such as single class inheritance and much stricter typing).

loading to name just a few. These 'legacies' will be total strangers to Java developers with no C/C++ background.

In addition to C/C++ 'legacies' and Java 'add-ons', C# spots several new useful features not found in both languages – examples include C# indexes, properties, attributes, delegates and events. A summary is shown in Figure 2.1.

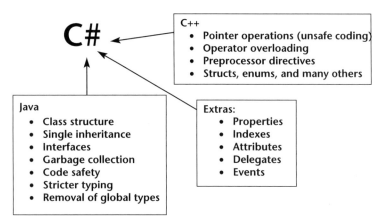

FIGURE 2.1   C# has not only extracted the cream features from both C++ and Java, it has come up with several new extras to aid the powerful developer. These extras come at a price – a steeper learning curve and the possibility of 'abuse' by weaker developers who use them for the wrong purposes.

Microsoft calls C# "a combination of the ease of use of VB and the power of C++". I would rather view it as having the elegance and simplicity of Java coupled with the power and convenience of C++ (see Figure 2.2). The C# team obviously had the

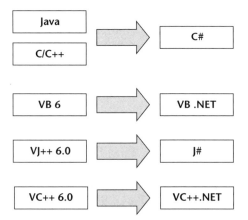

FIGURE 2.2   The new .NET programming languages and their predecessors in VS .NET. C# is a brand new language targeted primarily at the .NET platform. C# inherited elegance and simplicity from Java, and power and convenience from C++.

advantage of benefit from the experience of both Java and C++ when they came up with a whole new programming language (and I think they have done a good job having seen the product.)

Because of C#'s similarity to Java, learning C# will be relatively easy if you have a good Java foundation (compared to learning C# with a VB background, for example). Despite the initial "Hey-that's-a-feature-of-Java!", as you go along you will realize that C# is, after all, not so much like Java in certain aspects. There is a learning curve to climb even if you are a Java expert (and especially if you have never been exposed to C or C++). Nevertheless, it is the objective of this book to bridge this gap.

2.1.1   Is C# superior to Java?

It is difficult to say if Java or C# is the superior language because their purposes are vastly different in the first place.[6] Java emphasizes portability, platform independence, and simplicity. C# is commonly viewed as the most powerful .NET language used for writing web applications, Windows applications, and web services on the .NET platform. For C#, portability is of low value – rather, the emphasis is on giving the programmer as much power and convenience as needed, even if it takes more effort to master the language.

One thing is for sure, learning C# can involve a steeper climb than learning Java if you start from scratch. In addition to the 'convenience features' added into C#, C# has also preserved several features from C++ which the Java designers left out deliberately (such as operator overloading and the enum keyword), thus making learning C# more difficult compared to Java.

Table 2.1 compares the features of C# and Java. Where feature richness and power is concerned, I would say that C# is the clear winner. But Java wins in ease of use and learning. In my personal opinion, C# will succeed if, and only if, .NET succeeds. This language has been created from the ground up just for the .NET platform – if vendors do not use .NET for their implementations, there is little reason for software engineers around the world to learn a new language.

One important advantage of C# is the ability to write unsafe codes. Java codes must run within the JVM, and that is a severe limitation when it comes to real time programming. It is also impossible to write to memory-mapped devices using Java. JNI – which comes with performance overheads – is needed for Java codes to 'talk to' native components. It all boils down to the same engineering problem – where is the appropriate balance between portability and efficiency.

---

6. Always keep this point in mind when you read articles comparing the two languages (especially marketing material). The basis of comparison must be made very clear so that the comparison is fair. For example, you can say that Java's inability to make use of native operating system features is a disadvantage, but that is actually an engineering trade-off for portability. Likewise, the inability to use pointer operations in Java to access memory directly can be viewed as both an advantage and disadvantage.

TABLE 2.1 Comparing some aspects of Java and C#

Feature	Java	C#
Platform portability	Generally portable in the spirit of Java's "write once, run anywhere" vision	Portable to other .NET platforms – currently, .NET runs on Windows only, though this might change in the future
Unsafe codes	Not able to write unsafe codes – Java codes cannot perform pointer operations	Can be used to write unsafe codes in code blocks marked with the `unsafe` keyword
Simplicity	Very simple and easy to learn. The feature set has been kept to a minimum so that features that help productivity are not present. You can still write powerful OO Java codes without these convenience features	More difficult to learn because the language has many features – several productivity (convenience) features, such as operator overloading, are retained
Standardization	Regulated and evolved by the JCP	Standardized by ECMA
Post compilation codes	Java bytecodes in class files which runs on a JVM	IL in .NET assemblies which runs on a .NET CLR

The next chapter will discuss Microsoft's JUMP to .NET strategy specially tailored for Java developers.

chapter 3

JUMP to .NET and J#

If you are a Java developer who is picking up C# (and .NET), it will be nice to know a bit more about Microsoft's JUMP to .NET[1] initiative and J# – even if you have chosen to learn C# instead of J# for programming .NET.

Microsoft apparently decided that in order to woo the 2.5 million Java developers over to .NET, more had to be done in the way of encouragement. JUMP to .NET (which aptly stands for Java User Migration Path to .NET[2]) is Microsoft's initiative to make it easier for current Java developers to move over.

JUMP to .NET consists of two important components:

- Java Language Conversion Assistant.[3]
- J#

3.1 Java Language Conversion Assistant

The JLCA is a tool that converts Java source codes into C# codes automatically. I suppose writing such a tool is much easier than writing a C# to Java code conversion tool because Java was designed to be platform independent, so there are no operating system-specific codes in the Java core API classes.

I can't write much about this tool until it goes final and its feature set solidifies.[4]

3.2 The J# language

Announced only late in 2001, J# is the official successor of Visual J++. Like J++, J# follows Java's syntax and rules. But unlike Java, applications written using J# can

1. Check out the official website at http://msdn.microsoft.com/visualj/jump
2. I wonder who came up with this acronym. I think it's very clever indeed!
3. At the time of writing, this tool is in the beta stage. It can be downloaded at http://msdn.microsoft.com/vstudio/downloads/jca/default.asp
4. At time of writing, the final version of J# has just been released while JLCA is still in beta.

run only on the CLR, and *not* on a JVM. A J# compiler does not compile `.java` source files to `.class` byte codes.

Being a true blue .NET language as well, J# is like C# in many ways:

- Like C#, J# source codes are compiled into IL assemblies, which are then JIT-compiled into native Windows machine codes by the CLR during runtime.

- J# codes can consume .NET BCLs (instead of Java's core API classes).

- Being a .NET language, you can integrate .NET functionality such as ADO .NET, web services, Windows forms, and ASP .NET into a J# module.

- J# interoperates with other .NET languages – for example, your J# class can inherit from another class written in C# and vice versa.

Visual J#.NET includes `Jbimp.exe`. Jbimp is a tool which can convert prewritten Java `.class` byte codes into IL assemblies directly.

If you have a Javabean in the form of a `.class` file which you wish to convert into C# codes, you can do either of the following:

- use the Jbimp tool to convert the `.class` file into a .NET assembly;

- use a Java decompiler to convert the `.class` file back into a `.java` file, then use JLCA to convert the `.java` source codes into C# source codes.

One huge caveat – the use of Jbimp is limited to only JDK 1.1.4 (or earlier) Java byte codes, such as those created using J++'s `jvc.exe` tool.

For J++ developers, there is a migration path for porting a J++ program into J#. Most J++ applications can be ported over quite easily. J# supports legacy J++ features such as J/Direct, Java COM integration, delegates, conditional compilation, and some of the J++ @ directives.[5]

J# has a big limitation – it supports only Java 1.1.4 API classes. This means that if you have a Java source that uses Swing (or any other post-1.1.4 API class), you cannot simply open that `.java` file in VS .NET and compile it as a J# source file into IL codes directly. It is for this reason that it is extremely difficult to port pure Java applications which make use of any classes after JDK 1.1.4.[6] For `.java` files which make use of only 1.1.4 and earlier core Java classes, porting is as simple as opening that file in VS .NET and compiling it as a J# source.

5. If you are a pure Java developer who has never touched J++ before, you will be scratching your head over these J++ features. J/Direct is an API provided by Microsoft which allows Java code to call Windows operating system services and methods in third party COM components. Unlike JNI, J/Direct does not require a wrapper to bridge the communication between Java and native DLLs. J/Direct was first supported with the Microsoft Virtual Machine that shipped with Microsoft Internet Explorer 4.0. There are other Microsoft technologies to enable communication between Java codes and COM components such as using a CCW for Java objects in COM, and JCW, for COM objects in Java. For more information, see www.microsoft.com/java/resource/jdirectworkshop.htm

6. Java 1.1.4 is ancient by any standard (it is not even Java 2!). Visual J++ 6.0 was also 'stuck' at this stage and stopped evolving due to the court case between Sun and Microsoft. I was quite disappointed with this limitation.

Compared to C#, Java – and hence J# – has a poorer language feature set. For example, J# lacks features such as operator overloading and support for C# properties, events, and delegates. Otherwise, both C# and J# can utilize .NET BCL, and you can write programs in either language with the same functionalities provided by the BCL.

3.2.1 Why learn C# instead of J#?

If you discount project requirements and specific client instructions, choosing to pick up either C# or J# for developers with a Java foundation is probably a personal choice.

If you are a pure (non-J++) Java programmer, I would recommend that you spend a little more time picking up C# instead of J#, even if you have never programmed in C/C++ before. For such cases, I estimate that the learning time needed to pick up C# will be a just little longer than learning J#. Personally, I think the additional language features provided by C# is worth that extra learning time.

On the other hand, if you are (or have been) a J++ developer, then the migration path from J++ to J# would be significantly shorter. I would still recommend C# as a more powerful language than J# if you are really serious about .NET.[7]

The advantages of C# over J# are listed below.

- C# boasts a richer set of language features.[8]
- C# is not the only language for .NET, but it has been widely regarded as the de facto language.
- C# will be more widely used than J# for programming on .NET. As such, I am expecting C# developers to have easier access to technical support, more discussion forums, and definitely more published literature.
- C# is regulated by a standards body but J# is not (yet).[9]
- You can write unsafe codes with C# but not with J#.[10]
- The learning effort needed for a Java programmer to learn C# may not be very much more significant than that needed to learn J# (especially since you have this book).

7. I suppose many people will disagree with this recommendation. But, as I have mentioned, it's more a personal preference. What I am attempting to do here is point out the trade-offs of learning C# and J# so that an informed decision can be made.
8. Note that both J# and C# (and any other .NET language) has access to the same set of .NET BCLs. This implies that what you can do with .NET languages is quite uniform (if you are writing safe codes; you cannot write unsafe codes with J#). However C# has more language features that make programming easier, more efficient, and more elegant.
9. There has not been any official announcement from Microsoft as to whether J# will be submitted to ECMA for standardization. VB .NET isn't, and probably will not be.
10. This may be a minor point depending on whether your project requires you to write unsafe codes. Most application project teams will never use this feature (even as a C# developer, you should not use unsafe codes unless absolutely necessary).

The advantages of J# over C# are fewer.

- As a Java developer, learning J# is the fastest way to pick up a .NET programming language. J# uses Java syntax and grammar rules which you should already be familiar with.

- Being a fully fledged .NET language, J# code uses the same .NET BCL and hence it is fair to say that a J# program can do almost anything a C# program can, except for special features such as writing unsafe codes. By choosing J# over C#, your program should be able to achieve the same functionality set.

One of the first things a developer starting on .NET has to do is to pick one .NET language from the many available. Assuming no other influencing factors (such as client preference), Figure 3.1 shows *my* recommended migration path.

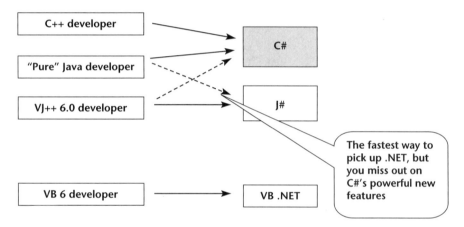

FIGURE 3.1   Recommended migration paths to .NET when selecting a language.

Hello C#!

Even before we start off with C# syntax and semantics in Part 2, let's do the traditional "Hello World" example just to warm up. This is Hello World, C# version:[1]

```
// HelloWorld.cs
public class TestClass{
  public static void Main (){
    System.Console.WriteLine("Hello C#! Here I come!");
  }
}
```

4.1 How to compile and run the code examples in this book

If you have VS .NET, you can choose either to write and compile the codes within the VS .NET IDE, or via command line.

You *cannot* run the VS .NET command line tools from your usual Windows DOS prompt (which is activated by START → run, type in "cmd" or START → Programs → Accessories → Command Prompt) because certain configuration settings are required.

You need to use the special VS .NET command prompt if you want to use the command line tools. After you have installed VS .NET, click on START → Programs → Microsoft Visual Studio .NET → Visual Studio .NET tools → Visual Studio Command Prompt.

Type in your codes using a text editor (e.g. Notepad) and compile it using the command line C# compiler csc.exe like this:

```
c:\expt>csc HelloWorld.cs
```

---

1. Doesn't this look like Java? This familiarity sure gives some confidence doesn't it? At first glance, the Hello World program makes C# look more 'Java-ish' than 'C-ish', but the differences between C# and Java will become more obvious as we progress.

Capitalization of the file name here doesn't matter. C# is case sensitive, but not at command line. If everything goes smoothly, `HelloWorld.exe` will be generated. `HelloWorld.exe` contains IL codes and is what is called a .NET assembly.

C# compiler

FIGURE 4.1   Compilation into IL.

Figure 4.1 shows what happens during compilation.

To run the program, you can either type in the full file name (i.e. `HelloWorld.exe`) or simply `HelloWorld`:

    c:\expt>HelloWorld

The output is:

    c:\expt>C#! Here I come!

Figure 4.2 shows what happens during runtime.

The screen output in this exercise is shown in Figure 4.3.

.NET CLR

FIGURE 4.2   Runtime JIT-compilation.

```
Visual Studio .NET Command Prompt                              _ □ ×

C:\expt>csc HelloWorld.cs
Microsoft (R) Visual C# .NET Compiler version 7.00.9466
for Microsoft (R) .NET Framework version 1.0.3705
Copyright (C) Microsoft Corporation 2001. All rights reserved.


C:\expt>dir
 Volume in drive C is BABYBLUES
 Volume Serial Number is E0D2-A7C8

 Directory of C:\expt

03/28/2002  04:02 PM    <DIR>          .
03/28/2002  04:02 PM    <DIR>          ..
03/28/2002  04:03 PM                144 HelloWorld.cs
03/28/2002  04:04 PM              3,072 HelloWorld.exe
               2 File(s)          3,216 bytes
               2 Dir(s)   3,188,830,208 bytes free

C:\expt>HelloWorld
Hello C#! Here I come!

C:\expt>_
```

FIGURE 4.3   Compiling and running `Helloworld.cs`

4.2   Some .NET specifics

During the compilation phase, a new file `Hello.exe` is created. Although it may seem so, remember that this particular 'executable' is unlike the other `.exe` files that are created using a conventional non-.NET compiler (such as Visual Studio 6 or the ancient Turbo C++). This `.exe` file is a *NET assembly* – it can only run if the .NET framework has been installed on the local machine. If you copy `HelloWorld.exe` to another Windows PC which does not have the .NET framework installed and try to execute it, it will not run.

The .NET framework[2] would have been installed if either of the following had been previously installed:

- Visual Studio .NET
- .NET Framework SDK
- `dotnetfx.exe` (.NET Framework installer)
- a .NET application which has been distributed together with the .NET framework together as one package.[3]

A .NET assembly (which is usually post-fixed with a `.exe` or `.dll` file extension) is actually IL code bundled together with a manifest file.[4] Remember that a .NET assembly is quite different from a normal Windows DLL or EXE file though the file extensions can be the same.

4.3   Disassembling an assembly file

VS .NET comes with a GUI-based disassembler tool which can be used to view the contents of the IL file. The IL disassembler can be really useful if you are really interested in understanding how things really work underneath, how different .NET compilers optimize their codes, and similar issues.

---

2. At the time of writing, the .NET Framework Service Pack 2 has been released. This takes care of some security issues and should be downloaded and set up after the .NET framework has been installed. Get it from http://msdn.microsoft.com/netframework/downloads/updates/sp
3. Using VS .NET, it is possible to 'package' a .NET application together with the whole .NET framework for distribution. Needless to say, this inflates the whole distribution but gives the client the convenience of having to obtain and install the .NET framework separately. A .NET EXE needs the .NET framework to run.
4. The assembly manifest contains some information (metadata) about the assembly itself such as the methods it contains, and even a hash value of the contents of the assembly. It is quite unlike the `manifest.mf` file in a Java `.jar` file – the assembly manifest contains so much more information.

Fire up IL disassembler from the command prompt by typing:

```
c:\expt>ildasm HelloWorld.exe
```

Figure 4.4 shows a screenshot of the disassembler at work. This book does not go into IL specifics.

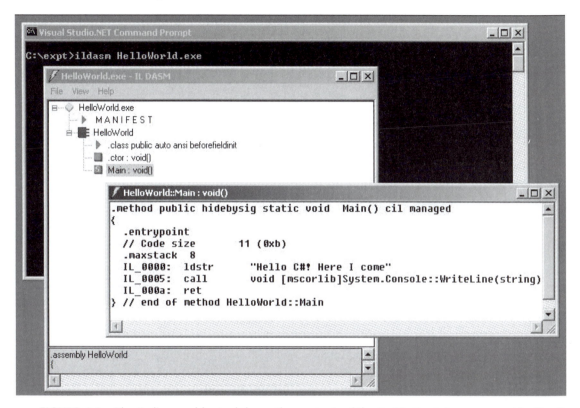

FIGURE 4.4   The IL disassembler tool shows the contents of the HelloWorld.exe assembly. The IL equivalent of the Main() method in HelloWorld.cs is shown here.

part 2

Classes, methods and other OO stuff

Introduction

The chapters in this part are:

- Chapter 5: Getting started
- Chapter 6: Class issues
- Chapter 7: Method issues
- Chapter 8: Miscellaneous issues.

This part builds the OO foundation for programming in C#. In the following chapters, I have made comparisons between how both C# and Java fulfill their support for object-oriented programming. This part has been written with the assumption that you are a Java developer. Hence I will not go through basic OO concepts and those 'why' questions (such as 'why do we want abstract methods?'; 'why are interfaces good?'; 'why do we need constants?'; etc.) but zoom in on the differences between the two languages.

I would suggest that you start with Chapter 5 which dissects the Hello World program you wrote in Chapter 4. The other chapters in this part can be read in any order. When you start on C# programming, you can always refer to the relevant sections for reference.

Language comparisons, in terms of their operators and flow control, will be covered in Part 3.

chapter 5

Getting started

This chapter explains basic C# semantics. You need to read and understand this in order to understand the codes presented in the other chapters in this part.

5.1 Basic class structure

Please attempt to write, compile, and execute `HelloWorld.cs` in the previous chapter[1] if you haven't already done so.

Let's review `HelloWorld.cs`. Notice that it is structurally very similar to a Java class:

```
1: // HelloWorld.cs
2: public class TestClass{
3:    public static void Main (){
4:       System.Console.WriteLine("Hello C#! Here I come!");
5:    }
6: }
```

Like Java

- The `Main` method, and all other methods, must be inside a class[2] (or a struct – the struct will be explained in Chapter 26).

- The `Main` method must be declared as static and is the 'entry point', or the first method the runtime will look for when your class executes.

- `Main` takes in a string array, which corresponds to the command line argu-

---

1. See Chapter 4: Hello C#! on page 34.
2. In C/C++, the `Main` method is defined outside a class as a global method. Like Java, and unlike C/C++, C# does not support global methods or variables. Declarations of methods/variables must always be contained within a class or struct.

ments.[3] The implementation of `Main` in the class above does not take in any argument. We can replace line 3 with:

```
3:    public static void Main (string [ ]args){
```

so that the program can receive command line arguments. Like Java, there is no need to use `args` as the string array variable name – any other valid identifier would do.

Unlike Java

- The `Main` method can be declared to take in no parameter instead of a string array. In other words, we can declare `Main` like this:

```
3:    public static void Main(){
```

instead of

```
3:    public static void Main(string [ ]args){
```

In the former case, command line arguments are simply ignored.
- The `Main` method may return an `int` instead of `void`. For example,

```
3:    public static int Main(){
```

This returned `int` will be useful if you invoke your program from a DOS script which requires a return value for further decision-making purposes.
- In C#, the `Main` method must start with a capital 'M'. You can have a `main` method (with a small 'm') in your class, but that will not be recognized as the starting point method. In Java, `main` must start with a small 'm'. Remember that both Java and C# are case sensitive.

5.1.1   Another example

Let's take a look at another C# source file so that we can discuss further similarities and differences.

```
1: // Test.cs
2:
3: class TestClass{
4:    public static void Main (){
```

_____

3. In C/C++, the first element in the array is the application name (e.g. "Hello" in our example), but in the case of C# (like Java), the first element in the array is the command line argument after the application's name.

```
 5:        MyClass m = new MyClass();
 6:        System.Console.WriteLine(m.Double(99));
 7:    }
 8: }
 9: class MyClass{
10:    public int Double(int value){
11:       return value*2;
12:    }
13: }
```

Like Java

You can define as many classes (and interfaces) as you want in a single source file.

Unlike Java

- There is no requirement for the file name (in this case, `Test.cs`) to be identical to any class defined in the source file. You can give your source file any legal name which the operating system accepts. There is no need even to give your source file a `.cs` extension, though you should do that to avoid confusion.
- You can have as many public classes/interfaces as you want in each source file. In Java, only up to one public class/interface can be defined in each source file.
- In addition to that, each of these classes (whether public or not) can have its own `Main` method.

In such cases however, there is a need to indicate to the compiler which `Main` method is to be the 'starting point' when the file executes. This is done by running the compiler like this:

```
c:\expt>csc Hello.cs /main:Class1
```

where `Class1` is the name of the class containing the `Main` method which you want to start off with when the assembly runs. The class name specified here is case sensitive as you can have two classes of the same name with different capitalization in the same source file.[4]

If you do not specify which `Main` method the program is to start with, and there is more than one class in the same source file containing a `Main` method, the C# compiler will give a compilation error. The following compiler error appeared when I tried to compile a source file containing three C# classes (`Class1`, `Class2` and `Class3`) – each with its own `Main` method – without the /main option.

---

4. Please do not do this even though it is legal. Common software sense will tell you not to have identical identifiers differing only in capitalization within the same scope, unless your objective is to introduce software mayhem and sabotage your co-workers.

```
c:\expt>csc test.cs
test.cs(2,22): error CS0017: Program 'test.exe' has more than
one entry point defined: 'Class1.Main()'
test.cs(6,22): error CS0017: Program 'test.exe' has more than
one entry point defined: 'Class2.Main()'
test.cs(10,22): error CS0017: Program 'test.exe' has more
than one entry point defined: 'Class3.Main()'
```

On the other hand, the following will compile correctly and produce `test.exe`. When `test.exe` is executed, the `Main` method of `Class2` will run.

```
c:\expt>csc test.cs /main:Class2
```

One possible purpose of having multiple `Main` methods in each class in a single source file is for debugging purposes. For the same reason, some Java developers like to write `main` methods for multiple classes within the same package, even though only one of them is meant to be executed.

A source file must have at least one `Main` method defined in one of the classes in the source file to act as the entry point if it is to be built into an EXE assembly. A compiler error is given if you try to compile a source file which does not contain a `Main` method:

```
1: // Test.cs
2: class TestClass{
3: }
```

An attempt to compile `Test.cs` above into an EXE assembly like this:

```
c:\expt>csc Test.cs
```

results in a compile time error:

```
error CS5001: Program 'test.exe' does not have an entry point
defined
```

You can compile `test.cs` into a DLL assembly though. Use the `/target:library` option of the C# compiler:

```
c:\expt>csc /target:library Test.cs
```

This time, compilation succeeds and results in the DLL assembly `test.dll`.

A source file which is to be built into a DLL assembly (or a .DLL library) does not need a `Main()` method (since DLLs, like Java classes without a `main()` method, are not executable).

This is a good point to briefly introduce EXE and DLL assemblies. .NET assemblies can be classified broadly into two groups:

- EXE assemblies which can be executed. EXE assemblies are somewhat similar to Java classes with a `main()` method. You compile a C# source file into an EXE assembly like this:

```
csc Hello.cs
```

The compiled assembly file will be `Hello.exe`.

- DLL assemblies which cannot be executed, but which contain classes or interfaces which an EXE assembly, or other DLL assemblies, may use. DLL assemblies can be thought of as Java classes without a `main()` method. You compile a C# source file into a DLL assembly like this:

```
csc /target:library Hello.cs
```

The compiled assembly file will be `Hello.dll`.

Let's look at a third basic C# class which introduces the C# keyword `using`.

```
1: // HelloWorld2.cs
2: using System;
3:
4: public class TestClass{
5:    public static void Main (){
6:        Console.WriteLine("Hello C#! Here I come!");
7:    }
8: }
```

`HelloWorld2.cs` is identical to `HelloWorld.cs` except for the inclusion of line 2 and a slight alteration to line 6, the statement used to print the `Hello World` line.

You can use the `using` keyword to 'import' the `System` namespace (see section 5.3), so that you can refer to `System.Console.WriteLine()` as `Console.WriteLine()` in your codes. `Console` is one of the core classes within the `System` namespace, and `WriteLine()` is a static method of the `System.Console` class.

Doesn't the `using` keyword sound like Java's `import`? There are some differences though, as you will see later (section 5.3).

5.2 Basic console I/O

5.2.1 Writing to console

For non-GUI Java programs, you use `System.out.println()` to output something to the command line console. For C#, you use `System.Console.WriteLine()`.

WriteLine is a static method of the Console class, which is found in the System namespace (see section 5.3). Both methods are similar – you can pass in a string, a numeric value, or a combination of strings and numeric values (using the + concatenation operator).

This example should make things clear.

```
 1: using System;
 2:
 3: class TestClass{
 4:    public static void Main(){
 5:        Console.WriteLine
 6:            ("Words\n" + "and " + 99 + " numbers.");
 7:        Console.WriteLine
 8:            ("Interesting {0} of WriteLine","usage");
 9:        Console.WriteLine
10:            ("{0} plus {1} gives {2}", 10, 20, 10+20);
11:
12:        TestClass c = new TestClass();
13:        Console.WriteLine(c);
14:    }
15: }
```

This generates the following output.

```
c:\expt>test
Words
and 99 numbers.
Interesting usage of WriteLine
10 plus 20 gives 30
TestClass
```

Like Java

- Like Java's System.out.println(), System.Console.WriteLine() adds a line feed automatically after the line is printed out. You can also use special characters such as \n inside strings to insert a line break.

- In addition to WriteLine(), the Console class also has a Write() method. Write() does not insert a newline character at the end of the printed statement as WriteLine() does. Console.Write() and Console.WriteLine() are similar to System.out.println() and System.out.print(), respectively.

- Like Java, the string concatenation operator (+) in C# works from left to right. When only one of the two operands of the string concatenation operator is a string, the other operand will be implicitly cast into a string before concatenation occurs.

Study the following `WriteLine` statements and their results.

```
Console.WriteLine("1"+2);    // Output: "12"
Console.WriteLine("1"+"2");  // Output: "12"
Console.WriteLine(1+"2");    // Output: "12"
Console.WriteLine(1+2+"3");  // Output: "33", since 1+2 is
                             // evaluated first.
Console.WriteLine("1"+2+3);  // Output: "123", since "1"+2
                             // is evaluated first.
```

● When you try to print out an object reference (line 13), the `ToString()` method of that class is called. In this case, the class type (`TestClass`) is displayed.

For Java, when you try to print out the value of an object reference variable, the `toString()` method of the object is invoked automatically to return a `String` for printing. For C#, the `ToString()` method of the object is also automatically invoked when you do the same thing. Your C# class can override `ToString()` (using the method signature `public override string ToString();`) to return something more meaningful if you want.

By default, Java's `java.lang.Object`'s `toString()` method returns a hash value of the object (in the form `typename@hashcode`). C#'s `System.Object`'s `ToString()` method (which has been inherited by `TestClass` in this case) returns the class type.

Unlike Java

● Take note of lines 7–10. Here is some legacy stuff borrowed from C. The format is similar to traditional C's `printf` statement in which `{0}` will be matched to the first element after the comma, `{1}` will correspond to the second, and so forth. Study lines 9–10:

```
 9:     Console.WriteLine
10:        ("{0} plus {1} gives {2}", 10, 20, 10+20);
```

Here `{0}` is matched with the first value after the string (10), `{1}` is matched with the second (20), and `{2}` will be matched with the third, (10+20), resulting in the output:

```
10 plus 20 gives 30
```

● You can also use variables instead of values. Assuming that a and b are `int` variables, this statement:

```
Console.WriteLine
   ("{0} plus {1} gives {2}", a, b, a+b);
```

and the following:

```
Console.WriteLine
    (a + " plus " + b + " gives " + (a+b));
```

do exactly the same thing.

● Java converts will definitely find using the + operator much more intuitive – choosing either way is largely a personal preference.

However, if you are printing out floating-point values, using {} to print out variable values has one big advantage. You can specify the number of digits you want to be shown after the decimal point with the appropriate rounding using #es.[5] Examine the code fragment below and its output.

```
float f = 3.87769f;
Console.WriteLine
    ("{0}, {1:#}, {2:#.#},{3:#.##}",f,f,f,f);
```

Output:

```
3.87769, 4, 3.9, 3.88
```

One limitation of using #es is that trailing zeros are not displayed:

```
float f = 3.8f;
Console.WriteLine
    ("{0}, {1:#}, {2:#.#}, {3:#.##}",f,f,f,f);
```

Output:

3.8, 4, 3.8, 3.8

5.2.2   Reading from console

Java has I/O classes to support the reading of user inputs from the keyboard[6] for console applications. In C#, this is even easier with System.Console.ReadLine().

Examine this example:

```
1: using System;
2:
3: class TestClass{
4:    public static void Main(){
```

5. To do this in Java would require use of the DecimalFormat class.
6. Most Java developers will do something like this to read user input via the command line console:
```
BufferedReader r = new BufferedReader
 (new InputStreamReader(System.in));
String s = r.readLine();
```

```
5:        Console.Write("Enter your name: ");
6:        string name = Console.ReadLine();
7:        Console.WriteLine("Hi " + name + "!");
8:    }
9: }
```

Output:

```
c:\expt>test
Enter your name: Mok
Hi Mok!
```

5.2.3 Converting a `string` to an `int`

You can use the `System.Convert` class for common type conversions. Useful methods in the `Convert` class include `ToInt32()`, `ToBoolean()`, and `ToDouble()`.

An example of how a string is converted to an `int` is shown here.

```
 1: using System;
 2:
 3: class TestClass{
 4:    public static void Main(){
 5:
 6:        Console.Write("Enter a number: ");
 7:        string userInput = Console.ReadLine();
 8:
 9:        try{
10:           int number = Convert.ToInt32(userInput);
11:           Console.WriteLine(number+10);
12:        }
13:        catch (System.FormatException){
14:           // exception handler
15:        }
16:
17:    }
18: }
```

Output:

```
c:\expt>test
Enter a number: 9
19
```

5.3   C# namespaces (Java packages)

Like the Java world, we always want to pack our C# classes into neat groups or packages. Besides making things much more organized, one important reason for packaging is to prevent naming conflicts when you are using classes from two separate developers who chose the same names for their classes.

In Java, you package classes using the `package` keyword. In C#, you use the `namespace` keyword to do exactly the same thing. In the example below, `MyClass` has been placed into a namespace called `MyNameSpace`.

```
1: using System;
2: namespace MyNameSpace{
3:    class MyClass{
4:       static void Main(string[] args){
5:       }
6:    }
7: }
```

When you want to access `MyClass` from another class, you can refer to it by its fully qualified class name (i.e. `MyNameSpace.MyClass`). Alternatively, to save some coding (especially if the namespace name is lengthy), you can use the `using` keyword. C#'s `using` keyword is similar to Java's `import` keyword.

Like Java

- You can group C# classes into namespaces using the `namespace` keyword.
- You can import C# classes using the `using` keyword.
- You can have multiple `using` statements in a C# file, but they must be right at the top of the source file before any class or namespace declaration.
- It is recommended that you name your namespaces after your company name to prevent namespace conflicts. For example, you could name your namespace `Mok.project1`. (Java users recommend that you use the reverse of your company's registered DNS name for your package names.)
- Both the importing of Java packages and the using of C# namespaces are not recursive. For Java, importing package `java.awt` does not imply the importing of subpackage `java.awt.event`. For C#, the statement `using System;` also does not imply recursive 'usage' of subnamespaces of `System`.
- You cannot use an invalid namespace which the C# compiler cannot find. That's the same as for newer Java compilers.[7] The C# compiler gives a compile

7. Older Java compilers generally ignore invalid `import` statements, but Java 2 SDK 1.4 from Sun actually gives a compilation error when it cannot find all the packages specified in your `import` statements.

time error when it cannot find that namespace referred to in your using statements.

The statement: using System.FakeNameSpace; results in the compile-time error (if the compiler cannot resolve System.FakeNameSpace):

```
error CS0246: The type or namespace name 'FakeNameSpace' could
not be found (are you missing a using directive or an assembly
reference?)
```

Unlike Java

- In Java, java.lang is automatically imported in every Java class. Although C# developers make extensive use of classes from the System namespace, System is not automatically 'used'. The statement 'using System;' is not implicitly inserted into your C# codes.

- It is compulsory to envelope all the classes in a particular namespace within curly braces. The statement namespace MyNameSpace; causes a compilation error.

- In Java, all the classes in a single source file must belong to the same package (if the package statement is used). In a single C# source file, you can have classes placed in different namespaces.

  The following C# source file can compile successfully (compile with the /target:library compiler option, since none of the classes contains a Main method).

```
 1: // NameSpaceTest.cs
 2:
 3: namespace MyNameSpace1{
 4:    public class MyClass1{
 5:    }
 6:    public class MyClass2{
 7:    }
 8: }
 9:
10: namespace MyNameSpace2{
11:    public class MyClass1{
12:    }
13:    public class MyClass2{
14:    }
15: }
```

NameSpaceTest.cs defines four classes – two in the MyNameSpace1 namespace, and another two in the MyNameSpace2 namespace. Note that it is legal to have classes of the same name in the same source file as long as they are defined in separate namespaces. Their fully qualified class names are:

```
MyNameSpace1.MyClass1, MyNameSpace1.MyClass2,
MyNameSpace2.MyClass1, and MyNameSpace2. MyClass2.
```

- You cannot include class names in your using statement. In Java, you can import only specific classes in a particular package. For example, the Java statement import java.io.IOException; imports only the IOException class and excludes all other classes in the java.io package. In C#, you can only 'use' a particular namespace. All the classes in that namespace become automatically 'imported'. If you import a specific class in the namespace, a compile-time error is shown.

  The statement using System.Console; results in the compile-time error:

  ```
  error CS0138: A using namespace directive can only be applied
  to namespaces; 'System.Console' is a class not a namespace
  ```

- Namespace hierarchies do not map into actual directory hierarchies. In Java, if you package your class in com.mok, and compile with the –d flag (using Sun's javac.exe command line compiler), the directories com and com\mok are created automatically. The actual class file is then placed in com\mok. This is not the case for C# – there is no correlation between directory hierarchy and namespace hierarchy.

- C# namespaces can be nested. The following source code compiles fine (compile with the /target:library compiler option, since MyClass1 does not contain a Main method):

  ```
   1: // NameSpaceTest.cs
   2:
   3: namespace A{
   4:    namespace B{
   5:      namespace C{
   6:        public class MyClass1{
   7:        }
   8:      }
   9:    }
  10: }
  ```

  The fully qualified name of MyClass1 is A.B.C.MyClass1. You can't do this in Java.

- The using keyword can be used in a namespace, in which case its scope is only in this particular namespace. It can be used outside any namespace (before any namespace declaration in the source file) and have a scope which spans all namespaces in the source file. Study the example below.

  ```
   1: // test.cs
   2: using System;
   3:
  ```

```
 4: namespace MyNameSpace1{
 5:     class MyClass{
 6:     }
 7: }
 8: namespace MyNameSpace2{
 9:     using MyNameSpace1;
10:     class TestClass{
11:         public static void Main(){
12:             MyClass c = new MyClass();
13:         }
14:     }
15: }
```

The using statement in line 2 has file-wide scope. You can use any class within the System namespace from any class in this file. On the other hand, the using statement in line 9 applies only for classes within MyNameSpace2. MyClass in line 12 is resolved to MyNameSpace1.MyClass.

5.3.1 A further example

This example demonstrates namespace nesting again, and introduces the /reference option of csc.exe.

The following shows the contents of two source files, Source1.cs and Source2.cs. The ExecuteMe class in Source2.cs contains a Main method which invokes the static DoThis() method of Class2 in Source1.cs. Pay close attention to how the source files are compiled.

```
 1: // Source1.cs
 2:
 3: namespace A{
 4:     public class Class1{
 5:     }
 6:
 7:     namespace B{
 8:         public class Class2{
 9:             public static void DoThis(){
10:                 System.Console.WriteLine("doing this");
11:             }
12:         }
13:     }
14: }
```

When compiling Source1.cs, remember to use the /target:library option because Source1.cs does not contain a class which has a Main method:

```
c:\expt>csc /target:library Source1.cs
```

If compilation succeeds, Source1.dll will be created. Source1.dll contains two classes with the fully qualified class names A.Class1 and A.B.Class2 (note that namespace B is nested within namespace A).

```
 1: // Source2.cs
 2: using A.B;
 3:
 4: namespace C{
 5:   public class ExecuteMe{
 6:     public static void Main(){
 7:       Class2.DoThis();
 8:     }
 9:   }
10: }
```

You must compile Source2.cs with the /reference option. The /reference option tells the compiler where to find A.B.Class2 (in this case, Class2 is in the Source1.dll DLL library):

```
c:\expt>csc /reference:Source1.dll Source2.cs
```

If compilation succeeds, Source2.exe will be created. When executed, Source2.exe's output looks like this:

```
c:\expt>Source2
doing this
```

If you do not use the /reference option when compiling Source2.cs, the following compile-time error is shown:

```
c:\expt>csc Source2.cs
Source2.cs(2,7): error CS0246: The type or namespace name 'A'
could not be found(are you missing a using directive or an
assembly reference?)
```

You can specify multiple DLL files using the /reference option. For example:

```
c:\expt>csc /reference:Library1.dll,Library2.dll,Library3.dll
SourceToCompile.cs
```

5.3.2 Creating your own alias

Another interesting use of the keyword using is to create namespace shortcuts. This example shows how you can create your own namespace shortcuts using the using keyword. Study this short piece of code.

```
1 using C = System.Console; //creating alias
2
3 class TestClass{
4    public static void Main(){
5       C.WriteLine("Hullo Dude!");
6    }
7 }
```

Output:

```
c:\expt>test
Hullo Dude!
```

In this example, we have created an alias called C for System.Console, so that instead of having to type System.Console.WriteLine on line 5, we can use the alias C.WriteLine. A word of good software engineering advice here – use aliases sparingly and carefully because, like abbreviated identifiers, everybody will start scratching their heads over what 'C' represents a few weeks down the road.

chapter 6

Class issues

Topics under this heading pertain to C# classes. It starts with a discussion on how to create new objects from classes, and moves on to the class hierarchy in C#, class inheritance, and interface implementation. It ends by covering sealed, abstract, and nested classes.

6.1 Class modifiers

A C# class can have the modifiers listed in Table 6.1.

TABLE 6.1 Valid class modifiers in C#

Class modifier	Comments
new	Only applicable for nested (inner) classes – Non-nested classes cannot have a new modifier (see section 6.9)
abstract	Makes the class an abstract class (see section 6.8)
sealed	Makes the class a sealed class – a sealed class is a final class in Java-speak (see section 6.7)
public	
protected	Access modifiers – modify the accessibility of the class (see section 8.1)
internal	
private	

6.2 Class members

In addition to instance and static variables, other classes (inner classes), and methods, a C# class can include many other different members. Class members can be divided into two categories:

- data members
- function[1] members.

Members that can contain executable code are known as *function members* of the class.

Like Java

All methods and variables must be declared within a class.[2] The only C# statements that can be outside a class's curly braces are:

- C# preprocessor directives (see Chapter 24);
- using statements (similar to Java's import statement);
- namespace statements (similar to Java's package statement);
- code comments (of course).

Unlike Java

There are several new class members not heard of in Java. Examples include properties, events, indexers, operators, delegates, destructors, and static constructors. Table 6.2 gives a brief description of C# class members. Note the new members which do not have equivalents in Java.

The following C# class contains all the possible members mentioned above:[3]

```
 1: using System;
 2:
 3: public class MyClass{
 4:
 5:    // constant
 6:    public const string MyConstant = "C Sharp is fun!";
 7:
 8:    // instance field
 9:    public int MyField = 2;
10:
11:    // another instance field
```

1. This is a terminology thing – the word 'function' (as in function member) does not mean just 'methods'. In OO languages, a method is simply another name for 'function', and some OO developers who graduated from traditional structured programming schools still use the term function to refer to method. In C#, function members include methods *and* properties, events, indexers, operators, instance constructors, destructors, and static constructors.
2. Like Java, C# has got rid of global methods or variables – a feature in C/C++.
3. You might notice (probably with unease) that I have named all my identifiers – except for local variable names – with an initial capital letter. In accordance to C#'s naming convention, only local variable names start with a lower case letter. This might take some getting used to.

TABLE 6.2   C# class members

C# Class Member	Nearest equivalent in Java	Comments
Data Members		
Constant	Final variable	You can declare a C# constant using the `const` modifier (see section 8.3)
Read-only variable	Final variable	A read-only variable is somewhat similar to a constant, except that its value can be set in a constructor (see section 8.3.2)
Event	No direct equivalent	An event is a special delegate instance used for event handling in C# (see Chapter 15)
Field	Class/instance variable	A field is similar to non-local variables in Java – fields can be static (belongs to the class) or non-static (belongs to the object/instance of the class)
Function Members		
Destructor	Java finalizer (finalize method)	A destructor is a special method in a class which is invoked by the garbage collector before the object is garbage collected – in this aspect, a C# destructor is similar to the Java finalizer (see section 7.5)
Indexer	No direct equivalent	An indexer is a convenient way to treat an object encapsulating an array field as an array itself (see Chapter 21)
Instance constructor	Class constructor	The instance constructor is a special method invoked during instantiation of a class (see section 7.3)
Static constructor	Static initializer	The static constructor is a special method invoked before any static methods/fields are utilized (see section 7.4)
Method	Method	C# methods are similar to Java methods. A method can be static (belongs to the class) or non-static (belongs to the object/instance of the class) – there are significant differences between how C# methods take in parameters though (see section 7.2)
Nested type declarations	Inner classes	Both C# and Java support inner/nested classes (see section 6.9)
Operator (or operator method)	No equivalent	C# supports operator overloading but Java does not – operator overloading is accomplished by having special operator methods in the C# class (see Chapter 22)
Property	Accessor/mutator methods	A property can be treated as a field which has optional accessor/mutator methods (see Chapter 20)

```
12:    private string[] MyArray = new string[10];
13:
14:    // instance constructor
15:    public MyClass(){
16:      Console.WriteLine("1st instance constructor running");
17:    }
18:
19:    // overloaded instance constructor
20:    public MyClass(int newMyField){
21:      Console.WriteLine("2nd instance constructor running");
22:      MyField = newMyField;
23:    }
24:
25:    // static constructor
26:    static MyClass(){
27:      Console.WriteLine("static constructor running");
28:    }
29:
30:    // destructor
31:    ~MyClass(){
32:      Console.WriteLine("destructor running");
33:    }
34:
35:    // instance method
36:    public void DoSomething(){
37:      Console.WriteLine("instance method running");
38:    }
39:
40:    // static Main method
41:    public static void Main(){
42:      Console.WriteLine("Main method running");
43:      MyClass mc = new MyClass();
44:      mc = null;
45:    }
46:
47:    // property
48:    public int MyProperty{
49:      get{
50:        return MyField;
51:      }
52:      set{
```

```
53:        MyField = value;
54:      }
55:    }
56:
57:    // indexer
58:    public string this [int index]{
59:      get{
60:        return MyArray[index];
61:      }
62:      set{
63:        MyArray[index] = value;
64:      }
65:    }
66:
67:    // event
68:    public event EventHandler MyEvent;
69:
70:    // operator method
71:    public static MyClass operator + (MyClass a, MyClass
b){
72:      return new MyClass(a.MyField + b.MyField);
73:    }
74:
75:    // nested class
76:    class MyNestedClass{
77:    }
78: } // end class
```

6.3 Creating an object with the new operator

Like Java, there is only one way[4] to create a new object in C# – by using the new keyword.

Like Java

Creating an object in C# is very similar to creating an object in Java. The following statement creates a new object object (object with a small 'o' is an alias for the

---

4. There are two ways to create a new object in C++. Car c(); (creates a Car object on the stack), and Car *c = new Car(); (creates a Car object on the heap). For the case of C#, you can only create an instance of an object using the new keyword. There is no way for the C# developer to control whether a new object is to be created on the heap or stack. All C# objects (reference types) are created on the heap, and all value types are created on the stack.

`System.Object` class in C#):

```
new object();
```

The expression returns an object reference to the new object created on the heap, which you should assign to a variable of an appropriate reference type.

The following works fine:

```
object o = new object();
```

Unlike Java

In C#, the keyword new can also be used to create a method which hides a method of the same signature in a superclass. So, don't be surprised to see a *method* being declared like 'new public void DoSomething();' in C#. This is called 'name hiding', or in this case 'method hiding'.

6.4 Looking at `System.Object`

Here's something that makes C# look more like Java than its official ancestor C++.

Like Java

- Only single class inheritance is supported in C#. A C# class can implement multiple interfaces.[5]
- All Java classes are implicitly subclasses of `java.lang.Object`. In C#, all classes are implicitly subclasses of `System.Object`.[6] This implies that all C# classes must have one, and only one direct superclass, except for `System.Object`.
- Like `java.lang.Object`, `System.Object` has several useful methods which are inherited by all C# classes, and can be overridden for more specific functionality in their respective contexts.

Table 6.3 gives a list of the important methods of `System.Object` (note that this class has three different methods for comparing object equality!).

Additional note

`System.Object` is represented by the alias `object` in C#. You can just use `object` instead of spelling out the full name `System.Object` in your codes (in very much the same way that you can use the C# alias `string` instead of `System.String`, or `int` instead of `System.Int32`).

---

5. C++ supports multiple class inheritance and does not support interfaces.
6. There are several advantages of having all your classes share a common ancestry. At the very least, you are assured that whatever object a method returns can be referenced by a variable of type `System.Object`. Also, there are several useful methods in `System.Object` that are inherited to every single class.

TABLE 6.3   The methods of `System.Object`

Method signature	Comments
`public virtual string` `ToString()`	Similar to `java.lang.Object`'s `toString()`. By default, in C#, this method returns the type of the object rather than a hash code (as in the case for Java[1]). This method can be overridden in a subclass.[2]
`public virtual int` `GetHashCode()`	Similar to `java.lang.Object`'s `hashCode()`. Returns the hash code for this object. An object's hash code will be useful for uniquely identifying an object in a collection (such as a dictionary).
`public virtual bool` `Equals(object a)`	These three methods are similar to `java.lang.Object`'s `equals()`. They are all used to compare two objects (see section 10.5).
`public static bool` `Equals(object a, object b)`	Here are the differences:
`public static bool` `ReferenceEquals(object a,` `object b)`	• The virtual `Equals()` method is to be overridden in subclasses for custom equality comparisons. In C#, only methods declared with the `virtual` keyword can be overridden in subclasses, hence this is the only `Equals()` method you can override.

The static `Equals()` method checks if the parameters are `null`. If both are `null`, it returns `true`. If only one of them is `null`, it returns `false`. If neither is `null`, it invokes the virtual `Equals()` method described above.

• `ReferenceEquals()` is used to compare if two variables are referring to the same object instance.[3] Note that when two nulls are passed as parameters, `ReferenceEquals` returns `true`. When only one of the parameters is `null`, the method returns `false`. The following code fragment should clarify the use of `ReferenceEquals()`:

```
MyClass c1 = new MyClass();

MyClass c2 = new MyClass();

MyClass c3 = c1;

bool b1 =ReferenceEquals(null,null);//true

bool b2 =ReferenceEquals(c1,c2); // false

bool b3 =ReferenceEquals(c1,c3); // true

bool b4 =ReferenceEquals(c1,null); //false
```

(Continued)

TABLE 6.3 Continued

Method signature	Comments
public Type GetType()	Similar to java.lang.Object's getClass(). GetType() returns an instance of System.Type which you can use for extracting more information about the object's type via the reflection API.
protected object MemberwiseClone()	Similar to java.lang.Object's clone(). This method returns a new object of the same type. Simple value variables (e.g. int, long) of the returned object are copied over. If the object contains references to other 'embedded' objects, only the references are copied over to the returned object. No new embedded objects are created.[4]
protected virtual Finalize()	Similar to java.lang.Object's finalize(). Put clean-up code here.

[1] In Java's case, the toString() method defined in java.lang.Object returns a String with the type name, followed by an '@' symbol, followed by the hash value for the object (something like 'Test@720eeb' where Test is this object's class type).

[2] Notice that the method has a virtual modifier. The virtual modifier will be covered later, but for now, all you need to know is that a virtual method is one which can be overridden in subclasses. A method declared without the virtual modifier cannot be overridden.

[3] The ReferenceEquals method is similar to using == operator for comparing object reference variables in Java.

[4] Both System.Object.MemberwiseClone() and java.lang.Object.clone() perform what is called 'shallow copying' instead of 'deep copying'.

6.5 Class inheritance

Inheritance in C# works in very much the same way as in Java, except for some differences in method overriding (see section 7.10). A class can inherit from only one superclass, and can implement multiple interfaces. Note the syntactical differences between the two languages though.[7]

To inherit one class from another, use the following syntax:

```
class <class_name>:<super_class>
```

The code below contains two classes, Child and Parent. Child is a subclass of Parent, and inherits the DoSomething() method.

```
1: using System;
2:
```

7. C# resembles C++ syntax when it comes to inheritance. There is no extends or implements keyword like in Java, just the colon.

```
 3: public class Parent{
 4:   protected void DoSomething(){
 5:     Console.WriteLine("inherited from Parent ");
 6:   }
 7: }
 8: public class Child:Parent{
 9:   static public void Main (){
10:     new Child().DoSomething();
11:   }
12: }
```

Output:

```
c:\expt>test
inherited from Parent
```

Like Java

● Every C# class must have one (and only one) superclass, except for `System.Object` which has no superclass. If no superclass is specified, a C# class implicitly subclasses `System.Object` directly.

● All class members are inherited except private members, constructors (both instance constructors and static constructors), and the special C# destructors.[8]

● Multiple class inheritance[9] is not supported. You should look at implementing multiple interfaces as a rough substitute for multiple class inheritance.

Unlike Java

● C# has a keyword `virtual` which is not found in Java. Methods, properties, and indexers can be declared `virtual` if they are intended to be overridden in subclasses. Only methods, properties, and indexers are class members whose implementation can be overridden in subclasses. (See section 7.7 for more information on virtual methods.)

8. Destructors are special methods in C#. Constructors are invoked when an instance of a class is created – destructors are invoked when that instance is destroyed and reclaimed.
9. Multiple inheritance, which is a notable feature in C++, brings several big problems, the biggest of which is resolution. When a class has two unrelated superclasses, and these two parents each contain an inheritable variable (or method) of the same name, a resolution mechanism is required to decide which should be inherited to the subclass. Single inheritance removes such problems. Instead of multiple inheritance, C# (and Java) supports multiple interface implementation. Like Java, a C# class can extend from one superclass, but implement as many interfaces as the programmer desires.

- The direct superclass of a class type must be at least as accessible as the class type itself. For example, the following two line C# file does not compile:

```
1. public class Child:Parent{}
2: class Parent{}
```

The compilation error given is:

```
test.cs(1,14): error CS0060: Inconsistent accessibility: base
class 'Parent' is less accessible than class 'Child'
```

Java does not have this requirement. The following Java file compiles properly:

```
1: public class Child extends Parent{}
2: class Parent{}
```

Additional note

The direct superclass of a user-defined class type must *not* be any of the following types:

- `System.Array`
- `System.Delegate`
- `System.Enum`
- `System.ValueType`

These are special classes of the BCL.[10]

6.6 Implementing interfaces

Interfaces, though new to C++ developers, is already a well-used and well-understood concept in the Java world. The idea of interfaces in C# is the same as for Java, except for the minor differences described below.

To implement one or more interfaces, use the following syntax when declaring your class:

```
class <class_name>:<interface1>[,<interface2>,<interface3>...]
```

---

10. All arrays in C# are automatically subclasses of `System.Array`. All delegates are subclasses of `System.Delegate`, all enums are subclasses of `System.Enum` and all structs are subclasses of `System.ValueType`. You cannot write your own class which extends these special `System` classes directly – they are meant to act as common superclasses of these special types.

Like Java

- C# does *not* support multiple class inheritance, but it does allow a class to implement multiple interfaces.[11]

- A C# interface can extend another C# interface.

- You use the keyword `interface` to define an interface, much as you define a class. The code which follows shows an example of how to write a class which implements an interface. `ISpeedBehavior`[12] is an interface which contains an abstract method called `TopSpeed()` which returns an int. Two classes, `Car` and `Van`, implement the `ISpeedBehavior` interface and override `TopSpeed()` to provide the code body.

```
 1: using System;
 2:
 3: interface ISpeedBehavior {
 4:    int TopSpeed();
 5: }
 6:
 7: class Car:ISpeedBehavior{
 8:    public int TopSpeed(){
 9:       return 200;
10:    }
11: }
12:
13: class Van:ISpeedBehavior{
14:    public int TopSpeed(){
15:       return 80;
16:    }
17: }
18:
19: class TestClass{
20:    public static void Main(){
21:       Car c = new Car();
22:       Console.WriteLine(c.TopSpeed());
23:       Van v = new Van();
24:       Console.WriteLine(v.TopSpeed());
25:    }
26: }
```

11. We can say that both Java and C# support multiple interface inheritance, but only single implementation inheritance. Though it can be confusing to use the term 'inheriting an interface' instead of 'implementing an interface', both terms are technically correct and interchangeable.

12. By convention, interface names are prefixed with an 'I' in C#. This is not mandatory, but highly recommended.

- All methods in an interface are implicitly public and abstract.
- If a class implements certain interfaces, it must override to provide concrete implementations for all the abstract methods in the interfaces. Otherwise the class has to be declared as an abstract class.
- You can use an interface object type variable to refer to an object which implemented that interface. In the code example above, since 'Car is a ISpeedBehavior' and a 'Van is a ISpeedBehavior' the following assignment works:

```
ISpeedBehavior temp = new Car();
```

Unlike Java

- There is no keyword for extending from a superclass (such as the extends keyword in Java), or an interface (such as the implements keyword in Java). Instead, you place the name of the interface(s) after the colon and the superclass name. If you have more than one interface, separate the interface names using commas.
- There is a significant difference between C# and Java interfaces – C# interfaces cannot contain fields (including C# constants and read-only fields). In Java, you can declare variables (which are implicitly public static and final) in interfaces, but not for C#. Declaring a field in a C# interface will result in a compilation error.
- Most Java naming conventions (including Sun Microsystem's official recommendations) do not require that interfaces be named with an 'I' in front. C# encourages (but does not mandate) that interfaces be named with an 'I' prefix (for example, I prefer to name an interface ISerializable instead of Serializable).
- Although methods in an interface are implicitly public and abstract, you cannot declare a method definition in an interface with either the public or abstract keywords in C# (doing so will result in a compilation error). On the other hand, Java allows you to declare methods inside an interface using the public or abstract modifiers, although that is superfluous.

Additional notes

- If your class is to extend a superclass, and implement one or more interfaces, the name of the superclass must be the first after the colon in the class definition. In the next code example, replacing

```
1: public class Child:Parent,I1,I2
```

with

```
1: public class Child:I1,Parent,I2
```

results in a compilation error. Otherwise, the order of the interfaces in the list does not matter. If the Child class directly extends System.Object, but implements I1 and I2, the declaration statement Child:I1,I2 will be just fine – there is no need to explicitly extend System.Object.

```
 1: public class Child:Parent,I1,I2{
 2:    static public void Main (){
 3:    }
 4:    public void MustImplement1(){
 5:      // code here
 6:    }
 7:    public void MustImplement2(){
 8:      // code here
 9:    }
10: }
11:
12: public class Parent{
13: }
14:
15: public interface I1{
16:    void MustImplement1();
17: }
18:
19: public interface I2{
20:    void MustImplement2();
21: }
```

In the example above, if either method MustImplement1() or MustImplement2() is not coded in Child, there will be a compilation error.

● C# interfaces can contain methods and the following C# members: properties, indexers, and events – all of which are to be implemented by the non-abstract class implementing this interface. There are no such members in Java (see section 6.2).

Here is an interface which contains a property, event, and indexer to be implemented by a class:

```
1: interface IAccelerate {
2:    double IncreaseSpeed();              // method
3:    int Speed { get; }                   // get property
4:    string this [int index] {get; set;} // indexer
5:    event TestEvent Changed;             // event
6: }
```

6.6.1 More about interfaces

Name hiding of interface methods is an interesting C# feature not found in Java. Do not confuse this with name hiding of normal methods which is described in section 7.11. Before describing name hiding of interface methods, the potential problem of interface name conflict resolution is first described so that you can understand how name hiding of interface methods can help prevent a potential pitfall in C#.

6.6.1.1 Interface name conflict resolution

Naming conflicts are possible in two scenarios.

● A superclass `Parent` already contains a method called `Method1()`, and an interface `ITest` contains the same method definition. A subclass `Child` inherits from this superclass and implements the interface. The scenario is shown in Figure 6.1 as a UML class diagram:

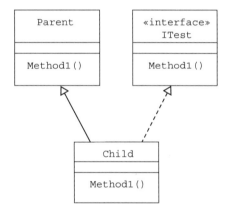

FIGURE 6.1 `Child` subclasses `Parent` and implements `ITest`.

Here are the codes which reflect this scenario:

```
 1: using System;
 2:
 3: interface ITest {
 4:    void Method1();
 5: }
 6:
 7: class Parent {
 8:    public void Method1(){
 9:       Console.WriteLine("running Parent.Method1");
10:    }
```

```
11: }
12:
13: class Child: Parent, ITest{
14:    public static void Main(){
15:       Child c = new Child();
16:       c.Method1();
17:    }
18: }
```

This gives the output:

```
c:\expt>test
running Parent.Method1
```

The code above compiles and runs perfectly, which means that inheriting a method of the same name signature can fulfill interface inheritance. Be aware of this because this may not be what you want.

● Two interfaces, `ITest1` and `ITest2` are shown in Figure 6.2. They contain the same abstract method `Method1()`, and a class `TestClass` implements both these interfaces.

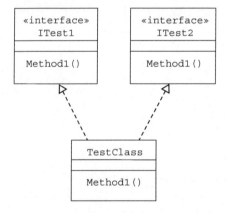

FIGURE 6.2   `TestClass` implements both `ITest1` and `ITest2`.

Here are the codes:

```
1: using System;
2:
3: interface ITest1 {
4:    void Method1();
5: }
6:
7: interface ITest2 {
```

```
 8:    void Method1();
 9: }
10:
11: class TestClass: ITest1, ITest2{
12:
13:    public void Method1() {
14:       Console.WriteLine("running Method1");
15:    }
16:
17:    public static void Main(){
18:       TestClass tc = new TestClass();
19:       tc.Method1();
20:    }
21: }
```

Output:

```
c:\expt>test
running Method1
```

The single Method1() method in TestClass has satisfactorily passed the requirements of both interfaces.

All is fine if this is exactly what you had wanted. But what if Method1() of ITest1 and Method1() of ITest2 are meant to do different things, or exact different behavior on TestClass? If this is the case, you may want to perform *name hiding of interface methods*.

6.6.1.2   Name hiding of interface methods

You can hide a method in an interface so that it is no longer 'truly public' by

- removing the public keyword of the method when declaring the implemented method in the class; *and*
- prefixing the name of the method with the interface name.

If this is done, your method will only be visible when the type of the variable referring to the object is of the interface's type. Examine the next program in which two Method1()s have been implemented in TestClass (thus fulfilling both interfaces) but they are hidden so that both cannot be invoked on an instance of type TestClass.

```
1: using System;
2:
3: interface ITest1 {
4:    void Method1();   // implicitly public
```

```
 5: }
 6:
 7: interface ITest2 {
 8:    void Method1();  // implicitly public
 9: }
10:
11: class TestClass: ITest1, ITest2{
12:
13:    void ITest1.Method1() { // was 'public void Method1()'
14:       Console.WriteLine("running ITest1.Method1");
15:    }
16:
17:    void ITest2.Method1() {
18:       Console.WriteLine("running ITest2.Method1");
19:    }
20:
21:    public static void Main(){
22:       TestClass tc = new TestClass();
23:       // tc.Method1(); // will cause compilation error
24:    }
25: }
```

In this case, Method1() is no longer visible to tc, because tc is of type TestClass. Invoking Method1() by tc.Method1() will cause a compilation error. Let's change Main() a bit.

```
21:    public static void Main(){
22:       TestClass tc = new TestClass();
23:       ITest1 it1 = (ITest1)tc;
24:       it1.Method1();  // prints out 'running
                                     ITest2.Method1'
25:       ITest2 it2 = (ITest2)tc;
26:       it2.Method1();  // prints out 'running
                                     ITest2.Method1'
27:    }
```

Output:

```
c:\expt>test
running ITest1.Method1
running ITest2.Method1
```

You need to cast tc to the correct interface type (ITest1 or ITest2) before you can invoke the respective implemented method.

6.7   Sealed classes (Java final classes)

A sealed class is the C# version of a Java final class. Sealing classes prevent unintended or unauthorized subclassing. It also enables certain runtime optimizations by the underlying runtime environment.

Lines 7–8 in the program which follows declares a sealed class called `Parent`. Being sealed, no other class is allowed to subclass it, hence explaining the compilation error.

```
1:  // Negative example
2:  class Child:Parent{
3:      public static void Main(){
4:      }
5:  }
6:
7:  sealed class Parent{
8:  }
```

Compilation error:

```
test.cs(2,7): error CS0509: 'Child' : cannot inherit from sealed
class 'Parent'
```

Like Java:

- Sealed classes cannot be derived from.
- Abstract classes cannot be sealed.[13]

6.8   Abstract classes

The idea of abstract classes in C# is pretty much identical to that in Java – a class which cannot be instantiated, and which may contain abstract methods.

There follows an example of an abstract class, `MyAbstractClass`, which contains one abstract method, `DoSomething()`. `MyClass` inherits from `MyAbstractClass` and provides an implementation of the method.[14]

13. Abstract classes are meant to be subclassed, while sealed classes cannot be subclassed. So it makes sense that a class cannot be abstract and sealed. The same argument goes for methods – there is no such thing as an abstract sealed method.
14. On line 8, the `override` modifier is used to declare that `DoSomething()` is overriding the abstract method of the same name in the superclass.

```
 1: using System;
 2:
 3: public abstract class MyAbstractClass{
 4:    public abstract int DoSomething();
 5: }
 6:
 7: public class MyClass:MyAbstractClass{
 8:    public override int DoSomething(){
 9:       return 0;
10:    }
11:
12:    public static void Main(){
13:       MyClass mc = new MyClass();
14:       Console.WriteLine(mc.DoSomething());
15:    }
16: }
```

Like Java

- An abstract class is one which cannot be instantiated. The only reason for the existence of an abstract class is for it to be subclassed.

- An abstract class may contain zero or any number of abstract members. On the other hand, a class with at least one abstract member *must* be declared as an abstract class.

- Subclasses of an abstract class must implement all abstract members (if any), or they will have to be declared as abstract themselves.

- Abstract classes cannot be sealed.[15]

6.9 Nested classes (Java inner classes)

C# allows you to write inner classes too. However, the rules are much simpler than in Java[16] when it comes to this. Java allows you to write four types of inner classes:

- static inner classes;
- member inner classes (non-static inner classes – also known as *nested classes*);
- local inner classes (a class within a method);
- anonymous inner classes[17] (a class within a method without a name).

---

15. A sealed class is similar to a final class in Java (see section 6.7).
16. Java has complex access privileges and scope for inner classes indeed.
17. This type of Java inner class is very commonly used in AWT and Swing.

The first two are inner classes declared at class scope, while the others are inner classes declared at method scope. C# only supports the second type of inner classes (nested classes).

This fragment shows a simple nested class in C#:

```
1: class MyClass{
2:    class MyNestedClass{
3:    }
4: }
```

The fully qualified class name for the nested class is `MyClass.MyInnerClass`.

Like Java

- A nested class has access to all members (external to its enclosing class) that are accessible to its enclosing class.
- A nested class has access to all members of the enclosing class including those declared as private and protected.

Unlike Java

- Only non-static nested classes are supported. Other forms of inner classes are not available in C#. You cannot have a static nested class, nor can you have a class declared within a method.
- In addition to nested classes, you can have nested structs (see Chapter 26). A nested struct is a `struct` type declared within a class. The rules for nested structs is very much the same as for nested classes. The following shows an example of a nested struct:

```
1: class MyClass{
2:    struct MyNestedStruct{
3:    }
4:}
```

- A nested class (or struct) can have any of three[18] forms of declared accessibility:

    - `public`
    - `internal`
    - `private`

As with all other class members, if no access modifier is specified, the default accessibility of the nested class is `private`.

---

18. A non-nested class can have any of five forms of declared accessibility: `public`, `protected internal`, `protected`, `internal`, or `private`.

● For Java (non-static) member inner classes, you can access the enclosing class's members directly. For C# nested classes, where a nested class needs access to the instance members of the enclosing class, access is provided by passing a reference of itself (this) as a constructor parameter when creating a new instance of the nested class. This example explains this.

```
 1: using System;
 2:
 3: class HumanBody{
 4:     private int noOfArms = 2;
 5:     private Arm a;
 6:
 7:     private void CreateArm(){
 8:        a = new Arm(this);
 9:     }
10:
11:     public static void Main(){
12:        HumanBody humanBody = new HumanBody();
13:        humanBody.CreateArm();
14:        humanBody.a.ShowNoOfArms();
15:     }
16:
17:     // nested class
18:     class Arm{
19:
20:        HumanBody refToBody;
21:
22:        // constructor
23:        public Arm(HumanBody r){
24:           refToBody = r;
25:        }
26:
27:        public void ShowNoOfArms(){
28:           Console.WriteLine(refToBody.noOfArms);
29:        }
30:     }
31: }
```

Output:

```
c:\expt>test
2
```

The constructor of the nested class (lines 23–25) takes in a reference to the enclosing class instance, so that it can invoke or access the members of the enclosing class (on line 28). Line 14 invokes a method of an instance of the nested class, which makes use of this reference to access the enclosing instance's private field. [19]

19. Of course you won't do this in a real application since this field of the enclosing class is easily accessible from the enclosing class instance itself. The aim of this example is to demonstrate how instances of a nested class should obtain a reference to the instance of its enclosing class.

chapter 7

Method issues

This section discusses C# methods. I will cover C# methods in general, such as how parameters are passed into C# methods, special method members of C# classes (such as static constructors and destructors), method overloading, and method overriding.

7.1 Method modifiers

A C# method can have the modifiers listed in Table 7.1

TABLE 7.1 Valid method modifiers

Method modifier	Comments
new	Besides using new to create new instances of a class, C# uses the same keyword for *name hiding* (in this case, *method hiding*) – a method declared with the new modifier hides (not overrides) an inherited method from the superclass of the same signature
abstract	An abstract C# method is similar to a Java abstract method
static	A static C# method is similar to a Java static method
override	You declare a method with the override modifier if this method is overriding a virtual method in the superclass
virtual	A virtual method is one that can be overridden in a subclass
sealed	A C# sealed method is similar to a Java final method – the sealed modifier is usually used together with the override modifier (see section 7.13)
public	Access modifiers (see section 8.1)
protected	
internal	
private	

7.2 Method basics

I shall cover method structure and method parameters before going into other aspects of methods.

7.2.1 Method structure

A C# method is structured in the same way as a Java method:[1]

```
[assess_modifier][other_modifiers] return_type
method_name ([parameter(s)]){
  //method code
}
```

For example, the method:

```
private void DoThis (int j, string s, object o){ }
```

takes in three parameters – an `int` object, a `string` object, and an `object` object – and returns nothing. This method has private access protection, so that it can only be invoked from with the same class.

Unlike Java

- Remember that if the access modifier is omitted, C#'s default access level is `private`.
- The return type and parameter type(s) of a method must be at least as accessible as the method itself.

  The following code compiles:

```
1: class B{}
2:
3: class A{
4:    public B DoSomething(){ // method returns type B
5:       return new B();
6:    }
7: }
```

  However, just by changing the accessibility of class `A` to `public`, as shown below (line 3), a compilation error occurs:

1. The textbook definition of 'method signature' in C# comprises only of the method identifier (the name) and the type and kind (reference, value or output) of its parameters. All modifiers and the method's return type are not considered to be part of the method signature. The `params` keyword, if used in the parameter list, is also not part of the signature.

```
1: class B{}
2:
3: public class A{
4:    public B DoSomething(){
5:      return new B();
6:    }
7: }
```

Compilation error:

```
test.cs(4,12): error CS0050: Inconsistent
accessibility: return type 'B' is less accessible
than method 'A. DoSomething()'
```

The reason for this is by making A a public class, the accessibility of DoSomething() is now weaker (less strict) than the return type (class B). This violates the rule under discussion.

7.2.2 Method parameters

There are some differences between Java and C# where method parameters are concerned.[2]

In Java, if you pass a primitive variable (or variable of simple/primitive type) to a method, the original primitive variable's value in the calling method will not be affected. Only a copy of the value stored in the calling method's primitive variable is being sent over. The output of the following Java program demonstrates that simple types are 'passed by value':

```
1: // Test.java
2: public class Test{
3:    public static void main(String args[]){
4:      int a=0;
5:      Test.doSomething(a);
6:      System.out.println(a);
7:    }
8:    static void doSomething(int y){
9:      y=99; //does not affect calling method's variable
10:   }
11: }
```

2. C/C++ programmers who love to pass pointers and references using * s and &s will realize that C#, like Java, has got rid of such messy stuff. Unless you are writing C# unsafe codes, there will be no more passing the-address-of-the-address of that integer variable over to a method, or performing deferencing n-levels down to get your value. Personally, I view this as a change for the better and am eternally grateful. Java developers who have never done C/C++ before (and hence do not understand what I am talking about here) well, just be thankful.

Output:

```
c:\expt>java Test
0
```

The same thing happens with C# when you pass over a value type[3] object. Examine the output of this C# program:

```
1:  // Test.cs
2:  public class Test{
3:    public static void Main(){
4:      int a=0;
5:      Test.DoSomething(a);
6:      System.Console.WriteLine(a);
7:    }
8:    static void DoSomething(int y){
9:      y=99;
10:   }
11: }
```

Output:

```
c:\expt>test
0
```

7.2.3 The `ref` keyword

Unlike Java, in C#, you can pass a value object by reference instead of by value.

If you want to pass value type a over to method `DoSomething`, such that `DoSomething` is able to permanently change the value stored in a of the calling method, C# provides two keywords, `ref` and `out`. We shall study `ref` first.

All you need to do is to insert in the `ref` keyword in the method invocation statement, and the method signature of `DoSomething()`:

---

3. The C# specification uses the term 'simple type' to refer to a primitive type. As far as this book is concerned, the terms 'primitive type' and 'simple type' are synonyms – they all refer to types such as `int`, `long`, `float`, `double`, etc. However the term 'value type' has a special meaning in C#. A 'value type' in C# includes all simple/primitive types and some other special types in C# (enum types and struct types, which will be covered in Chapters 25 and 26, respectively). A simple type is a subset of value type. The term 'value type' does not make sense in Java simply because there are no enums and structs in Java. Hence, as far as this discussion is concerned (especially if you are unsure about what enums and structs are) just remember that the term value types encompasses all simple types. (So much for techno-jumbo – get more of it in Chapter 9.) Furthermore, don't be surprised to see me use the term 'value type object' or 'value object' because, in C#, even your `int`s, `long`s and `float`s can be treated as objects and will be converted into objects when necessary automatically.

```
1: // Test.cs
2: public class Test{
3:   public static void Main(){
4:     int a = 0; // a is initialized
5:     Test.DoSomething(ref a);
6:     System.Console.WriteLine(a);
7:   }
8:   static void DoSomething(ref int y){
9:     y=99;
10:  }
11: }
```

Output:

```
c:\expt>test
99
```

The ref keyword passes a reference to the actual int object over to the invoked method so that its value can be altered there directly. In Java, there is no way you can 'pass by reference' a primitive type to a method – primitive types will always be passed 'by value'.

7.2.4 The out keyword

The keyword out is identical to ref, except for one difference – before you pass over a value type variable using ref, that variable must already have been initialized with a value. However, when you pass a variable over using out, it is not necessary for it to be initialized with a value.

The previous code example works well if you replace ref with out on lines 5 and 8 – out doesn't care if a has already been initialized with a value.

But the ref keyword does care. Let's alter line 4 so that a is not given a value.

```
1: // Test.cs
2: public class Test{
3:   public static void Main(){
4:     int a;  // a is not initialized
5:     Test.DoSomething(ref a);
6:     System.Console.WriteLine(a);
7:   }
8:   static void DoSomething(ref int y){
9:     y=99;
10:  }
11: }
```

Output:

```
c:\expt>test
Test.cs(5,26): error CS0165: Use of unassigned local
variable 'a'
```

A runtime error occurs because a has not been initialized with a value before being 'handed over' to DoSomething.

Just think of out as a more lenient alternative of ref. You must ensure that variables passed over using ref are assigned a value first. For out, it doesn't matter.[4]

7.2.5 Passing object references

Passing method parameters by ref and out apply only to the passing of value types such as int, bool, double, etc. In both Java and C#, passing a reference type actually passes the address of the object being referenced over to the invoked method.

Any alterations to the object in the called method are permanent, since the alterations are performed on the actual object itself. The C# example below demonstrates this.

```
 1: public class Test{
 2:    int i;
 3:
 4:    public static void Main(){
 5:       Test t = new Test();
 6:       t.i = 0;
 7:       Test.DoSomething(t);
 8:       System.Console.WriteLine(t.i);
 9:    }
10:    static void DoSomething(Test z){
11:       z.i=99;
12:    }
13: }
```

Output:

```
c:\expt>test
99
```

4. ref is useful if the called method will use the value stored in the passed-over variable. If you use out, the called method will then have to perform manual checks to see if the variable has been initialized with a value.

7.3 Instance constructors

Instance constructors in C# are simply Java constructors. The reason for the name is because there is another group of constructors in C# called *static* constructors (see section 7.4).

Here is an example of a class with overloaded instance constructors.

```
 1: using System;
 2:
 3: public class Test{
 4:    public static void Main(){
 5:       Test t1 = new Test();
 6:       Test t2 = new Test("Here is a string");
 7:    }
 8:
 9:    // overloaded instance constructors
10:    public Test(){
11:       Console.WriteLine("Running default constructor");
12:    }
13:    public Test(string i){
14:       Console.WriteLine("Running constructor with param");
15:    }
16: }
```

Output:

```
c:\expt>test
Running default constructor
Running constructor with param
```

Like Java

- Instance constructors must have the same name (and case) as the immediately enclosing class, and cannot return a value.

- Constructors are special methods of a class that will always be called when an instance of that class is first created.

- The rule of constructor chaining still applies – invoking the constructor of a class always invokes the constructor of its superclass recursively all the way to System.Object.

- Unlike other methods, constructors are not inherited to subclasses.

- You can overload constructors.

- A default constructor[5] is provided if no constructor is explicitly coded in the class. However, when at least one constructor is coded in a class, the default constructor will not be provided implicitly.
- You can use the this keyword to invoke an overloaded constructor in the same class (see section 7.6).

7.4 Static constructors (Java static initializers)

C# has two different kinds of constructors, static and instance – depending on whether they are declared with the static keyword or not. While C# instance constructors are similar to Java constructors, C#'s static constructors are similar to Java static initializers. Static constructors, like their instance counterparts, must have the same name and case as the class of which it is a member.

However, unlike instance constructors, static constructors:

- cannot have parameters;
- cannot have accessibility modifiers;
- cannot be called explicitly.

Static constructors are automatically invoked before the first static class member is utilized. Here is an example of a static constructor.

```
 1: using System;
 2:
 3: public class Test{
 4:    private static string StaticField;
 5:
 6:    public static void Main(){
 7:      Console.WriteLine(Test.StaticField);
 8:    }
 9:
10:    // static constructor
11:    static Test(){
12:      StaticField = "i am initialized";
13:      Console.WriteLine("running static constructor");
14:    }
15: }
```

Output:

```
c:\expt>test
running static constructor
i am initialized
```

5. A default constructor refers to the constructor which takes in no parameters.

In the example above, even if lines 4 and 12 are commented out, the output still indicates that the static constructor has executed (output shows 'running static constructor'). The reason?[6] Well, because Main itself is static, and is considered to be a static member. When Main runs, the static constructor of the class of which it is a member needs to run first.

A static constructor is executed before an instance constructor when a new instance of the class is created, regardless of whether the class has any static member or not. The following example demonstrates this.

```
 1: using System;
 2:
 3: class Test{
 4:    public static void Main(){
 5:       Demo d = new Demo();
 6:    }
 7: }
 8:
 9: class Demo{
10:    // static constructor
11:    static Demo(){
12:       Console.WriteLine("running static constructor");
13:    }
14:    // instance constructor
15:    public Demo(){
16:       Console.WriteLine("running instance constructor");
17:    }
18: }
```

Output:

```
c:\expt>test
running static constructor
running instance constructor
```

Like Java

Both Java static initializers and C# static constructors cannot be called explicitly. Both do not take in parameters, and overloading doesn't make sense in both cases.

Unlike Java

- The difference between a Java static initializer and a C# static constructor is that

6. This is a trick question!

you can have multiple static initializers in a Java class which will be executed in order. You can have only one static constructor in any C# class.

● Other differences are largely syntactical.

7.5 Destructors

A destructor is a special method which is somewhat similar to Java's finalizer method.[7] Traditionally, in C++ codes, clean-up code is placed in the destructor. The destructor for an instance is called automatically during garbage collection, when the instance is destroyed. You usually release resources not managed by the .NET runtime in the destructor (such as file or database connections).

A destructor must have the same name and case as the class it is a member of. Destructors are declared with a tilde:

```
~<class_name>() {
  // codes
}
```

Here is an example of destructor usage.

```
 1: using System;
 2:
 3: public class Test{
 4:   public static void Main(){
 5:     Test t1 = new Test();
 6:   }
 7:
 8:   // instance constructor
 9:   public Test(){
10:     Console.WriteLine("running default constructor");
11:   }
12:
13:   // destructor
14:   ~Test(){
15:     Console.WriteLine("running destructor");
```

7. Destructors came from C++. In C++ classes, destructors are called when the object is manually deleted using the C++ delete keyword. That's where you would recursively delete other objects created and referenced exclusively by the current object. Poor destructor programming in C++ leads to memory-leaky applications. Unlike C++, C# (and Java) has the luxury of automatic memory management. Destructors are no longer as important since any lingering objects which cannot be referenced will be cleaned up by the garbage collector.

```
16:    }
17: }
```

Output:

```
c:\expt>test
running default constructor
running destructor
```

Before the program ends, the destructor of the `Test` object is invoked before it is garbage collected.

Additional notes

- Destructors cannot have parameters and access modifiers. And since destructors cannot have parameters, it follows that each class can have only up to one destructor.

- They cannot be called explicitly. Since garbage collection is non-deterministic, it cannot be predicted when the destructor of an instance will run.

7.6 Constructor initializers and constructor chaining

Called 'constructor initializers' in C#, the two keywords `this` (similar to Java's `this`) and `base` (similar to Java's `super`) allow the programmer to invoke an overloaded constructor in the same class and a constructor in the superclass, respectively.

Like Java

- You can use `this()` to call an overloaded constructor in the same class by passing into `this()` the correct parameters. Instead of a separate `this()` statement, in C#, the `this` keyword is used like an extension of the constructor declaration as shown in the example below.

```
 1: using System;
 2:
 3: public class Test{
 4:    public static void Main(){
 5:      Test t = new Test(0);
 6:    }
 7:
 8:    public Test(int i):this("a string"){
 9:      Console.WriteLine("constructor with int param");
10:    }
```

```
11:
12:    public Test(string s){
13:       Console.WriteLine("constructor with string param");
14:    }
15: }
```

Output:

```
c:\expt>test
constructor with string param
constructor with int param
```

The `this` keyword is used on line 8 so that when this constructor is invoked, it first invokes the overloaded constructor which takes in a string parameter (on lines 12–14).

● You can use `base()` to call a specific constructor in the superclass by passing into `base()` the correct parameters which match one of the constructors in the superclass. Like `this()`, `base()` is an extension of the constructor's method declaration. Examine this example.

```
 1: using System;
 2:
 3: public class Child:Parent{
 4:    public static void Main(){
 5:       Child c = new Child(0);
 6:    }
 7:
 8:    public Child(int i):base("hello!"){
 9:       Console.WriteLine("Child with int param");
10:    }
11: }
12:
13: public class Parent{
14:    public Parent(string s){
15:       Console.WriteLine("Parent with string param");
16:    }
17:    public Parent(){
18:       Console.WriteLine("Parent with no param");
19:    }
20: }
```

Output:

```
c:\expt>test
Parent with string param
Child with int param
```

Constructor chaining up the inheritance hierarchy, as seen in Java, still happens in C#. If none of the superclass's constructor is explicitly invoked via the base() extension of the method declaration, the constructor of a subclass will always invoke the *default* constructor[8] of the immediate superclass before executing the rest of its statements, as this example shows:

```
 1: using System;
 2:
 3: public class Child:Parent{
 4:    public static void Main(){
 5:       Child c = new Child(0);
 6:    }
 7:
 8:    public Child(int i){ // invoked last
 9:       Console.WriteLine("Child with 1 param");
10:    }
11: }
12:
13: public class Parent:GrandParent{
14:    public Parent(){ // invoked 2nd
15:       Console.WriteLine("Parent");
16:    }
17: }
18:
19: public class GrandParent{
20:    public GrandParent(){ // invoked 1st
21:       Console.WriteLine("GrandParent");
22:    }
23: }
```

Output:

```
c:\expt>test
GrandParent
Parent
Child with 1 param
```

Unlike Java

The differences between Java's this() and super() compared to C#'s this() and base() are largely syntactical when used in constructors. In Java, you can only use this() and super() as a statement in the first line of the constructor, if they are used. In C#, the keywords are extensions of the constructor's method declaration.

---

8. The default constructor is the constructor with no parameters.

7.7 Method overloading

There isn't much difference between method overloading in Java and in C#. You have multiple methods of the same name and return type in the same class.

Like Java

- You cannot consider two methods with the same name and parameters but with a different return type as method overloading. For example, having

  ```
  public void DoThis (int j) {}
  ```

  and

  ```
  public int DoThis (int j) {return 0;}
  ```

  in the same class is illegal.

- Constructors can be similarly overloaded. Like Java, you can invoke overloaded constructors from another constructor using the `this` keyword (see section 7.6).

7.8 Passing variable numbers of parameters into C# methods

This is a useful feature in C# which is not found in Java. Using the C# `params` keyword, a method can take in a variable number of parameters (which may not be known until runtime).

The `params` keyword will be useful for writing methods in shared codes, in which the programmer wants to provide maximum convenience and flexibility for users. The parameters are taken in as an array (you can take in an array of `object` types[9] – which means it can accept anything since every C# object is a subclass of `object`).

This is how you declare a method called `Test1` which takes in an arbitrary number of `int` parameters:

```
public static void Test1(params int[] list)
```

You can invoke `Test1` like this:

```
Test1(9, 23, 34);
```

in which case the local variable, `list` will be initialized to an `int` array of size three with `list[0]`, `list[1]`, and `list[2]` set to 9, 23, and 34 respectively.

---

9. `object` is an alias for the `System.Object` class, which is the ultimate superclass for all classes in C#.

You can also invoke `Test1` like this:

```
Test1(9);
```

in which case the local variable `list` will be initialized to an `int` array of size one with `list[0]` set to 9 only.

Let's consider the example of another method called `Test3` which is declared as follows:

```
public static void Test3(string temp, params double[] list)
```

`Test3` takes in a string followed by an arbitrary number of `double` values.

You can invoke `Test3` like this:

```
Test3("Hello!", 3.4, 4.5);
```

in which case the local variable `temp` will be set to `Hello`, and `list` will be a double array of size 2 with `list[0]` and `list[1]` set to `3.4` and `4.5`, respectively.

Examine the full example below showing how params is used. It should be self-explanatory.

```
 1: using System;
 2:
 3: public class TestClass{
 4:
 5:   public static void Test1(params int[] list){
 6:      Console.WriteLine("running Test1 ----------");
 7:      for(int i=0; i<list.Length; i++)
 8:        Console.WriteLine(i + ": " + list[i]);
 9:   }
10:
11:   public static void Test2(params object[] list){
12:      Console.WriteLine("running Test2 ----------");
13:      for(int i=0 ;i<list.Length ;i++)
14:        Console.WriteLine(i + ": " + (object)list[i]);
15:   }
16:
17:   public static void Test3(string temp, params double[] list){
18:      Console.WriteLine("running Test3 ----------");
19:      Console.WriteLine("temp: " + temp);
20:      for(int i=0 ;i<list.Length ;i++)
21:        Console.WriteLine(i + ": " + list[i]);
```

```
22:     }
23:
24:     public static void Main(){
25:
26:         // passing in variable number of parameters
27:         Test1(1, 2, 3, 4, 5);
28:         Test2("hot", 99, 'c', "weather");
29:         Test3("apple", 4.5, 1.2, 8.88, 9.001);
30:
31:         // passing in an array
32:         int [] array = {3, 6, 9, 12};
33:         Test1(array);
34: }
35: }
```

Output:

```
c:\expt>test
running Test1 ----------
0: 1
1: 2
2: 3
3: 4
4: 5
running Test2 ----------
0: hot
1: 99
2: c
3: weather
running Test3 ----------
temp: apple
0: 4.5
1: 1.2
2: 8.88
3: 9.001
running Test1 ----------
0: 3
1: 6
2: 9
3: 12
```

Not only can you pass a variable number of parameters when invoking a method which takes in a params parameter, you can also pass over an array object. The array's type must match the params's type.

On line 33 of the example above, an array object is passed over to method `Test1`

Additional notes

- Only one `params` keyword is allowed in each method declaration. This implies that only one of your method parameters can take in a variable number of elements.
- If your method takes in more than one parameter, the one which uses the `params` keyword must be the last one.
- The first two rules above prevent ambiguity in circumstances such as:

```
void DoThis (param string []list1,
             string temp,
             param string []list2)
```

If you have such a method, it will be impossible to match the string parameters passed in with the parameters taken in.

- You can implement the same functionality in Java (or in C# without using `params`) by writing a similar method which takes in an array. The calling method needs to create a new array, initialize it with the individual objects you want to pass over, and then pass the array object over – `params` is just much more convenient for all the calling methods.

7.9 Abstract methods

Abstract methods in C# are pretty much the same as abstract methods in Java, except for some additional rules. Here is an example.

```
1: abstract class A{
2:    protected abstract int ProcessInt(int i);
3: }
4:
5: class B:A{
6:    protected override int ProcessInt(int i){
7:       return i*2;
8:    }
9: }
```

Like Java

- No implementation of that method is provided – overriding methods of non-abstract subclasses are expected to provide the method implementation.

- Abstract methods cannot be private.[10]
- Classes with one or more abstract methods must be declared as an abstract class (although abstract classes need not contain any abstract methods at all).

Unlike Java

- Remember to use the `override` keyword[11] when overriding the abstract method in the subclass. (If you omit the `override` keyword on line 6, you will be performing *name hiding*, not method overriding. The code still compiles, but a warning is given.)
- Java allows you to change the access modifier in the overridden method to be of weaker (less strict) access. In C# you are not allowed to change the access modifier of the abstract or virtual method in the overridden method. In the previous code example, if you change line 6 to:

```
6: public override int ProcessInt(int i){
```

you will get a compiler error:

```
test.cs(6,23): error CS0507: 'B.ProcessInt(int)':
cannot change access modifiers when overriding
'protected' inherited member 'A.ProcessInt(int)'
```

Additional notes

- Abstract methods are implicitly virtual, but you cannot use the `virtual` modifier when declaring abstract methods (you will get a compilation error).
- An abstract method declaration can override a method which is already implemented in the superclass. In this way, an abstract class can 'force' a reimplementation of that method in a subclass. Examine the example below.

```
1: abstract class A{
2:    protected abstract int ProcessInt(int i);
3: }
4:
5: class B:A{ // class B extends A
6:    protected override int ProcessInt(int i){
7:       return i*2;
8:    }
9: }
```

10. Abstract private methods don't make sense at all since abstract methods are intended to be overridden, and private methods cannot be overridden in subclasses.
11. An overriding method in C# must be declared with the `override` keyword. See section 7.10.

```
10:
11: abstract class C:B{ // class C extends B
12:    protected abstract override int ProcessInt(int i);
13: }
14:
15: class D:C{ // class D extends C
16:    protected override int ProcessInt(int i){
17:       return i*3;
18:    }
19: }
```

In this case, class C contains another method which is abstract, yet overrides the implementation in B. This forces non-abstract class D to contain an implementation for that method.

7.10   Method overriding using the `virtual` and `override` Modifiers

There are some significant differences here between Java and C#. Method overriding in C# involves two keywords borrowed from C++ with no equivalents in Java – virtual and override. Take note of them carefully.

Like Java

● Private methods in the superclass cannot be overridden in a subclass. If a subclass has a method of the same signature as a private method in the superclass, this is not considered to be a method override.[12]

● You can invoke the superclass's method, which has been overwritten in the subclass, by using the C# keyword base – this is similar to Java's super keyword. Here is an example.

```
1: using System;
2:
3: class Child:Parent{ // Child extends Parent
4:    public static void Main(){
```

12. Take note that if a method is declared as private in the superclass, and there is a method of the same signature (name and parameters only – the method signature excludes the return type) in the subclass, this does not constitute 'method overriding'. The reason is that private methods are not visible to subclasses anyway, and hence cannot be overridden. I am bringing this out here because in your experiments you may declare a method without any access modifier (remember that in C#, default accessibility is private) in the superclass without using the virtual keyword. When you write a method of the same signature in the subclass and compile it, there will be no warnings or errors at all. C#'s method overriding rules still apply – it's just that you are not performing method overriding in this case.

```
 5:       new Child().DoThis();
 6:    }
 7:    public override void DoThis(){
 8:       Console.WriteLine("DoThis of child");
 9:       base.DoThis();
10:    }
11: }
12:
13: class Parent{
14:    public virtual void DoThis(){
15:       Console.WriteLine("DoThis of parent");
16:    }
17: }
```

Output:

```
c:\expt>test
DoThis of child
DoThis of parent
```

Unlike Java

● If you want to override a method in C#, you need to declare the method which is intended to be overridden using the `virtual` keyword in the superclass. You have to declare the overriding method with the `override` keyword in the sub-class.

In Java, You override a method like this:

```
 1: // Child.java
 2: public class Child extends Parent{
 3:    public static void main(String args[]){
 4:       new Child().doSomething();
 5:    }
 6:    void doSomething(){ // no special keyword
 7:       System.out.println("running Child's version");
 8:    }
 9: }
10:
11: class Parent{
12:    void doSomething(){ // no special keyword
13:       System.out.println("running Parent's version");
14:    }
15: }
```

Output:

```
c:\expt>java Child
running Child's version
```

If you want to override a method in C#, you *must* use the virtual and override keywords. A method in the superclass to be overridden must be declared as a virtual method. A method which is overriding a virtual method must be declared as an override method. A non-virtual method (methods are non-virtual by default) cannot be overridden.[13]

This is the correct way to do it using the virtual and override keywords in C#:

```
 1: using System;
 2: public class Child:Parent{
 3:    public static void Main(){
 4:      new Child().DoSomething();
 5:    }
 6:    public override void DoSomething(){
 7:      Console.WriteLine("running Child's version");
 8:    }
 9: }
10:
11: public class Parent{
12:    public virtual void DoSomething(){
13:      Console.WriteLine("running Parent's version");
14:    }
15: }
```

- For Java, an overriding method can have weaker (less strict) accessibility than the overridden method. The following code compiles and works in Java.

```
 1: // Child.java
 2: public class Child extends Parent{
 3:    public static void main(String args[]){
 4:      new Child().doSomething();
 5:    }
 6:    public void doSomething(){
 7:      System.out.println("running Child's version");
```

13. Without the virtual and override keywords, C# does what is similar to 'early binding'. During compilation into MSIL, C# relates a call to an overridden method in any subclass to a jump to the superclass's version of the method. In a virtual method invocation, the runtime type of the instance for which the invocation takes place determines the actual method implementation to invoke. In a non-virtual method invocation, the compile-time type of the instance is the determining factor.

```
 8:    }
 9: }
10:
11: class Parent{
12:    protected void doSomething(){
13:       System.out.println("running Parent's version");
14:    }
15: }
```

However, C# insists that the overriding method must have the *same* accessibility as the overridden method. Examine the following C# class and its corresponding compilation error.

```
 1: using System;
 2: public class Child:Parent{
 3:    public static void Main(){
 4:       Child c = new Child();
 5:       c.DoSomething();
 6:    }
 7:    public override void DoSomething(){
 8:       Console.WriteLine("running Child's version");
 9:    }
10: }
11:
12: public class Parent{
13:    protected virtual void DoSomething(){
14:       Console.WriteLine("running Parent's version");
15:    }
16: }
```

Compilation error:

```
Source1.cs(7,24): error CS0507: 'Child.DoSomething()':
cannot change access modifiers when overriding
'protected' inherited member 'Parent.DoSomething()'
```

Additional notes on virtual methods

- By default (if you do not declare a method with the virtual keyword), methods are non-virtual, and non-virtual methods cannot be overridden.
- Although a virtual method can be overridden, it doesn't have to be. It doesn't matter if a virtual method is not overridden in a subclass – it will be inherited by the subclass and can be invoked normally just like other inherited non-virtual methods.

- A virtual method cannot be declared with the following keywords – `static`, `abstract`, or `override`.

  – Abstract methods are implicitly virtual (they must be overridden in a subclass before they can of use), but you cannot declare a method using both the `abstract` and `virtual` modifiers (this results in a compilation error). Just declare an abstract method with the `abstract` modifier alone.
  – Although an overriding method cannot have the `virtual` modifier, a method declared with the `override` modifier is 'automatically virtual' (in a sense) and you can still override that method in a future subclass.

- Virtual methods cannot be declared as private.[14]

- If you come across the term 'most derived method', it refers to what the name implies. A virtual method can be overridden in a subclass, which in turn can be overridden by another subclass, and so forth. The most derived method is the 'latest overridden version' in the subclass lowest in the hierarchy which has this method implemented.

Method hiding versus method overriding

Try something like this in C# without the `virtual` and `override` keywords (which looks like method overriding in Java):

```
 1: using System;
 2: public class Child:Parent{
 3:   public static void Main(){
 4:     new Child().DoSomething();
 5:   }
 6:   public void DoSomething(){ // override not used
 7:     Console.WriteLine("running Child's version");
 8:   }
 9: }
10:
11: public class Parent{
12:   public void DoSomething(){ // virtual not used
13:     Console.WriteLine("running Parent's version");
14:   }
15: }
```

14. This follows logically – a private method is not visible in a subclass, and a virtual method is meant to be visible so that it can be overridden. So, a virtual private method simply doesn't make any sense.

A compilation *warning* appears, but the assembly file is still created:

```
Test.cs(5,15): warning CS0108: The keyword new is required on
'Child.DoSomething()' because it hides inherited member
'Parent.DoSomething()'
```

The resultant EXE runs as expected too:

```
c:\expt>test
running Child's version
```

It may *seem* that the DoSomething method has been successfully overridden in the subclass despite a warning message. Far from being a discrepancy between the C# standard and the behavior of the C# compiler,[15] you are actually doing something called *method hiding* here, rather than *method overriding* (see section 7.11).

7.11 Method hiding with the new keyword

Please make sure that you understand section 7.10 before you read this section.

Name hiding in C# will be a new concept to Java developers. In C#, the new keyword can be used for two purposes, the first of which is well understood:

- as an operator – to create a new instance of a class or struct;
- as a modifier – to create a new class member (method, field, constant, property, type) which hides an inherited member from a superclass.

I will concentrate on the second use in this section.

You can use the new keyword to hide a class member. In this case, we shall be concentrating on method hiding (hence the name of this section). However, the same idea can be applied to other class members (property hiding, field hiding, etc.).

Examine the program which follows. It shows two classes A and B – both contain the DoThis() method, and B is a subclass of A.

```
1: using System;
2:
3: class A{
4:    public virtual void DoThis(){
5:        Console.WriteLine("A");
6:    }
7: }
```

15. Initially I thought that this behavior was due to a bug in my C# compiler. I have never heard of 'method hiding' in all my years as a Java developer!

```
 8:
 9: class B:A{ // B extends A
10:    public override void DoThis(){
11:       Console.WriteLine("B");
12:    }
13: }
14:
15: class TestClass{
16:    public static void Main(){
17:
18:       A temp1 = new A();
19:       temp1.DoThis(); // output: A
20:
21:       B temp2 = new B();
22:       temp2.DoThis(); // output: B
23:
24:       A temp3 = new B();
25:       temp3.DoThis(); // output: B
26:
27:       A temp4 = (A)temp2;
28:       temp4.DoThis(); // output: B
29:    }
30: }
```

Output:

```
c:\expt>test
A
B
B
B
```

Lines 1–13 give a proper example of method overriding in C#. You need to use the virtual and override keywords. Now examine the output results. The output from lines 19 and 22 is expected – I have included it in the example for completeness. Examine line 24 in which a new instance of the B class is created, and referenced via a variable of type A. Regardless of the variable's type, when DoThis() on the instance is invoked, the overridden one executes.[16] The output from line 28 simply serves to reinforce the same idea. Regardless of what supertype the instance of B is cast into, the overridden DoThis() method coded in class B runs.

16. From within class B, you can invoke the overridden method in A by using the base keyword (as in base.DoThis()) in the overriding DoThis() method.

What happens if you omit the `virtual` and `override` keywords in C#? Replacing lines 1–13 with the following still gives a successful compilation (with a warning) that produces a different output althogether.

```
 1: using System;
 2:
 3: class A{
 4:    public void DoThis(){
 5:       Console.WriteLine("A");
 6:    }
 7: }
 8:
 9: class B:A{
10:    public void DoThis(){
11:       Console.WriteLine("B");
12:    }
13: }
```

Compilation warning:

```
test.cs(10,15): warning CS0108: The keyword new is required on
'B.DoThis()' because it hides inherited member 'A.DoThis()'
```

Output:

```
c:\expt>test
A
B
A
A
```

Despite the compiler warning, compilation continues to completion to produce `test.exe`. What the compiler warning says is that because `DoThis()` in class `A` (line 4) hasn't been declared with the `virtual` modifier, it is not a method which can be overridden. (If you insert the `override` modifier on line 10 in an attempt to perform an override, you will get a compilation error, not a warning.) Hence, what we are doing here is 'method hiding' in which the new method declared in class `B` (lines 10–12) hides the old method of the same name in the superclass.

What this means is that the data type of the variable used to reference the object is taken into consideration when determining which of the two methods to invoke. As demonstrated, if the reference variable is of type `A`, it doesn't matter if the actual instance being referred to is of class `A` or `B`, the `DoThis()` method which is coded in `A` is invoked. It hasn't been overridden in `B`, simply hidden.

The proper way to perform method hiding is to use the new keyword. Replace line 10 with this:

```
10:    public new void DoThis(){
```

and there will be no compiler warning. The compiler is assured that you know that you are performing method hiding rather than method overriding.

Additional notes

- A class member cannot be declared with both the override and new modifiers. They are antagonistic.
- A new point of specialization is created when new and virtual are used together. This means if you write another class C, which subclasses B, C can contain another DoThis() method of the same signature which either overrides the method in B, or hides the method in B.

Examine these three classes:

```
class A   {public void DoThis(){}}
class B:A{public virtual new void DoThis(){}}
class C:B{public override void DoThis(){}}
```

In this case, B is hiding A's method, and C is overriding B's method.

Now examine these three classes:

```
class A   {public void DoThis(){}}
class B:A{public new void DoThis(){}}
class C:B{public new void DoThis(){}}
```

Here we have B hiding A's method, and C hiding B's method again. If an instance of C is cast into type A, invoking DoThis() on this object will execute A's method – not B's or C's.

Method overriding in Java

For those who are not very sure of what will happen during method overriding in Java, I have included the next example in Java as a reference. Remember that Java does not have this method hiding feature, only method overriding.

```
1: // Test.java
2:
3: class A{
4:    public void doThis(){
5:       System.out.println("A");
```

```
 6:    }
 7: }
 8:
 9: class B extends A{
10:    public void doThis(){ // properly overridden
11:        System.out.println("B");
12:    }
13: }
14:
15: public class Test{
16:    public static void main(String args[]){
17:        A temp1 = new A();
18:        temp1.doThis();
19:
20:        B temp2 = new B();
21:        temp2.doThis();
22:
23:        A temp3 = new B();
24:        temp3.doThis();
25:
26:        A temp4 = (A)temp2;
27:        temp4.doThis();
28:    }
29: }
```

Output:

```
c:\expt>java Test
A
B
B
B
```

7.12 Static methods

Static methods in C# are very similar to static methods in Java. You declare a static method using the `static` keyword. A static method belongs to the class as a whole, rather than to a single instance of the class.

Similarly, you invoke a static method by prefixing the method name with the class name followed by a dot.

```
1: using System;
2:
```

```
 3: class MainClass{
 4:    static void Main(){
 5:       TestClass.DoSomething();
 6:    }
 7: }
 8:
 9: class TestClass{
10:    static public void DoSomething (){
11:       Console.WriteLine("running static method");
12:    }
13: }
```

Output:

```
c:\expt>test
running static method
```

Like Java

A static method cannot refer to non-static methods or other non-static members.

Unlike Java

You cannot invoke a static method using a reference to an instance of that class. You need to use the class name to invoke a static method, or access a static member. Java allows you to invoke a static method using a variable referring to an instance of the class, as shown in the example below.

You can do this in Java:

```
 1: // TestMain.java
 2: public class TestMain{
 3:    public static void main(String args[]){
 4:       TestClass c = new TestClass();
 5:       c.doSomething(); // or TestClass.doSomething();
 6:    }
 7: }
 8: class TestClass{
 9:    public static void doSomething(){
10:       System.out.println("running static method");
11:    }
12: }
```

However in C#, this will give a compilation error:

```
 1: using System;
 2: public class TestMain{
 3:   public static void Main(){
 4:     TestClass c = new TestClass();
 5:     c.DoSomething(); // use TestClass.DoSomething();
 6:   }
 7: }
 8: class TestClass{
 9:   public static void DoSomething(){
10:     Console.WriteLine("running static method");
11:   }
12: }
```

Compilation error:

```
Test.cs(4,5): error CS0176: Static member
'TestClass.DoSomething()' cannot be accessed with an
instance reference; qualify it with a type name instead
```

Additional notes

● The `static` keyword can be used with fields, methods, properties, operators, and constructors, but *cannot* be used with indexers, destructors, or types.

● Static function members (methods, instance constructors, properties, and operators) are always non-virtual.

● A static member *cannot* be declared with the following modifiers: `virtual`, `override`, and `abstract`.

7.13 Sealed methods (Java final methods)

It will be wise to make sure you understand section 7.10 before reading this section.

C# sealed methods are simply Java final methods – methods which cannot be overridden in subclasses. Here is an example of how an attempt to override a sealed method will result in a compilation error:

```
1: using System;
2:
3: class GrandChild:Child{
4:   public static void Main(){
```

```
5:    }
6:
7:    // this will cause a compilation error.
8:    public override void DoSomething(){
9:       Console.WriteLine("running version 3");
10:   }
11: }
12:
13: class Child:Parent{
14:    public override sealed void DoSomething(){
15:       Console.WriteLine("running version 2");
16:  }
17: }
18:
19: class Parent{
20:    public virtual void DoSomething(){
21:       Console.WriteLine("running version 1");
22:  }
23: }
```

Compilation error:

```
test.cs(8,24): error CS0239: 'GrandChild.DoSomething()' :
cannot override inherited member 'Child.DoSomething()'
because it is sealed
```

Like Java

Sealed methods cannot be overridden in subclasses.

Additional note

It doesn't make sense to declare a method as sealed unless it is itself an overridden method of a subclass. If you are defining a new method in a class, and do not want subclasses to override it, simply do not declare the method using the virtual modifier. Non-virtual methods cannot be overridden in subclasses, though they can be hidden (see section 7.11). In other words, you almost always use the sealed modifier together with the override modifier in a method declaration.

chapter 8

Miscellaneous issues

This chapter discusses miscellaneous topics not covered in previous chapters. In particular, it covers C# access modifiers, static members, volatile fields, C# constants, and read-only variables.

8.1 Access modifiers

Java has four categories of protection access for methods and variables:

- `private`
- `protected`
- (default, or package – no access modifier specified)
- `public`.

C# has five categories of protection access:[1]

- `private`
- `protected`
- `internal`
- `internal protected`
- `public`.

Java's default (also known as package) accessibility is no longer there, and there is a new accessibility category based on the `internal` modifier in C#.

Table 8.1 shows more information about C#'s accessibility options.

Table 8.2 shows the applicable accessibility modifiers for the various types/members in C#, together with their default accessibility if no accessibility modifier is specified in their declarations. Note that no access modifiers are allowed in the

---

1. If you have done C++ before, you might have heard of C++'s `friend` keyword. Both Java and C# have discarded the 'friend function' feature of C++. `friend` is not a keyword in both Java and C#.

Table 8.1   Declared accessibility of C# type members and their meanings

Access modifier	Meaning
`public`	Access unlimited (same as Java)
`protected`	Access limited to enclosing type and subtypes (same as Java)
`internal`	Access limited to this program (i.e. all codes in the same source file)
`protected internal`	Access limited to this program and types derived from the enclosing type (even if it is coded outside this program)
`private`	Access limited to the enclosing type only (same as Java)

Table 8.2   Applicable access modifiers for types and their members

Category	Applicable accessibility modifiers	Default accessibility
Namespaces[1]	(implicit) `public`	`public`
Classes, interfaces, and structs declared within a namespace	`public, internal`	`internal`
Class members[2]	`public, protected, internal, protected internal, private`	`private`
Struct members[3]	`public, internal, private`	`private`
Interface members[1]	(implicit) `public`	`public`
Enumeration members[1]	(implicit) `public`	`public`

1. No access modifiers are allowed in the declaration of namespaces, interface members, and enumeration members.

2. Class members include constants, fields, methods, properties, events, indexers, operators, constructors, destructors, and other methods.

3. structs are implicitly sealed.

declaration of namespaces, interface members, and enumeration members – although these types/members do have a default implicit accessibility level.

Like Java

The accessibility of a type member is established by both:

- the declared accessibility of the member itself; *and*
- the accessibility of its enclosing type.

For example, a field declared as `public` in a class which has `internal` accessibility will not be accessible from another class written in a separate program. You must be able to have access to the class before you can access its members even though it may seem that a member's accessibility is less strict (more accessible) than its enclosing type. Both factors have to be considered when determining the final accessibility of a member.

Unlike Java

● For Java, variables or methods declared with no access modifiers will be given 'default' accessibility protection. For C#, if no access modifiers are used in the declaration of variables and methods, the default protection is private.[2] Refer to Table 8.2 for the default accessibility levels for other types in C#.

● You will realize that unlike Java, whereby accessibility is often affected by whether a class is in a particular package, namespaces in C# do not play a role in accessibility.

8.1.1   Further examples

I have presented several examples below to illustrate the accessibility domain of a class member declared as `internal` and `protected  internal` because these are the special accessibility levels not applicable in Java.

Let's explore the `internal` accessibility modifier first. Study `Source1.cs` below:

```
 1:  // Source1.cs
 2:
 3:  namespace NameSpace1{
 4:    public class A{
 5:       internal static int X;
 6:       protected internal static int Y;
 7:       public static int Z;
 8:
 9:       static void DoThis(){
10:          X = 1;
11:       }
12:
13:       class NestedA{
14:         static void DoThis(){
15:            A.X = 1;
16:         }
17:       }
18:    }
19:
20:    class B{
21:      static void DoThis(){
```

---

2. I think that this is a good move on the part of C#. Good OO programming principles dictate that class members should be 'as private as possible', and this feature of C# helps developers who omit the accessibility modifier (whether on purpose or through laziness) attain this goal whether they like it or not!

```
22:          A.X = 1;
23:        }
24:      }
25:  }
26:
27:  namespace NameSpace2{
28:     internal class C{
29:
30:       public static int W;
31:
32:       static void DoThis(){
33:         NameSpace1.A.X = 1;
34:       }
35:     }
36:  }
```

This program compiles properly. Remember to compile with the /target: library option if you are using csc.exe since there is no Main() method:

```
c:\expt>csc /target:library Source1.cs
```

In this program, the accessibility of the field X in class A of the NameSpace1 namespace (declared on line 5) is being tested on line 33.

The program shows that NameSpace1.A.X is accessible from:

● within the same class (line 10);

● a nested class of the same class (line 15);

● another class of the same namespace in the same source file (line 22);

● another class of a different namespace in the same source file (line 33).

In fact, X is accessible from anywhere inside the same program (codes in the same source file). However, X is *not* accessible from another class defined in a separate source file regardless of whether that class is in the same namespace as A. The following program, Source2.cs, written in another source file demonstrates this. Remember to compile Source2.cs using the /reference option if you are using csc.exe so that it can find the classes you have just written in Source1.dll:

```
c:\expt>csc /reference:Source1.dll /target:library Source2.cs
```

```
1:   // Source2.cs
2:
3:   using NameSpace1;
4:   using NameSpace2;
```

```
 5:
 6:   // default namespace
 7:   class D:A{
 8:     static void DoThis() {
 9:       A.X = 1; // compilation error
10:     }
11:   }
12:
13:   namespace NameSpace1 {
14:     class E{
15:       static void DoThis() {
16:         A.X = 1; // compilation error
17:       }
18:     }
19:   }
```

Compilation error:

```
Source2.cs(9,5): error CS0122: 'NameSpace1.A.X' is inaccessible
due to its protection level
Source2.cs(16,7): error CS0122: 'NameSpace1.A.X' is inaccessible
due to its protection level
```

NameSpace1.A.X is only accessible to code written in Source1.cs only. Even a class in the same namespace (class E in Source2.cs) cannot access it if it is in another program (source file).

Having understood internal accessibility, let's try out protected internal. Line 6 of Source1.cs declares field Y as protected internal. This time, Y is accessible to a class in an external program which is a subclass of NameSpace1.A. I have modified Source2.cs to prove this point:

```
 1:   // Source2.cs
 2:
 3:   using NameSpace1;
 4:
 5:   namespace NameSpace3 {
 6:     class D:A{ // subclass
 7:       static void DoThis() {
 8:         A.Y = 1; // ok
 9:       }
10:     }
11:     class E{ // non-subclass
12:       static void DoThis() {
13:         A.Y = 1; // compilation error
14:       }
```

```
15:    }
16:  }
```

Compilation error:

```
Source2.cs(13,7): error CS0122: 'NameSpace1.A.Y' is inaccessible
due to its protection level
```

Here, `A.Y` is accessible by a class in another program (source file) as long as that class is a subclass of `NameSpace1.A`.

As a final note, notice that although both fields `NameSpace1.A.Z` and `NameSpace2.C.W` in `Source1.cs` (declared on lines 7 and 30 respectively) have been declared as `public`, their resultant accessibility is different because class `A` is a `public` class, while class `C` is an `internal` class.

Because class `C` is internal, you cannot access the class from another program. So despite `C.W` being declared as `public`, it is inaccessible from a class written in, say, `Source2.cs`. On the other hand, `A.Z` is truly free for all to use.

8.2 Static members

This section covers static members in general. More information on static methods can be found in section 7.12.

The use of `static` in C# is almost identical to the use of the same keyword in Java. A class member declared without the `static` modifier is considered non-static or belonging to an instance. A static member of a class does not belong to an instance of this class, but rather to the whole class itself. A non-static member of a class is also known as an instance member.

A static field identifies only one storage location so that no matter how many instances of this class are created, there is only one copy of this static field for a particular application domain.[3] The following is an example showing the use of static fields and methods in C#.

```
1:  class TestClass{
2:
3:    int InstField;         // instance field
4:    static int StatField;  // static field
5:
6:    void DoThis() {
7:      InstField = 1; // same as this.InstField=1
8:      StatField = 1; // same as TestClass.StatField=1
9:    }
```

3. A .NET application domain is similar to a Win32 process.

```
10:
11:     static void DoThat(){
12:        // InstField = 1; // compilation error
13:        StatField = 1;     // same as TestClass.StatField=1
14:     }
15:
16:     static void Main() {
17:        TestClass t = new TestClass();
18:        t.InstField = 1;
19:        TestClass.StatField = 1;
20:
21:        // t.StatField = 1;           // compilation error
22:        // TestClass.InstField = 1; // compilation error
23:     }
24: }
```

Line 12 will result in a compilation error because method DoThis is static. You cannot access a non-static member from a static context. Line 22 results in a compilation error because you cannot refer to a non-static member via its class name. A non-static member belongs to an instance of the class and should be referred to by an object reference variable referring to an instance of this class.

Line 21 results in a compilation error (this statement is okay in Java) because in C# you can only refer to a static member via its class name, never by an object reference variable.

Like Java

Static members of a class can only access other static members of the class. It is not legal for a static method to access a non-static (instance) field, or for a static field to refer to another non-static field. The reverse is not true though – a non-static member can invoke or access both non-static and static members.

Unlike Java

Java allows you to refer to a class's static variable via a variable which references an instance of that class. In the case of C#, you cannot access a static member via an object reference variable. You can only access a static field using the class name.

Additional notes

- In C#, a static member *cannot* be declared with the following modifiers: virtual, override, and abstract.
- All C# constants (declared with the C# const keyword) are implicitly static.

8.3   C# constants and read-only fields (Java final variables)

In Java, a final variable is one whose value cannot be reassigned once it has been given a value. You can only use a final variable after it has been assigned a value – all final variables must be assigned values at some point in time before its first use, otherwise the compiler complains.

In Java:

```
1:  // FinalTest.java
2:  public class FinalTest{
3:     final int FINAL_VAR;
4:
5:     public FinalTest(int newValue){
6:       FINAL_VAR = newValue; // compilation error if
                                           omitted.
7:     }
8:
9:     public static void main(String args[]){
10:       FinalTest f = new FinalTest(4);
11:     }
12:  }
```

If FINAL_VAR has been declared with the static modifier too on line 3, you will have to either:

● initialize it in the same statement it is declared in (e.g. final static int FINAL_VAR = 3;); or

● initialize it in a static initializer (e.g. static { FINAL_VAR = 3; }) somewhere in the class.

This is because you cannot assign a value to a static variable from outside a static context, and the constructor coded above (lines 5–7) is an instance method.

In C#, instead of final variables, there are C# constants, and read-only fields.[4]

8.3.1   C# constants

A C# constant is like a final variable which *must* be initialized in the same declaration statement. What this means is that you cannot declare a constant and initialize it in a separate statement. You use the C# const keyword to declare a constant.

---

4. C# constants are more similar to Java final variables than readonly fields. However both constants and read-only variables will be discussed here.

Unlike Java

- Constants in C# are always implicitly static. However, you cannot declare a constant with both the const and static keywords.
- The value assigned to a constant must be a literal, and cannot be decided on during runtime.
- You *must* assign a constant a value during declaration. You cannot even declare a constant and assign a value to it in a static constructor.[5] The compiler will complain once it sees a constant variable being declared but not initialized in the same statement:

```
class MyClass{
  const int FinalVar;
}
```

Compilation error:

```
test.cs(2,22): error CS0145: A const field requires a value to
be provided
```

Like Java

A constant is similar to a Java final static variable except that it must be initialized in the same statement as the one that it has been declared in.

```
1:   using System;
2:   class TestClass{
3:     const int FinalVar = 5;
4:
5:     public static void Main(){
6:        Console.WriteLine(FinalVar);
7:     }
8:   }
```

In the code above, you can use TestClass.FinalVar instead of FinalVar within the class itself (on line 6), since all constants are implicitly static members of the class.

8.3.2   C# read-only fields

The main difference between a C# constant and a C# read-only field is that a read-only field can be initialized in a separate statement (in a constructor) from the one

5. A C# static constructor is similar to a Java static initializer.

in which it is declared.[6] Hence, unlike a constant, a read-only field's value can be determined at runtime, as long as the read-only field is initialized before it is used.

Direct assignments to read-only fields can only occur:

- in an instance constructor (for non-static read-only fields);
- in a static constructor (for static read-only fields);
- in the declaration statement itself.[7]

A read-only field can be reassigned a new value any number of times, as long as the condition above is satisfied. Read-only fields are generally used instead of constants if the value of that field cannot be determined before runtime.

Use the C# `readonly` keyword to declare a read-only variable:

```
 1:  class TestReadOnly{
 2:     readonly int FinalVar;
 3:
 4:     TestReadOnly(int newValue){
 5:        // assignment in an instance constructor
 6:        FinalVar = newValue;
 7:     }
 8:
 9:     public static void Main(){
10:        TestReadOnly tro = new TestReadOnly(9);
11:        System.Console.WriteLine(tro.FinalVar);
12:     }
13:  }
```

Output:

```
c:\expt>test
9
```

The code below produces a compilation error because an attempt is made to assign `FinalVar` with a value *outside a constructor*.

```
 1: class TestReadOnly{
 2:    readonly int FinalVar;
```

6. If you are wondering why C# differentiates constants from read-only fields, I believe it has to do with performance optimization. Theoretically, the CLR can optimize constants if it is known that their values are fixed even before runtime. For the same reason, it is good programming practice to declare a non-changing variable as a constant (or read-only variable) not only to prevent some code from accidentally altering that value (leading to mysterious bugs), but also because a clever compiler can take advantage of this fact to squeeze out a few more milliseconds.

7. The part of the declaration statement whereby a value is assigned to the declared field is known as a variable initializer. For example, in the statement `int i = 3;`, `i = 3` is the variable initializer.

```
3:
4:     public static void Main(){
5:        TestReadOnly tro = new TestReadOnly();
6:        tro.FinalVar = 1; // illegal assignment
7:     }
8:  }
```

Compilation error:

```
test.cs(6,5): error CS0191: A readonly field cannot be assigned
to (except in a constructor or a variable initializer)
```

You can assign a value to a read-only variable when it is being declared (as part of the variable initializer). For example, you can replace line 2 with:

```
2: readonly int FinalVar = 9;
```

Additional Notes

● Read-only variables are somewhat similar to Java final variables in that once they have been assigned a value (in a constructor, or in the declaration statement) you cannot reassign a new value outside the constructor.

● Read-only variables are *not* implicitly static. Compare this with C# constants – C# constants are implicitly static. Java final variables are also not implicitly static.

● You can declare a read-only variable as static (e.g. `static readonly int j;`), and initialize it either:

    – on the same statement as the declaration; or
    – in a static constructor (see section 7.4).

8.4 Volatile fields

Like Java, C# has a `volatile` keyword for modifying fields only. This special modifier is usually used only in multi-threaded programming. Threads might cache the values of member fields for efficiency and, since threads can share the same field, it might be possible that a particular thread's cache field value is out of sync with the actual field's value. This is especially so if other concurrently running threads update the field of a shared object.

In both Java and C#, declaring a field as volatile tells the compiler that it should not attempt to perform optimizations (such as caching) on the field. The system always reads the current (latest) value of a volatile field at the point it is requested, and writes the value of the field immediately on assignment.

You declare a field as volatile by inserting the `volatile` keyword in front, as with all other modifiers. The following statement declares `temp` as a public static `int` variable which is also volatile: `public static` **`volatile`** `int temp;`

Like Java

- You inform the compiler not to optimize a shared field by declaring it as volatile.

- You should declare fields which are shared by multiple concurrently-running threads as volatile – this is especially so if this field is not synchronized within a `lock` block.[8]

Additional notes

- A volatile field cannot be passed to a `ref` or `out` parameter of a method (see section 7.2.2).

The following will cause a compilation error:

```
 1: class TestClass{
 2:     private volatile int MyInt;
 3:
 4:     public void DoThis(ref int i){
 5:     }
 6:
 7:     public static void Main(){
 8:       TestClass tc = new TestClass();
 9:       tc.MyInt = 3;
10:       tc.DoThis(ref tc.MyInt);
11:     }
12:  }
```

Compilation error:

```
test.cs(10,19):  error  CS0676: Cannot  pass  volatile  field
'TestClass.MyInt' as ref or out, or take its address
```

- A volatile field cannot be read-only as well. The following declaration results in the compilation error 'A field can not be both volatile and read-only':

```
public readonly volatile bool b;
```

Likewise, you cannot declare a constant as volatile.[9]

---

8. A C# `lock` block is similar to a `synchronized` block in Java. A locked block is protected by an object mutex, and can only be assessed by any single thread at only one time. See Chapter 17.
9. A volatile constant doesn't make sense since you cannot change a constant's value.

● The type of a field marked as volatile can only be of the following:

- any reference type;
- a pointer type (within an unsafe context) – see section 9.1;
- the following simple (primitive) types only: `sbyte`, `byte`, `short`, `ushort`, `int`, `uint`, `char`, `float`, `bool`;
- an enum (see Chapter 25) type with an enum base type of `sbyte`, `byte`, `short`, `ushort`, `int` and `uint`.

part 3

Types, operators, and flow control

Introduction

The chapters in this part are:

- Chapter 9: C# types
- Chapter 10: C# operators
- Chapter 11: Iteration and flow control.

This part deals with C# types and operators. I shall be covering topics such as the different predefined types in C#, the ranges of the different numeric and floating point types, how to use the various operators, new C# operator keywords and their equivalent in Java (if any), and how operators are used in flow control.

Like the chapters in Part 2, special emphasis will be placed on the differences between C# and Java where operators and types are concerned.

I suggest that the chapters in this part are read quickly from beginning to end. It will be useful to know which operators are provided by C# so that you can come back to the relevant sections when you actually use them in your development work.

9

C# types

Object-oriented purists will argue that C# is 'more OO' than Java in a few ways. One can say that Java is not a pure OO language because it supports primitive types – and primitive types such as Java's `int`, `long`, and `double` are not real objects. (There is, however, a really good reason for not making your `int`s and `long`s objects.[1])

In C#, everything can be treated like an object. Even your `int`s, `char`s, and `long`s – primitive types in C# (primitive types are known officially as 'simple types') – are also subclasses of `System.Object` together with all other C# classes.

Java types are grouped into two main categories:

- primitive types (e.g. `int i`→i is a primitive variable);
- object reference types (e.g. `Object o;`→o is an object reference variable).

In C#, all types are categorized into three groups:

- pointer types
- reference types
- value types.

Table 9.1 shows a brief comparison between types in Java and C#. More detailed information about C# types follows.

---

1. Instantiating objects is an expensive process. When you want to perform a simple arithmetic addition, you want to perform the operation on the stack quickly and efficiently. Some programming languages do not have primitives; even integers are represented as objects. When two integers are to be added, two integer objects are actually created in the heap. The process is wasteful if all you want to do is to perform a simple arithmetic computation (in which case, there is no need to take advantage of the integer object's methods or properties).

So, we have a performance issue if we convert every little thing into objects. Anyway the Java core API includes nice wrapper classes for each of the eight Java primitive types if you really do need them. Read more in section 9.8.3.

TABLE 9.1   Comparing Java and C# types

Java types	C# types
Primitive type	**Value type**
● Java has only eight primitive types: `byte`, `short`, `int`, `long`, `float`, `double`, `boolean`, `char`. ● Primitive types are not objects, and cannot be manipulated as if they are objects. ● Each primitive type variable stores its own copy of the value.	● Types such as `int`, `byte`, `short`, `float`, etc. are known as 'simple types'. All simple types are value types in C#. Value types include other special types (such as enum types and struct types) which are not applicable in Java. ● C# has thirteen simple value types. In addition to those of Java, C# supports unsigned types, and a new `decimal` type for high precision mathematical/financial calculations. ● Value types will be converted into objects when necessary. They can be manipulated as objects and are direct subclasses of `System.Object`.
Reference type Stores a reference to an object on the heap. Can also be assigned a `null` value. It is possible for many reference type variables to refer to the same object.	**Reference type** Similar to Java's reference type.
No equivalent – pointer operations are absolutely impossible in Java.	**Pointer type** Used for pointer operations only in unsafe codes. Pointer types allow the programmer to retrieve address locations of objects, and manipulate the bytes stored in memory directly.

Figure 9.1 shows how C# types are categorized.

9.1   Pointer types

Pointer types are special – they are only used in unsafe codes (code blocks marked with the `unsafe` keyword) and are not usually used in most applications. Pointer types will not be discussed here (see Chapter 29).

9.2   Reference types

Reference types in C# are identical to Java reference types – they refer to objects on the heap. You can skip to the next section if you are already clear about Java reference types – I have included the following paragraphs just to make the text more complete.

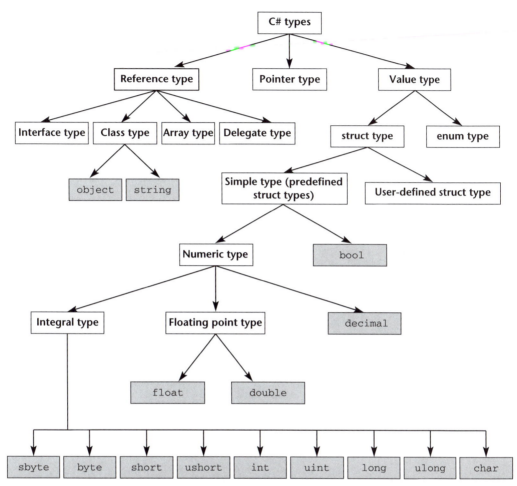

FIGURE 9.1 C# type categorization. The shaded boxes are C# keywords. Besides `object` and `string` (which are aliases for `System.Object` and `System.String`, respectively), the other shaded boxes are simple value types.

Like Java, and unlike C/C++, C# reference types are type-safe, meaning that it is impossible for a reference type variable to refer to some unallocated or random memory space which you can corrupt. Such type-safety means that a C# application cannot corrupt memory which has not been allocated for that application running on the Windows operating system (which supports multi-programming). The only way a C# program can access memory locations directly is via pointer operations in unsafe codes.

Reference types may be:

- class type
- interface type

- array type
- delegate type.

Like Java reference types, C# reference types can be either:

- referring to an instance of the type or subtype stored on the heap;[2] or
- null.

Reference types store references to their objects. With reference types, you can have two reference type variables referring to the same object on the heap, so that performing operations on one variable will affect the object referenced by the other variable (since they are referring to the same object). The code below shows an example of this scenario.

```
 1: using System;
 2:
 3: public class Test{
 4:     public int i=0;
 5:
 6:     public static void Main(){
 7:         Test t1 = new Test();
 8:         Test t2 = new Test();
 9:         t1.i = 1;
10:         t2.i = 2;
11:         Console.WriteLine("t1.i is " + t1.i);
12:         Console.WriteLine("t2.i is " + t2.i);
13:
14:         Console.WriteLine(" --------- ");
15:
16:         Test t3 = new Test();
17:         Test t4 = t3;
18:         t3.i = 1;
19:         t4.i = 2;
20:         Console.WriteLine("t3.i is " + t3.i);
21:         Console.WriteLine("t4.i is " + t4.i);
22:     }
23: }
```

---

2. C++ developers: C# no longer allows you to choose if you want your object to be created on the stack or heap. All C# objects are created on the heap with the new keyword.

Output:

```
c:\expt>test
t1.i is 1
t2.i is 2
---------
t3.i is 2
t4.i is 2
```

In the example above, reference types t3 and t4 refer to the same object due to the assignment on line 17. Hence changing t3's i value will also result in t4's i being changed. Figure 9.2 shows a representation of this scenario.

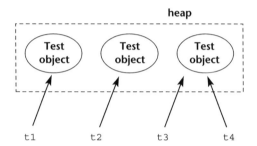

FIGURE 9.2   Only three Test objects are actually created on the heap.

9.3 Value types

C# value types are close to Java primitives, but there are significant differences. Value types will be your enums (see Chapter 25) and structs (see Chapter 26). Simple types (or primitive types of Java) such as int, byte, and float are special predefined struct types which you can use directly.

While reference types store a reference to an object on the heap, value types directly contain their data. As such, similar to the case of Java's primitives, when you assign one value type to another, a new value is created. Each of the value type variables will store their own copy of the values, and changing the value of one will not affect the value stored in the other. The code below illustrates this:

```
1: using System;
2:
3: public class Test{
4:
5:    public static void Main(){
```

```
 6:        int k = 0;
 7:        int j = k;
 8:        k = 1;
 9:        Console.WriteLine("k is " + k);
10:        Console.WriteLine("j is " + j);
20:    }
21: }
```

Output:

```
c:\expt>test
k is 1
j is 0
```

Both value type variables k and j store their own copy of their value due to the assignment on line 7. Assignment of a value type to a variable creates a copy of the value being assigned.

Value types may not be null and operations involving value types are performed on the stack instead of the heap. Value types are 'passed by value' across methods while reference types are 'passed by reference'.[3]

In the discussion here, I shall focus on the predefined simple types of C#. Looking at the type categorization diagram given in Figure 9.1, you will realize that simple types are actually struct types, which are, in turn, value types. Structs will be introduced in Chapter 26.

C# has many more predefined simple types than Java – these are shown in Table 9.2.

Like Java

● You can specify that a number be a long by appending L (or l) after it. You can specify that a floating point number be a float by appending an F (or f). Table 9.3 shows the special character you should put after a number to specify its type in C#.

● If the special character is not specified, by default all floating point numbers are considered to be double values and all integral numbers are considered to be int values.

In both Java and C#, the statement float f = 9.9; causes a compiler error

---

3. The phrase 'pass by reference' across methods can be controversial and is the source of confusion in several programming books. Since a reference type variable stores the address of an object, when you pass a reference type *value* over to a method you are actually passing the address of the object over, thus prompting some to argue that a reference type variable is also passed 'by value'. So when Mughal and Rasmussen stated in their book *A Programmer's Guide to Java Certification* that "in Java, all parameters are passed by value", it is not incorrect.

TABLE 9.2   Comparing simple types in C# and Java

Simple type category	Java	C#	Size (in bytes)	Comments
Non-numeric	boolean	bool	–	Stores only true or false
Numeric: integral	byte	sbyte	1	Range: -2^7 to $+2^7-1$
	–	byte	1	Range: 0 to $+2^8-1$
	short	short	2	Range: -2^{15} to $+2^{15}-1$
	–	ushort	2	Range: 0 to $+2^{16}-1$
	int	int	3	Range: -2^{31} to $+2^{31}-1$
	–	uint	3	Range: 0 to $+2^{32}-1$
	long	long	4	Range: -2^{63} to $+2^{63}-1$
	–	ulong	4	Range: 0 to $+2^{64}-1$
Numeric: floating point	float	float	4	Single precision floating point
	double	double	8	Double precision floating point
	–	decimal	16	High precision decimal notation with 28 significant digits
(Numeric) character	char	char	2	Single Unicode character

TABLE 9.3   Special postfix characters on numbers to depict its type. The character to append is not case sensitive – ul is the same as UL

Append character	Type	Example	Comments
L	long	long temp = 999L;	–
U	uint	uint temp = 999U;	N/A in Java – Java has no unsigned type
UL	ulong	ulong temp = 999UL	N/A in Java – Java has no unsigned type
F	float	float temp = 9.99F	–
M	decimal	decimal temp = 9.99M	N/A in Java – Java has no decimal type

because 9.9 is defaulted to a double value, and an attempt is made to perform an illegal implicit cast of a double to a float (a narrowing cast like this requires explicit casting).

- You can use the hexadecimal representation 0xYYYY (where YYYY represents the hexadecimal value) instead of the common base 10 decimal value.

```
int temp1 = 65;
int temp2 = 0x41;
```

In this case, the expression (temp1==temp2) will be true for both Java and C# since 41_{16} is equivalent to 65_{10}.

- You can use the Unicode representation \uYYYY (where YYYY represents the Unicode value) for character assignment or in string literals. Like Java, characters in C# are 16-bit Unicode values instead of 8-bit ASCII values.

```
char temp4 = '\u0041'; //Unicode char 41(hex) is 'A'
System.Console.WriteLine(temp4); // prints out A;
```

Unlike Java

- Note however, that C# does not support Java's octal representation 0YYY (where YYY is the octal value), and instead ignores any preceding zeros on any numbers.

```
// in Java
int temp3 = 065; // 65 base 8
System.out.println(temp3); // prints out 53
```

```
// in C#
int temp3 = 065; // treated as 65 base 10
```

```
System.Console.WriteLine(temp3);// prints out 65
```

- C# has unsigned integral types while Java does not.
- While the short, int, and long integral types of Java and C# are identical in range, the Java byte is signed but the C# byte is unsigned. C#'s signed 8-bit integral type is sbyte.

9.4 Unsigned types in C#

Unsigned types are types which cannot store values in the negative range (hence unsigned – the values stored are always positive).[4] The unsigned integral types in C# are: byte (*not* ubyte!), ushort, uint, and ulong.[5]

Attempting to assign a negative value to an unsigned numeric type results in a compilation or runtime error, depending on when the assignment is performed. For example, the statement

```
uint i = -3;
```

4. The reason for unsigned types is that you can store twice as many values in the positive range with the same number of bits because one bit is no longer required for storing the sign. Signed types always 'waste' one bit for determining if the value stored is positive or negative. There is no way in Java we can 'save' on the wasted bit, even if we know for certain that a particular value can never be negative. Anyway, this is probably not a significant issue given the amount of memory available to applications today.
5. C/C++ programmers: there is no separate unsigned keyword in C#.

results in a compilation error:

```
Constant value '-3' cannot be converted to a 'uint'
```

9.5 The `decimal` type

The decimal type is unique to C#. It is a 128-bit data type which can represent values from 1.0×10^{-28} to approximately 7.9×10^{28} with 28–29 significant digits, and is particularly suitable for financial or scientific calculations requiring a high level of precision.

According to the C# specification, for decimals with an absolute value smaller than 1.0M,[6] the value represented is exact to the 28th decimal place. For decimals with an absolute value equal to or greater than 1.0M, the value is exact to 28 or 29 significant figures.

At first sight, it may appear that you can implicitly cast a `float` or `double` into a `decimal`. But note that the `decimal` type has a greater precision but a *smaller* range than the `float` or `double` types. As a result, you cannot implicitly cast a `float` or `double` to a `decimal`, and a `decimal` *cannot* be implicitly cast into a `float` or `double`, or any other numeric type. Table 9.4 gives the ranges of the different types.

TABLE 9.4 C# floating type ranges

Simple type	Approximate range
float	$\pm 1.5 \times 10^{-45}$ to $\pm 3.4 \times 10^{38}$
double	$\pm 5.0 \times 10^{-324}$ to $\pm 11.7 \times 10^{308}$
decimal	$\pm 1.0 \times 10^{-28}$ to $\pm 7.9 \times 10^{28}$

9.6 The `char` type

Like Java, a `char` in C# is a 16-bit Unicode character instead of the traditional 8-bit ASCII character of older programming languages. Table 9.5 shows escape the sequences supported by C# which can be used in character assignments or within string literals.

---

6. You put an M or m behind a number or floating point number to indicate that this value should be interpreted as a decimal.

TABLE 9.5   Escape sequences for characters and strings

Escape sequence	Character represented	Comments
\'	single quote	
\"	double quote	Same as in Java
\\	backslash	
\0	null	
\a	alert (beep sound)	No such escape sequence in Java – For example, `System.Console.WriteLine("\a ");` causes a beep.
\b	backspace	
\f	form feed	Same as in Java
\n	new line	
\r	carriage return	
\t	horizontal tab	
\v	vertical tab	No such escape sequence in Java

9.7 The `string` type and string literals

There are two types of string literals in C#:

- regular string literals;
- verbatim string literals.

What we have seen and used so far are regular string literals. These consist of characters enclosed in double quotation marks and may contain escape sequences, hexadecimal (\x) and Unicode (\u) escape sequences within. Examples of regular string literals include the following:

- `"Hello!"`
- `"My \tname is\nMok"`
- `"Apple starts with the letter \u0041, Banana starts with the letter \x42"`

Verbatim string literals are string literals which are 'what they seem'. If you include a @ sign in front of a string literal, everything between the double quotes will be considered part of the string 'as they are'. The @ symbol, in this case, is acting as a verbatim string prefix.

For example, the string temp1 in the statement below will represent a "Hello", followed by a tab, and a "World":

```
string temp1 = "Hello\tWorld"; // regular string literal
```

If you want to include the two characters '\' and 't' in between the two words, you have to use the backslash escape sequence and do something like this:

```
string temp1 = "Hello\\tWorld"; // regular string literal
```

You can also use verbatim strings to do the same thing. The string temp2 in the statement below will represent "Hello\tWorld" – with the '\' and the 't' right in the middle of the two words.

```
string temp2 = @"Hello\tWorld"; //verbatim string literal
```

String literals are useful if you don't want \something to be treated as escape sequences in your string. The simple program below gives more examples showing how to use string literals.

```
 1: using System;
 2:
 3: public class TestClass{
 4:    public static void Main(){
 5:
 6:       string a,b,c,d,e,f,g,h,i,j;
 7:
 8:       a = "hello, world";
 9:       b = @"hello, world";
10:       c = "hello\t world";
11:       d = @"hello\t world";
12:       e = "\\\\server\\share\\file.txt";
13:       f = @"\\server\share\file.txt";
14:       g = "one\ntwo\nthree";
15:       h = @"one
16:    two
17:    three";
18:       i = "\u0041 is for \x41pple";
19:       j = @"\u0041 is for \x41pple";
20:
21:
```

hello, world

hello,   world

hello\t world

\\server\share\file.txt

one
two
three

A is for Apple

\u0041 is for \x41pple

```
22:        Console.WriteLine(a);
23:        Console.WriteLine(b);
24:        Console.WriteLine(c);
25:        Console.WriteLine(d);
26:        Console.WriteLine(e);
27:        Console.WriteLine(f);
28:        Console.WriteLine(g);
29:        Console.WriteLine(h);
30:        Console.WriteLine(i);
31:        Console.WriteLine(j);
32:    }
33: }
```

Output:

```
c:\expt>test
hello, world
hello, world
hello     world
hello\t world
\\server\share\file.txt
\\server\share\file.txt
one
two
three
one
two
three
A is for Apple
\u0041 is for \x41pple
```

9.8 All types are objects

As well as additional unsigned types and a new decimal type, there is another big difference between C# simple types and Java primitive types – C# allows you to treat all types, including value types, as objects. In Java, primitive types are not objects, do not behave like objects, and cannot be treated like objects. If you need an object representation of a primitive type, the Java core library has the following wrapper java.lang classes which can be used in place of the primitives: Byte, Short, Integer, Long, Float, Double, Character, and Boolean.

All types in C# are ultimately objects derived from System.Object. The process whereby CLR converts a simple value type into an object is called *boxing*. Boxing bridges the gap between value types and reference types. It enables a unified view of the type system whereby a value of any type can be treated as an object.

9.8.1 Boxing

Boxing can be performed implicitly or explicitly. The following shows an example of explicit boxing. An `int` simple value type is being boxed when line 7 is executed.

```
 1: using System;
 2:
 3: public class Test{
 4:
 5:   public static void Main(string []args){
 6:     int i = 99;
 7:     object o = (object)i;
 8:     Console.WriteLine(o.ToString());
 9:     Console.WriteLine(o.GetType());
10:   }
11: }
```

Output:

```
c:\expt>test
99
System.Int32
```

`ToString()` and `GetType()` are methods of the `System.Object` (object) class, which return a string representation and type of the object respectively.

You can replace lines 7–9 with the following statements:

```
7:     // remove line 7
8:     Console.WriteLine(i.ToString());
9:     Console.WriteLine(i.GetType());
```

The program compiles and, when executed, produces the same output. In this case, i has been implicitly boxed into an object type. Since all types (including `int`) are subclasses of `object`, such implicit conversions are legal.

The code fragment below does *not* show boxing.

```
// Test is a user-defined class.
Test t = new Test();
object o = t;
```

Boxing is different from converting or casting a reference type (such as `Test` in this example) to the `object` type. In this case, no new object is created. The same instance is used, and is simply regarded as a less derived `object` type. In the case of real boxing, a new object is created and a copy of the value type copied over to this new object.

9.8.2   Unboxing

The opposite of boxing, *unboxing* is the conversion from the object type to any value type. Unlike boxing, unboxing is usually explicit. During unboxing, the object instance that is being unboxed is first checked to see if its original type matches the target value type. Unboxing an object to a wrong value type, or attempting to unbox a null, results in a System.InvalidCastException. The following code fragment shows an int being boxed and unboxed explicitly:

```
int i = 99;
object boxed = (object)i; // boxing
int j = (int)boxed; // unboxing
```

The following gives an InvalidCastException during runtime because the original type of the boxed object does not match a short.

```
int i = 99;
object boxed = (object)i; // boxing
short j = (short)boxed; // InvalidCastException
```

Even if you are trying to cast a boxed up int into a double, or something 'wider' in range, you will still get the exception:

```
int i = 99;
object boxed = (object)i; // boxing
double j = (double)boxed; // InvalidCastException
```

In this case, you need to obtain the initial int value first, and then perform a cast of the int into your desired simple type.

9.8.3   Why the boxing and unboxing?

At this point, you could (and should) be wondering what the purpose of the boxing mechanism is. It might seem better just to make all value types – including the simple types int, long, float, and so on – real object types.

Efficiency is the reason. It is definitely an advantage for all simple types to be objects. Objects come with all the goodness of OO technology – for one thing, you can invoke methods on object types, something you cannot do with Java primitives. However, one big performance issue to consider is that object creation is naturally expensive.

In Java, primitive operations (such as the declaration, assignment, and addition of two int primitive types) are performed totally on the stack. No object is created on the heap if all you want to do is to perform a simple arithmetic addition of two numbers (which translates to no overheads corresponding to object creation). Subsequently the garbage collector will also not need to reclaim anything since no object has been created in the first place.

You can perform the same addition by creating two `java.lang.Integer` objects which encapsulate the two `int` values. The difference is that not only is the latter technique more expensive, it will also be slower because instead of working on the stack, the objects are created and manipulated on the heap. Worse still, you do not even need to take advantage of the OO features of the `Integer` class in this case. You have to live with the overheads of object creation, without even requiring the benefits it brings.

C# wants you to have the best of both worlds – the ability to treat even simple types like objects, and yet avoid the overheads of object creation and destruction unless absolutely necessary.

When simple types are declared and assigned values in C#, no object is created and things are performed quickly on the stack. Only when the type is explicitly boxed, or if a method operation is applied on it (thus causing implicit boxing), will a real object be created on the heap and the value copied over to this object (see Figure 9.3).

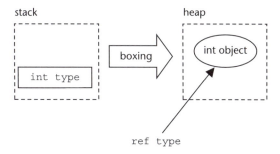

FIGURE 9.3   Only when a value type is boxed is an object created on the heap, and the value copied over. Object creation is expensive and should be avoided if not necessary.

That's how C# gives you the best of both worlds and, best of all, everything is done transparently without the developer's intervention.

9.9 Casting for reference types

Like Java, both C#'s variables and objects are typed.[7] Assuming that there are two classes `Vehicle` and `Car`, and `Vehicle` is the superclass of `Car`, you can have an

---

7. This is not the case for some OO programming languages. In Ruby, for example, variables have no types. A variable can refer to any object of any class.

object of class `Car` being referred to by a variable of type `Vehicle`. And, like Java, you cannot have a `Vehicle` object (object of a super type) referenced by a variable of type `Car` (variable of subtype). Similarly, you can explicitly cast an object to a superclass type.

9.10 Casting for value types

Like Java, casting in C# can be implicit as well as explicit. Widening casts[8] can be performed implicitly, while narrowing casts have to be stated explicitly.

Figure 9.4 shows the allowed implicit casts in C#. Unlike Java, which has only eight primitive types, the C# picture is more complex with four more types.

Figure 9.4 is very useful in determining whether you are performing a narrowing or widening conversion. A type at the start of the arrow can be implicitly cast to a type at the end of the arrow without any loss of precision or overflow. The diagram can be read recursively – for example, a `byte` can be cast into a `decimal` because a forward path exists from `byte` to `decimal`. Alternatively, a `uint` can be implicitly cast into a `long`, `float`, `double`, `ulong`, or `decimal`.

Explicit casting is done in the same way as in Java. Examine the program following.

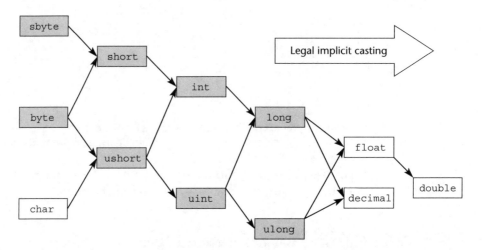

FIGURE 9.4 Direction of arrows shows legal implicit casting. The shaded boxes are integral simple types.

8. A widening cast is a cast from a simple type of lower range to one of higher range. Examples include casting a `short` to an `int`, an `int` to a `long`, a `float` to a `double`. A narrowing cast is the opposite. Casting a `long` to an `int` is a narrowing cast.

```
 1: using System;
 2:
 3: public class Test{
 4:
 5:    public static void Main(string []args){
 6:       double d = 1.11111111;
 7:       float f = (float)d;
 8:       ulong ul = (ulong)f;
 9:       System.Console.WriteLine(d);
10:       System.Console.WriteLine(f);
11:       System.Console.WriteLine(ul);
12:    }
13: }
```

Output:

```
c:\expt>test
1.11111111
1.111111
1
```

Line 7 in the program above performs an explicit cast of a double to a float. Line 8 shows an explicit cast from a float to a ulong. Both are narrowing casts.

Note that although decimal is also used to store floating point values, the decimal type is structured differently from a float or double, and explicit casting is required between decimal and a float or a double in either direction.

Remember that (like Java) an explicit narrowing cast may result in some unexpected results because of overflow or underflow. The code below shows some explicit casts which result in meaningless values because the narrowing cast results in an underflow.

```
 1: using System;
 2:
 3: public class Test{
 4:
 5:    public static void Main(string []args){
 6:       int i = -32769;
 7:       short s = (short)i; // range of s is -32768 to 32767
 8:       uint ui = (uint)i; // range of ui is 0 to 4294967295
 9:       System.Console.WriteLine(i);
10:       System.Console.WriteLine(s);
11:       System.Console.WriteLine(ui);
12:    }
13: }
```

Output:

```
c:\expt>test
-32769
32767
4294934527
```

C# has a special `checked` operator (which has no equivalent in Java) that can be used to throw an exception if an explicit cast causes an overflow (see section 10.4).

9.11 Common typing with other .NET languages

Adherence to the CTS enables all .NET languages to interoperate. Having a common type system enables codes from different languages to integrate seamlessly. You can easily pass a variable of a common type between methods written in different .NET languages. You can even write a class in C# which inherits from a class written in VB .NET. One factor that makes such interoperability possible is the adherence of each .NET programming language to the CTS.

The CTS specifies a set of common types shared by all the .NET programming languages. You can either use the full .NET framework type name or the C# alias[9] in your C# programs. Table 9.6 shows the available C# aliases for types defined in the CTS.

This implies that the following two statements are equivalent, except that the first is easier to read:

```
ulong temp = 99L; // usage of C# alias
System.UInt64 temp = 99L; // usage of full type name
```

Other .NET languages may have their own aliases for the .NET types too, so that writing in those languages will be more natural. For example, for VB .NET developers, their familiar `Integer` type maps to `System.Int32`. And for J# developers, J#'s `int` type also maps to `System.Int32`. VB .NET's `Integer` type and J#'s `int` type refer to exactly the same type as C#'s `int` – a 32-bit signed integer.

Additional notes:

- All the types listed in Table 9.6, except `object` and `string`, are referred to as *simple* types. Simple types are value types – on the other hand, `object` and `string` are reference types.

9. Needless to say, this will be the more popular (and recommended) choice. Who would prefer to write 'System.String' instead of 'string'?

TABLE 9.6 C# aliases for BCL types

C# alias	.NET framework type
bool	System.Boolean
byte	System.Byte
sbyte	System.SByte
char	System.Char
decimal	System.Decimal
double	System.Double
float	System.Single
int	System.Int32
uint	System.UInt32
long	System.Int64
ulong	System.UInt64
long	System.Int64
ulong	System.UInt64
object	System.Object
short	System.Int16
ushort	System.UInt16
string	System.String

● To display the actual type a C# variable represents, use the `GetType()` [10] method of `System.Object`. For example, the following statement displays the system alias that represents the type of `myVariable`:

```
Console.WriteLine(myVariable.GetType());
```

10. `System.Object` is the superclass of all C# classes (very much like `java.lang.Object`). As such, all methods declared within are inherited to every C# class – `GetType()` is one such method.

10

C# operators

Learning about C# operators will be easy for Java developers since most of those in C# have been borrowed from C/C++ and Java. I have listed them in Table 10.1 and made remarks where there are differences. There are a few special operator keywords – typeof, checked, unchecked, is, and as – which should be noted carefully.

10.1 Operators and their precedence in C#

TABLE 10.1 C# operators in decreasing order of precedence

Higher precedence	
Operator category	**Operators**
Primary	`x.y  f(x)  a[x]  x++  x--  new typeof` `checked unchecked`
Unary	`+  -  !  ~  ++x  --x  (T)x`
Multiplicative	`*  /  %`
Additive	`+  -`
Shift	`<<  >>`
Relational and type testing	`<  >  <=  >=  is  as`
Equality	`==  !=`
Logical AND	`&`
Logical XOR	`^`
Logical OR	`|`
Conditional AND	`&&`
Conditional OR	`||`
Conditional (ternary)	`?:`
Assignment	`=  *=  /=  %=  +=  -=  <<=  >>=  &=  ^=  |=`

All operators in the same category have the same precedence. To decide which operator in a particular group takes precedence, follow these associative rules:

- except for the assignment operators, all other binary operators are left associative – for example, a+b-c is the same as (a+b)-c;
- the assignment operators and conditional (ternary) operator are right associative – for example, if a, b, and c are non-boolean variables of the same type, a=b=c is the same as a=(b=c) [1];
- you can use brackets to enforce precedence. [2]

Each operator is described in Table 10.2:

TABLE 10.2 C# operators with brief descriptions – operators which require special attention for Java developers are shaded and are detailed in later sections

Category	Operator	Comments
Primary	x.y	*Dot operator*[1] Used to specify the member of an object/class – x is the object, y is the member
	f(x)	Used to list the arguments or parameters to a method – f is the method name, and x represents the method parameter(s)
	a[x]	Used to index an array or an C# indexer (see Chapter 21)
	x++	*Post increment operator* Same as Java
	x--	*Post decrement operator* Same as Java
	new	*new operator* Used to create an instance of a class – besides being an operator keyword, note that the new keyword can also be used as a modifier in C# for name hiding (see section 7.11)
	typeof	*typeof operator* Returns the System.Type object representing the type of the object it is applied to – similar to java.lang.Object's getClass() method
	checked	*checked operator* Control overflow checking for mathematical operations – no equivalent in Java
	unchecked	*unchecked operator* Control overflow checking for mathematical operations – no equivalent in Java

(Continued)

1. The value of c is assigned to b. This is followed by the value of b being assigned to a.
2. Please *do* use brackets to make your codes look clearer if you are using multiple operators in a single expression. Expressions containing many operators are very difficult to read and, if there are no brackets to specify precedence, it becomes necessary to refer to the precedence table.

TABLE 10.2 Continued

Category	Operator	Comments
Unary	+	*Unary plus* Same as Java – example: +3
	–	*Unary minus* Same as Java – example: –3
	!	*(Boolean) logical negation operator* Only to be used on `boolean` values – returns `true` or `false` only. Same as Java's ! operator
	~	*Bitwise complement operator* Only to be used on the following C# simple types – `int`, `uint`, `long`, `ulong`. Same as Java's ~ operator
	++x	*Prefix increment operator* Same as Java
	--x	*Prefix decrement operator* Same as Java
	`(T)expression`	*Cast operator* Used to explicitly cast an expression into another type – `T` denotes the new type. Same as Java
Multiplicative	*	*Mathematical multiplication* (also used for dereferencing pointers in unsafe codes) Same as Java
	/	*Mathematical integral division* Same as Java
	%	*Mathematical remainder (modulus)* Same as Java
Additive	+	*Mathematical addition (binary add)* Same as Java
	–	*Mathematical subtraction (binary minus)* Same as Java
Shift	<<	*(Bitwise) Left-shift operator* Same as Java
	>>	*(Bitwise) Right-shift operator*[2] Same as Java *(Continued)*

TABLE 10.2 Continued

Category	Operator	Comments
Relational and type testing	<	*Smaller-than operator* Same as Java
	>	*Bigger-than operator* Same as Java
	<=	*Smaller-than or equals operator* Same as Java
	>=	*Bigger-than or equals operator* Same as Java
	`is`	*is operator* Used to check if an object is of a particular type – similar to Java's `instanceof` operator
	`as`	*as operator* Can be viewed as a combination of the `is` operator and a cast – no equivalent in Java
Equality	==	*Equality operator* Slightly different from Java's == when used to compare string objects – otherwise very similar to Java's == operator
	!=	*Inequality operator* Because the == operator behaves slightly differently in C# and Java, the != operator, which returns the complementary result of the == operator is also different – returns the complementary result of the == operator
Bitwise/ boolean AND	&	*&-operator* Like Java, can be used for both `bool` (boolean AND) and integral (bitwise AND) types
Bitwise/ boolean XOR	^	*XOR operator* Like Java, can be used for both `bool` (boolean AND) and integral (bitwise AND) types
Bitwise/ boolean OR	|	*| operator* Like Java, can be used for both `bool` (boolean AND) and integral (bitwise AND) types
Conditional AND (also known as short-circuit boolean AND)	&&	*Conditional & operator* Similar to Java's && operator – will only evaluate second operand if first operand is true. Like Java's &&, this operator applies only for `bool` types (not for integral types)

(Continued)

TABLE 10.2 Continued

Category	Operator	Comments
Conditional OR (also known as short-circuit boolean OR)	‖	*Conditional	operator* Similar to Java's ‖ operator – will not evaluate second operand if first operand is true. Like Java's ‖, this operator applies only for `bool` types (not for integral types)
Conditional	?:	*Conditional operator* Only operator which requires three operands (hence, also popularly known as the 'ternary operator') – same as Java's ternary operator
Assignment[3]	=	*Assignment operator* Same as Java
	*=	*Multiplication assignment operator* Same as Java
	/=	*(Integral) Division assignment operator* Same as Java
	%=	*Remainder assignment operator* Same as Java
	+=	*Addition assignment operator* Same as Java
	-=	*Subtraction assignment operator* Same as Java
	<<=	*Left shift assignment operator* Same as Java
	>>=	*Right shift assignment operator* Same as Java
	&=	*AND assignment operator* Same as Java
	^=	*XOR assignment operator* Same as Java
	‖=	*OR assignment operator* Same as Java

Additional C# operators used for unsafe code (see Chapter 29):

Operators for unsafe coding	*	*Pointer operator* Used to declare pointer types and for dereferencing pointers (same symbol is used as the mathematical multiplication operator) – no equivalent in Java *(Continued)*

TABLE 10.2   Continued

Category	Operator	Comments
	&	*Address of operator* Used to retrieve the address of a particular object (same symbol is used as the bitwise and boolean AND operator) – no equivalent in Java
	sizeof	*sizeof operator* Returns the size (number of bytes) of a simple type or other structs – no equivalent in Java
	-	*Member-of operator* Used for accessing a member of a class via pointers, like the . operator – Can only be applied to a pointer type. No equivalent in Java

[1] C++'s :: (class reference operator) has been removed from C#. Use the dot operator instead to refer to a class member.
[2] C# has no >>> operator.
[3] The current implementation of C# converts code like j+=2; into more efficient MSIL codes than j=j+2;. Hence if possible, use +=, -=, /=, etc. in your codes.

10.2   Operator overloading

Operator overloading is a new concept to Java developers since Java doesn't allow operator overloading.[3, 4]

In brief, operator overloading allows you to write special methods (called operators, or operator methods) which are invoked when an overloaded operator is used to perform an operation on one or more operands. For example, you can overload the + operator so that you can 'add up' two objects of type `Matrix` (`Matrix` may be a user-defined class which represents a matrix). The following statements will then make sense:

```
Matrix m1 = new Matrix();
Matrix m2 = new Matrix();
// + operator overloaded to accept Matrix operands
Matrix m3 = m1 + m2;
```

Operator overloading is an elegant way of allowing programmers to perform 'operations' on classes in a more intuitive way. Java does not support operator overloading.

More information about operator overloading can be found in Chapter 22.

3. Some Java programmers may want to argue that the + operator in Java is a pseudo-overloaded operator when it is used for concatenating strings. This is a special case whereby the compiler actually decides if you are doing a numerical addition or a string concatenation depending on the operand types, and hence shows a little 'operator overloading' behavior.
4. Operator overloading is a feature in C++ though.

10.3 `typeof` operator

The `typeof` operator is used to get a representative `System.Type` object of a type or object. There is only one `System.Type` object for each type. C#'s `typeof` is very similar to `java.lang.Object`'s `getClass()` method. `getClass()` returns a `java.lang.Class` object that represents the runtime type of a Java object.

Study this example.

```
 1: using System;
 2: namespace Mok.Book{
 3:    class Test{
 4:      public static void Main(){
 5:         Type t1 = typeof(int);
 6:         Type t2 = typeof(decimal);
 7:         Type t3 = typeof(string);
 8:         Type t4 = typeof(object);
 9:         Type t5 = typeof(Test);
10:
11:         Console.WriteLine(t1);
12:         Console.WriteLine(t2);
13:         Console.WriteLine(t3);
14:         Console.WriteLine(t4);
15:         Console.WriteLine(t5);
16:      }
17:    }
18: } // end namespace
```

Output:

```
c:\expt>test
System.Int32
System.Decimal
System.String
System.Object
Mok.Book.Test
```

`int` and `decimal` are special simple value types which correspond to the .NET `System.Int32` and `System.Decimal` classes respectively. `string` and `object` are C# aliases for the `System.String` and `System.Object` classes too.

One important point to note is that the `typeof` operator can be applied only on type names – it cannot take in an object. For example, the following code fragment will result in a compilation error:

```
// Test is a user defined class
```

```
Test tObject = new Test();
Type t1 = typeof(tObject); // compilation error
```

The compiler will attempt to search for the type definition of t, and on not finding it will throw an exception which says:

```
The type or namespace name 'tObject' could not be found (are you
missing a using directive or an assembly reference?)
```

Here is another example to illustrate how typeof can also work with interfaces and structs (see Chapter 26 for structs).

```
1: using System;
2:
3: interface IMyInterface {}
4: struct MyStruct {}
5:
6: namespace MyNamespace{
7:    class ClassA:IMyInterface {}
8: }
9:
10: class ClassB{
11:    public static void Main(){
12:       Type a = typeof(IMyInterface);
13:       Type b = typeof(MyStruct);
14:       Type c = typeof(MyNamespace.ClassA);
15:       Type d = typeof(ClassB);
16:
17:       Console.WriteLine(a);
18:       Console.WriteLine(b);
19:       Console.WriteLine(c);
20:       Console.WriteLine(d);
21:    }
22: }
```

Output:

```
c:\expt>test
IMyInterface
MyStruct
MyNamespace.ClassA
ClassB
```

Getting a Type object of a class or interface will be useful when you are writing codes which make use of reflection. The Type class has several useful methods which enable you to find out more about a particular type dynamically.

10.3.1   Comparing `Object.GetType()`, `Type.GetType()`, and `typeof`

You might have noticed that `System.Object` (which is the superclass for all classes in C#) has a `GetType()` method which also returns a `Type` object. Study the program below.

```
1: using System;
2: class Test{
3:   public static void Main(){
4:     Test tObject = new Test();
5:     Type t = tObject.GetType();
6:     Console.WriteLine(t);
7:   }
8: }
```

Output:

```
c:\expt>test
Test
```

So what's the difference between using `GetType()` and the `typeof` operator? Notice that `GetType()` works on an object, while the `typeof` operator takes in a type name as the operand.

Replacing line 5 with

```
5:     Type t = typeof(tObject);
```

will result in a compilation error because `tObject` is not a type name, but a variable.

The `System.Type` class also has a static `GetType()` method which takes in a type name (a string) as a method parameter. Assuming `MyClass` is a user-defined class, this statement is valid:

```
Type t = Type.GetType("MyClass");
```

The above statement is functionally identical to:

```
Type t = typeof(MyClass);
```

There are two main differences between `Type.GetType()` and `typeof`:

- `typeof` cannot take in a variable as an operand (even a constant), while you can pass in string variables into `Type.GetType()`.
- `typeof` is evaluated during compile time and hence is faster during execution, while `Type.GetType()` is evaluated during runtime – this also explains why `typeof` cannot operate on a variable.

Table 10.3 summarizes the differences.

TABLE 10.3   Comparing the `typeof` operator with `Type.GetType()` and `Object.GetType()` – all of them return a `System.Type` object

	typeof operator	**Object.GetType()**	**Type.GetType()**
Parameter	Type name	Object name	Type name (as a string)
Execution	Compile time	Runtime	Runtime
Example	`typeof(MyClass)`	`myClass.GetType()`	`Type.GetType("MyClass")`

10.4 checked and unchecked operators and statements

The checked keyword is useful for detecting overflows[5] in integral-type arithmetic operations and conversions.

10.4.1 The checked keyword

The checked keyword can be used in one of two ways:

- checked {<code block>}
- checked (<expression>),

where `<expression>` or `<code block>` contains codes that perform any of the following operations (provided that operands are integral types only):

- ++ and -- unary operators – Example: `int i = j++;` where j is an `int` type;
- – unary operator – Example: `int i = -j;` where j is an `int` type;
- +, –, *, / binary operators – Example: `int i = j + k;` where j and k are both `int` types;
- explicit numeric conversions (or casting) from one integral type to another integral type – Example: `int i = (int)j;` where j is of a `long` type.

Statements within the `()` or `{}` brackets are considered to be within a checked context.

In cases where any of the above operations results in an overflow:

- if the operation happens within a checked context, a `System.OverflowException` is thrown;

5. An overflow results when you are trying to store an integer value which is beyond the range of the integral variable. For example, the short type's range is only –32 768 to +32 767. An attempt to store a value greater than 32 767 into a short type causes an overflow. An attempt to store a value smaller than –32 768 into a short type causes an underflow. No distinction is made between underflow and overflow in this book. When I use the term 'overflow', I am referring to both overflow and underflow scenarios.

● if the operation happens outside a checked context (i.e. within an unchecked context), no exception is thrown and the program continues. However, a 'wrong' value will be stored in the integral variable due to the overflow.

Study the program below.

```
1: using System;
2: class MyClass{
3:   public static void Main(){
4:     int i = 32768;
5:     // a short can take up to +32767 only
6:     short s = (short)i;
7:     Console.WriteLine(s);
8:   }
9: }
```

Output:

```
c:\expt>test
-32768
```

When you try to explicitly cast 32768 into a short type, an overflow occurs. Nevertheless, because this is an explicit cast the compiler assumes that you know what you are doing,[6] and stores a 'wrong' value in s. In this case, it 'wraps around' by 1 and stores the smallest negative value a short can take.

If you insert the checked operator, you can be notified via a System.OverflowException during runtime if an overflow does occur. Here is how the checked operator can be used:

```
1: using System;
2: class MyClass{
3:   public static void Main(){
4:     int i = 32768;
5:     checked{
6:       short s = (short)i; // --> OverflowException
7:       Console.WriteLine(s);
8:     }
9:   }
10: }
```

Output:

```
c:\expt>test
Unhandled Exception: System.OverflowException: Arithmetic
operation resulted in an overflow at MyClass.Main()
```

6. Which is obviously a bad assumption for some developers.

Within the checked context (lines 6–7), an explicit cast from an int to a short happens (line 6). In this case, an overflow results and, since the cast occurs within a checked context, an OverflowException is thrown. If no overflow occurs during the cast, no exception is thrown. The exception error seen in the output is a runtime error, not a compilation error. If you change line 4 to:

```
4:      int i = 100;
```

the program executes properly and prints out 100.

You should try to catch the exception and provide an appropriate exception handler. The program has been modified so that it exits gracefully.[7]

```
 1: using System;
 2: class MyClass{
 3:   public static void Main(){
 4:     int i = 32768;
 5:     try{
 6:       checked{
 7:         short s = (short)i; // --> OverflowException
 8:         Console.WriteLine(s);
 9:       }
10:     }
11:     catch (OverflowException e){
12:         Console.WriteLine("exception caught:" + e);
13:     }
14:   } // end main
15: } // end class
```

Output:

```
c:\expt>test
exception caught: System.OverflowException: Arithmetic operation
resulted in an overflow at MyClass.Main()
```

You can delimit the checked expression in round brackets too. The example below shows a method, DoThis(), which may throw the OverflowException if the expression x*y results in an overflow:

```
40: public static int DoThis(int x, int y){
41:   return checked(x*y);
42: }
```

Line 41 may throw an OverflowException if the result of x*y is beyond the range

---

7. This is a highly construed example structured in quite an unwieldy style. The purpose is simply to showcase how the checked operator works.

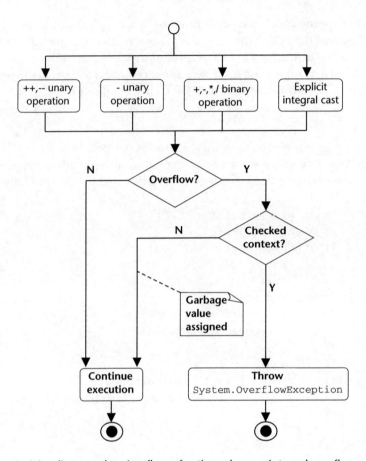

FIGURE 10.1   Activity diagram showing flow of action when an integral overflow occurs.

of an `int`. The calling method may want to catch this exception and deal with it. Figure 10.1 summarizes what has been discussed so far.

If you are using `csc.exe` as your C# compiler, you can enforce overflow checking for all unmarked code using the `/checked` option:

```
c:\expt>csc /checked test.cs
```

Using the `/checked` option is equivalent to putting all your codes in a huge checked block. All your codes will be within a checked context except for those sections specifically marked as unchecked (see the next section).

10.4.2   The unchecked keyword

Study the following program.

```
1: using System;
2: class MyClass{
3:    public static void Main(){
4:      // max positive value for int is 2147483647
5:      int i = 2147483647;
6:      int j = i + 1; // overflow
7:      Console.WriteLine(j);
8:    }
9: }
```

Output:

-2147483648

The class above compiles, performs an overflow operation (on line 6), and displays the results. Line 6 is outside a checked context and hence does not cause an OverflowException to be thrown. It is important to note that overflow checking (for the statement on line 6) is *performed during runtime*.

I have changed the program above slightly. Examine it carefully now:

```
1: using System;
2: class MyClass{
3:    public static void Main(){
4:      int j = 2147483647+1; // overflow
5:      Console.WriteLine(j);
6:    }
7: }
```

Compilation error:

test.cs(4,13): error CS0220: The operation overflows at compile time in checked mode

In this case, the class above fails to compile because of line 4. The only difference between the previous class and this one is that for this class, overflow checking on line 4 is performed *during compile time*. The reason for this is that the program is dealing with constant or fixed values, and it is possible to determine during compile time if an overflow occurs.

Let's alter the first class which successfully compiled by shifting the variable i outside the Main() method and declare it using the const modifier, so that it becomes a class constant:

```
1: using System;
2: class MyClass{
3:    // i is a constant this time
4:    const int i = 2147483647;
```

```
 5:
 6:    public static void Main(){
 7:     int j = MyClass.i+1; // overflow
 8:     Console.WriteLine(j);
 9:    }
10: }
```

Compilation error:

```
test.cs(7,12): error CS0220: The operation overflows at compile
time in checked mode
```

This time, compilation fails because the compiler is able to determine that an overflow is expected on line 7, since we are dealing with constants.

By default, if an overflow can be determined during compile time, you will not be able to compile it. In order to force your codes to compile, despite the fact that the compiler has determined an overflow even during compilation, you have to put the statements causing the predetermined overflow in an unchecked context.

This is accomplished by using the unchecked operator. Like the checked operator, you can use it in one of two ways:

- unchecked {<code block>}

- unchecked (<expression>),

where <expression> or <code block> contains codes that you want to place in an unchecked context.

Although seldom used, you suppress compile-time overflow checking with the unchecked keyword.

One last note before this section closes – it is possible to nest checked sections within unchecked sections and vice versa. Whether overflow checking is performed on a statement or not depends on whether it is within a checked or unchecked context. The following program shows a checked block within an unchecked block.

```
1: using System;
2: class MyClass{
3:    public static void Main(){
4:      int i = 32768;
5:      unchecked{
6:        short s1 = (short)i; // no problem
7:        Console.WriteLine("checkpoint 1");
8:
9:        checked{
```

```
10:             short s2 = (short)i; // --> OverflowException
11:             Console.WriteLine("checkpoint 2");
12:         }
13:      }
14:   } // end Main
15: }
```

Output:

```
c:\expt>test
checkpoint 1
Unhandled Exception: System.OverflowException: Arithmetic
operation resulted in an overflow at MyClass.Main()
```

In this example, lines 6–7 are in an unchecked context, and lines 10–11 are in a checked context.

10.5 The == operator

The == operator in C# deserves some attention from Java developers. It works in exactly the same way the == operator works in Java except for one case – when the operands are string objects.

The == operator behaves differently depending on what its operands are:

● when used to check the equality of two value types,[8] the operator returns true if both operands have the same value – this is the same for Java;

● when used to check the equality of two reference types, the operator returns true only if the types refer to the same object in memory – this is the same for Java too.

The program below demonstrates these points.

```
1: using System;
2:
3: class TestClass {
4:
5:   public static void Main(){
6:      int i=5;
7:      int j=5;
8:      // comparison of value types
9:      Console.WriteLine(i==j); // true
10:
```

8. Simple types (such as int, long, char, etc.) are value types.

```
11:      object o1 = (object)i;
12:      object o2 = (object)j;
13:      object o3 = o2;
14:      // comparison of reference types
15:      Console.WriteLine(o1==o2); // false
16:      Console.WriteLine(o2==o3); // true
17:   }
18: }
```

Output:

```
c:\expt>test
True
False
True
```

Both o2 and o3 refer to the same object on the heap, and that's the reason why the expression (o2==o3) is true. Even though all the fields of the objects referenced by o1 and o2 have the same values, (o1==o2) is false because they refer to distinct objects on the heap.

10.5.1   Comparing string objects

So far, the use and behavior of the == operator has been the same in C# as in Java. The significant difference between the == operator in C# and Java arises when it is used to compare string objects. In this case, the *values* of the two strings are compared instead of whether they refer to the same string object on the heap, despite the fact that a string is a reference type, not a value type. The program below demonstrates this.

```
 1: using System;
 2:
 3: class TestClass {
 4:
 5:    public static void Main(){
 6:       string s1 = "apple";
 7:       string s2 = "apple";
 8:       Console.WriteLine(s1==s2); // true
 9:       s1 = "orange";
10:       Console.WriteLine(s1==s2); // false
11:       s1 = "apple";
12:       Console.WriteLine(s1==s2); // true
13:    }
14: }
```

Output:

```
True
False
True
```

In this program, two unique string objects are created on lines 6 and 7. The == operator returns true if the string literals encapsulated by the string objects which are used as the operands are the same.

Here is a short note to dispel some confusion for Java developers experimenting with Java Strings. Unlike C#, strings objects are not singled out as exceptional cases when compared using the == operator. When used to compare string objects, the == operator in Java returns true if the string variables used as the operands refer to the same string object, and false if two unique string objects are being compared, even if they both encapsulate the same string literal. Examine the Java program below.

```
1: // Test.java
2: public class Test{
3:    public static void main(String args[]){
4:        String a = "apple";
5:        String b = "apple";
6:        System.out.println(a==b); // true
7:    }
8: }
```

Output:

```
true
```

The output from the Java program above does not seem to follow this rule. The reason for this strange output is because the statements on lines 4 and 5 actually produced only one string object, rather than two separate string objects each encapsulating identical string literals. String declarations made like this in Java result in only one string object being created. (a==b) returns true because a and b are both referring to the same string object on the heap.

To prove this, change line 5 a little to force a new String object to be created:

```
5:        String b = new String("apple");
```

This time, the output will show false. The statement above actually forces a new string object referenced by b to be created. In this case, object reference variables a and b refer to separate string objects both encapsulating the same string literal. A comparison with the == operator hence returns false as expected.

10.6   The `is` operator (Java's `instanceof` operator)

C#'s `is` operator is used to determine if the runtime type of an object is equivalent to another, much like how Java's `instanceof` is used.

It goes like this:

```
<expression> is <type>
```

The `is` operator returns a boolean result (`true` or `false`).

The `is` operator returns `true` if:

● `<expression>` is not null AND

● `<expression>` is an object which is either a subclass of `<type>` or is a class that implemented `<type>` (in this case, `<type>` is an interface) – in other words, if `<expression>` can be successfully cast into `<type>`.

Let's study an example. The output is shown as comments. For convenience, the inheritance relations between the classes in this example are shown in Figure 10.2.

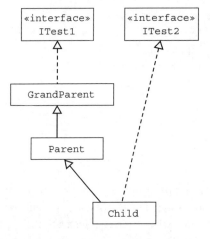

FIGURE 10.2   Class diagram showing inheritance relations between the classes in this example.

```
1: using System;
2:
3: interface ITest1 {}
4: interface ITest2 {}
5: class GrandParent:ITest1{}
6: class Parent:GrandParent {}
7:
8: class Child: Parent,ITest2 {
9:    public static void Main(){
```

```
10:
11:        Child c = new Child();
12:        Console.WriteLine(c is Child);          // True
13:        Console.WriteLine(c is ITest1);         // True
14:        Console.WriteLine(c is ITest2);         // True
15:        Console.WriteLine(c is Parent);         // True
16:        Console.WriteLine(c is GrandParent);    // True
17:
18:        Parent p = new Parent();
19:        Console.WriteLine(p is Child);          // False
20:        Console.WriteLine(p is ITest1);         // True
21:        Console.WriteLine(p is ITest2);         // False
22:        Console.WriteLine(p is Parent);         // True
23:        Console.WriteLine(p is GrandParent);    // True
24:
25:        ITest2 it2 = new Child();
26:        Console.WriteLine(it2 is Child);        // True
27:        Console.WriteLine(it2 is ITest1);       // True
28:        Console.WriteLine(it2 is ITest2);       // True
29:        Console.WriteLine(it2 is Parent);       // True
30:        Console.WriteLine(it2 is GrandParent);  // True
31:    }
32: }
```

Compilation warning:

```
test.cs(12,23): warning CS0183: The given expression is always
of the provided ('Child') type
test.cs(13,23): warning CS0183: The given expression is always
of the provided ('ITest1') type
test.cs(14,23): warning CS0183: The given expression is always
of the provided ('ITest2') type
test.cs(15,23): warning CS0183: The given expression is always
of the provided ('Parent') type
test.cs(16,23): warning CS0183: The given expression is always
of the provided ('GrandParent') type
test.cs(20,23): warning CS0183: The given expression is always
of the provided ('ITest1') type
test.cs(22,23): warning CS0183: The given expression is always
of the provided ('Parent') type
test.cs(23,23): warning CS0183: The given expression is always
of the provided ('GrandParent') type
test.cs(28,23): warning CS0183: The given expression is always
of the provided ('ITest2') type
```

The compilation warnings warn that some of the statements containing the is operator can already be determined during compile time.

Output:

```
c:\expt>test
True
True
True
True
True
False
True
False
True
True
True
True
True
True
True
```

If you want to perform a cast of <expression> to <type> if (<expression> is <type>), C# has a convenient as operator which you can use.

10.7 The as operator

The as operator is a convenient shortcut in C# not found in Java. It can be viewed as the is operator combined with a type cast. It is used like this:

```
<expression> as <type>
```

First as checks if the <expression> can be cast into <type> – another way to phrase this is that a check is made to see if (<expression> is <type>) is true. If so, it casts <expression> to <type>, and then returns the result of the cast. If casting is not possible, the operator returns null. Study this example:

```
1: using System;
2:
3: class Parent {}
4: class Child:Parent {}  // Child extends Parent
5:
6: class MainClass{
```

```
7:    public static void Main(){
8:       Child c = new Child();
9:       Parent p = c as Parent;
10:
11:      if (p==null)
12:         Console.WriteLine("cast failed");
13:      else{
14:         Console.WriteLine("cast successful");
15:      }
16:   }
17: }
```

Output:

```
c:\expt>test
cast successful
```

Assuming that a is a reference variable which we want to check, the two methods below are functionally identical:

```
40: // implementation 1: using is operator
41: public MyClass PerformCast(object a){
42:    if (a is MyClass)
43:       return (MyClass)a;
44:    else
45:       return null;
46: }
```

```
40: // implementation 2: using as operator
41: public MyClass PerformCast(object a){
42:    return a as MyClass;
43: }
```

Using the as operator for this purpose is obviously more efficient.

If it is known during compile time that the as operator is used to attempt to perform an invalid cast, a compiler error will be produced. The following code fragment will not compile, because there is no way that i can be cast into a string, and this fact is known during compile time:

```
int i = 99;
string s = i as string;
```

On the other hand, the following fragment compiles fine because it is possible that o be reassigned to refer to a string object during runtime:

```
object o = 99;
string s = o as string;
```

During runtime, s is assigned a null value, because the casting cannot be performed. Figure 10.3 summarizes how the as operator works.

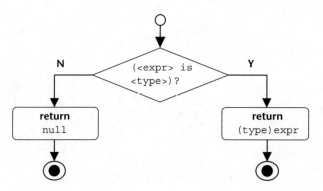

FIGURE 10.3   Activity diagram showing the flow of action for the as operator.

11

Iteration and flow control

This chapter deals with the basic issue of iteration (looping) and flow control in C#.

Like Java

- In C#, the `while` (in while loops), `do` and `while` (in do...while loops), and `for` (in for loops) keywords work in exactly the same way as in Java.

- You can `break` and `continue` from within loops to terminate iteration prematurely (except that you cannot use them with labels).

Unlike Java

Flow control in C# is very much the same as Java, except for:

- a new and useful `foreach` keyword;
- some changes to how `switch-case` is used;
- C# retains the `goto` keyword;[1]
- you cannot use `break` and `continue` with labels.

Short examples are given showing while/do...while/for loops and the use of continue and break, but they will not be described in detail because they are used the same way in Java. The later sections emphasize the new stuff that came with C#.

11.1 Looping with the `while`, `do`, `for`, `continue` and `break` keywords

The use of these keywords in looping is identical in Java and C# (with some exceptions with the `break` and `continue` keywords). There follows some examples for completeness. Feel free to skip this section if you are already familiar using looping with these keywords in Java.

---

1. `goto` is a reserved word in Java, but has no functionality. The usage of `goto` in C/C++ has often been criticized as poor structural programming. Use it with care in C#.

11.1.1   Use of `while` in loops

Here is an example of a while loop in C#.

```
30:   public static void PrintNumbersUsingWhile(){
31:     int i=0;
32:     while (i<10)
33:        Console.WriteLine(i++);
34:   }
```

`PrintNumbersUsingWhile()` prints out the numbers 0 to 9.
   Here is another example.

```
30:   public static void GetUserInputUsingWhile(){
31:     Console.WriteLine("You must enter Y to return");
32:     string UserInput = Console.ReadLine(); //read keyboard
33:     while (true){
34:       if (UserInput.Equals("Y"))
35:         break;
36:       Console.WriteLine("You must enter Y to return");
37:       UserInput = Console.ReadLine();
38:     }
39:     return;
40:   }
```

`GetUserInputUsingWhile()` reads a string from the keyboard (line 32), and goes into a infinite while loop (line 33), breaking out only when the string the user enters is a capital 'Y'.

Like Java

● You can break out of a while loop using the `break` keyword.

● You can bypass the remaining statements in a loop and go directly to the conditional using the `continue` keyword.

● `while` takes in only a boolean value, or an expression which evaluates to a boolean type only.[2]

2. `while` in C/C++ takes in both booleans and integers. Zero is considered 'false' and any other integer – regardless of sign – is considered 'true'. Lots of programming bugs have been attributed to this 'loose typing' feature of C/C++. We have the classic mistake of accidentally leaving out one equal character in `while(intX==intY)` to become `while(intX=intY)`. This compiles in C/C++ and during runtime the value stored in `intY` is assigned to `intX`, and if `intX` is a non-zero integer the `while` condition is fulfilled. Such bugs are extremely difficult to detect, but often deadly. Fortunately, the `while` construct is extremely strict in this aspect for both Java and C# – we would prefer a compilation error than difficult-to-find logic errors.

Unlike Java

You cannot use the `break` and `continue` keywords together with labels (see section 11.5).

11.1.2   Use of `do` and `while` in loops

Here is an example of a do ... while loop in C#.

```
30:    public static void GetUserInputUsingDoWhile(){
31:        string UserInput;
31:        do {
35:          Console.WriteLine("You must enter Y to return");
32:          UserInput = Console.ReadLine();
36:        } while (!UserInput.Equals("Y"));
38:        return;
39:    }
```

`GetUserInputUsingDoWhile()` is functionally identical to `GetUserInput UsingWhile()` in the previous section, except that the former uses do...while instead of just a `while` construct.

11.1.3   Use of `for` in loops

Here is an example of a for loop in C#.

```
30:    public static void PrintNumbersUsingFor(){
31:        for (int i=0; i<10; i++)
32:            Console.WriteLine(i++);
33:    }
```

`PrintNumbersUsingFor()` prints out the numbers 0 to 9.

Like Java

- The initialization expression, loop condition expression, and increment expression[3] are all optional. The following is perfectly valid in both C# and Java, and results in a infinite loop:

```
// similar to while (true) {}
for (;;) {
  // code here
}
```

3. for syntax: for(initialization expression; loop condition expression; increment expression){...}

11.2 Conditional statements using the `if` and `else` keywords

The use of these keywords in conditional statements is identical in Java and C#. There follows some examples for completeness. Feel free to skip this section if you are already familiar with writing conditional statements using these keywords in Java.

Below is an example usage of `if` and `else` in conditional statements. It is self-explanatory.

```
30:  public static void ConditionalDemo(int i){
31:    if (i==0){
32:      Console.WriteLine("is a zero");
33:    }
34:    else if (i==1){
35:      Console.WriteLine("is a one");
36:    }
37:    else {
38:      Console.WriteLine("is not a zero or one");
39:    }
40:  }
```

Like Java

● You can omit the curly braces if there is only one statement within your conditional block:

```
31:  if (i==0)
32:    Console.WriteLine("is a zero");
```

is as good as:

```
31:  if (i==0){
32:    Console.WriteLine("is a zero");
33:  }
```

● Like `while`, the `if` construct accepts only a boolean value, or expressions which will evaluate to a boolean. `if` does not take in integral values.[4]

You may have seen the use of `#if` and `#else` in C# (or C/C++ codes) – these special keywords which start with a hex sign are called preprocessor directives, and are used

---

4. In C/C++, the `if` construct can take in integral values or expressions that evaluate to integral values. Zero is considered 'false' and any other integer is considered 'true'. In C/C++, statements such as `if(1)` instead of `if(true)` are considered legal.

only by the compiler during compilation. Preprocessor directives are not converted into IL code during compilation (see Chapter 24).

11.3 Looping with the `foreach` keyword

C# comes with a new and convenient `foreach` keyword used for looping. What you can do with `foreach`, you can do with `for` (or `while`), but `foreach` is very convenient indeed for certain scenarios. For instance, you do not need to create a temporary loop counter variable to keep track of looping. `foreach` works only for repeating a bunch of statements (or looping through) once for *every* element of an array or object collection.[5]

`foreach` is only good for retrieving information from the array elements – you should not attempt to assign values to the array elements. Remember that you do not have a counter variable in the loop (unless you create one yourself – in which case you would be better off using `for` instead of `foreach`).

This is how array elements are retrieved sequentially from the first to the last using the classic `for` keyword:

```
1:  class TestClass{
2:
3:    public static void Main(){
4:      int []array = {11,12,13,14,15};
5:
6:      for (int i=0; i<array.Length; i++)
7:        System.Console.WriteLine(array[i]);
8:    }
9:  }
```

Output (as expected):

```
c:\expt>test
11
12
13
14
15
```

5. I will cover only using `foreach` for arrays in this section. You can iterate through a collection type using `foreach` too, but quite some work has to be done to prepare a class so that you can iterate through it using `foreach`. This special class has to implement `System.Collections.IEnumerable` and you need to write codes for the abstract methods declared in this interface.

You can do the same thing using `foreach` like this:

```
1:  class TestClass{
2:
3:     public static void Main(){
4:        int []array = {11,12,13,14,15};
5:
6:        foreach (int i in array)
7:           System.Console.WriteLine(i);
8:     }
9:  }
```

In the program above, in the `foreach` loop, i is a local variable (the scope of i is only within the `foreach` loop) which is automatically assigned the value of the next int element in the array. i is *not* a loop iteration counter. Of course, the type of i declared in the `foreach` statement must match the element type stored in the array (or at least the array elements can be *implicitly* cast into i's type).

Replacing lines 6–7 with this:

```
6:  foreach (double d in array)
7:     System.Console.WriteLine(d);
```

will work just fine, since an int can be implicitly cast to a double. In each iteration, the array elements (of type int) are implicitly cast into type double before the first statement of the iteration (line 7) starts. If there is a casting problem, the compiler will complain.

Lines 4–7 have been replaced in the following code fragment to illustrate another example. This time a string array is being dealt with:

```
4:  string []array = {"apple","orange","banana","chiku"};
5:
6:  foreach (string s in array)
7:     System.Console.WriteLine(s);
```

If array is null, line 6 will throw a `System.NullReferenceException` (which, by its name, should suggest that it is the C# equivalent of Java's `java.lang.NullPointerException`).

`foreach` comes with limitations too. The following actions cannot be done without additional workarounds:

- Since there is no loop counter, you cannot assign values to individual array elements or perform any operation requiring a loop counter.
- You can only use `foreach` if you intend to iterate from the first to the last

element in the array or collection. You cannot, for example, loop from element 3 to element 5 of the array.

If all you want to do is to retrieve all the values in an array or collection, foreach is clear, clean, and easy to use. Otherwise go back to the classic for loop if you need to perform more complex operations involving a counter, or jump out of the loop prematurely.

11.4 Conditional statements with the switch and case keywords

C# has made one efficient change for the switch clause to accept strings in addition to integral expressions. The switch statement in Java can only accept the byte, short, char, and int primitive types.

Examine the following program which uses switch to compare a string (ignore the goto statement for now, it will be explained later).

```
 1:  using System;
 2:
 3:  class TestClass{
 4:     public static void Main(string []args){
 5:        string s = args[0];
 6:
 7:     switch(s){
 8:           case "jam" : Console.WriteLine("BUTTER");
 9:                        goto case "butter";
10:
11:           case "cake": Console.WriteLine("CAKE");
12:                        break;
13:
14:           case "bug" : Console.WriteLine("BUG");
15:                        break;
16:
17:           case "fly" : Console.WriteLine("FLY");
18:                        break;
19:
20:           default    : Console.WriteLine("DEFAULT");
21:                        break;
22:        }
23:     }
24:  }
```

Output:

```
c:\expt>test bug
BUG
```

Note that capitalization is taken into consideration when comparing strings using `switch`. Check out the output when I used a different command line argument:

```
c:\expt>test BUG
DEFAULT
```

Another change is that you *must* end each case block with a `break;` statement. Java and C/C++ have this 'fall through' behavior in which if you omit the `break;` the subsequent statements in the next `case` block actually execute all the way down until a `break;` is encountered (or the `switch` block ends).

In C#, you must end your `case` blocks either with a `break` statement or a `goto` statement. Otherwise there will be a compiler error.[6]

With the removal of this 'fall through' feature, are we condemned to write repeated code in multiple `case` blocks? Definitely not! How, then, do we force the execution of multiple `case` blocks for a particular situation? The solution is to use the `goto` keyword to jump from one `case` block to another.

Let's use another command line parameter and examine the output:

```
c:\expt>test butter
BUTTER
FLY
```

What has happened is that the `case "butter"` block (lines 8–9) executes and prints out BUTTER). On line 9, the flow of execution meets the `goto` statement: `goto case "fly";`. The flow of execution jumps to the `case "fly"` block (lines 17–18) and carries on executing from there (thereby printing out 'FLY').

Even if you want your program to flow from one case block to the next consecutive case block, you will need to use the `goto` keyword to accomplish that (see section 11.6).

11.5 Flow control with the `break` and `continue` keywords

In Java, you cannot `goto` some statement, but you can label certain loops with a valid identifier and `break` or `continue` to that loop. An example of using the

---

6. I believe the removal of this fall-through behavior was to prevent careless programmers from bugging up their programs. Some Java programmers always forgot to insert the break statement after each case block when it really was meant to be there.

break keyword to terminate a loop prematurely is shown in the Java program below.

```java
1:   // Test.java
2:   public class Test{
3:     public static void main(String []args){
4:
5:       outerLoop: // loop label
6:       while(true){
7:         for (int i=0; i<10; i++){
8:           System.out.println(i);
9:           if (i==3)
10:             break outerLoop;
11:         }
12:       }
13:       System.out.println("end");
14:     }
15:   }
```

In C#, both break and continue cannot be used with a label. You cannot break <expression> or continue <expression> as you can in Java.

But you can still do that – use C#'s goto if you want to break out of an inner loop (see section 11.6.2).

11.6 Flow control with the goto keyword

Yes, goto is still there in C#, although the makers of Java got rid of its functionality (still reserving the goto keyword) when they designed Java from C++. Nevertheless, do you realize that if you have been using labels in Java, and break-ing or continue-ing to such labels, you are actually performing a pseudo goto (without the goto keyword)?

There are three ways to use C#'s goto:

● goto case <expression>;
● goto <label>;
● goto default;

11.6.1 Using goto in switch-case blocks

goto can be quite useful in switch-case blocks too, since 'falling-through' case blocks is no longer supported in C#.

Their use should be clear from this example (see section 11.4):

```
 1:   using System;
 2:
 3:   class TestClass{
 4:     public static void Main(){
 5:       int i = 1;
 6:
 7:       switch(i){
 8:             case 1 : Console.WriteLine("ONE");
 9:                      goto case 3;
10:
11:             case 2 : Console.WriteLine("TWO");
12:                      break;
13:
14:             case 3 : Console.WriteLine("THREE");
15:                      goto default;
16:
17:             default : Console.WriteLine("DEFAULT");
18:                       break;
19:       }
20:     }
21:   }
```

Output:

```
c:\expt>test
ONE
THREE
DEFAULT
```

Study line 9 which shows how the goto case expression is used to force both the case 1 and case 3 blocks to be executed in the event when i==1.

11.6.2   Using goto <label>

If you use labels in Java, you can use the break and continue statements to force execution flow to continue from a particular label. C#'s break and continue keywords do not take in a label – you use C#'s goto <label> to exit an outer loop from an inner loop prematurely. Instead of labeling the loop (which you do in Java), you label a statement outside the loop you want to break out of, and goto that statement.

Study this example:

```
 1:  using System;
 2:
 3:  class TestClass{
 4:     public static void Main(){
 5:
 6:        for (int i=0; i<5; i++){
 7:          for (int j=0; j<5; j++){
 8:             Console.WriteLine(i+","+j);
 9:             if (j==3)
10:                goto End;
11:          }
12:          Console.WriteLine("skipped");
13:        }
14:
15:        End: // arbitrary label
16:          Console.WriteLine("end");
17:     }
18:  }
```

Output:

```
c:\expt>test
0,0
0,1
0,2
0,3
end
```

Because of the goto End; statement on line 10, line 12 will never get to execute since the inner for loop never completes.

However, the following code does *not* compile:

```
 1:  using System;
 2:
 3:  class TestClass{
 4:
 5:     public static void Main(){
 6:
 7:        goto InsideLoop;
 8:        for (int i=0; i<5; i++){
 9:          InsideLoop:
10:             Console.WriteLine("looping");
```

```
11:      }
12:    }
13:  }
```

Compilation warnings and error:

```
test.cs(8,5): warning CS0162: Unreachable code detected
test.cs(7,5): error CS0159: No such label 'InsideLoop' within
the scope of the goto statement
test.cs(9,7): warning CS0162: Unreachable code detected
test.cs(9,7): warning CS0164: This label has not been referenced
```

Line 8 is unreachable, and the compiler generates a warning (not an error though). The error thrown by the compiler is what I want to draw your attention to – 'InsideLoop' is not within the scope of the goto statement, since it is in a for loop. You can jump from inside a loop to outside, but not from outside to inside.[7] Even if you shift line 7 to between lines 11 and 12, you will still get the same compilation error.

If a label is specified but not used, the compiler will give a warning that the label has not been referenced. In the code example above, if line 7 is deleted but the label of line 9 is kept, the class compiles with a compilation warning, but runs fine.

11.6.3 Misusing the goto keyword

Although you can jump around blocks of code using labels and the goto <label> statement, you should restrict its use to breaking out from inner loops.

Here's an example of how the goto <label> statement can be legally abused.

```
 1:  using System;
 2:
 3:  class TestClass{
 4:
 5:    public static void Main(){
 6:
 7:      Label1:
 8:        Console.WriteLine("never ");
 9:        goto Label2;
10:
11:      Label2:
12:        Console.WriteLine("ending ");
13:        goto Label1;
```

7. Wouldn't it be messy if you could jump right into the middle of a loop? Obvious ambiguities include deciding which iteration it will be. It's for that reason that you are not allowed to hop into a statement in the middle of a loop using goto <label>.

```
14:      }
15:   }
```

Output:

```
c:\expt>test
never
ending
never
ending
never
ending
never
ending
never
ending
```

(etc ...)

The output has been truncated. It carries on printing 'never' and 'ending' on alternate lines until you force a termination (by hitting Ctrl-C if running from the command line).

part 4

Core topics

Introduction

The chapters in this part are:

- Chapter 12: Arrays
- Chapter 13: Exception handling
- Chapter 14: C# delegates
- Chapter 15: C# events
- Chapter 16: Reflection and dynamic method invocation
- Chapter 17: Multi-threaded programming
- Chapter 18: File I/O
- Chapter 19: C# collection classes.

Core topics are 'intermediate-level' topics that are beyond the basic class features and operator functions. Topics covered in this part include arrays, exception handling, event handling (which is quite different in C# from Java), reflection, multi-threaded programming, file I/O and the .NET collection classes.

I suggest that particular attention is paid to Chapter 14, where I shall introduce the idea of delegates. Delegates are special types which encapsulate methods, and are used in C# events and multi-threaded programming.

Chapters 16–18 (reflection, multi-threaded programming, and file I/O) are written in a more 'how-to' style. I will not cover the basics (such as what reflection is, what multi-threading is, and what the difference is between a binary file and a text file, etc). Rather, I will emphasize how to perform the different operations (how to read from a text file, how to get the type name of an object during runtime) using .NET's rich framework API. For these chapters, there are few new concepts to learn, simply new classes to be acquainted with.

Chapter 19 introduces several useful classes of the C# collection API by giving coded examples showing how they can be used. Though not important, this chapter serves as a helpful reference when using an array is not good enough.

Strictly speaking, the last four chapters deal with topics not really related to the C# language itself, but more with the functionality provided by the .NET BCL. I have decided to cover them in this book because you will need to know about these subjects eventually if you are to become a C# developer (and also to make my book thicker ;).

12

Arrays

Arrays in C# is a more complex topic than in Java. Java has only one category of multi-dimensional array. C# groups multi-dimensional arrays into two distinct categories: 'normal' rectangular arrays, and jagged arrays (see Figure 12.1). Things can be a bit confusing because you can view a Java multi-dimensional array as in either category, though I personally think that it fits a little better into 'rectangular arrays'.

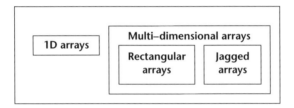

FIGURE 12.1   The different types of arrays in C#.

We will start with the simplest, one dimensional (1D) arrays. Then rectangular multi-dimensional arrays will be covered followed by the more complex jagged multi-dimensional arrays. I shall limit my discussion to 2D arrays for the sections on multi-dimensional arrays – you can extend the idea to *n*-levels once you have understood the discussion. This chapter ends with some suggestions on how rectangular and jagged arrays can be used together.

I will discuss some general characteristics of arrays in C# first.

Like Java

● Arrays are objects in C#. All arrays are subclasses of `System.Array` in C#.[1]

● An array's index starts from 0.

1. In Java, array objects are direct subclasses of `java.lang.Object`.

- You cannot access beyond the allocated size of an array. If a 1D array has been declared with a size of 6, attempting to access the array through `ArrayName[6]` or `ArrayName[-1]` will cause a runtime exception to be thrown.[2]

Unlike Java

- The syntax for declaring arrays is different in C#. This will be elaborated on in the next few sections.
- Be careful here – the `Length` property of an array in C# gives the total size of an array. For a multi-dimensional array, it gives the total size of the whole array, instead of just the size of the 'first-level array'. An example will be provided to illustrate this in section 12.2.

Additional note

C# comes with a new useful looping keyword, `foreach`, which is very convenient for looping through an array (see section 11.1).

12.1 One-dimensional arrays

The syntax for array declaration is the same in C# as in Java, except for one difference – when declaring an array, Java permits putting the square brackets either in front of or behind the array's type. C# only allows the former – Putting the square brackets after an array identifier will cause a compilation error.[3]

Both the following declarations are okay in Java:

- `int MyArray[];`
- `int []MyArray;`

However, only `int []MyArray;` is legal in C#.

Other than that, the syntax for array declaration, instantiation, and initialization are identical in C# and Java as far as *1D arrays* are concerned. Examples are shown below as a refresher and for reference.

- Declaring a 1D array (without instantiating it):

  ```
  int []MyArray1;
  object[] MyArray2;
  ```

  It doesn't matter if the space is between the type and the square brackets, or between the square brackets and the array identifier.

---

2. The exception thrown in `System.IndexArrayOutOfRangeException` – the equivalent of Java's `java.lang.ArrayIndexOutOfBoundsException`. Accessing beyond an array's range is allowed in C/C++, where the array boundaries are not checked during runtime.
3. C/C++ mandates that the square brackets be *behind* the array type (as in `int array[];`).

- Declaring and instantiating a 1D array in a single statement:

  ```
  int []MyArray1 = new int[3];
  object[] MyArray2 = new object[2];
  ```

  The statements declare and instantiate `MyArray1` as an `int` array with a size of 3, and `MyArray2` as an `object` array of size 2.

- Declaring, instantiating and initializing a 1D array in a single statement:

  ```
  int[] MyArray1 = {1,2,3};
  object[] MyArray2 = {"apple",9};
  ```

- Accessing a value in a 1D array:

  ```
  int Temp = MyArray1[1];
  MyArray1[2] = 99;
  ```

Beyond 1D arrays, C# supports two types of multi-dimensional arrays – rectangular arrays and jagged arrays. Because Java's multi-dimensional arrays do not map directly into either category, I have chosen to compare Java's implementation with the simpler rectangular arrays.

12.2 Multi-dimensional arrays: rectangular arrays

Rectangular arrays are, as the name implies, arrays which look like a table. A 2D rectangular array can be represented as a plane rectangle, and a 3D rectangular array can be represented as a cuboid.[4] Whatever the case, the idea is the same – in rectangular arrays, every row has the same number of columns. Jagged arrays differ from this as you will see later.

The syntax for rectangular arrays is different from Java. Study the statements below and note the syntactical differences.

- Declaring a 2D rectangular array (without instantiating it):

  In Java: `int [][]MyArray1;`
  In C#: **`int [,]MyArray1;`**

- Declaring and instantiating a 2D rectangular array in one statement:

  In Java: `int [][]MyArray1 = new int[2][5];`
  In C#: **`int [,]MyArray1 = new int[2,5];`**

  The statement above declares `MyArray1` as a 2D int array with 2 rows and 5 cells in each row.[5]

---

4. Some people have great difficulty understanding 4D arrays and above because it is difficult to picture a 4D rectangular array as represented by a simple object (a 4D shape?) in our 3D world.
5. Like most people, I am visualizing the 2D array as a table. The first level array is the row, while the second level array is the number of cells in each row.

Figure 12.2 shows what `MyArray1` looks like (default values for each 'cell' is 0).

[0] [0]	[0] [1]	[0] [2]	[0] [3]	[0] [4]
0	0	0	0	0
[1] [0]	[1] [1]	[1] [2]	[1] [3]	[1] [4]
0	0	0	0	0

FIGURE 12.2   `MyArray1`.

● Declaring, instantiating and initializing a 2D rectangular array in one statement:

In Java: `int [][]MyArray2 = {{1,2,3},{4,5,6}};`
In C#: **`int [,]MyArray2 = {{1,2,3},{4,5,6}};`**

The statement above declares a 2D int array called `MyArray2`. `MyArray2` is a 2×3 array with 2 rows and 3 cells in each row. Figure 12.3 gives a visual representation of the array.

[0] [0]	[0] [1]	[0] [2]
1	2	3
[1] [0]	[1] [1]	[1] [2]
4	5	6

FIGURE 12.3   `MyArray2`.

● Accessing a value in a 2D rectangular array:

In Java: `int Temp = MyArray1[1][0];`
In C#: **`int Temp = MyArray1[1,0];`**

● Assigning a value to an array element:

In Java: `MyArray1[2][3] = 99;`
In C#: **`MyArray1[2,3] = 99;`**

12.2.1   Using the `Length` property

I mentioned earlier that the `Length` (with a capital 'L') property of an array in C# gives the total size of an array. For a multi-dimensional array, it gives the total size of the whole array instead of just the size of the 'first-level array'.

For example, if you have a 2D rectangular array of 2 rows of 5 cells each created by this statement:

```
int [,] MyArray = new int[2,5];
```

In Java, `MyArray.length` will return 2. In C#, `MyArray.Length` will return 10 (2×5). To obtain the size of the first-level array (the number of rows), use `MyArray.GetLength(0)` (which returns 2). To obtain the size of the second-level array (the number of cells in each row), use `MyArray.GetLength(1)` (which returns 5).

Study the output of the following class to confirm your understanding:

```
 1: using System;
 2:
 3: public class TestClass{
 4:    int [,]MyArray = new int[2,5]; // new 2D array
 5:
 6:    public static void Main(){
 7:      TestClass c = new TestClass();
 8:      Console.WriteLine(c.MyArray.Length);
 9:      Console.WriteLine(c.MyArray.GetLength(0));
10:      Console.WriteLine(c.MyArray.GetLength(1));
11:    }
12: }
```

Output:

```
c:\expt>test
10
2
5
```

12.3 Multi-dimensional arrays: jagged arrays

Unlike rectangular arrays, jagged arrays are arrays of arrays.[6] In the case of rectangular arrays, we can think of a 2D array as a planar rectangular table, where the first-level array specifies a row, and the second-level array specifies a cell in the row. Notice that the number of cells in each row has to be the same. If row 0 has 10 cells, row 1 will have 10 cells – a rectangular array is always a neat rectangle (hence the name).

The statement:

```
int [,] Array = new int[3,5]; // rectangular array
```

will produce the array shown in Figure 12.4.

6. Since Java doesn't differentiate between rectangular and jagged arrays, you may have heard your Java instructor telling you that multi-dimensional arrays in Java are arrays of arrays too. But, as you shall see, there's a difference between jagged and rectangular arrays.

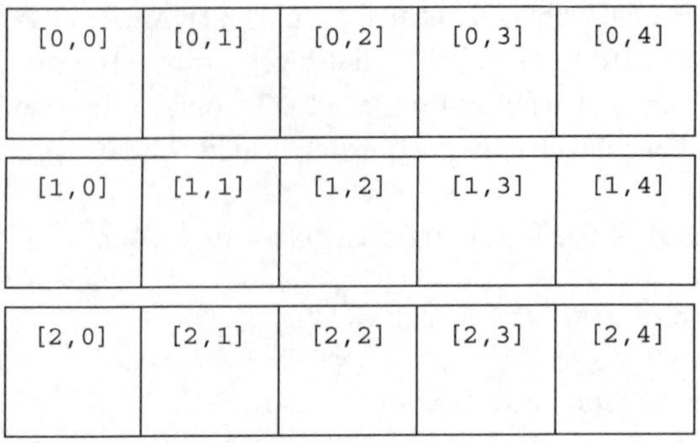

[0,0]	[0,1]	[0,2]	[0,3]	[0,4]
[1,0]	[1,1]	[1,2]	[1,3]	[1,4]
[2,0]	[2,1]	[2,2]	[2,3]	[2,4]

FIGURE 12.4   A 3 × 5 rectangular array.

A jagged array, on the other hand, can have rows with different numbers of cells. A 2D jagged float array is declared like this:

```
float [][] MyJaggedArray; // jagged array declaration
```

Note that this is how a 2D array is declared in Java!

The following code fragment creates a 2D jagged int array called JArray containing two separate int arrays.

```
// JArray contains 2 arrays: JArray[0] and JArray[1]
int [][] JArray = new int[2][];

// JArray[0] is an array with 3 slots
JArray[0] = new int[3];
JArray[0][0] = 1;
JArray[0][1] = 2;
JArray[0][2] = 3;

// JArray[1] is an array with 5 slots
JArray[1] = new int [5];
JArray[1][0] = 4;
JArray[1][1] = 5;
JArray[1][2] = 6;
JArray[1][3] = 7;
JArray[1][4] = 8;
```

The first array (JArray[0]) is a 3-element int array containing the values 1, 2, and 3. The second array (JArray[1]) is a 5-element int array containing the values 4, 5, 6, 7, and 8.

Diagrammatically, the jagged array created is shown in Figure 12.5 (with the assigned values shown).

[0] [0]	[0] [1]	[0] [2]
1	2	3

[1] [0]	[1] [1]	[1] [2]	[1] [3]	[1] [4]
4	5	6	7	8

FIGURE 12.5   JArray.

It is no longer a rectangle, but a shape with a jagged edge.

You can declare and initialize a jagged int array in a single statement too:

```
int[][] JArray = new int[2][]
   {new int[] {1,2,3}, new int[]{4,5,6,7,8} };

int[][] JArray = new int[] []
   {new int[] {1,2,3}, new int[]{4,5,6,7,8} };

int[][] JArray =
   {new int[]{1,2,3}, new int[]{4,5,6,7,8} };
```

The above three statements are alternatives – they all do the same thing as the code fragment above.

Accessing a value in a jagged array is done in the same way as accessing a 2D array in Java:

```
int Temp = JArray [1][0]; // Temp is assigned the value 4
JArray[1][3] = 99;        // replaces value 7 with 99
```

12.4 Mixing jagged and rectangular arrays

Developers who have mastered arrays, and want to put some complexity into their multi-dimensional arrays, can mix jagged and rectangular arrays.[7] Here is an example.

```
int[][,] MessyArray = new int [3][,]

{

new int[,] { {1,3}, {5,7} },

new int[,] { {0,2}, {4,6}, {8,10} },

new int[,] { {11,22,33}, {77,88,99} }

};
```

7. I personally wouldn't do too much of this unless there really is good justification for doing so (such as sabotaging your colleague who is taking over your codes!).

This statement creates an `int` array called `MessyArray`, which is an array of two arrays. The first is an array of size 3 – call them 3a, 3b, and 3c. 3a is a 2D array containing 2 rows of 2 cells each. 3b is a 2D array containing 3 rows of 2 cells each, and 2c is a 2D array of 2 rows of 3 cells each.

Figure 12.6 shows what `MessyArray` looks like.

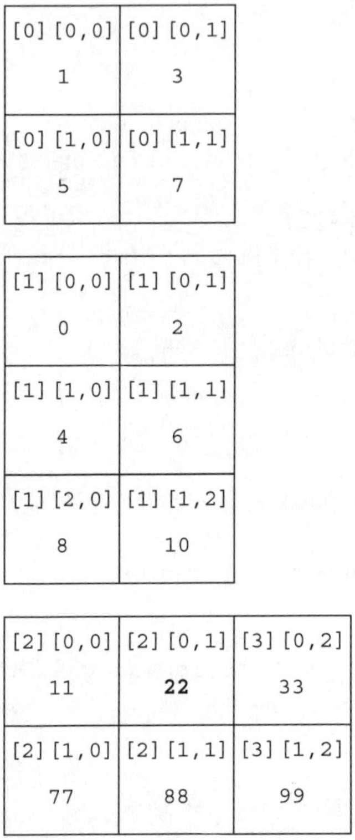

[0] [0,0]	[0] [0,1]
1	3
[0] [1,0]	[0] [1,1]
5	7

[1] [0,0]	[1] [0,1]
0	2
[1] [1,0]	[1] [1,1]
4	6
[1] [2,0]	[1] [1,2]
8	10

[2] [0,0]	[2] [0,1]	[3] [0,2]
11	**22**	33
[2] [1,0]	[2] [1,1]	[3] [1,2]
77	88	99

FIGURE 12.6   `MessyArray`.

As an example, you can access the cell containing the value 22 via the expression:

```
MessyArray[2][0,1]
```

Despite the increased complexity of C# arrays, no matter how you declare them, arrays in C# can store only elements of the same type (as with Java arrays).

12.5   Using the `System.Array` class

I mentioned that all array objects in C# are implicitly objects of the `System.Array` class. `System.Array` contains useful methods and properties which you can use.

The Length property,[8] discussed earlier, is actually inherited from System.Array. Other methods can be used for creating, manipulating, searching, and sorting arrays.

I shall introduce the following static methods in System.Array which can be useful for 1D arrays:

- public static void **Reverse** (Array array)
- public static void **Sort** (Array array)
- public static int **IndexOf** (Array array, Object value)

Check out the API documentation for more details.

Reverse() takes in a 1D array and reverses the sequence of the elements stored in it. Here is a simple example of its use:

```
 1: using System;
 2:
 3: public class TestClass{
 4:    public static void Main(){
 5:       string []Fruits ="apple","orange","banana","coconut"};
 6:       Array.Reverse(Fruits);
 7:
 8:       for (int i=0; i<4; i++)
 9:          Console.WriteLine(i + ":" + Fruits[i]);
10:    }
11: }
```

Output:

```
c:\expt>test
0:coconut
1:banana
2:orange
3:apple
```

Likewise, Sort() takes in a 1D array and sorts the elements in order. Replacing line 6 of the program above with this statement:

```
 6:       Array.Sort(Fruits);
```

results in this output:

```
c:\expt>test
0:apple
1:banana
2:coconut
3:orange
```

---

8. If you are not sure of C# properties, just treat a property as a public field for now. See Chapter 20 for more information.

IndexOf() takes in a 1D array and an object to be matched against the elements in the array. It returns the array index of the first match or −1 if no match is found. Examine the following program:

```
1: using System;
2: public class TestClass{
3:    public static void Main(){
4:        string []Fruits={"apple","orange","banana","coconut"};
5:        Console.WriteLine(Array.IndexOf(Fruits,"banana"));
6:    }
7: }
```

Output:

```
c:\expt>test
2
```

13

Exception handling

If you are a Java developer, C#'s exception handling mechanism is very similar to Java's, and you will feel very comfortable.[1] There are, of course, new things to learn – C# has done away with checked exceptions and built in something called inner exceptions, as well as other minor improvements.

C# has four keywords for exception handling – try, catch, finally, and throw. Notice that C# does not have the throws keyword which Java developers use when declaring methods.

I shall start with a general example of exception handling in C# just to warm up a bit. This will be followed by examples on nested try blocks and user-defined exceptions.[2] Then I will discuss the following topics:

- The C# exception class hierarchy;
- System.Exception class;
- inner exceptions;
- general catch block;
- catching generic exceptions.

13.1 Exception examples

Three examples are given here as a refresher:

- basic try-catch-finally;
- nested try;
- user-defined exception.

Read through these examples to familiarize yourself with the different types of exception objects thrown for each scenario. Note the comments I have made at the end of each example.

1. VB 6 developers will find exception handling a totally new thing to pick up when they move over to VB .NET. VB 6 has no proper exception handling mechanism, and developers rely on the ancient On Error Goto construct to handle errors.
2. User-defined exceptions are exception classes written by the developer.

13.1.1   Exception example 1: basic try-catch-finally

Here is a basic example of exception handling in C#. Try to trace the program flow based on your knowledge of Java's exception handling.

```
1: using System;
2:
3: class TestClass{
4:    public static void Main(){
5:
6:        Console.Write("Enter a number :");
7:        string userInput = Console.ReadLine();
8:
9:        try{
10:          int number1 = Convert.ToInt32(userInput);
11:          int number2 = 1/number1;
12:        }
13:        catch (FormatException e){
14:          Console.WriteLine("check point 1");
15:          Console.WriteLine(e.Message);
16:          Console.WriteLine(e.StackTrace);
17:        }
18:        catch (DivideByZeroException e){
19:          Console.WriteLine("check point 2");
20:          Console.WriteLine(e.Message);
21:          Console.WriteLine(e.StackTrace);
22:        }
23:        finally {
24:          Console.WriteLine("running finally block");
25:        }
26:    }
27: }
```

Convert.ToInt32() on line 10 is a static method of the System.Convert class. Like Java's Integer.parseInt(), Convert.ToInt32() takes in a string and returns an int. While Integer.parseInt() throws a java.lang.NumberFormatException if the string passed in contains non-numeric characters, Convert.ToInt32() throws a System.FormatException when that happens.

Line 11 may throw a System.DivideByZeroException if a division by 0 is performed. As the name implies, System.DivideByZeroException is the C# equivalent of java.lang.ArithmeticException.

You can execute the program, key in different inputs, observe the output, and trace through the code.

First case: enter a non-numeric string

```
c:\expt>test
Enter a number: not_a_number
check point 1
Input string was not in a correct format at
System.Number.ParseInt32(String s, NumberStyles style,
NumberFormatInfo info) at TestClass.Main()
running finally block
```

This user input will cause line 10 to throw a `System.FormatException`. The exception is caught at the first catch block (line 13). The `finally` block (line 23) runs after that. The program flow goes like this:

- lines 5–10 (exception object created on line 10);
- lines 13–17 (catch block);
- lines 23–25 (finally block).

Second case: enter the number zero

```
c:\expt>test
Enter a number: 0
check point 2
Attempted to divide by zero at TestClass.Main()
running finally block
```

The statement on line 11 throws a `System.DivideByZeroException` exception. Similarly, the finally block runs after the second exception block finishes. The program flow goes like this:

- lines 5–11 (exception object created on line 11);
- lines 18–22 (catch block);
- lines 23–25 (finally block).

Third case: enter a proper integer

```
c:\expt>test
Enter a number: 70
running finally block
```

No exceptions were thrown, the two catch blocks were skipped, and the finally block executes. The program flow goes like this:

- lines 5–12;
- lines 23–25 (finally block).

13.1.2 Exception example 2: nested try

Like Java, you can have multiple levels of try-catch nesting. Instead of a fully fledged code example, I will step through a skeletal code fragment, and discuss the program flow when an exception occurs at different points in the code.

I am using an example of one try-catch block immediately enclosed within another. Though you usually do not write nested try blocks within a single method, this exercise will clarify any conceptual uncertainties.

```
10: try{
11:        // statement 1
12:        // statement 2
13:        try{
14:            // statement 3
15:            // statement 4
16:        }
17:        catch(Exception1 e){
18:           // statement 5
19:           // statement 6
20:        }
21:        catch(Exception2 e){
22:           // statement 7
23:           // statement 8
24:        }
25:        finally{
26:           // statement 9
27:           // statement 10
28:        }
29:        // statement 11
30:        // statement 12
31:    }
32:    catch (Exception1 e){
33:       // statement 13
34:       // statement 14
35:    }
36:    catch (Exception2 e){
37:       // statement 15
38:       // statement 16
39:    }
40:    catch (Exception3 e){
41:       // statement 17
42:       // statement 18
43:    }
```

```
44:    finally{
45:       // statement 19
46:       // statement 20
47:    }
```

First case: **Exception2** *thrown on statement 3 only*

Figure 13.1 shows the program flow.

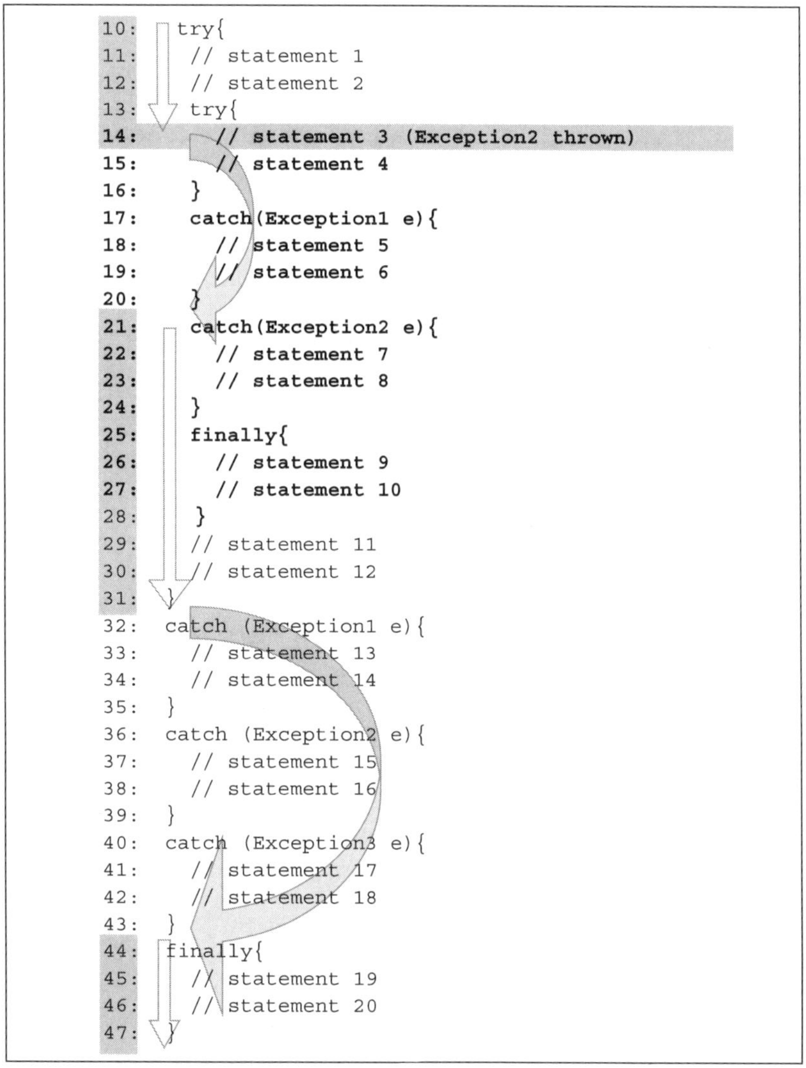

```
10:    try{
11:       // statement 1
12:       // statement 2
13:       try{
14:          // statement 3 (Exception2 thrown)
15:          // statement 4
16:       }
17:       catch(Exception1 e){
18:          // statement 5
19:          // statement 6
20:       }
21:       catch(Exception2 e){
22:          // statement 7
23:          // statement 8
24:       }
25:       finally{
26:          // statement 9
27:          // statement 10
28:       }
29:       // statement 11
30:       // statement 12
31:    }
32:    catch (Exception1 e){
33:       // statement 13
34:       // statement 14
35:    }
36:    catch (Exception2 e){
37:       // statement 15
38:       // statement 16
39:    }
40:    catch (Exception3 e){
41:       // statement 17
42:       // statement 18
43:    }
44:    finally{
45:       // statement 19
46:       // statement 20
47:    }
```

FIGURE 13.1   Program flow: Exception2 thrown on statement 3.

The exception is caught at line 21. The finally block completes and, since the exception has been handled properly in the inner try-catch block, the exception is not propagated to the next enclosing try block.

Second case: statement 3 throws **Exception3** *only*

Figure 13.2 shows the program flow for this case.

```
10:    try{
11:       // statement 1
12:       // statement 2
13:       try{
14:          // statement 3 (Exception3 thrown)
15:          // statement 4
16:       }
17:       catch(Exception1 e){
18:          // statement 5
19:          // statement 6
20:       }
21:       catch(Exception2 e){
22:          // statement 7
23:          // statement 8
24:       }
25:       finally{
26:          // statement 9
27:          // statement 10
28:       }
29:       // statement 11
30:       // statement 12
31:    }
32:    catch (Exception1 e){
33:       // statement 13
34:       // statement 14
35:    }
36:    catch (Exception2 e){
37:       // statement 15
38:       // statement 16
39:    }
40:    catch (Exception3 e){
41:       // statement 17
42:       // statement 18
43:    }
44:    finally{
45:       // statement 19
46:       // statement 20
47:    }
```

FIGURE 13.2   Program flow: Exception3 thrown on statement 3.

Since the inner try-catch block cannot handle Exception3, it is propagated to the next enclosing try block. Note that the inner finally block (lines 25–28) executes first before control leaves the inner block. The exception is caught on line 40, and the enclosing finally block executes after the exception is handled.

Third case: statement 3 throws **Exception1** *and statement 5 throws* **Exception2**

Figure 13.3 shows the program flow.

```
10:  try{
11:      // statement 1
12:      // statement 2
13:      try{
14:          // statement 3  (Exception1 thrown)
15:          // statement 4
16:      }
17:      catch(Exception1 e){
18:          // statement 5  (Exception2 thrown)
19:          // statement 6
20:      }
21:      catch(Exception2 e){
22:          // statement 7
23:          // statement 8
24:      }
25:      finally{
26:          // statement 9
27:          // statement 10
28:      }
29:      // statement 11
30:      // statement 12
31:  }
32:  catch (Exception1 e){
33:      // statement 13
34:      // statement 14
35:  }
36:  catch (Exception2 e){
37:      // statement 15
38:      // statement 16
39:  }
40:  catch (Exception3 e){
41:      // statement 17
42:      // statement 18
43:  }
44:  finally{
45:      // statement 19
46:      // statement 20
47:  }
```

FIGURE 13.3   Two exceptions thrown.

This is a pretty interesting scenario. An exception is thrown within the inner catch block itself. (Some programmers do practice this deliberately when they want to propagate the exception 'outwards'. After catching an exception, and performing some initial handling, a more descriptive new exception is created and thrown out to be handled by a higher-level exception handler.)

At line 18 (statement 5), note that when `Exception2` is thrown it will no longer be handled by the inner catch block on line 21. Any exception thrown in lines 17–28 will be propagated to the next enclosing try block for processing. Nevertheless, the inner finally block (lines 25–28) will be executed first before control goes out to the next enclosing try block.

13.1.3   Exception example 3: user-defined exception

Here is a more complex example showing how new user-defined exception objects are created and 'thrown back several levels'.

```
 1: using System;
 2:
 3: class NotEnuffMoneyException:Exception{
 4:    public float Debt;
 5:    public NotEnuffMoneyException(float debt){
 6:       this.Debt = debt;
 7:    }
 8: }
 9:
10: class TestClass{
11:    public static void Main(){
12:
13:       try{
14:          CollectFood();
15:       }
16:       catch (NotEnuffMoneyException e){
17:          Console.WriteLine(e.Message);
18:          Console.WriteLine("Debt: $" + e.Debt);
19:       }
20:    }
21:
22:    static void CollectFood(){
23:       PayForFood();
24:    }
25:
26:    static void PayForFood(){
27:       throw new NotEnuffMoneyException(2.5f);
28:    }
29: }
```

Output:

```
c:\expt>test
Exception of type NotEnuffMoneyException was thrown.
$2.5
```

A new exception class called NotEnuffMoneyException[3] is created (on lines 3–8). Notice that NotEnuffMoneyException is a subclass of System.Exception. In C#, all exception classes must be subclasses of System.Exception, directly or indirectly. Main() calls CollectFood(), which in turn calls BuyFood(). BuyFood() throws a new NotEnuffMoneyException to CollectFood(). CollectFood() hasn't got the necessary exception handling mechanism to handle this, and so it automatically throws it backwards (or upwards) to Main(), where it is handled.[4]

Hopefully, the three exception examples above have 'warmed you up' a bit. There haven't really been any distinctive differences between C# and Java yet. I shall now discuss some general similarities first, followed by the differences.

Like Java

● You place code which may produce an exception into a try block, and can use one or more catch blocks to catch any exceptions.

● The principle of exception shadowing still applies – if you have multiple catch blocks, you must ensure that the catch blocks in front cannot catch exceptions which are superclasses of the exceptions caught in later catch blocks. For example, the code fragment which follows will not compile because System.FormatException is a subclass of System.Exception. You must catch System.FormatException *before* System.Exception.

```
10: // will not compile
11: try{
12:    int number1=System.Convert.ToInt32(userInput);
13: }
14: catch (Exception e){
15:    // do something
16: }
17: catch (FormatException e){
18:    // do something
19: }
```

3. Although not compulsory, it is customary to name your exception classes Something*Exception*. I would suggest that you stick to this convention, which is followed by most C# and Java communities.
4. In my example here, NotEnuffMoneyException obviously wasn't well encapsulated. In a real program, I would have chosen to make Debt a private field, which is accessible via a public C# property (see Chapter 20) or accessor method. I didn't want to bring in properties and encapsulation to dilute the focus – which is exception handling.

- The finally block executes regardless of whether an exception happens or not.
- Both the catch and the finally blocks are optional. However, you cannot have a try block without at least a catch or a finally block. You need not have any catch blocks, as long as there is a finally block. In this case, the finally block will execute before the exception object is propagated backwards/upwards.

```
10: // perfectly legal - try without catch block
11: try{
12:    // do something
13: }
14: finally{
15:    // do something
16: }
```

- All exception classes are subclasses of one main exception class. In C#, this is System.Exception. If you want to write your own exception class, it must extend System.Exception or one of its subclasses. More information about the C# exception hierarchy will be given in the next section.

Unlike Java

- In Java, exception classes are categorized into two types – checked[5] and unchecked exceptions. In C#, no such differentiation exists. All C# exceptions are unchecked.[6]
- Java insists that checked exceptions be handled or thrown. In C#, there is no need to trap for any type of exception at all. The following code opens temp.txt and prints to the console the contents of the file.[7] A System.IO.FileNotFoundException is thrown if the file is not found (on line 6), but there is no need to write codes for exception handling.

```
1: using System;
2: using System.IO;
3:
```

5. Java's java.io.FileNotFoundException and java.io.IOException are the most famous examples of checked exceptions. Here is a refresher on Java's checked and unchecked exceptions – checked exceptions are exceptions that must be handled or thrown out explicitly from the method (using the Java throws keyword). Unchecked exceptions are exceptions which do not need to be explicitly handled or thrown out of the method. Unchecked exceptions in Java are java.lang.RuntimeException and its subclasses. All other exceptions in Java are considered checked.
6. I have come across literature which states that all C# exceptions are runtime exceptions (which are unchecked exceptions). This is not wrong, but since C# does not categorize exceptions into checked or unchecked, the terms 'checked' and 'unchecked' do not make sense from a C# perspective.
7. See Chapter 18 for more information on File I/O. Although file I/O will not be discussed here, the use of any I/O related class should be clear enough to be understood in this chapter.

```
 4: class TestClass{
 5:    public static void Main(){
 6:       StreamReader sr = File.OpenText("temp.txt");
 7:       String input;
 8:       while ((input=sr.ReadLine())!=null) {
 9:          Console.WriteLine(input);
10:       }
11:    }
12: }
```

- It follows then that C# has no `throws` keyword. Java uses the `throws` keyword in the method declaration to pass *checked* exceptions to the calling method for processing. In C#, all exceptions are unchecked, and are hence automatically propagated if not handled locally.

- It is permissible (and encouraged) not to assign the exception object with a variable name if it is not needed. The following code fragment actually causes a compiler warning because e is declared but never used:

```
10: try{
11:    // do something
12: }
13: catch (Exception e){
14:    Console.WriteLine("an exception occurred");
15: }
```

Compiler warning:

```
test.cs(13,1): warning CS0168: The variable 'e' is
declared but never used.
```

In such cases, you can replace line 13 with

```
13: catch (Exception){
```

so that no unused local variable is declared. In contrast, Java insists that the local variable referring to the caught exception object be specified, regardless of whether it is used in the catch block.

- Within a catch block, you can just use the `throw` keyword to re-throw the caught exception to the calling method. There is no need to specify the exception variable (as in `throw e`, where e is a reference to the caught exception object). This removes the need to declare the local variable referring to the exception object in the catch block if it is never used (as explained in the previous point).

```
10: try{
11:    // do something
12: }
13: catch (Exception){
```

```
14:    // do some local processing here
15:    throw; // throw to calling method the same exception
16: }
```

13.2 C# exception hierarchy

Like Java, all exception classes are subclasses of one special exception class.[8] In Java, it is `java.lang.Exception`;[9] in C# the grandfather of all exception classes is `System.Exception`.

Figure 13.4 shows some significant predefined exception classes in C#.

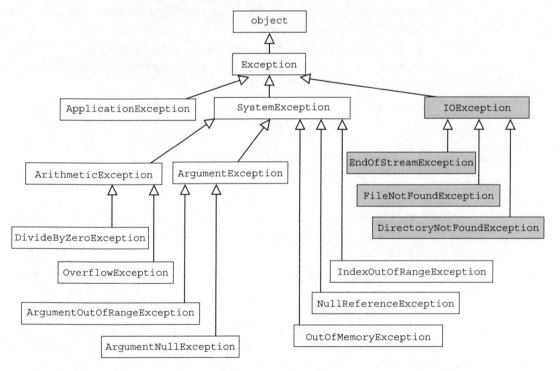

FIGURE 13.4   `System.Object` and some C# exception classes. Shaded exception classes are of the namespace `System.IO`. All other classes shown here are of the `System` namespace.

Table 13.1 briefly describes some of the predefined exceptions. It should be evident from their names what each exception does.

8. C++ developers will find this a new idea. In C++, anything can be an exception – there is no rule to say that exceptions must be instances of any special class.
9. Which is in turn a direct subclass of `java.lang.Throwable`. For Java, `Throwable` is a direct subclass of `java.lang.Object`. From `Throwable`, we have `java.lang.Error` and `java.lang.Exception`. C# does not differentiate between exceptions and errors.

TABLE 13.1 Some common exceptions and their descriptions

Exception class	Comments
ApplicationException	Thrown by a user program (not by the CLR) when a non-fatal error occurs. If you are writing your own exception classes, derive them from this class. Although this exception extends `System.Exception`, it does not add new functionality – rather, its main purpose is to differentiate user-written application exceptions from those thrown by the CLR.
ArgumentException	Thrown when a method is invoked and at least one of the passed arguments does not meet the parameter specification of the called method. Instances of this exception should carry a meaningful error message describing the invalid argument, as well as the expected range of values for the argument.
ArgumentNullException	Thrown when a method is invoked and at least one of the passed arguments is a `null` reference which should not be `null`.
ArithmeticException	Base class for `DivideByZeroException`, `NotFiniteNumberException`, and `OverflowException`.
DirectoryNotFoundException	Thrown when part of a file or directory cannot be found.
FileNotFoundException	Thrown on an attempt to access a file that does not exist.
IndexOutOfRangeException	Thrown when an attempt is made to access an element of an array with an index outside the bounds of the array. Similar to `java.lang.ArrayIndexOutOfBoundsException`.
InvalidCastException	Thrown for invalid casting or explicit conversion. Similar to `java.lang.ClassCastException`.
IOException	Base class for exceptions thrown while accessing information using streams, files, and directories. Subclasses of `IOException` include `DirectoryNotFoundException`, `EndOfStreamException`, `FileNotFoundException`, `FileLoadException`, and `PathTooLongException`. I/O exceptions are in the `System.IO` namespace.
NullReferenceException	Thrown when there is an attempt to dereference a `null` object reference. Similar to the infamous `java.lang.NullPointerException`.

(Continued)

TABLE 13.1   Continued

Exception class	Comments
OutOfMemoryException	Thrown when there is not enough memory to continue the execution of a program. Similar to `java.lang.OutOfMemoryError`.[1]
SystemException	Thrown by the CLR when errors occur that are non-fatal and recoverable by user programs. Although this exception extends `System.Exception`, it does not add new functionality – rather, its main purpose is to differentiate exceptions thrown by the CLR and user-written application exceptions

[1] Unlike Java, C# does not differentiate between errors and exceptions, hence the name OutOfMemory*Exception*.

13.3   Examining `System.Exception`

Since `System.Exception` is an important class, I shall examine some of its methods and properties[10] that all other C# exception classes will inherit. Table 13.2 shows the public properties[11] of this class.

Take particular notice of `StackTrace`, `Message`, and `InnerException`. These three public properties are used frequently. The values of these properties can be specified in the constructor when creating a new instance of the exception. Make use of these properties as if they are public fields of the exception object. Here is an example.

```
1: using System;
2:
3: class MyException:ApplicationException{
4:    public MyException(string msg):base(msg){}
5: }
6:
7: class TestClass{
8:    public static void Main(){
9:       try{
```

10. If you are unsure about C# properties, just treat them as public class attributes which you can access. C# properties are different from C# fields. C# properties are not class attributes, but implemented like methods. See Chapter 20 for more information.

11. Besides the public properties listed, there is one `int` property of protected accessibility called HResult. HResult represents the HRESULT value of an exception. HRESULT is a 32-bit integer with coded information on the severity (information, warning, or error-type exception), the facility (which part of the system is responsible for this exception), and a unique error code. Each exception has a unique HRESULT value. You will not be dealing with the HRESULT value most of the time.

TABLE 13.2 `System.Exception` public properties

Public property (type)	Comments
StackTrace (string)	StackTrace carries a stack trace that shows where the exception occurred. Similar to Java's `Throwable.printStackTrace()` method.
InnerException (exception)	Some exceptions may encapsulate another exception object (the inner exception). `InnerException` returns this encapsulated exception, or `null` if there is no inner exception. Inner exceptions will be discussed later.
Message (string)	Textual description of the exception. Similar to Java's `Throwable.getMessage()` method.
HelpLink (string)	HelpLink is a string that can contain a URL to a help file which provides information on why the exception occurred. For example, it may contain the value `"file:///c:/error.htm#err99"`.
Source (string)	Name of the object or application which caused the exception. If not explicitly set, `Source` defaults to the name of the .NET assembly (exe or dll file) from which the exception originated.
TargetSite (MethodBase)	The `MethodBase` object that threw the exception. The `MethodBase` class encapsulates a method and is commonly used in reflection.

```
10:        TestException();
11:     }
12:     catch (Exception e){
13:        Console.WriteLine("Message        :"+e.Message);
14:        Console.WriteLine("StackTrace     :"+e.StackTrace);
15:        Console.WriteLine("HelpLink       :"+e.HelpLink);
16:        Console.WriteLine("TargetSite     :"+e.TargetSite);
17:        Console.WriteLine("InnerException:"+e.InnerException);
18:        Console.WriteLine("Source         :"+e.Source);
19:     }
20:  }
21:
22:  static void TestException(){
23:      MyException me = new MyException("help me!");
24:      me.HelpLink = "http://helpme.com/help";
25:      throw me;
26:  }
27: }
```

Output:

```
c:\expt>test
Message      :help me!
StackTrace   :   at TestClass.TestException()
   at TestClass.Main()
HelpLink     :http://helpme.com/help
TargetSite   :Void TestException()
InnerException:
Source       :test
```

Lines 3–5 contains the code for a user-defined exception class which extends `System.ApplicationException`. `MyException` has one constructor which takes in a string (the message description of the exception) and passes the string to its superclass's constructor (using the `base` keyword) which also takes in a string.

The output shows the `InnerException` property to be `null` (nothing is printed out). In this case, `Source` has the value `test` because I saved this source file as `Test.cs`, and `test.exe` is the assembly which I executed. `Source` will show the name of the application which was being executed when the exception occurred.

`System.Exception` has three[12] important overloaded constructors. These are shown in Table 13.3.

TABLE 13.3 Overloaded constructors of `System.Exception`

Constructor	Comments
`public Exception (string)`	The passed-in string is the error message that is retrievable via the exception object's `Message` property.
`public Exception()`	The default constructor. The exception object is created with a default error message. The default error message goes like this: "`Exception of type <type> was thrown`", where `<type>` is the exception's class name.
`public Exception (string, Exception)`	Takes in a specified error message, and another `Exception` instance (the inner exception object).

13.4 Inner exceptions

C# came out with something called an inner exception – effectively one exception encapsulated within another.[13]

---

12. This class has four overloaded constructors altogether. The last one enables you to create an instance of the exception class with serialized data.
13. Inner exceptions can be implemented in Java too, but it requires extra manual coding effort. In C#, support for inner exceptions is deeply 'entrenched' high up in the exception hierarchy in `System.Exception`.

System.Exception's third constructor shown in Table 13.3 enables you to pass in another exception object to the constructor. Think of it as stuffing a smaller envelope with a message into a bigger envelope (which may contain its own message too). To create an new exception object which encapsulates an inner exception object, use the third constructor in Table 13.3.

Inner exceptions are useful when you have multiple levels of exception throwing (such as when you have nested try-catch blocks). They may be useful if you want to keep the original exception instance, and create a new exception object at the next level, so that at the highest level it is possible to extract the first exception (the inner exception) from the second one.

Going back to the envelope analogy,[14] let's have three people to assist us in our understanding – Abigail, Betsy, and Charlotte. Abigail writes Betsy a message on a piece of paper and hands it over in an envelope. Betsy can read this message if she wants to, then puts it in a larger envelope with her own message (which may contain her interpretation of Abigail's message). Betsy hands this larger envelope over to Charlotte. Charlotte is able to read Betsy's message, and also Abigail's message in the original form.

Abigail's message is the inner exception which is thrown to Betsy, who creates a new exception with Abigail's exception passed into the constructor. Betsy then throws it to Charlotte.

Of course, inner exceptions make sense only if Betsy has something to add on. If not, she can simply forward Abigail's envelope directly to Charlotte just by using a throw statement. Alternatively, in the case where Betsy doesn't even have to be aware of Abigail's message, Betsy may not even bother to catch it. Under such circumstances, there is really no need (except to mess things up) to use inner exceptions.

You can obtain the inner exception of an exception object via the public InnerException property. The following code example should clarify your understanding of inner exceptions.

```
 1: using System;
 2:
 3: class TestClass{
 4:    public static void Main(){
 5:
 6:       try{
 7:          DoSomething();
 8:       }
 9:       catch (Exception e){
10:          Console.WriteLine(e.Message);
11:          Exception innerE = e.InnerException;
12:          Console.WriteLine(innerE.Message);
13:       }
14:    }
```

14. I am quite pleased with myself for coming up with this analogy to explain inner exceptions.

```
15:
16:    static void DoSomething(){
17:      try{
18:        DoSomethingElse();
19:      }
20:      catch (Exception e){
21:        // do some local exception processing
22:        throw new Exception("exception in DoSomething",e);
23:      }
24:    }
25:
26:    static void DoSomethingElse(){
27:      throw new Exception("exception in DoSomethingElse");
28:    }
29: }
```

Output:

```
c:\expt>test
exception in DoSomething
exception in DoSomethingElse
```

A new exception is thrown from DoSomethingElse() (line 27) from DoSomethingElse() to DoSomething() at line 18 – a new exception object is created which encapsulates the original exception as an inner exception (line 22). This new exception object is then thrown back to Main(). In Main(), it is possible to recover the first (inner) exception from the second exception object. Hence, Main() can extract the original (inner) exceptions recursively to obtain every single exception thrown right from the very beginning of the exception chain. It is up to Main() to make use of this information in a creative and useful way.

13.5 Catching generic exceptions

It may seem that a catch block specified with the System.Exception type (i.e. catch(System.Exception)) can handle any type of exception object thrown, since all exception classes are subclasses of System.Exception. This is true only if the exception is thrown from C# code.

Since C# may work with other .NET languages (or even non-.NET languages, such as a COM object written in VB 6 or VC++ 6), it is possible that these codes might throw their own exception objects. And since they may not be .NET-compliant, it is possible that these exception objects are not subclasses of System.Exception. Under such circumstances, you can omit the exception type altogether after the catch keyword. Examine line 16 in this code fragment:

```
10: try{
11:    // method which invokes a legacy COM object
12: }
13: catch(Exception e){
14:    Console.WriteLine("Object of type Exception caught");
15: }
16: catch{
17:    Console.WriteLine("Object of unknown type caught");
18: }
```

The exception handler from lines 16–18 will be able to catch any type of exception object regardless of its type. You can't really do much exception handling with this type of catch block though, since the exception object caught is of an unknown type. Nevertheless, at least C# provides a way for you to deal with it.

14

C# delegates

Delegates will be something new to Java developers, and understanding them is important for understanding events.[1] And since events are an important part of any event-driven language, mastering delegates is a prerequisite if you want to be proficient in C#.

14.1 What are delegates?

Think of a delegate as a special type – something like a class.[2] A delegate type is a class type that is derived from `System.Delegate`. When you declare a delegate using the `delegate` keyword, you do not have to specify that you are deriving from `System.Delegate`; that is implicit.

A delegate type's main job is to encapsulate one or more methods (see Figure 14.1). A delegate instance is an instance of a delegate type. You can view delegate instances as representations of methods, so that when you invoke a delegate instance, the method(s) it encapsulates is also invoked.[3]

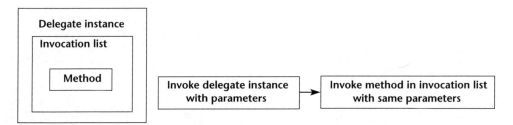

FIGURE 14.1   A delegate instance has an invocation list which contains one or more methods. When the delegate instance is invoked, the method in its invocation list is invoked.

---

1. I have read C# books which do not make a distinction between delegates and events, and (worse still) some which use delegates instead of events for event handling. Events can be viewed as one special type of delegate, but they are definitely not identical!
2. A note for C++ developers: C# delegates are similar to C++ function pointers. However, unlike function pointers, delegates are object-oriented.
3. Hence the name 'delegate'.

All delegate types are implicitly sealed[4] (which means that you cannot derive a subdelegate from any delegate). System.Delegate is also special in the sense that you cannot subclass it into any other class except a delegate. System.Delegate is itself not a delegate, but the superclass of all delegate types. See Figure 14.2.

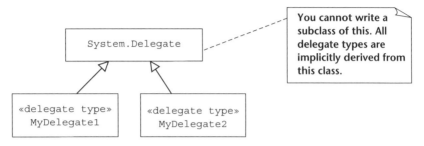

FIGURE 14.2   All delegate types are subclasses of System.Delegate.

Like other types, you perform the following steps to use a delegate:

● declaration of the delegate type;

● instantiation of a delegate type to create a delegate instance;

● invocation of a delegate instance.

14.1.1 Declaration

You need to declare a delegate type before you can use it. The syntax for this looks like a method signature:

```
[accessibility_modifier] delegate return_type
delegate_identifier (parameter list);
```

Here is an example:

```
public delegate int MyDelegate (string s, int i);
```

The statement above declares a delegate type called MyDelegate with public accessibility. MyDelegate returns an int, and takes in two parameters: a string and an int.

Unlike a class type, a delegate type declaration does not start and end with curly braces. You can declare a delegate type within another type (inside another class, or inside an interface), or outside any classes.[5]

I mentioned just now that a delegate instance is used to encapsulate one method. Only methods with:

● the same return type,

---

4. A sealed class in C# is what is called a final class in Java. See section 6.7.
5. The location of declaration, together with its accessibility modifier, will affect the delegate's accessibility. OO common sense still applies concerning accessibility issues for delegates.

- the same number of parameters,
- the same parameter types, in the same order,

as the delegate type declaration can be represented by a delegate instance of this delegate type.

In this case, methods that can be encapsulated by an instance of the `MyDelegate` delegate type must:

- return an `int` AND
- take in a `string` and an `int` as parameters (in that order).

Examples of methods which are compatible with `MyDelegate` are:

- `private int MyMethod1 (string a, int b){...}`
- `public static int MyMethod2 (string a_string, int an_int){...}`

14.1.2 Instantiation

Each delegate instance maintains an invocation list internally. This list contains the ordered list of methods the delegate instance represents. I shall discuss inserting more than one method into the invocation list in section 14.3. For now, just assume that each delegate instance has only one method in its invocation list.

Like classes, you create an instance of a delegate using the `new` keyword. The delegate type constructor takes in either a method reference or another delegate instance.

A newly created delegate instance can refer to any of:

- a static method;
- an instance method (in which case, both the class instance and its method are encapsulated);
- another delegate.

Assuming that `MyClass` is a user-defined class which contains a static method called `MyStaticMethod` and a non-static method called `MyMethod1`, and `mc` is an instance of `MyClass`, here is an example of how to create instances of the `MyDelegate` type:

```
MyDelegate d1 = new MyDelegate(MyClass.MyStaticMethod);
```

In this statement, a delegate instance d1 is created. d1 encapsulates a static method of `MyClass` called `MyStaticMethod`.

Let's consider another statement:

```
MyDelegate d2 = new MyDelegate(mc.MyMethod1);
```

In this statement, a delegate instance d2 is created which encapsulates an instance method of a particular instance of `MyClass` called `MyMethod1`.

Both `MyStaticMethod` and `MyMethod1` *must* have compatible return types (in this case, an int) and method parameters (a `string` and an int, in that order) as the `MyDelegate` delegate type.

14.1.3 Invocation

Invoking a delegate instance simply results in the invocation of the method it represents – or methods, if there is more than one in the delegate instance's invocation list.

Hence, invoking a delegate instance is similar to invoking the method. The parameters passed into the delegate invocation statement are in turn passed into the method as method parameters by the delegate instance.

The following statement invokes the delegate instance d1, created previously with a `string` and an int:

```
d1("test string", 99);
```

This will cause the static method `MyClass.MyStaticMethod` to be invoked with the same parameters.

Hence, since d1 is a delegate instance that encapsulates the static method `MyClass.MyStaticMethod`, the two statements below produce the same effect:

```
d1("test string", 99);
MyClass.MyStaticMethod("test string", 99);
```

And also, since d2 is a delegate instance that encapsulates the instance method `MyMethod1` of mc, the two statements below produce the same effect:

```
d2("hello", 123);
mc.MyMethod1("hello", 123);
```

14.2 A first delegate example

Let's combine what we have done so far into a full concrete example. Study the program below.

```
 1:  using System;
 2:
 3:  delegate int MyDelegate (int i);
 4:
 5:  class TestClass{
 6:
 7:     static int Double (int val){
 8:        Console.WriteLine("running Double");
 9:        return val*2;
10:     }
11:
```

```
12:     int Triple (int val){
13:         Console.WriteLine("running Triple");
14:         return val*3;
15:     }
16:
17:     public static void Main(){
18:
19:         TestClass tc = new TestClass();
20:         MyDelegate d1, d2;
21:
22:         d1 = new MyDelegate(TestClass.Double);
23:         d2 = new MyDelegate(tc.Triple);
24:
25:         Console.WriteLine(d1(3));
26:         Console.WriteLine(" ---------- ");
27:         Console.WriteLine(d2(5));
28:     }
29: }
```

Output:

```
c:\expt>test
Running Double
6
----------
Running Triple
15
```

The MyDelegate type is declared on line 3 outside the scope of any class. MyDelegate is compatible with any method that returns an int, and takes in a single int as parameter. TestClass has two methods: a static Double, and a non-static Triple. Since both Double and Triple return an int, and take in a single int as parameter, both methods are compatible with the MyDelegate type. Two delegate instances of MyDelegate are created on lines 22–23 – d1 encapsulates the static method Double, while d2 encapsulates the instance method Triple.

On lines 25 and 27, both delegate instances are invoked with different int parameters. When d1 is invoked (line 25), the static method Double is invoked with 3 as the input parameter – the value of 6 is returned and printed out. When d2 is invoked (line 27), the instance method Triple is invoked with the parameter 5 – the value 15 is returned and printed out.

14.3 Combining delegates

If each delegate instance is only good for encapsulating one method, then its use will be very limited. The good news is that you can have one delegate instance encapsulating multiple methods in its invocation list.[6] It does not matter whether the methods in a delegate instance's invocation list are static or not. It also does not matter if these methods are totally unrelated and belong to classes in unrelated namespaces. All that matters is that each method matches the delegate type's return type and parameters.

You can use the + and – operators (as well as += and –=) to combine delegate instances, each of which represent one method, to get a delegate instance which represents multiple methods. The statements below create delegate instances of `MyDelegate` called d1 and d2:

```
MyDelegate d1 = new MyDelegate(TestClass.Double);
TestClass tc = new TestClass();
MyDelegate d2 = new MyDelegate(tc.Triple);
```

We can 'add' d1 and d2 together to get a new delegate instance which contains both methods `TestClass.Double` and `tc.Triple` in its invocation list. The new delegate instance is called `compositeDelegate`:

```
MyDelegate compositeDelegate = d1 + d2;
```

Now, delegate instance `compositeDelegate`'s invocation list contains the two methods `TestClass.Double` and `tc.Triple`.

You can also do something like this to achieve the same effect:

```
MyDelegate compositeDelegate =
    new MyDelegate(TestClass.Double) +
    new MyDelegate(tc.Triple);
```

Note that the invocation list of a delegate instance is ordered. In the scenario above, `TestClass.Double` comes before `tc.Triple` on `compositeDelegate`'s invocation list.

When you invoke `compositeDelegate` with a suitable int parameter, all the methods on the invocation list are invoked in that order with the same parameter.

If the methods on the invocation list return a value, only the last invoked method's return value is returned by the invocation of the delegate instance. Figure 14.3 summarizes this idea.

A full coded example is shown below.

```
1:  using System;
2:
3:  delegate int MyDelegate (int i);
4:
5:  class TestClass{
```

---

6. Some books use the terms 'composite delegate' or 'multi-cast delegate' to refer to delegate instances with more than one method in their invocation list.

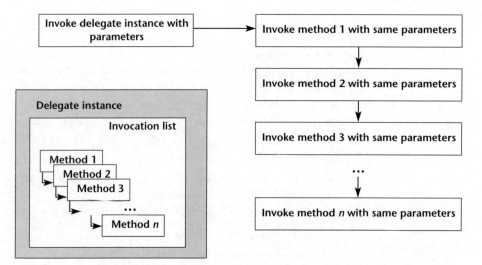

FIGURE 14.3 A delegate instance's invocation list can contain multiple methods. When the delegate instance is invoked, the methods in its invocation list are invoked sequentially with the same parameters that were used to invoke the delegate instance.

```
 6:
 7:    static int Double (int val){
 8:       Console.WriteLine("running Double");
 9:       return val*2;
10:    }
11:
12:    int Triple (int val){
13:       Console.WriteLine("running Triple");
14:       return val*3;
15:    }
16:
17:    public static void Main(){
18:
19:       TestClass tc = new TestClass();
20:       MyDelegate d1, d2, compositeDelegate;
21:
22:       d1 = new MyDelegate(TestClass.Double);
23:       d2 = new MyDelegate(tc.Triple);
24:       compositeDelegate = d1 + d2;
25:
26:       int retVal = compositeDelegate(3);
27:       Console.WriteLine(retVal);
27:    }
28: }
```

Output:

```
c:\expt>test
running Double
running Triple
9
```

In line 24, a new delegate instance is created (`compositeDelegate`) which has `TestClass.Double` and `tc.Triple` in its invocation list (in that order). When invoked on line 26, `TestClass.Double` is invoked first with parameter 3 (which prints out "`running Double`"), followed by `tc.Triple` with the same parameter (which prints out "`running Triple`"). Only the return value of the last invoked method (i.e. the value 9 from `tc.Triple`) is returned by `compositeDelegate`. This return value is then assigned to the variable `retVal` (line 26) and printed out (line 27).

14.4 Removing delegates

As well as combining, you can also remove methods from a delegate instance using the – operator. It is possible to have a delegate instance with no method in its invocation list. However, when such a delegate instance is invoked, a `System.NullReferenceException` is thrown.

It is also possible to have a method in the list more than once. For example, this statement is perfectly legal:

```
MyDelegate compositeDelegate = d1 + d1;
```

When you attempt to remove a method which does not exist in the invocation list, nothing happens.

When you remove a method which occurs more than once in the list, the last is removed. Assuming that d1, d2, and d3 represent delegate instances encapsulating `Method1`, `Method2`, and `Method3` respectively, you can put them all into `compositeDelegate` like this:

```
MyDelegate compositeDelegate = d1 + d2 + d3 + d2 + d1;
```

Invoking `compositeDelegate` will invoke `Method1`, `Method2`, `Method3`, `Method2` and `Method1` in that order.

The statement:

```
compositeDelegate -= d2;
```

will result in the last `Method2` (the one between d3 and d1) to be removed from the invocation list. Thereafter, invoking `compositeDelegate` will invoke only `Method1`, `Method2`, `Method3`, and `Method1` in that order.

An example is given here to clarify and summarize the concepts of combining and removing delegates discussed so far.

Assume that methods M1, M2, and M3 are compatible with `MyDelegate` and study the following code fragment. The corresponding comments show the ordered list of methods in the invocation list of `compositeDelegate`.

```
10:  MyDelegate d1 = new MyDelegate(M1);

11:  MyDelegate d2 = new MyDelegate(M2);

12:  MyDelegate d3 = new MyDelegate(M3);

13:

14:  MyDelegate compositeDelegate = d1 + d2; // M1,M2

15:  compositeDelegate(2); // invoked in order: M1,M2

16:

17:  compositeDelegate += d3; // M1,M2,M3

18:  compositeDelegate(2); // invoked in order: M1,M2,M3

19:

20:  compositeDelegate -= d2; // M1,M3. (M2 removed)

21:  compositeDelegate(2); // invoked in order: M1,M3

22:

23:  compositeDelegate -= d2; // nothing happens.

24:

25:  compositeDelegate -= d3; // M1. (M3 removed)

26:  compositeDelegate(2); // invoked: M1

27:

28:  compositeDelegate -= d1; // nothing on list

29:  compositeDelegate(2);//throws
                                    System.NullReferenceException
```

Composite delegates can be very useful. Effectively, we have one delegate instance representing multiple unrelated methods. By invoking this single delegate instance, all the methods in the invocation list get invoked.

Looking at things from an event point of view, can you see that a delegate instance can be used to store event handler methods? Interested event consumers[7] can register their interest by adding their event handler method to a single delegate instance. This delegate instance is 'offered' by an event source.[8] The event source maintains

---

7. Event consumers are also known as 'event listeners' or 'event sinks' in different literature. The event consumer consumes an event. Typically, the event consumer registers with an event source about an event it is interested in. When the event occurs, the event source will notify the event consumer about the event by passing over an event object.
8. Event sources are also known as 'event generators'. The event source generates an event object for interested event consumers who wish to be notified when that event occurs.

one delegate instance for each potential event, and invokes the relevant delegate instance when that particular event occurs. This will in turn invoke all the event handler methods which are in the invocation list of the relevant delegate instance.

If you understand this, you are beginning to understand events in C#. Keep this in mind when you move on to the events chapter.

14.5   Exception throwing in delegates

When a delegate instance is invoked, and an unhandled exception occurs in one of the methods on the instance's invocation list, the remaining methods will not be invoked and the exception is thrown to the delegate instance's context (see Figure 14.4). The diagram shows the scenario whereby a delegate instance contains five methods in its invocation list. When this instance is invoked, `Method1` and `Method2` are invoked in turn. Let's assume that when `Method3` is invoked, an unhandled exception occurs. As a result, `Method4` and `Method5` will not execute and the exception object is thrown to the delegate instance's context.

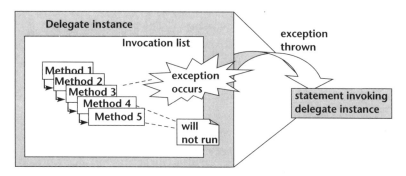

FIGURE 14.4   `Method4` and `Method5` will not execute if an exception occurs when `Method3` is invoked.

14.6   Passing method parameters by reference in delegates

It is possible for methods to take in parameters by reference instead of by value using either the `ref` or `out` keywords (see section 7.2).

In the case of a composite delegate instance, the methods in the invocation list are invoked in sequence. Since each method is invoked with the same set of parameters as that given to the delegate instance, for passed-by-reference parameters, each method invocation will be passed the same reference. This means that changes to that variable by one method in the invocation list will be passed in to the remaining methods. Study the example below:

```
1:   using System;
2:
3:   delegate void MyDelegate (ref int i);
4:
5:   class TestClass{
6:
7:     static void MyMethod(ref int val){
8:       Console.WriteLine("running M1 with parameter "+val);
9:       val+=1;
10:    }
11:
12:    public static void Main(){
13:
14:      MyDelegate d1 = new MyDelegate(TestClass.MyMethod);
15:      MyDelegate compositeDelegate = d1 + d1 + d1 + d1;
16:
17:      int i = 1;
18:      compositeDelegate(ref i);
19:    }
20:  }
```

Output:

```
c:\expt>test
running M1 with parameter 1
running M1 with parameter 2
running M1 with parameter 3
running M1 with parameter 4
```

On line 15, a composite delegate instance is created which encapsulates four references to TestClass.MyMethod. When the first MyMethod in the invocation list is invoked on line 18, it increments the value of the int passed to it by reference so that when the MyMethod is called a second time, it is passed a reference to the same int variable (which now contains the value of 2). This explains the output.

15

C# events

I recommend that you read and understand Chapter 14 before proceeding.

Any modern programming language has an efficient event model, and C# is no exception. The concepts in C#'s event model are quite similar to Java 2's event delegation model: – we still have the event source, the event consumer, and the event object. However, unlike Java 2's event delegation model, C#'s model uses an event object which is a special type of C# delegate.

I will start by examining the generic event model, then zoom in to C# specifics. If you are familiar with events, jump to section 15.2.

15.1 Generic event model

Table 15.1 gives a review of the major roles in a generic event model. Figure 15.1 shows them in a schematic way.

TABLE 15.1 Description of different roles in a generic event model

Role	Description
Event source	The object which potentially causes an event to happen – an event can be any special occurrence. The event source provides a way for interested event consumers to register their interest with this event source. The event source typically keeps a list of registered event consumers, so that when the event occurs the registered consumers in the list are notified.
Event consumer	The object which is interested in listening to a particular event. An event consumer contains a special method called the event handler. This method takes in the event object as a parameter. Event sources and event consumers can have a many-to-many relationship – one event consumer can register with many event sources, and one event source can have multiple event consumers registered for the same event.
Event object	When an event occurs in the event source, a new event object is created. This event object is then passed over to the event consumer's event handler method as a parameter. An event object encapsulates event-specific information (e.g. the label of the button clicked) which the event consumer can extract.

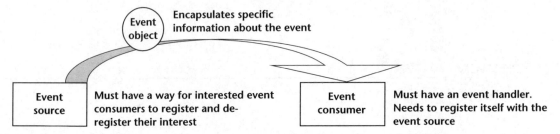

FIGURE 15.1   Characteristics of the event source, object and consumer in a generic event model.

Let us examine the sequence of actions in the generic event model.

1 The event consumer registers its interest with an event source and provides the name of the event handler that should be invoked when the event occurs.

2 The event source keeps a reference to each registered event consumer in an internal list.

3 When the event occurs, the event source creates a new instance of an event object and passes into it event-specific information.

4 The event source goes down the list of registered event consumers and invokes each event handler, passing in the event object as a parameter.

5 The event handler of the event consumer runs. Event information can be obtained from the event object passed in.

Figure 15.2 depicts this sequence.

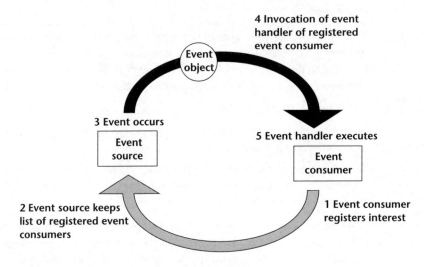

FIGURE 15.2   Sequence of action in a generic event model.

15.2 What are C# events?

Having reviewed the generic event model, I shall introduce C# events, and map C#'s implementation to the generic model.

A delegate instance encapsulates one or more (static or non-static) methods with the same return type and parameters, so that when the delegate instance is invoked all the methods in its invocation list are invoked in order with the same set of parameter values.

A C# event is a special type of delegate. It too encapsulates one or more methods – in this case, event handlers – so that when the event occurs, all these event handlers are invoked.

Event handlers usually take in two parameters, though this is not mandatory:

- one `object` type which references the event source; and

- one event object of type `System.EventArgs`, or a subclass of it.

Before you can do anything with events, you need to declare an event instance. But even before doing that, you must have a delegate type which matches the event handlers of your event consumers.

The statement below declares a delegate type which returns nothing, and takes in two parameters – a reference to the event source of type `object`, and the event object of type `EventArgs`.

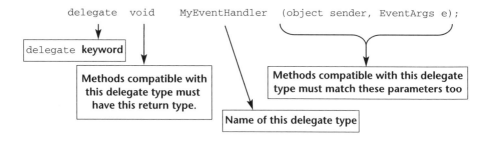

Since it is unlikely that your event consumer's event handlers will return any other thing besides `void`, you would want to declare your delegate type to return `void` too. Remember that the return type and the method parameters of your event handlers must match those of the delegate type.

Once you have the delegate type declared, you are ready to roll.

15.2.1 Event source class

The event source has to do two things.

- Declare the event object.

You use the event keyword to do this. The following statement declares an event instance called SomethingHappened of type MyEventHandler:
Note that the event's type must be a delegate type.[1]

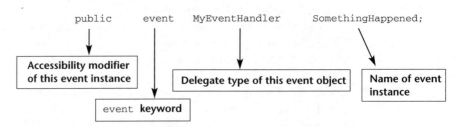

- Invoke the event when the event occurs.
  When the event occurs in the source, the source can fire the event by invoking it. Invoking an event is similar to invoking a delegate – just pass in the correct parameters like this:

```
SomethingHappened (this, new EventArgs());
```

  This statement will cause all the event handler methods in SomethingHappened's invocation list to be invoked with the parameters this and a new EventArgs object. For the object parameter, this is passed in so that the consumer can have a reference to the source object. For the EventArgs parameter, a new event object is created and sent over.

15.2.2   Event consumer class

The event consumer also has do to two things:

- Provide an event handler.
  Here is an event handler called TellMe, coded in the consumer class:

```
public void TellMe (object sender, EventArgs e){
   Console.WriteLine("***** i am being notified! *****");
}
```

  The return type and method parameters of TellMe must match those of the delegate type MyEventHandler. What this event handler does is simply print out a message to indicate that it is running.

- Register the event handler with the event source's event.
  You have got to tell the SomethingHappened event (of the event source) that you want to be notified when the event fires. This is done by using the += operator.

1. That's why I said that an event is some kind of delegate. There is no separate event type – all event instances are of a delegate type.

Assuming that the event source class's name is `EventSource`, and the `EventSource` class has a public event instance called `SomethingHappened`, the following statements perform the registration:

```
EventSource source = new EventSource();
source.SomethingHappened += new MyEventHandler(TellMe);
```

An event instance (in this case `source.SomethingHappened`) can be used as the left-hand operand of the `+=` and `-=` operators. You can register as many methods as you like with each event instance in the same manner using `+=`.

This 'hooking up' of the event source to the event consumer can be done anywhere in your code as long as you have a reference to both the source object and the consumer object, though this registration of interest usually occurs in the event consumer. In this case, the consumer object has to either create an instance of the source, or obtain a reference to it in some way or other.

15.2.3   Event object class

`System.EventArgs` is the base class for predefined event objects in the BCL. You can subclass it to add in event-specific fields and accessor methods, but it is *not* mandatory that all event objects be subclasses of `EventArgs`.

In the first example below, I will simply use `EventArgs` as the event object class instead of writing a new subclass.

15.3   A full example

After examining the various pieces of the whole picture, it is time to put them all together. Here is a fully coded example consisting of three classes – the source, the consumer, and an execution class containing the `Main()` method. To keep things simple, I am not going to write a custom-made subclass of `EventArgs` for the event object, and I have purposely placed the `Main()` method in a separate class so that the role of each class can be clearly seen.

Lines 1–7 code the delegate declaration:

```
1:  using System;
2:
3:  /* ------------------------------------------------
4:   * Delegate declaration
5:   *------------------------------------------------ */
6:  delegate void MyEventHandler (object sender, EventArgs e);
7:
```

Lines 8–29 code the event source class. Line 12 declares the event instance called `SomethingHappened`. This is of delegate type `MyEventHandler`. In the example here, when the `Run()` method is called, it produces and prints out 200 random `int`s between 0 and 99 (lines 20–21) in a `for` loop. Take note of lines 24–26 – in this trivial example, we are interested in the event whereby a 9 appears as one of the random `int`s. When such an event occurs, the `SomethingHappened` event is fired.

```
 8:   /* -----------------------------------------------
 9:    * Event Source
10:    * -----------------------------------------------*/
11:  class MySource{
12:      public event MyEventHandler SomethingHappened;
13:
14:      public void Run(){
15:          // produce random numbers
16:          Random r = new Random();
17:          int rnd;
18:
19:          for (int i=0; i<200; i++){
20:            rnd = r.Next() % 100; // between 0 and 99
21:            Console.Write(rnd + ", ");
22:
23:            // event happened! Fire event
24:            if (rnd==9){
25:                SomethingHappened(this, new EventArgs());
26:            }
27:          }
28:      } // end Run
29:  } // end class
30:
```

Lines 31–39 code the event consumer. It contains only one event handler method called `TellMe`. `TellMe`'s return type and parameters must match that of delegate type `MyEventHandler` in order for this event handler to be registered with the source's `SomethingHappened` event. This trivial event handler simply prints out a message.

```
31:   /* -----------------------------------------------
32:    * Event consumer
33:    * -----------------------------------------------*/
34:  class MyConsumer{
35:      // event handler
36:      public void TellMe (object sender, EventArgs e){
37:        Console.Write("***** i am being notified *****");
38:      }
39:  }
40:
```

Lines 41–53 code the main class where the action happens. On lines 47–48, new consumer and source objects are created. Event registration is performed on lines 49–50 – here the event handler of consumer is 'hooked to' the SomethingHappened event, so that when SomethingHappened fires consumer.TellMe runs. Finally, on line 51, Run() of the source object is invoked, so that random number generation starts.

```
41:  /* ----------------------------------------
42:   * Main class
43:   * ---------------------------------------*/
44:  class TestClass{
45:
46:    public static void Main(){
47:      MyConsumer consumer = new MyConsumer();
48:      MySource source = new MySource();
49:      source.SomethingHappened +=
50:        new MyEventHandler(consumer.TellMe);
51:      source.Run();
52:    }
53:  }
```

Output:[2]

```
c:\expt>test
4, 78, 65, 66, 64, 20, 59, 27, 28, 29, 34, 68, 21, 12, 98, 56,
64, 52, 42, 93, 44, 40, 6, 14, 31, 96, 83, 48, 96, 25, 59, 86,
17, 58, 68, 70, 78, 21, 47, 88, 24, 86, 79, 69, 95, 35, 68, 9,
***** i am being notified ***** 63, 40, 48, 32, 1, 66, 74, 64,
19, 51, 82, 68, 37, 58, 31, 50, 70, 48, 51, 10, 91, 28, 25, 90,
5, 1, 69, 5, 8, 37, 66, 96, 28, 74, 32, 56, 24, 74, 85, 98, 31,
4, 98, 27, 86, 26, 51, 13, 55, 76, 99, 47, 31, 5, 65, 35, 62, 5,
27, 47, 97, 69, 3, 82, 32, 33, 40, 10, 73, 22, 73, 43, 10, 53,
79, 34, 77, 98, 4, 26, 50, 3, 97, 79, 38, 19, 65, 70, 56, 97,
94, 19, 47, 85, 1, 62, 1, 16, 95, 0, 86, 88, 87, 33, 3, 3, 84,
78, 73, 31, 58, 11, 1, 48, 97, 41, 19, 71, 91, 13, 68, 17, 54,
76, 28, 54, 43, 25, 99, 64, 33, 8, 3, 51, 87, 9, ***** i am
being notified ***** 63, 64, 76, 82, 82, 34, 44, 72, 86, 30, 65,
46, 88, 60, 43, 77,
```

Observe the output. When Run() executes and produces random ints, a SomethingHappened event gets fired when a 9 appears. The event handler TellMe() runs and prints out a message.

---

2. Of course your output will vary because the numbers generated are random.

15.4 Another full example

This scenario involves three consumers and two events from the same event source. Two of the consumers will be listening to the same event, while the third consumer will be monitoring another event.

In this example, a `WaterTank` (the event source) fills up slowly. Two interested consumers, the `EmergencyAlarm` and the `FlashingLight`, want to be notified when the water level reaches 20 m so that they can start ringing and flashing to attract attention. The warnings are supposed to prompt the duty officer to rush over, pump out the water manually, and turn off the alarm and light. If he has had too much alcohol the night before and does not respond to the din, an `Electrode` (somehow attached to his body) should fire small electric shocks so that he awakes. The `Electrode` is the third consumer which wants to be notified when the water level reaches 25 m – just before the `WaterTank` overflows at 30 m.

To make things a bit different from the previous example, each consumer class has its own constructor which takes in a `WaterTank` object. Registration of the event handler to the appropriate event is done in these constructors.

I have also coded a special event object class, `OverflowRiskEventArgs`, which contains a string message field and an `int` field indicating the water level. Figure 15.3 shows the scenario and the code follows.

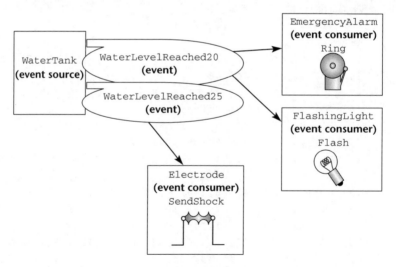

FIGURE 15.3   Pictorial representation of the coded example.

```
1:   using System;
2:   /* ------------------------------------------
3:    * Delegate declaration
4:    * ------------------------------------------*/
5:   delegate void WaterTankEventHandler
```

```
 6:        (object sender, OverflowRiskEventArgs e);
 7:
 8:    /* --------------___-      .===----------------
 9:     * Event object
10:     * -------------------------------------*/
11:    class OverflowRiskEventArgs:EventArgs{
12:      private string Message;
13:      private int WaterLevel;
14:
15:      // constructor
16:      public OverflowRiskEventArgs(string Message, int WaterLevel):base(){
17:        this.Message = Message;
18:        this.WaterLevel = WaterLevel;
19:      }
20:
21:      // accessor methods
22:      public string getMessage(){
23:        return Message;
24:      }
25:
26:      public int getWaterLevel(){
27:        return WaterLevel;
28:      }
29:    }
30:
31:    /* ---------------------------------------
32:     * Event Source
33:     * -------------------------------------*/
34:    class WaterTank{
35:      public event WaterTankEventHandler WaterLevelReached20;
36:      public event WaterTankEventHandler WaterLevelReached25;
37:
38:      private int WaterLevel = 0;
39:
40:      public void Run(){
41:        // water level increases in steps of 1
42:        while (WaterLevel<30){
43:          WaterLevel += 1;
44:
45:          Console.WriteLine("tank: Current water level: "+WaterLevel);
```

```
46:
47:        // Fire WaterLevelReached20 event
48:        if (WaterLevel==20)
49:          WaterLevelReached20(this,
50:            new OverflowRiskEventArgs("Please bail out",WaterLevel));
51:
52:        // Fire WaterLevelReached25 event
53:        if (WaterLevel==25)
54:          WaterLevelReached25(this,
55:            new OverflowRiskEventArgs("Overflow imminent",WaterLevel));
56:      }
57:      Console.WriteLine("tank: Overflowed.");
58:    }
59: }
60:
61: /* ----------------------------------------
62:  * Event consumer 1
63:  * ----------------------------------------*/
64: class EmergencyAlarm{
65:
66:    // constructor
67:    public EmergencyAlarm (WaterTank wt){
68:      wt.WaterLevelReached20 += new WaterTankEventHandler(this.Ring);
69:    }
70:
71:    // event handler
72:    public void Ring (object sender, OverflowRiskEventArgs e){
73:      Console.WriteLine("alarm: Message : "+e.getMessage());
74:      Console.WriteLine("alarm: WaterLevel: "+e.getWaterLevel());
75:      Console.WriteLine("alarm: Ringing ...");
76:    }
77: }
78:
79: /* ----------------------------------------
80:  * Event consumer 2
81:  * ----------------------------------------*/
82: class FlashingLight{
```

```
 83:
 84:     // constructor
 85:     public FlashingLight (WaterTank wt){
 86:       wt.WaterLevelReached20 += new WaterTankEventHandler(this.Flash);
 87:     }
 88:
 89:     // event handler
 90:     public void Flash (object sender, OverflowRiskEventArgs e){
 91:       Console.WriteLine("light: Message : "+e.getMessage());
 92:       Console.WriteLine("light: WaterLevel: "+e.getWaterLevel());
 93:       Console.WriteLine("light: Flashing light ...");
 94:     }
 95:  }
 96:
 97:  /* ----------------------------------------
 98:   * Event consumer 3
 99:   * ---------------------------------------*/
100:  class Electrode{
101:
102:     // constructor
103:     public Electrode (WaterTank wt){
104:       wt.WaterLevelReached25 +=new WaterTankEventHandler(this.SendShock);
105:     }
106:
107:     // event handler
108:     public void SendShock (object sender, OverflowRiskEventArgs e){
109:       Console.WriteLine("electrode: Message : "+e.getMessage());
110:       Console.WriteLine("electrode: WaterLevel: "+e.getWaterLevel());
111:       Console.WriteLine("electrode: Sending Shocks ...");
112:     }
113:  }
114:  /* ----------------------------------------
115:   * Main class
116:   * ---------------------------------------*/
117:  class TestClass{
```

```
118:
119:    public static void Main(){
120:      WaterTank wt = new WaterTank();
121:      EmergencyAlarm alarm = new EmergencyAlarm (wt);
122:      FlashingLight light = new FlashingLight (wt);
123:      Electrode electrode = new Electrode (wt);
124:
125:      // the fun starts
126:      wt.Run();
127:    }
128: }
```

Output:

```
c:\expt>test
tank: Current water level: 1
tank: Current water level: 2
tank: Current water level: 3
tank: Current water level: 4
tank: Current water level: 5
tank: Current water level: 6
tank: Current water level: 7
tank: Current water level: 8
tank: Current water level: 9
tank: Current water level: 10
tank: Current water level: 11
tank: Current water level: 12
tank: Current water level: 13
tank: Current water level: 14
tank: Current water level: 15
tank: Current water level: 16
tank: Current water level: 17
tank: Current water level: 18
tank: Current water level: 19
tank: Current water level: 20
alarm: Message : Please bail out
alarm: WaterLevel: 20
alarm: Ringing ...
light: Message : Please bail out
light: WaterLevel: 20
light: Flashing light ...
tank: Current water level: 21
tank: Current water level: 22
tank: Current water level: 23
```

```
tank: Current water level: 24
tank: Current water level: 25
electrode: Message : Overflow imminent
electrode: WaterLevel: 25
electrode: Sending shocks ...
tank: Current water level: 26
tank: Current water level: 27
tank: Current water level: 28
tank: Current water level: 29
tank: Current water level: 30
tank: Overflowed.
```

chapter 16

Reflection and dynamic method invocation

Reflection has always been considered an 'advanced' topic in most programming books, probably because you seldom use it unless you are in the business of writing debuggers and introspection tools such as the Javabean Development Kit. I myself would try to avoid using reflection as much as possible if there are alternative ways to do things.

This particular chapter has been written in a very 'dry' style. I have simply included lots of short code examples showing how to perform certain reflection operations using reflection classes in the BCL. The intention is that you can refer back here when there is a need to write reflection codes. Like Java, reflection is largely dependent on the class libraries provided. There are no new C# keywords to be learnt in this chapter – all you have to do is to become familiar with the C# reflection API. You could skip this chapter altogether and come back when you need 'how-to' reflection examples quickly.

Reflection is possible in C# because the metadata stored, together with IL codes, in a .NET assembly provides information about the assembly itself.

Most of the classes related to reflection operations are in the following namespaces: `System.Reflection` and `System.Reflection.Emit`. They are listed in Tables 16.1 and 16.2.

TABLE 16.1 Description of the namespaces which contain significant classes for reflection

Namespace	Description
`System.Reflection`	Contains classes/interfaces that provide a managed view of loaded types, methods and fields with the ability to dynamically create and invoke types
`System.Reflection.Emit`	Contains classes that allow a compiler or tool to emit metadata and IL codes, and optionally generate an assembly file on disk – script engines and compilers will use classes of this namespace

System.Type is the most important class here. Type is an abstract base class that represents a type in the CTS – which can be a class or interface.

From the view-of-classes shown in Figure 16.1, I have extracted those classes which represent different entities in C# – these are shown in Figure 16.2.

TABLE 16.2   Description of the significant classes for reflection

Class	Description
System namespace	
Type	Represents type declaration (class types, interface types, array types, value types, enum types)
Activator	Contains methods to create types of objects locally or remotely, or obtain references to existing remote objects
AppDomain	Represents an application domain – an application domain is an isolated environment where applications execute within. Application domains are also separated by security boundaries for executing managed code
System.Reflection namespace	
Assembly	Represents an assembly – an assembly is a reusable and self-describing block of .NET codes which can be versioned
Module	Represents a module, and contains methods which permit reflection on a module – an assembly can consist of multiple modules
PropertyInfo	Discovers the attributes of a property and provides access to property metadata
EventInfo	Discovers the attributes of an event and provides access to event metadata
FieldInfo	Discovers the attributes of a field and provides access to field metadata
MethodInfo	Discovers the attributes of a method and provides access to method metadata
System.Reflection.Emit namespace	
AssemblyBuilder	Defines and represents a dynamic assembly
ModuleBuilder	Defines and represents a module
PropertyBuilder	Defines the properties for a type
EventBuilder	Defines events for a class
FieldBuilder	Defines and represents a field
ILGenerator	Generates IL codes

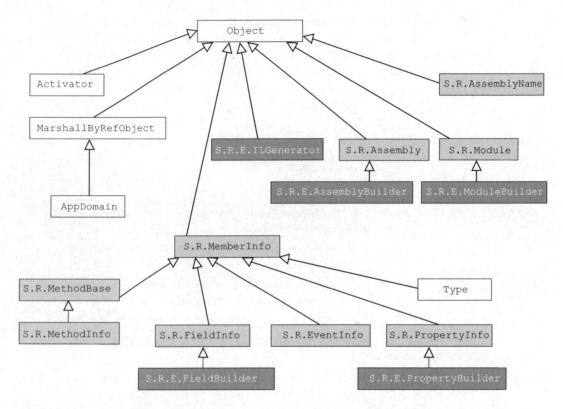

FIGURE 16.1   Classes which are significant in reflection. S.R. stands for the `System.Reflection` namespace; and S.R.E. stands for the `System.Reflection.Emit` namespace. Classes in unshaded boxes are found in the `System` namespace.

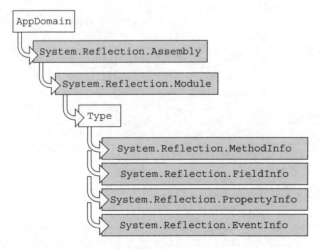

FIGURE 16.2   Classes which represent .NET entities.

An `AppDomain` object is the root of the type hierarchy of a .NET application during runtime. The `AppDomain` class represents a .NET application domain which is similar to a Win32 process. You can have multiple .NET assemblies executing in separate application domains simultaneously. A .NET assembly can contain one or more modules. Each module contains one or more `Types` (classes, interfaces) and, of course, you can find properties, events, fields, and methods within a `Type`.

In the following sections, I shall show how to perform various reflection tasks. If you follow the code examples given, performing reflection operations in C# should be straightforward.

16.1   Retrieving the type of an instance

To retrieve the `Type` of an object, use `System.Object`'s `GetType()` method. `System.Type` has a `Name` field which tells you the type's name. Examine the following example:

```
 1: using System;
 2: using System.Reflection;
 3:
 4: public class MyClass {
 5: }
 6:
 7: public class MainClass {
 8:    public static void Main () {
 9:       MyClass c = new MyClass();
10:       Type t = c.GetType(); // GetType() of Object
11:       Console.WriteLine(t);
12:    }
13: }
```

Output:

```
c:\expt>test
MyClass
```

Line 11 can be replaced by

```
11:       Console.WriteLine(t.Name);
```

to produce the same output. The `ToString()` method of the `Type` class prints out its `Name` property automatically, so passing t or t.Name to `Console.WriteLine()` does not make a difference.

16.2 Retrieving the type from a name of a class

If you want to retrieve the Type of a class represented by a string instead, you can use the static GetType() method of the Type class. Examine the following code.

```
1: using System;
2: using System.Reflection;
3:
4: public class MyClass {
5: }
6:
7: public class MainClass {
8:    public static void Main () {
9:       Type t = Type.GetType("MyClass");
10:       Console.WriteLine(t);
11:    }
12: }
```

You can try this to retrieve the Type representation of an int:

```
Type t = Type.GetType("System.Int32");
```

It is illegal to do the following though:

```
Type t = Type.GetType("int");
```

because int is just a C# alias for System.Int32. Type.GetType only takes in strings representing types of the CTS.

Alternatively, you can use C#'s typeof operator instead of Type.GetType() to do the same trick:

```
1: public class TestClass {
2:    public static void Main () {
3:       Type t = typeof("MyClass");
4:       Console.WriteLine(t);
5:    }
6: }
```

The main difference between using typeof and Type.GetType() is that the former is evaluated at compile time (and hence is faster during execution) while the latter is evaluated during runtime (See section 10.3.1).

System.Type has several methods which are useful for telling us more about the type. The method names are self-explanatory: FullName, IsAbstract, IsClass, IsInterface, IsPublic, IsSerializable, IsSealed, etc. Consult the BCL API documentation for the other members of Type.

16.3 Retrieving methods from a type

You can retrieve a single MethodInfo object, if you already know the name of the method, or an array of MethodInfo objects.

In the following example, MyClass contains a method called DoThis() which takes in no parameters. Some useful methods of MethodInfo are demonstrated.

```
 1: using System;
 2: using System.Reflection;
 3:
 4: public class MyClass{
 5:   public static void DoThis(){
 6:     Console.WriteLine("doing this");
 7:   }
 8:   public static void DoThat(){
 9:     Console.WriteLine("doing that");
10:   }
11: }
12:
13: public class TestClass{
14:   public static void Main(){
15:
16:     Type t = Type.GetType("MyClass");
17:     MethodInfo m = t.GetMethod("DoThis");
18:     Console.WriteLine("method       :" + m);
19:     Console.WriteLine("Name         :" + m.Name);
20:     Console.WriteLine("IsPublic     :" + m.IsPublic);
21:     Console.WriteLine("IsStatic     :" + m.IsStatic);
22:     Console.WriteLine("IsConstructor:" + m.IsConstructor);
23:     Console.WriteLine("ReturnType   :" + m.ReturnType);
24:   }
25: }
```

Output:

```
c:\expt>test
method       :Void DoThis()
Name         :DoThis
```

```
IsPublic      :True
IsStatic      :True
IsConstructor:False
ReturnType    :System.Void
```

If you don't know the method name in the type, you can obtain an array of all
`MethodInfo` objects in a particular type:

```
 1: using System;
 2: using System.Reflection;
 3:
 4: public class MyClass{
 5:   public static void DoThis(){
 6:      Console.WriteLine("doing this");
 7:   }
 8:   public void DoThat(int a, int b){
 9:      Console.WriteLine("doing that " + (a*b));
10:   }
11: }
12:
13: public class TestClass{
14:   public static void Main(){
15:
16:      Type t = Type.GetType("MyClass");
17:      MethodInfo[] methods = t.GetMethods();
18:
19:      foreach (MethodInfo m in methods)
20:        Console.WriteLine("method: " + m);
21:   }
22: }
```

Output:

```
c:\expt>test
method: Int32 GetHashCode()
method: Boolean Equals(System.Object)
method: System.String ToString()
method: Void DoThis()
method: Void DoThat(Int32, Int32)
method: System.Type GetType()
```

Notice that several methods such as `GetHashCode`, `Equals`, and `ToString` inherited from `System.Object` to `MyClass` are also retrieved.

16.4 Retrieving modules from an assembly

An assembly can consist of one or more modules.[1] To obtain an array of modules in an assembly, you use `System.Reflection.Assembly`'s `GetModules` method.

Let's create an assembly (called `Assm`) containing two modules (`Mod1` and `Mod2`) first. The following three code fragments do just that.

```
1: // Mod1.cs
2: public class Mod1{}
```

```
1: // Mod2.cs
2: public class Mod2{}
```

```
 1: // Assm.cs
 2: using System;
 3: using System.Reflection;
 4:
 5: public class Assm{
 6:    public static void Main(){
 7:       Assembly a = Assembly.LoadFrom("Assm.exe");
 8:       Module[] modules = a.GetModules();
 9:       foreach(Module m in modules)
10:          Console.WriteLine(m);
11:    }
12: }
```

If you are using `csc.exe`, compile the two module files `Mod1.cs` and `Mod2.cs` into module files first (module files end with a `.netmodule` extension). Use the `/target:module` option of `csc.exe`:

```
c:\expt>csc /target:module Mod1.cs
c:\expt>csc /target:module Mod2.cs
```

`Mod1.netmodule` and `Mod2.netmodule` will be created.
(You can also use the option shortcut `/t:module` instead of `/target:module`.)

Then compile `Assm.cs` by adding into it the two module files you have just created. Use the `/addmodule` option to do this. If there is more than one module to be added into the final assembly file, separate them using commas without any spaces:

```
c:\expt>csc /addmodule:Mod1.netmodule,Mod2.netmodule Assm.cs
```

---

1. A module is a file containing IL codes but without a manifest. Each assembly must have one and only one manifest file regardless of the number of modules it contains.

The assembly file `Assm.exe` will be created. When executed, `Assm.exe` will produce the following output.

```
c:\expt>assm
Assm.exe
Mod1.netmodule
Mod2.netmodule
```

The `Assm` assembly contains three modules in all – the `Assm` class itself, `Mod1`, and `Mod2`. Their names are displayed by reflection.

16.5 Dynamically invoking methods in late bound objects

You should have read section 16.3 before embarking on this section.

Late bound objects are objects the type of which we are unsure until runtime. Late binding is more flexible but slower to perform. We use `System.Activator`'s `CreateInstance` method to create an instance of a class during runtime.

Examine the program below:

```
 1: using System;
 2: using System.Reflection;
 3:
 4: public class MyClass{
 5:   public void DoThis(){
 6:     Console.WriteLine("doing this");
 7:   }
 8:   public void DoThat(int a, int b){
 9:     Console.WriteLine("doing that " + (a*b));
10:   }
11: }
12:
13: public class TestClass{
14:   public static void Main(){
15:
16:     // can assign typeName to a type known during runtime
17:     string typeName = "MyClass";
18:
19:     Type t = Type.GetType(typeName);
20:     object o = Activator.CreateInstance(t);
21:
22:     MethodInfo m = t.GetMethod("DoThis");
23:     m.Invoke(o, null); // DoThis takes in no parameters
24:   }
25: }
```

Output:

```
c:\expt>test
doing this
```

We use `MethodInfo`'s `Invoke` method to dynamically invoke a method. `Invoke` is inherited from `MethodBase`, which is a superclass of `MethodInfo`.

The signature for `Invoke` is:

```
public object Invoke (object obj, object[] parameters);
```

It takes in the object instance containing the method (represented by `MethodInfo`) as the first parameter, and the parameters to be passed into that method via an `object` array as the second parameter.

On line 23 in the example above, o and `null` were passed into `Invoke` since `DoThis` does not take in any parameters.

`DoThat` is a little bit more complex than `DoThis` because `DoThat` takes in two `int`s as parameters. If you want to invoke `DoThat`, you need to create an object array with two `int`s first before passing it into `Invoke`.

You can replace lines 20–23 with the following to invoke `DoThat` instead:

```
20:      object o = Activator.CreateInstance(t);
21:      object []param = {2,3};
22:      MethodInfo m = t.GetMethod("DoThat");
23:      m.Invoke(o, param); // DoThat takes in two parameters
```

New output:

```
c:\expt>test
doing that 6
```

Line 21 creates a new `object` array containing two `int` elements. This array is then passed into `Invoke` as the second parameter on line 23.

16.6 Creating new types during runtime

`System.Reflection.Emit` contains classes such as `AssemblyBuilder`, `ModuleBuilder`, `TypeBuilder`, and `MethodBuilder` which are used to create new types during runtime. Rarely used in conventional programming, the ability to create new `Type`s during runtime may be useful when you want to dynamically create new proxy classes for remote operations.

Since this is an advanced topic, I will give only a simple code example to give a clue as to which classes to use. Refer to the API documentation for more information about each class in `System.Reflection.Emit`.

```
 1: using System;
 2: using System.Reflection;
 3: using System.Reflection.Emit;
 4:
 5: public class TestClass{
 6:
 7:   public static Type CreateType (){
 8:
 9:       AppDomain        ad;
10:       AssemblyName     an;
11:       AssemblyBuilder  ab;
12:       ModuleBuilder    mb;
13:       TypeBuilder      tb;
14:       MethodBuilder    methb;
15:       ILGenerator      ilg;
16:
17:       // AppDomain.CurrentDomain returns the current process
18:       // that is running
19:       ad = AppDomain.CurrentDomain;
20:
21:       // create a new assemby called 'MyAssembly'
22:       an     = new AssemblyName();
23:       an.Name = "MyAssembly";
24:       ab     = ad.DefineDynamicAssembly
25:             (an, AssemblyBuilderAccess.Run);
26:
27:       // create a new module called 'MyModule'
28:       mb = ab.DefineDynamicModule("MyModule");
29:
30:       // create new Type called 'MyType'
31:       tb = mb.DefineType("MyType", TypeAttributes.Public);
32:
33:       // create new method called DoThis which takes in no
34:       // parameters and is public.
35:       methb = tb.DefineMethod
36:         ("DoThis", MethodAttributes.Public, null, null);
37:
38:       // Generate IL codes for DoThis method.
39:       // All DoThis does is to print out a string and return.
40:       ilg = methb.GetILGenerator();
41:       ilg.EmitWriteLine("i love computers!");
```

```
42:         ilg.Emit(OpCodes.Ret);
43:
44:         // complete creating the Type. Call tb.CreateType only
45:         // after all the members within have been defined.
46:         return tb.CreateType();
47:    }
48:
49:    public static void Main(){
50:         // CreateType returns a dynamically generated Type
51:         Type t = CreateType();
52:
53:         // create new instance of the dynamically generated type
54:         object o = Activator.CreateInstance(t);
55:
56:         // retrieve and invoke the DoThis method of the object
57:         MethodInfo m = t.GetMethod("DoThis");
58:         m.Invoke(o, null);
59:    }
60: }
```

Output:

```
c:\expt>test
i love computers!
```

The action happens in the CreateType method. When CreateType runs, it dynamically creates an assembly (MyAssembly) (lines 22–25) which contains a module (MyModule) (line 28), which in turn contains a new Type (MyType) (line 31). MyType contains a single method (DoThis) which returns void and takes in no parameters (lines 35–42). All DoThis does is print out a string and return (coded in lines 41–42).

Reflection is also used extensively together with custom attributes to retrieve attribute values during runtime from an entity. Custom attributes are covered in Chapter 28.

17

Multi-threaded programming

The Java concepts of multi-threading can be generally applied here, though code-wise, there are significant differences in how to write a threaded class. To get started with writing threaded applications in C# quickly, all you need to do is get familiar with the relevant classes and their methods. This chapter assumes a basic knowledge of threads – topics such as what threads are, multi-threading versus multi-processing, etc. will not be covered.

17.1 Multi-threading

For those who need a quick reminder – a multi-processing operating system is one that can, apparently, execute more than one process simultaneously. Each process in turn can have multiple threads running at same time. The term 'multitasking' generally means running many tasks concurrently, and can be used for both multi-processing (also known as 'process-based multitasking') and multi-threading (also known as 'thread-based multitasking').

If a computer has only one CPU, we are talking about only one real processing sequence. Hence, any multi-processing on a single-CPU machine is 'apparent' only. Each CPU can only run one statement at a time, but it is switching between the different concurrent processes very quickly to give the appearance of handling multiple processes simultaneously. True multi-processing can happen only if you have more than one CPU with each executing its own statements.

Operating systems implement multitasking in one of two ways – cooperative or pre-emptive. In the former, each thread is responsible for relinquishing control of the CPU so that other threads will get a chance to execute. Older versions of Windows and MS-DOS are based on cooperative multitasking. On the other hand, in pre-emptive multitasking, the scheduler is responsible for allocating time slices to each thread. When a timeslice is up, the scheduler invokes the process of context switching so that the next thread is ready to run its allocated timeslice. Context switching involves copying out the 'state' of the current thread to the stack, and restoring the state of the next thread back from the stack. The 'state' of a thread includes register values and any other information needed by the thread for it to run.

Unlike older operating systems which practice cooperative multitasking, Windows NT/2000/XP works on the premise of pre-emptive multitasking. The Windows scheduler decides how many CPU time slices to give to each thread and process currently running, and performs context switching. Cooperative multitasking has the disadvantage that badly written applications, which refuse to give up their hold on the CPU, can hog the whole processor and eventually hang the whole operating system. .NET was designed to run only on pre-emptive multitasking operating systems.

C# has only one keyword specially reserved for threading purposes – `lock` (which is equivalent to Java's `synchronize` keyword). All other threading operations are done via classes in the BCL. In particular, the class which represents a threading object is the `System.Threading.Thread` class. This is C#'s counterpart of Java's `java.lang. Thread`.

Both `java.lang.Thread` and `System.Threading.Thread` have a number of similar methods for threading operations (such as start, sleep, join, wait, etc.). These methods are largely similar in functionality, and differ only in subtle ways.

This chapter introduces the significant methods of the `System.Thread` class, and you will have to refer to the API documentation for a full description of the other class members. The more advanced threading classes (such as `ThreadPool`, `Interlocked`, and `Timer`) will not be covered.

For basic threading operations in C#, three classes of the `System.Threading` namespace will be useful – `Thread`, `Monitor`, and `Mutex`. See Figure 17.1.

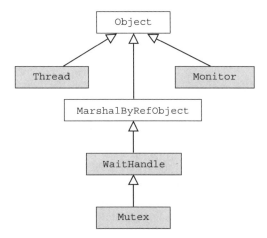

FIGURE 17.1   Important classes used for threading operations. Shaded classes are in the `System.Threading` namespace – unshaded classes are in the `System` namespace.

TABLE 17.1   Some classes, enums, and delegates involved in threading operations and their descriptions

Classes/enums/delegates	Description
Classes	
`Thread`	Represents a threading entity – contains methods for creating, starting, aborting, suspending, resuming, and other operations on the thread it encapsulates
`Mutex`	A synchronization primitive used for inter-process synchronization
`Monitor`	Provides a mechanism for synchronizing access to objects
Exception Classes	
`ThreadAbortException`	Thrown by the runtime when a thread is being aborted (i.e. when a call is made to the `Abort()` method of the thread)
`ThreadInterruptedException`	Thrown when a thread is interrupted while in waiting (WaitSleepJoin) state
`ThreadStateException`	Thrown when a thread operation is requested, but the thread is not in a suitable state for that operation – For example, when the `Start()` method of an aborted (dead) thread is invoked, or when the `Resume()` method of a non-suspended, unstarted, or aborted thread is invoked
Enums	
`ThreadPriority`	Used to specify the scheduling priority of a thread – often used as a parameter to the `Thread.Priority` public property
`ThreadState`	Used to specify the execution states of a thread – often used as a parameter for the `Thread.ThreadState` public property
Delegates	
`ThreadStart`	Encapsulates the starting point method when a thread is started

Table 17.1 gives a description of classes, enums, and delegates involved in threading operations.

17.2 Thread states and multi-threading in C#

In C#, a thread can exist in the states shown in Figure 17.2. A thread must be in one (and only one) of these seven states at any one time.

Some Java books may categorize threads which are 'ready to run' in a separate state, so that there are 'ready to run' threads (also known as 'runnable'), and 'running' threads. In a single-CPU machine, only one thread can be in the running state, while all the rest are in the ready to run pool. In Figure 17.2, I have not differentiated between ready to run and running. All threads which are ready to run, are con-

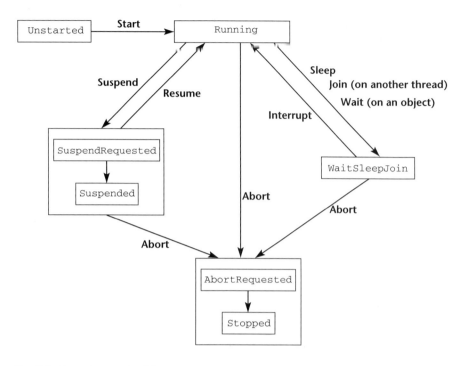

FIGURE 17.2   Possible thread states in C#.

sidered to be in the running state. However, only one of these can actually be hogging the CPU in a single-CPU machine at any one time.

Special mention must be made of the SuspendedRequested, Suspended, AbortRequested, and Stopped states. When a thread is suspended (via the invocation of its `Suspend()` method), it does not go into the Suspended state immediately. The .NET runtime will ensure that the thread executes to a point (called the 'safe point') before putting it into the Suspended state. The same thing happens when the `Abort()` method of a thread is invoked. The runtime ensures that the thread has reached a safe point before putting it into the Stop state.

In other words, suspension and abortion of a thread may not be immediate (and that is why we have the `Join()` method to deal with threads awaiting abortion).

Like Java, a thread in the Stopped state may not be started again. Attempting to call the `Start()` method of a stopped thread will throw a `ThreadStateException`. Once a thread has been stopped, you are holding on to a dead thread which you can't do much with.

17.2.1   How to multi-thread in C#

After all the 'administrative stuff' discussed above, its time to get your hands dirty.

In Java, you can write a thread class in one of two ways – subclass `java.lang.`

Thread, or write a class which implements the `java.lang.Runnable` interface. In both cases, you need to write an implementation of the `run()` method. When the `start()` method of the thread is called, the `run()` method will act as the starting point for your thread.

Though the ideas are similar, C# looks at things a bit differently. There is also a `System.Threading.Thread` class, but this class is sealed (or final, in Java-speak), and there is no interface to implement. What happens is that you create an instance of `System.Threading.Thread` and pass into it a delegate instance[1] of the `StartThread` delegate. This `StartThread` delegate instance encapsulates the method which will act as the starting point for this new thread when its `Start()` method is invoked.

This implies that you can name any method as the starting point when the thread runs. All you have to do is to pass this method name into the `StartThread` delegate.[2] Unlike C#, Java insists that the starting point for any thread is the `run()` method.

17.2.2 Instantiating the thread class

Before creating a `Thread` object, you need to create an instance of the `StartThread` delegate. The `StartThread` delegate has this method signature:

```
public delegate void StartThread ();
```

All methods which are to be compatible with the `StartThread` delegate must return `void`, and take in no parameters. This implies that your thread's starting method must return `void` and take in no parameters too.

Here a `StartThread` instance is declared by passing in the name of the `StartWithMe()` method:

```
StartThread st = new StartThread(StartWithMe);
```

You then create a new `Thread` object by passing in the delegate instance to its constructor:

```
Thread t = new Thread(st);
```

So far, what you have done is create a `Thread` object with a specified method as the starting point. To start the thread, invoke its `Start()` method:

```
t.Start();
```

1. If you are not sure about C# delegates, just treat it as a class which encapsulates a method for now. A delegate is a new C# type which is used to represent one or more methods. See Chapter 14.
2. Of course, the limitation is that this method designated as the starting point must match the delegate's declaration type. The `StartThread` delegate will be introduced next.

Here is a full simple example on threading:

```
 1: using System;
 2: using System.Threading;
 3:
 4: public class TestClass{
 5:    public static void PrintA(){
 6:       for (int i=0; i<1000; i++)
 7:          Console.Write("A");
 8:    }
 9:
10:    public static void PrintB(){
11:       for (int i=0; i<1000; i++)
12:          Console.Write("B");
13:    }
14:
15:    public static void Main(){
16:
17:       // create new delegate instances
18:       ThreadStart ts1 = new ThreadStart(PrintA);
19:       ThreadStart ts2 = new ThreadStart(PrintB);
20:
21:       // create new thread instances
22:       Thread t1 = new Thread(ts1);
23:       Thread t2 = new Thread(ts2);
24:
25:       // start the threads running
26:       t1.Start();
27:       t2.Start();
28:    }
29: }
```

Output:[3]

```
c:\expt>test
BBBBBBBBBBBBBBBBBBBBBBBBBBBBBBBBBBBBBBBBBBBBBBBBBBBBBBBBBBBBB
BBBBBBBBBBBBBBBBBBBBBBBBBBBBBBBBBBBBBBBBAAAAAAAAAAAAAAAAAAAAAAAA
AAAAAAAAAAAAAAAAAAAAAAAAAAAAAAAAAAAAAAAAAAAAAAAAAAAAAAAAAAAAA
AAAAAAAAAABBBBBBBBBBBBBBBBBBBBBBBBBBBBBBBBBBBBBBBBBBBBBBBBBBBBBB
BBBBBBBBBBBBBBBBBBBBBBBBBBBBBBBBBBBBBBBBBBBBBBBBBBBAAAAAAAAAAAA
AAAAAAAAAAAAA...
```

3. The output has been truncated – You don't want to see a screen full of As and Bs in this book!

Two thread instances are created (t1 and t2) on lines 22–23. Their respective entry point methods are PrintA() and PrintB() respectively.

The output shows the two threads running concurrently. For this particular run, the second thread (ts2) started first, and PrintB was invoked to print out a series of Bs. Halfway through, the first thread (ts1) kicked in and invoked PrintA to print out a series of As. After ts1's time slice expired, ts2 took over again and printed several Bs – and so on.

In this example, both the starting point methods of both threads are static. You can specify an instance method as the starting point of a thread too. If that is the case, you need to create an instance of the class and then pass the reference to the instance method into the delegate's constructor on lines 18–19. Assuming PrintA() and PrintB() are both instance methods of TestClass, you will have to replace lines 16–19 with this code:

```
16:    // create new delegate instances
17:    TestClass tc = new TestClass();
18:    ThreadStart ts1 = new ThreadStart(tc.PrintA);
19:    ThreadStart ts2 = new ThreadStart(tc.PrintB);
```

17.2.3 Thread methods

I have introduced the Start() method of Thread. Instead of listing all the methods of Thread, Table 17.2 shows the corresponding methods of java.lang.Thread with System.Threading.Thread along with appropriate comments. More details about each method follow.

After a thread has started running, you can suspend it by calling its Suspend() method. This is Suspend()'s method signature:

```
public void Suspend();
```

Calling Suspend() on a thread which is already in the Suspended state has no effect (no exception will be thrown).

You can resume the suspended thread by calling the Resume() method of that thread instance:

```
public void Resume();
```

Calling Resume() on a thread which is:

- not already in the Suspended state, or
- has been aborted, or
- has not been started yet

will throw a ThreadStateException.

TABLE 17.2   Methods of `java.lang.Thread` and `System.Threading.Thread` side by side

System.Threading.Thread	java.lang.Thread	Comments
Start()	start()	Starts a thread
Interrupt()	interrupt()[1]	Interrupts a thread in the sleeping/waiting/joining state
Sleep()	sleep()	Puts a thread in the sleeping state – Java: throws a `java.lang.InterruptedException` when interrupted. C#: throws a `Thread.Threading.ThreadInterruptedExc eption` when interrupted
Join()	join()	Puts a thread in the joining state until another thread has completed abortion. Although both methods allow you to specify a maximum waiting time (so that it returns after timeout even though the other thread is still not completely aborted) there is a difference in their return values. Java: all overloaded join methods return `void`. You can't tell if the return is due to a timeout or if the other thread has been successfully aborted. C#: join returns a boolean – `true` will mean that the join returned because the thread has aborted completely; `false` will mean that join returned because of a timeout
Suspend()	suspend()	suspend() in Java is deprecated because it is deadlock prone
Resume()	resume()	Resumes a thread which has been suspended – in Java `resume()` is deprecated
Abort()	stop()	Aborts (or stops or kills) a running thread. In both Java and .NET, threads which have been aborted cannot start again – In Java `stop()` is deprecated
IsBackground (get and set property)	setDaemon(), isDaemon()	Used to alter or get the current thread type. Terminology differences – a daemon thread in Java is a foreground thread in .NET: a non-daemon thread in Java is a background thread in .NET
IsAlive (get property)	isAlive()	Used to check if a thread is still alive or dead[2]

1. `java.lang.Thread` has an `isInterrupted()` method to check if the thread is currently in the interrupted state. C# has no such equivalent.
2. Within this context, there is no difference between a non-alive, dead, aborted, or stopped thread and the terms are used interchangeably. They all refer to a thread which is no longer in the active running state, and can never be resurrected again.

You can pause a thread's execution by calling `Sleep()`. `Sleep()` takes in an `int` value which represents the number of milliseconds you want the thread to sleep:

```
public static void Sleep(int millisecondsTimeout);
```

Unlike `Suspend()`, `Sleep()` is a static method and that implies that you cannot invoke the `Sleep()` method on any particular thread instance. You can only call the static `Thread.Sleep()` method so that the *current* thread sleeps. You can suspend another thread by calling the `Suspend()` method of that thread instance as long as you have a reference variable to it, but you cannot put *another* thread to sleep – only the currently running one. Unlike `Sleep()`, `Suspend()` has no timeout period.

You can abort a thread by calling `Abort()`:

```
public void Abort();
```

When a thread is aborted, it throws a `ThreadAbortException`. This is a very special exception in the sense that it cannot be caught using a `catch` block, but if there is a finally block, that finally block will still execute.

The difference between a suspended thread and an aborted one is that an aborted thread cannot start again. Calling `Start()` on a thread instance that has been aborted will throw a `ThreadStateException`. On the other hand, a suspended thread can still be resumed into its active running state by calling its `Resume()` method. `Resume`'s method signature looks like this:

```
public void Resume();
```

You can check if a thread instance has stopped (aborted) via its `IsAlive` (get-only) public property. [4] Assuming `t` is the thread instance, `b` will be true if `t` is not in the Stopped state.

```
bool b = t.IsAlive;
```

As previously mentioned, when `Abort()` or `Suspend()` of a thread instance has been invoked, the thread may not be aborted or suspended immediately. The scheduler will ensure that execution of the thread continues until a safe point is reached before stopping the thread's line of execution, and putting it into the Stopped state.

Because there is no way to determine when this safe point is reached when abort-

---

4. If you are not sure what a C# property is, just treat it as a public field for now. Unlike real fields however, properties can be designed so that you can obtain its value only (get property) or assign a value to it only (set property) or both. An example of a get-only property of the `Thread` class is `IsAlive`. You can check if the `IsAlive` property contains `true` or `false` (as in `bool b = threadInstance.IsAlive`), but you cannot change its value (`threadInstance.IsAlive = false`; causes a compilation error). See Chapter 20.

ing a thread, you can use the `Join()` method so that execution of the calling thread is blocked until the aborted thread has really stopped. `Join()` is useful if the calling thread's continued execution needs the aborted thread to be completely stopped before carrying on. `Join`'s method signature looks like this:

```
public void Join();
```

`Join()` is overloaded so that it can take in an `int` value representing the timeout (in the number of milliseconds). This overloaded method blocks the calling method until either the aborted thread has completely stopped, or if the timeout occurs, whichever happens first. `Join`'s other method signature looks like this:

```
public bool Join (int milliseconds);
```

This method returns `true` if the aborted thread has completely stopped (before the timeout), or `false` if a timeout has occurred (before the aborted thread has completely stopped).

To get a reference to the currently running thread, use the public property `CurrentThread` like this:

```
Thread current = Thread.CurrentThread;
```

This is similar to Java's static `Thread.currentThread()` method except that in C#'s case, `CurrentThread` is a property rather than a method.

17.2.4 Thread priorities

As for Java, threads can be assigned priorities in C# too. But unlike Java, which has ten priority levels, C# threads can have one of five:

- `Highest`
- `AboveNormal`
- `Normal`
- `BelowNormal`
- `Lowest`

In the case of Java, threads spawned off another thread 'inherit' the priority level of the parent thread. In C#, all threads are defaulted to `Normal` priority regardless of the priority level of the parent thread.

You can set or get a thread instance's priority level via its `Priority` public property. You can use the `ThreadPriority` enum to specify the priority level when setting a thread's priority level. The statement below changes the priority level of a thread instance t to `Highest`.

```
t.Priority = ThreadPriority.Highest;
```

I have modified the simple threading example in section 17.2.2 by inserting line 25 to make thread ts1 higher in priority than ts2. Here is the modified program.

```
1: using System;
2: using System.Threading;
3:
4: public class TestClass{
5:    public static void PrintA(){
6:      for (int i=0; i<1000; i++)
7:        Console.Write("A");
8:    }
9:
10:    public static void PrintB(){
11:      for (int i=0; i<1000; i++)
12:        Console.Write("B");
13:    }
14:
15:    public static void Main(){
16:
17:      // create new delegate instances
18:      ThreadStart ts1 = new ThreadStart(PrintA);
19:      ThreadStart ts2 = new ThreadStart(PrintB);
20:
21:      // create new thread instances
22:      Thread t1 = new Thread(ts1);
23:      Thread t2 = new Thread(ts2);
24:
25:      t1.Priority = ThreadPriority.AboveNormal;
26:      // start the threads running
27:      t1.Start();
28:      t2.Start();
29:    }
30: }
```

Output:[5]

```
c:\expt>test
AAAAAAAAAAAAAAAAAAAAAAAAAAAAAAAAAAAAAAAAAAAAAAAAAAAAAAAAAAAAA
AAAAAAAAAAAAAAAAAAAAAAAAAAAAAAAAAAAAAAAAAAAAAAAAAAAAAAAAAAAAA
AAAAAAAAAAAAA...BBBBBBBBBBBBBBBBBBBBBBBBBBBBBBBBBBBBBBBBBBBBBB
BBBBBBBBBBBBBBBBBBBBBBBBBBBBBBBBBBBBBBBBBBBBBBBBBBBBBBBBBBBB...
```

5. The output has been truncated. All the As are displayed before the first B gets printed out.

Instead of alternating between threads ts1 and ts2, it is apparent from the output that ts1 executes to completion before ts2 is given any time slice. The output shows all 1000 As being printed out even before a single B appears.

If there are threads of differing priorities, the general rule is that all the threads of the higher priorities *which are in the running state* will complete execution first, before the lower-prioritized threads have a chance to run. Be careful when assigning priorities to threads because of the possibility of unintended code starvation.[6]

The actual priority level of a thread depends not only on the assigned thread priority in relation to other threads in the same process, but also on the priority of the process the thread is running in compared to other processes. One point to note is that although C# and the BCLs have all these priority mechanisms built in, the C# language specification states that the underlying operating system is *not* required to honor a thread's priority level.

17.2.5   Foreground versus background threads

Like Java, C# groups threads into two categories – background and foreground. Foreground threads are like Java daemon threads – they are the more 'important' ones compared to background threads (or Java non-daemon threads).

A particular process may consist of multiple background and foreground threads running concurrently. If all foreground threads are aborted (stopped), the .NET runtime will automatically abort all other background threads which are still running by invoking their Abort() method.

You can check if a thread in C# is background or foreground via Thread's IsBackground public property. IsBackground is a getter and setter property – you can change a background thread to a foreground one (and vice versa) by changing the value of IsBackground directly. By default, all threads are foreground threads.

The program below creates and starts two threads, t1 and t2. Both are foreground threads by default.

```
 1: using System;
 2: using System.Threading;
 3:
 4: public class TestClass{
 5:
 6:    public static void PrintA(){
 7:      for (int i=0; i<100; i++)
 8:        Console.Write("A");
 9:      Console.Write(" Thread 1 complete ");
10:    }
11:
```

---

6. This is only a general rule. Different operating systems may behave differently concerning thread priorities.

```
12:    public static void PrintB(){
13:      while(true)
14:        Console.Write("B");
15:    }
16:
17:    public static void Main(){
18:      ThreadStart ts1 = new ThreadStart(PrintA);
19:      ThreadStart ts2 = new ThreadStart(PrintB);
20:
21:      Thread t1 = new Thread(ts1);
22:      Thread t2 = new Thread(ts2);
23:
24:      // t2.IsBackground = true;
25:      Console.WriteLine
26:        ("t1 is background: " +t1.IsBackground);
27:      Console.WriteLine
28:        ("t2 is background: " +t2.IsBackground);
29:
30:      t1.Start();
31:      t2.Start();
32:    }
33: }
```

Output:[7]

```
c:\expt>test
t1 is background: False
t2 is background: False
AAAAAAAAAAAAAAAAAAAAAAAAAAAAAAAAAAAAAAAAAAAAAAAAAAAAAAAA
AAAAAAAAAAAAAAAAAAAAAAAAAAAAAAAAAAAAAAAAAAAA Thread 1
complete BBBBBBBBBBBBBBBBBBBBBBBBBBBBBBBBBBBBBBBBBBBBB
BBBBBBBBBBBBBBBBBBBBBBBBBBBBBBBBBBBBBBBBBBBBBBBBBBBBBBBBBB
BBBBBBBBBBBBBBBBBBBBBBBBBBBBBBBBBBBBBBBBBBBBBBBBBBBBBBBBBBBB
BBBBBBBBBBBBBBBBBBBBBBBBBBBBBBBBBBBBBBBBBBBBBB......
```

When ts1 starts, PrintA prints out 100 As and terminates. When ts2 starts, PrintB goes into an infinite loop, and continues printing Bs until you force termination by hitting Ctrl-C.

If line 24 is uncommented, so that t2 becomes a background thread instead of a foreground one, the output changes:

```
c:\expt>test
t1 is background: False
```

7. The output truncated – the program continues to print Bs until a forced termination occurs.

```
t2 is background: True
BBBBBBBBBBBBBBBBBBBBBBBBBBBBBBBBBBBBBBBBBBBBRRRRRRDDDDDD
BBBBBBBRRRRRRRDDDDDDDDBBBBBBBBBBBBAAAAAAAAAAAAAAAAAAAAAAAAAAAAA
AAAAAAAAAAAAAAAAAAAAAAAAAAAAAAAAAAAAAAAAAAAAAAAAAAAAAAAAA
AAAAAAAAAAAAAAAA Thread 1 complete BBBBBBBBBBBBBBBBBB
```

What happens now is that once t1 finishes its for loop and terminates, the runtime realizes that no more foreground thread is running. It will then automatically invoke the Abort() method of all other background threads which are still running. If you examine the new output, you will realize that even after t1 terminates, t2 still runs for a very short while. This may be due to the delay between the termination of t1 and the invocation of t2's Abort() method, or the fact that the runtime is bringing t2 to a safe point before aborting it completely. Unlike the previous case, t2 no longer carries on running after t1 terminates.

17.3 Thread synchronization

Of course multithreading comes with a whole host of synchronization problems. There are concurrency problems which lead to indefinite states,[8] and other complicated 'programming traps' such as race conditions and deadlocks. Hence, it is important for a C# developer using threads to be well versed in thread synchronization.

In this section, I will introduce the lock keyword, and two more classes – Mutex and Monitor.

Table 17.3 gives some initial clues as to how thread synchronization compares in C# and Java.

17.3.1 Thread safety in .NET classes

According to documentation from Microsoft, all public and static methods, properties, or fields of the .NET BCL support concurrent access within a multi-threaded environment. This means that any such member can be invoked simultaneously

TABLE 17.3 Corresponding thread synchronization methods of Java and C#

C#	Java
lock keyword or Monitor.Enter()/Monitor.Exit()	synchronized keyword
Monitor.Wait()	Object.wait()
Monitor.Pulse()/Monitor.PulseAll()	Object.notify()/Object.notifyAll()

8. For example, if we have two concurrently running threads getting and setting the value of a shared variable, the exact value stored in this variable will be indefinite at any one time.

from multiple threads without problems of deadlocks, race conditions, or other syn-chronization problems. However, *not* all classes and structs of the BCL are thread safe.[9] If you intend to use non-thread safe classes within a multi-threaded context, and there is a possibility of synchronization problems with these classes, you can wrap the class instance within your own synchronization code.

17.3.2   Using the *lock* keyword

The C# equivalent of Java's `synchronize` keyword, is `lock`. However, unlike the `synchronize` keyword, which can be used to declare a synchronized block or method, C#'s `lock` can only be used to declare a synchronized block. You cannot use the `lock` keyword in a method declaration.

`lock` takes in an object which acts as the mutex.[10] When a thread attempts to enter the critical section,[11] it checks to see if the mutex object is available. If so, it obtains the mutex and enters the critical section – only to release it after it leaves the critical section. Another thread attempting to enter the critical section can only do so if no other thread is holding onto the mutex. If the mutex has been taken, the second thread will be blocked until the mutex is released. Here's the syntax.

```
lock (<expression>){
  // critical section code
}
```

`<expression>` is the mutex object for this critical section, and must be a reference type. Typically, expression is either:

- an object reference variable or
- `this` or
- `typeof(<class_name>)`.

The last expression is often used to protect a shared static variable from concurrent access.

---

9. When you say that a class is 'thread safe', it means that member of an instance of this class will always maintain a valid state when used simultaneously by concurrent threads. You will have to refer to the API documentation of each class under the *Thread Safety* section to determine if that class is thread safe or not. If all classes are made thread safe, you are going to get lousy performance indeed.
10. Mutex stands for 'mutual exclusion'. A mutex is a token used as a flag to determine if someone is already holding on to a particular resource (in our case, the resource is a block of code). If you have heard of the term 'semaphore', this is similar to a mutex, except that a semaphore maintains a counter so that n numbers of threads or processes can access a resource concurrently, and the $n + 1^{th}$ request will be rejected. (By the way, all this discussion reminds me of the 'operating system' module I did in my undergraduate days.)
11. The critical section is the group of statements delimited by the curly brackets of a `lock` statement.

Here is a slightly modified version of the first threading example (section 17.2.2). It has been modified to include a random sleep period for each thread, so that the results can be more easily observed. [12]

```
 1: using System;
 2: using System.Threading;
 3:
 4: public class TestClass{
 5:
 6:    public static void PrintA(){
 7:       for (int i=0; i<10; i++){
 8:          Random r = new Random();
 9:          Thread.Sleep(r.Next() % 2000);
10:          Console.Write("A");
11:       }
12:    }
13:
14:    public static void PrintB(){
15:       for (int i=0; i<10; i++){
16:          Random r = new Random();
17:          Thread.Sleep(r.Next() % 1000);
18:          Console.Write("B");
19:       }
20:    }
21:
22:    public static void Main(){
23:       ThreadStart ts1 = new ThreadStart(PrintA);
24:       ThreadStart ts2 = new ThreadStart(PrintB);
25:
26:       Thread t1 = new Thread(ts1);
27:       Thread t2 = new Thread(ts2);
28:
29:       t1.Start();
30:       t2.Start();
31:    }
32: }
```

Output:

c:\expt>test

ABBBBAABBABBABBAAAAA

12. Without the random sleep, chances are that each allocated time slice of my operating system is long enough for either thread to perform the whole for loop all at one shot. And the output will either be all As followed by all Bs, or vice versa.

Lines 8–9 and 16–17 are the random pauses introduced in both methods. Instead of an inconsequential `Console.Write` statement (on lines 10 and 18), you could have critical code there which involves the reading or updating of a static shared variable. If that is the case, you can lock both methods on a common mutex object so that only one of the two can execute concurrently.

In the fragment below, methods `PrintA()` and `PrintB()` have been altered to include the `lock` keyword demarcating the simulated critical section.

```
 6:    public static void PrintA(){
 7:      lock(typeof(TestClass)){
 8:        for (int i=0; i<10; i++){
 9:          Random r = new Random();
10:          Thread.Sleep(r.Next() % 2000);
11:          Console.Write("A");
12:        }
13:      }
14:    }
15:
16:    public static void PrintB(){
17:      lock(typeof(TestClass)){
18:        for (int i=0; i<10; i++){
19:          Random r = new Random();
20:          Thread.Sleep(r.Next() % 1000);
21:          Console.Write("B");
22:        }
23:      }
24:    }
```

Output:

```
c:\expt>test
BBBBBBBBBBAAAAAAAAAA
c:\expt>test
AAAAAAAAAABBBBBBBBBB
```

I have used the `typeof(TestClass)` as the mutex object.[13] If you are dealing with non-static methods, you can use a reference to any common object accessible by both methods as the mutex. (`this` is very commonly used if both threads are running on the same object instance.) Depending on which thread obtains the mutex first, either all the `B`s are printed out before an `A` appears, or vice versa. Both possible scenarios are shown in the output above.

---

13. `typeof` is a C# keyword which returns a `System.Type` object.

17.3.3 Using *Monitor*

System.Threading.Monitor is a sealed[14] class which contains several useful static methods for locking operations. The most commonly used methods of Monitor are Monitor.Enter() and Monitor.Exit(). Both take in a mutex object reference:

```
public static void Enter (object obj);
public static void Exit (object obj);
```

These two methods do exactly the same thing as the lock keyword. Assuming the mutex object in use is some reference type called lockingObj, the following two code fragments (lines 30–32 and lines 40–42) are thus functionally identical:

```
30      lock (lockingObj){
31          // critical section codes
32      }

40      Monitor.Enter(lockingObj);
41          // critical section codes
42      Monitor.Exit(lockingObj);
```

Probably one advantage of using these two Monitor methods over lock is that you can conditionally execute the Monitor.Exit() method within the critical section. Another advantage is that you can have the Monitor.Enter() statement in one method, and Monitor.Exit() coded in another method, thus having a critical section spanning multiple methods.[15]

The Monitor class has other useful static methods which you can use – Pulse, PulseAll, Wait, and TryEnter.

TryEnter is similar to Enter, except that TryEnter is overloaded to specify a timeout. If some other thread is already hogging the mutex object, using Enter will block the calling thread indefinitely. Using TryEnter, on the other hand, can cause the statement to return on timeout if the calling thread is still unable to obtain the mutex object after the specified time.

TryEnter's method signatures look like this:

```
public static bool TryEnter (object obj);
public static bool TryEnter (object obj, int
millisecondTimeout);
```

For the first overloaded TryEnter, the timeout is defaulted to 0. This means that the method returns immediately if it could not get the mutex object. Both methods

14. A sealed class in C# is a final class in Java.
15. This practice, although possible, is highly discouraged because it leads to unstructured code which is difficult to debug.

return `true` if the mutex object has been successfully acquired, and `false` if the acquisition has failed before the timeout expired. Java does not have this built-in mechanism.

`Monitor.Pulse()` and `Monitor.Wait()` are similar in functionality to Java's `java.lang.Object`'s `notify()` and `wait()`. Both `Wait()` and `Pulse()` should be called only within a critical section (delimited by the `lock` curly brackets, or in between the `Monitor.Enter()` and `Monitor.Exit()` statements.)

Here are the method signatures for `Wait()`:

```
public static bool Wait (object obj);
public static bool Wait (object obj, int
millisecondTimeout);
```

Invoking the first overloaded `Wait()` releases the mutex object currently being held[16] by the thread, and blocks itself indefinitely until it reacquires the mutex object. When `Wait()` is invoked, other threads waiting for this mutex object can acquire it and enter the critical section. The method returns `true` if the thread manages to reacquire the mutex object. It does not return until it has done so.[17]

The second overloaded `Wait()` enables you to specify the timeout in milliseconds. The method returns `true` if the thread manages to reacquire the mutex object within the specified time. If the calling thread does not manage to reacquire the mutex object before timeout expiry, the method will return `false`.

`Pulse()` works together with `Wait()`. It is invoked by the current thread to notify the next thread waiting for the particular mutex object that there might be a change in the mutex object's state. Essentially, `Pulse()` tells the waiting thread to 'please go and take a look at the mutex object, and get ready to acquire it if it is available'.

Here is the method signature for `Pulse()`:

```
public static void Pulse (object obj);
```

If you intend to notify all threads waiting on the mutex object, use the `PulseAll()` method instead:

```
public static void PulseAll (object obj);
```

Before concluding this section with a coded example, I have to mention that each object which is acting as a mutex keeps three references:

- reference to the thread that has currently acquired it;

16. A thread which is invoking this `wait` method should already be in the critical section and hence must be holding on to the mutex object.
17. Meaning that `false` will never be returned, and making the boolean return value superfluous.

- reference to a waiting queue – the waiting queue contains a list of threads waiting to be notified about the mutex object's change in state;
- reference to a ready queue – The ready queue contains a list of threads ready to acquire the mutex object once it is ready.

A `Wait()` invocation will place the thread currently holding the mutex object into the waiting queue, so that a thread from the ready queue can acquire it. A `Pulse()` invocation will cause a thread from the waiting queue to move over to the ready queue. `PulseAll()` causes a mass migration of all threads in the waiting queue to the ready queue.

Here is a construed example to demonstrate how a mutex object is released via `Wait()`.

```
 1: using System;
 2: using System.Threading;
 3:
 4: public class TestClass{
 5:
 6:    static object mutex = new object();
 7:
 8:    public static void PrintA(){
 9:      Monitor.Enter(mutex);
10:        for (int i=0; i<5; i++){
11:          Console.WriteLine("A:"+i);
12:          if (i==2){
13:            Monitor.Pulse(mutex);
14:            Monitor.Wait(mutex);
15:          }
16:        }
17:      Monitor.Exit(mutex);
18:    }
19:
20:    public static void PrintB(){
21:      Monitor.Enter(mutex);
22:        for (int i=0; i<5; i++)
23:          Console.WriteLine("B:"+i);
24:      Monitor.Pulse(mutex);
25:      Monitor.Exit(mutex);
26:    }
27:
28:    public static void Main(){
29:      ThreadStart ts1 = new ThreadStart(PrintA);
30:      ThreadStart ts2 = new ThreadStart(PrintB);
31:
```

```
32:      Thread t1 = new Thread(ts1);
33:      Thread t2 = new Thread(ts2);
34:
35:      t1.Priority = ThreadPriority.Highest;
36:      t1.Start();
37:      t2.Start();
38:  }
39: }
```

Output:

```
c:\expt>test
A:0
A:1
A:2
B:0
B:1
B:2
B:3
B:4
A:3
A:4
```

This code demonstrates two threads which are running two separate critical sections (one in PrintA, and the other in PrintB) both synchronized on the same static object.[18] The first thread which got the mutex object calls a Wait halfway (line 14), so that the second thread can obtain the mutex and execute the critical section.

An object to be used as the mutex is declared in line 6. Both the code in PrintA and PrintB are synchronized on the same static mutex object. In order to ensure that thread t1 starts first, I have set its priority so that it is higher than t2 on line 35. When t1 starts, it grabs hold of the mutex object on line 9, thus preventing t2 from going beyond line 21 in PrintB when it starts. Under normal circumstances, t2 has to wait for t1 to finish and release the mutex object before it can execute line 22. However, after PrintA has performed three iterations of the for loop (and printed out A:0, A:1 and A:2 to the console), the condition on line 12 becomes true and the thread invokes Wait (line 14). When that happens, t1 surrenders the mutex object and is itself blocked while t2 grabs hold of the mutex and completes its looping. After t2 is done, it notifies t1 that the mutex is about to be released (line 24), and releases it (line 25). t1 then takes off from where it left off previously and completes its for loop.

18. Of course, you can have multiple threads attempting to enter the same critical section of the same method of the same object too.

17.3.4 Using *Mutex*

The last[19] of the threading classes I am going to cover is System.Threading. Mutex. Mutex is a class which represents ... well, a mutex. You can create an instance of Mutex and use it in place of any other object as the mutex lock.

Mutex has 2 useful overloaded constructors:

```
public Mutex ();
public Mutex (bool initiallyOwned);
```

The first constructor creates a Mutex object which is owned by the thread which is currently running (and creating that instance of the Mutex). The second constructor creates a Mutex object with the option of whether the currently running thread shall own it. Passing in a false as parameter will create a Mutex object which is currently not owned by any thread yet.

Mutex has two useful methods:

```
public virtual bool WaitOne();
public virtual void Close();
```

Calling WaitOne() of the Mutex object will cause the calling thread to wait indefinitely until the Mutex object is available (i.e. not owned by any other thread). If the Mutex object is available, the calling thread becomes the new owner of the Mutex object, and WaitOne() returns true. The thread owning the Mutex object relinquishes it by calling the Close() method. WaitOne() is also overloaded to take in a timeout period so that, on expiry, the method will return regardless of whether the calling thread has successfully obtained the Mutex object.

Here is an example of how Mutex can be used:

```
 1: using System;
 2: using System.Threading;
 3:
 4: public class TestClass{
 5:
 6:    static Mutex m = new Mutex (false);
 7:
 8:    static void PrintString (string toPrint){
 9:      m.WaitOne();
10:      for (int i=0; i<10; i++)
```

---

19. There are other useful classes in the System.Threading namespace, such as Interlocked and ThreadPool. Most of these classes provide useful methods which help to make threading and synchronization more convenient.

```
11:          Console.Write(toPrint);
12:        m.Close();
13:      }
14:
15:    static void PrintA(){
16:        PrintString("A");
17:      }
18:
19:    static void PrintB(){
20:        PrintString("B");
21:      }
22:
23:    public static void Main(){
24:        ThreadStart ts1 = new ThreadStart(PrintA);
25:        ThreadStart ts2 = new ThreadStart(PrintB);
26:
27:        Thread t1 = new Thread(ts1);
28:        Thread t2 = new Thread(ts2);
29:
30:        t1.Start();
31:        t2.Start();
32:      }
33: }
```

Output:

```
c:\expt>test
AAAAAAAAAABBBBBBBBBB
c:\expt>test
BBBBBBBBBBAAAAAAAAAA
```

Using the Mutex class is one way of synchronizing code without using Monitor, or the lock keyword.

17.4 Threading guidelines

Use threads only when there is a real need for multi-threading, such as if you have multiple CPUs and are writing a computation intensive application which has a user interface portion. While one thread deals with user interaction, the other can be performing background computation concurrently.

Avoid using multiple threads unnecessarily because not only does writing such applications require a higher level of expertise, it is also often difficult to debug threaded applications.[20]

You have to keep in mind performance issues when writing multi-threaded applications – dividing a task amongst many threads can help if you have more than one CPU, and if some of these threads can be kept waiting (for example, threads awaiting user input). However, having too many critical section code blocks[21] or having too many mutex objects that require waiting on may slow things down considerably. A good rule of the thumb is to have as few critical section code blocks as possible, and to enclose as few statements as possible into each.

When searching for code to optimize, a good developer will pay special attention to how a multi-threaded application is written, and the justification for placing codes in critical sections.

20. This is true especially for bugs due to inconsistent state which resulted from thread synchronization problems. The difficulty is exacerbated by the fact that multi-threaded applications always give different outputs depending on various factors decided on by the operating system's scheduler and the current load on the CPU.
21. 'Critical section code blocks' are code blocks which only one thread can execute at any one time. They are usually delimited by lock's curly brace or Monitor.Enter() and Monitor.Exit().

chapter 18

File I/O

File I/O functionality in C# depends largely on the underlying BCL. There are no keywords in C# for dealing with file I/O specifically.[1] This chapter will familiarize you with some of the common file I/O operations so that you can start using them immediately.

The classes will not be described fully, and there is usually more than one way to accomplish something. You will be expected to refer to the API documentation for more information.

In order to execute the codes in this chapter, you need the necessary permissions to manipulate your file system.[2]

I shall discuss how to manipulate files and directories[3] using the `Directory`, `File`, `DirectoryInfo`, and `FileInfo` classes. This is followed by sections on how to read/write from text files and binary files.

Figure 18.1 lists the classes that are important in file I/O. Table 18.1 lists the classes involved in I/O operations and Table 18.2 gives some exception classes.

18.1 Copying, moving, and deleting files

When specifying the location of a file or directory, you can use an absolute path, a relative path, or a UNC share path. The following are acceptable paths to a file:[4]

- `c:\\expt\\loveletter.txt`

---

1. This is the same case for Java too. File I/O depends wholly on the underlying Java core classes rather than the language itself.
2. Permissions and security will not be discussed here, but if you are experimenting on your local Windows machine and you have administrator privileges, you should be able to run the codes without any security exceptions.
3. Directories are also known as 'folders' in Windows nomenclature. However, Microsoft has selected to use 'directory' instead of folder for naming purposes in the .NET class libraries.
4. I suggest using the @ string literal for path or file names so that the string appears neater. For example, instead of `c:\\expt\\loveletter.txt`, you can use `@"c:\expt\loveletter.txt"`.

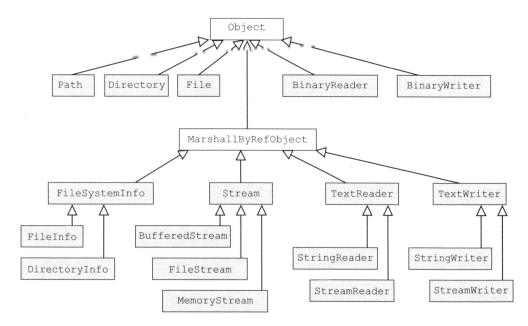

FIGURE 18.1   Important classes used for I/O operations. Shaded classes are in the `System.IO` name-space – unshaded classes are in the `System` namespace.

TABLE 18.1   Some classes involved in I/O operations and their description

Class	Description
FileInfo	Represents a file
File	Represents a file – contains only static methods, and cannot be instantiated
DirectoryInfo	Represents a directory – exposes instance methods for creating and moving through directories and subdirectories
Directory	Represents a directory – contains only static methods for creating and moving through directories and subdirectories; this class cannot be instantiated
Path	Contains static members for manipulating path names
StreamReader	Implements a `TextReader` that reads characters from a byte stream
StreamWriter	Implements a `TextWriter` that writes characters to a byte stream
StringReader	Implements a `TextReader` that reads from a string
StringWriter	Writes to a string
TextReader	A reader that reads a sequential series of characters
TextWriter	A writer that writes a sequential series of characters
FileStream	Exposes a Stream object around a file for synchronous and asynchronous read/write operations

TABLE 18.2 Important exception classes for I/O operations – all these exception classes are in the `System.IO` namespace

Exception class	Description
`FileNotFoundException`	Thrown when a file cannot be found
`DirectoryNotFoundException`	Thrown when part of a file or directory cannot be found
`EndOfStreamException`	Thrown when an attempt is made to read past end of a stream
`IOException`	Thrown when an general I/O error occurs – for example, when an attempt is made to copy a file to a target path which already contains a file of the same name
`PathTooLongException`	Thrown when a path or file name is longer than the maximum length defined by the system
`FileLoadException`	Thrown when file is found but cannot be loaded

TABLE 18.3 Methods to use for performing common file operations

Function	`System.IO.FileInfo`	`System.IO.File`
Copying a file	`CopyTo(string destination_path)`	`Copy (string source_path, string destination_path)`
	`CopyTo(string destination_path, boolean overwrite)`	`Copy (string source_path, string destination_path, boolean overwrite)`
Moving a file	`MoveTo(string destination_path)`	`Move(string source_path, string destination_path)`
Deleting a file	`Delete()`	`Delete(string path)`

- `expt\\loveletter.txt`
- `\\\\shareddrive\\loveletter.txt`

Table 18.3 shows the methods to use for performing copying, moving, and deletion of files. Code examples are given later.

The difference between using `File` and `FileInfo` to perform the operations is that `File` contains static methods which take in the file path, while `FileInfo` needs to be instantiated with the file path before you perform operations on it. `FileInfo` encapsulates a file, while `File` is more like a utility class.

`FileInfo` may take a bit longer to execute at first because of the object instantiation. If you simply want to perform a one-time file operation, it is preferable to use the static methods of `File`. However, if you want to perform multiple operations on a file, you might want to use `FileInfo` so that, after the initial instantiation, you can call other methods of that object.

18.1.1   Copying a file

To copy a file, use either the non-static `FileInfo.CopyTo` method:

```
FileInfo f = new FileInfo("c:\\expt\\loveletter.txt");
f.CopyTo("c:\\backup\\loveletter.txt");
```

or the static method `File.Copy`:

```
File.Copy("c:\\expt\\loveletter.txt",
          "c:\\backup\\loveletter.txt");
```

Both result in the file `c:\expt\loveletter.txt` being copied over to `c:\backup\loveletter.txt`.

Note that a `System.IO.IOException` is thrown if the target file already exists. Both methods are overloaded to take in an additional boolean parameter to indicate that you want to overwrite the target file if it exists without throwing the exception.

```
// overwrite target file even if it exists
f.CopyTo("c:\\backup\\loveletter.txt", true);
File.Copy("c:\\expt\\loveletter.txt",
          "c:\\backup\\loveletter.txt", true);
```

A `System.IO.FileNotFoundException` is thrown if the source file cannot be found.

18.1.2   Moving a file

To move a file, use either the non-static `FileInfo.MoveTo` method:

```
FileInfo f = new FileInfo("c:\\expt\\loveletter.txt");
f.MoveTo("c:\\backup\\loveletter.txt");
```

or the static method `File.Move`:

```
File.Move("c:\\expt\\loveletter.txt",
          "c:\\backup\\loveletter.txt");
```

Both result in the file `c:\expt\loveletter.txt` being moved (copied over and deleted) to `c:\backup\loveletter.txt`.

18.1.3   Deleting a file

To delete a file, use either the non-static `FileInfo.Delete` method:

```
FileInfo f = new FileInfo("c:\\expt\\loveletter.txt");
f.Delete();
```

or the static method `File.Delete`:

```
File.Delete ("c:\\expt\\loveletter.txt");
```

Both result in the file `c:\expt\loveletter.txt` being deleted.

18.2 Copying, moving, and deleting directories

For deleting and moving a directory and its contents, both `Directory` and `DirectoryInfo` contain the following methods shown in Table 18.4.

TABLE 18.4 Methods to use for performing common directory operations

Function	`System.IO.DirectoryInfo`	`System.IO.Directory`
Copying a directory	No method	No method
Moving a directory	`MoveTo(string destination_path)`	`Move(string source_path, string destination_path)`
Deleting a directory	`Delete()`	`Delete(string path)`

Note that there is no method for copying a whole directory and its contents. You will have to perform manual copying of each file within.

18.3 Reading from or writing to a binary file

You can use the `FileStream` class for reading from or writing to a binary file.

18.3.1 Creating a `FileStream` object

You create an instance of a `FileStream` object by passing in the path to the file you want to read. The `FileStream` class has several overloaded constructors which you can use to specify the following options:

- file mode
- file access
- file share.

Table 18.5 describes these options.

There are three useful constructors which you can use for `FileStream`.

- `public FileStream (string path, int fileMode);`
- `public FileStream (string path, int fileMode, int fileAccess);`

TABLE 18.5 The available file mode, access, and share options that can be used when instantiating a `FileStream`

Enumeration	Description
FileMode – how to open or create this file?	
`FileMode.Append`	Opens a file, if it exists, for appending. Moves the file pointer to the end of the existing file, so that the original data will not be overwritten – can only be used if file access has been set to `FileAccess.Write`
`FileMode.CreateNew`	Creates a new file if no such file exists – if the file already exists, an `IOException` is thrown
`FileMode.Create`	Creates a new file regardless of whether it currently exists – overwrites, the file if it exists (i.e. delete existing file if any) without throwing an exception
`FileMode.Open`	Opens an existing file – if file does not exist, throws a `FileNotFoundException`
`FileMode.OpenOrCreate`	Opens an existing file if there is one, or creates a new file if one does not currently exist – if writing to an existing file, writing starts from the first byte of the file and will overwrite existing bytes, but leaving the remaining bytes unchanged
`FileMode.Truncate`	Opens an existing file, and immediately truncates its contents
FileAccess – how the file can be accessed by the file stream	
`FileAccess.Read`	Opens a file for reading only
`FileAccess.ReadWrite`	Opens a file for reading and writing
`FileAccess.Write`	Opens a file for writing only
FileShare – how the file can be shared by other processes	
`FileShare.None`	File is not to be shared by another process until it is closed
`FileShare.Read`	File can be opened by another process for reading only
`FileShare.ReadWrite`	File can be opened by another process for reading and writing
`FileShare.Write`	File can be opened by another process for writing only

- `public FileStream (string path, int fileMode, int fileAccess, int fileShare);`

For example, the following statement:

```
FileStream fs = new
  FileStream("c:\\expt\\loveletter.dat",
            FileMode.OpenOrCreate);
```

creates a new file under the specified name if it does not exist, or opens it if it already exists. The default file access is `ReadWrite`, and the default file share is `Read`.

The following statement:

```
FileStream fs = new
    FileStream("c:\\expt\\loveletter.dat",
               FileMode.Create,
               FileAccess.Write,
               FileShare.None);
```

creates a new file for writing only. This file cannot be shared by another process until it has been closed. If the file already exists, it will be overwritten.

18.3.2 Reading from a `FileStream` object

With the `FileStream` object created, you can use either of the following methods for reading data from the stream:

- public override int **ReadByte**()
- public override int **Read**(in byte[] array, int offset, int count)

ReadByte() reads a single byte from the stream, casts it into an `int`, and returns an `int`. It returns –1 when the end of the stream has been reached.

The following statements open a stream and read in data one byte at a time.

```
 1:   using System;
 2:   using System.IO;
 3:
 4:   public class TestClass{
 5:
 6:     public static void Main(){
 7:       FileStream fs = new FileStream
 8:         ("c:\\expt\\loveletter.txt",
 9:          FileMode.Open,
10:          FileAccess.Read);
11:
12:       int i=0;
13:       while (i>-1){
14:         i = fs.ReadByte();
15:         Console.Write(i+",");
16:       }
17:       fs.Close();
18:     }
19:   }
```

Output:[5]

c:\expt>test
68,101,97,114,32,74,117,108,105,101,116,44,13,10,73,32,121,101,
97,114,110,32,102,111,114,32,117,33,13,10,89,111,117,114,32,82,
111,109,101,111,13,10,-1,

A `FileNotFoundException` is thrown if my `loveletter.txt` doesn't already exist in `c:\expt`. If there is no `expt` directory in `c:\`, a `DirectoryNotFoundException` is thrown instead. The integral equivalents of the characters are shown (68→D, 101→e, etc.). Of course, you can also explicitly cast the `int`s into `char` values if you are reading a text file.[6]

Read() gives you more control than `ReadByte()`. Read() takes in:

- a byte array which will be populated;
- a specified number of bytes from the stream into a byte array; and
- the array's index to start the population.

It returns the number of bytes actually read (this may differ from the number of bytes specified to be read, and is zero if the end of stream has been reached).

Let's look at an example. I have replaced the `Main` method of the code above with the following lines:

```
12:   byte []byteArray = new byte[50];
13:   int noBytesRead = fs.Read(byteArray,5,20);
14:
15:   Console.WriteLine("noBytesRead: "+noBytesRead);
16:   // display array contents
17:   for (int i=0; i<50; i++)
18:     Console.Write(byteArray[i] + ",");
```

Output:

c:\expt>test
noBytesRead: 20
0,0,0,0,0,68,101,97,114,32,74,117,108,105,101,116,44,13,10,73,
32,121,101,97,114,0,0,0,0,0,0,0,0,0,0,0,0,0,0,0,0,0,0,0,0,0,0,0,
0,0,0,

Line 13 instructs that the first 20 bytes are to be read from `loveletter.txt` into

---

5. The output shows the contents of the `loveletter.txt` file in *my* `c:\expt` folder. Of course, the output will differ if you put different stuff into yours!
6. If you are reading/writing a text file, use `StreamReader` and `StreamWriter` instead of `FileStream`. These classes have more convenient methods specially tailored for interacting with text files.

byteArray's sixth slot (byteArray[5]). The next time a Read or ReadByte is called on fs, reading carries on from the 21st byte in the file.

18.3.3   Writing to a FileStream object

With the FileStream object created, use either of the following methods to write data to the stream:

- public override void WriteByte(byte value)
- public override void Write(byte[] array, int offset, int count)

WriteByte simply takes in a byte and writes it to the FileStream object.

```
 1:   using System;
 2:   using System.I/O;
 3:
 4:   public class TestClass{
 5:
 6:     public static void Main(){
 7:       FileStream fs = new FileStream
 8:         ("c:\\expt\\alphabet.txt",
 9:           FileMode.Create,
10:           FileAccess.Write);
11:
12:       for (byte i=65; i<91; i++)
13:         fs.WriteByte(i);
14:
15:       fs.Close();
16:     }
17:   }
```

Contents of alphabet.txt:

c:\expt>type alphabet.txt
ABCDEFGHIJKLMNOPQRSTUVWXYZ

Lines 12–13 loops through 26 times and writes the alphabet (65→A, 66→B, etc.) to alphabet.txt.

Write() takes in:

- a byte array which contains the bytes to write in;
- the array offset (which element in the array do we start with?); and
- the count (the number of bytes to write).

Lines 12+ above have been modified to use Write instead of WriteByte:

```
12:        byte []array = {65,66,67,68,69,70,71,72,73,74};
13:        fs.Write (array, 2, 5);
14.
15:        fs.Close();
16:    }
17:  }
```

Contents of `alphabet.txt`:

```
c:\expt>type alphabet.txt
CDEFG
```

Line 13 says to take five bytes from `array` starting from `array[2]`, and write these into the `FileStream` object. `array[2]` is 67 (67→C).

18.3.3 Closing a `FileStream` object

Good developers close their files after use:

```
fs.Close();
```

You have already seen it in previous code examples.

18.4 Reading from and writing to text files

You can use the `StreamReader` class for reading, and `StreamWriter` for writing. Unlike the more generalized `FileStream` class, `StreamReader` and `StreamWriter` are specialized classes for text files containing ASCII or Unicode characters. There are useful methods which make text file access more convenient.

18.4.1 Reading using `StreamReader`

`StreamReader` has several overloaded constructors but here are the two most useful ones:

● `public StreamReader (string path)`
● `public StreamReader (string path, Encoding encoding)`

If the first constructor is used, `StreamReader` will try to determine the file's encoding format from the text file itself.[7]

---

7. It is possible to determine if a text file is encoded using Unicode by examining the first few bytes of the file, known as the byte code markers. Text files encoded in the older ASCII format will not have this byte code marker. Windows 9x does not support Unicode, but the other Windows operating systems do.

`StreamReader` supports the following text encoding formats:

- ASCII
- Unicode (both big and little Endian)
- UTF7
- UTF8

For the encoding parameter of your second `StreamReader` constructor, you can pass in either of the following properties of the `System.Text.Encoding` class:

- `System.Text.Encoding.ASCII`
- `System.Text.Encoding.Unicode`
- `System.Text.Encoding.UTF7`
- `System.Text.Encoding.UTF8`
- `System.Text.Encoding.BigEndianUnicode`

`StreamReader` has two methods useful for reading:

- `public override int Read()`
- `public override string ReadLine()`

Read() reads in a single character, and returns the `int` value of the character. ReadLine() reads the whole line until it reaches a newline character and returns the string or `null` if the end of file has been reached. ReadLine() does not include the newline character in the returned string.

Here is an example of how `StreamReader` can be used to read the loveletter.txt file.

```
1:   using System;
2:   using System.IO;
3:
4:   public class TestClass{
5:
6:     public static void Main(){
7:       StreamReader sr = new
8:         StreamReader("c:\\expt\\loveletter.txt");
9:
10:       int counter=0;
11:       string line = sr.ReadLine();
12:
13:       while (line!=null){
14:         counter++;
15:         Console.Write("line #"+counter+" :");
16:         Console.WriteLine(line);
17:         line = sr.ReadLine();
```

```
18:        }
19:
20:        sr.Close();
21:    }
22: }
```

Output:

```
c:\expt>test
line #1 :Dear Juliet,
line #2 :I yearn for u!
line #3 :Your Romeo
```

18.4.2 Writing using StreamWriter

StreamWriter has several overloaded constructors, but here are the two most useful ones:

- public StreamWriter (string path)
- public StreamWriter (string path, bool append, Encoding encoding)

If the first constructor is used, StreamWriter will use the UTF8 encoding format by default for writing. If the file indicated by path already exists, it is deleted first (not appended to).

The second constructor takes in a boolean value to indicate if you want to append your new characters (true) or overwrite the entire file if it exists (false). You can pass in the same encoding parameter as shown in the previous section.

StreamWriter has two methods useful for writing:

- public override void **Write**(string value)
- public override void **WriteLine**(string value)

The difference between them is that WriteLine appends a newline character automatically to the string. In fact, both methods are overloaded to take in a bool, char, decimal, double, int, long, float, uint, ulong, or char[] instead of a string.

Here is a code fragment showing how StreamWriter can be used:

```
80:  StreamWriter sw = new
81:     StreamWriter("c:\\expt\\reply.txt");
82:
83:  sw.WriteLine("Dear Romeo,");
84:  sw.WriteLine("you still owe me cash!");
85:  sw.WriteLine("Your Juliet");
86:  sw.Close();
```

chapter 19

C# collection classes

Collection classes are convenient classes acting as data structures for 'holding' multiple objects. Collection classes are often used instead of arrays because they have useful methods for manipulating the objects stored within. While not part of the C# language itself, I have included this chapter because collection classes are used very frequently.

Java 2 came with a whole set of useful collection classes so that we have more choices than `java.util.Vector`. The Java 2 Collection API includes classes in the `java.util` package such as `Stack`, `LinkedList`, `Set`, `ArrayList`, `Vector`, etc.

Of course the .NET framework comes with its own set of collection classes which can be used by any .NET language. They are found in the `System.Collections` namespace and include classes such as `ArrayList`, `Queue`, `SortedList`, and `Stack`. The following sections give a brief description of the more useful classes in `System.Collections` and examples of how they are used.

You can refer to the API documentation for more details on the classes and their other methods. The examples here are only meant to get you up and running with some of these classes quickly. The more commonly used methods are demonstrated and should be self-explanatory by their names.

19.1 ArrayList

An `ArrayList` encapsulates an ordered list of objects, much like Java's `Vector` or `ArrayList` classes. Each `ArrayList` object has an initial capacity (accessible via the public property `Capacity`) which automatically expands as more elements are inserted into the `ArrayList` object.

The example below shows some common methods which you can use with `ArrayList`.

```
1: using System;
2: using System.Collections;
3:
```

```
4: public class TestClass{
5:   public static void Main(){
6:
7:       String item1 = "apple",
8:               item2 = "orange",
9:               item3 = "banana",
10:              item4 = "durian",
11:              item5 = "strawberry";
12:
13:      ArrayList al = new ArrayList();
14:
15:      // Use of Add. New elements are inserted behind.
16:      al.Add(item1);
17:      al.Add(item2);
18:      al.Add(item3);
19:      al.Add(item4);
20:      al.Add(item5);
21:
22:      // Use of Contains and IndexOf
23:      Console.WriteLine
24:        ("al contains orange : " + al.Contains("orange"));
25:      Console.WriteLine
26:        ("Index of orange : " + al.IndexOf("orange"));
27:      PrintCollection(al);
28:      Console.WriteLine("-----------------------------");
29:
30:      // Use of Insert. Unlike Add, you can specify a
31:      // position to insert an element.
32:      Console.WriteLine("Inserting peach at index 1...");
33:      al.Insert(1,"peach");
34:      Console.WriteLine
35:        ("Index of peach  : " + al.IndexOf("peach"));
36:      Console.WriteLine
37:        ("Index of orange : " + al.IndexOf("orange"));
38:      PrintCollection(al);
39:      Console.WriteLine("-----------------------------");
40:
41:      // Use of Count public property
42:      Console.WriteLine("Count: " +al.Count);
43:
44:      // Use of Remove
45:      PrintCollection(al);
46:      Console.WriteLine("Removing banana...");
```

```
47:          al.Remove("banana");
48:          PrintCollection(al);
49:          Console.WriteLine("------------------------------");
50:
51:          // Use of Sort
52:          PrintCollection(al);
53:          Console.WriteLine("Sorting...");
54:          al.Sort();
55:          PrintCollection(al);
56:          Console.WriteLine("------------------------------");
57:
58:          // Use of ToArray. ToArray returns an object array
59:          Console.WriteLine("Creating new array...");
60:          object[] myArray = al.ToArray();
61:          Console.WriteLine("Array size: " + myArray.Length);
62:      }
63:
64:      // prints out all elements of the ArrayList object
65:      public static void PrintCollection(ArrayList al){
66:          Console.Write("Elements: ");
67:
68:          IEnumerator enumerator = al.GetEnumerator();
69:
70:          while (enumerator.MoveNext())
71:              Console.Write(enumerator.Current + ",");
72:
73:          Console.WriteLine(""); // new line
74:      }
75: }
```

Output:

```
c:\expt>test
al contains orange : True
Index of orange : 1
Elements: apple,orange,banana,durian,strawberry,
------------------------------
Inserting peach at index 1...
Index of peach  : 1
Index of orange : 2
Elements: apple,peach,orange,banana,durian,strawberry,
------------------------------
```

```
Count: 6
Elements: apple,peach,orange,banana,durian,strawberry,
Removing banana..
Elements: apple,peach,orange,durian,strawberry,
-----------------------------
Elements: apple,peach,orange,durian,strawberry,
Sorting...
Elements: apple,durian,orange,peach,strawberry,
-----------------------------
Creating new array...
Array size: 5
```

19.2 BitArray

A `BitArray` is similar to an `ArrayList`, except that it is used to store only bits represented as boolean values. A 1 bit is true, while a 0 bit is false. `BitArray` objects are extremely useful for mathematical operations such as those involving long encryption keys. The class has the following public methods which are useful for operations on the bits it encapsulates: Xor, Not, Or, And.

The program below demonstrates how a `BitArray` can be used. The output is interspersed with the code to show the outputs of the different sections.

```
 1: using System;
 2: using System.Collections;
 3:
 4: public class TestClass  {
 5:    public static void Main()  {
 6:
 7:        // By default, all bits are false if not specified
 8:        BitArray ba1 = new BitArray(4);
 9:        Console.WriteLine("ba1");
10:        Console.WriteLine("Length:" + ba1.Length);
11:        Console.WriteLine("Values:");
12:        PrintCollection(ba1);
13:
```

Output:

```
ba1
Length:4
Values:
False,False,False,False,
```

Line 8 creates a new `BitArray` object containing four bits.

```
14:             // Use of Set method
15:             Console.WriteLine("Setting elements 0 and 2");
16:             ba1.Set(0,true);
17:             ba1.Set(2,true);
18:             PrintCollection(ba1);
19:
```

Output:

```
Setting elements 0 and 2
True,False,True,False,
```

```
20:             // Accessing a BitArray like an index
21:             Console.WriteLine("ba1[0] : " + ba1[0]);
22:             Console.WriteLine("ba1[1] : " + ba1[1]);
23:             Console.WriteLine("ba1[2] : " + ba1[2]);
24:             Console.WriteLine("ba1[3] : " + ba1[3]);
25:
```

Output:

```
ba1[0] : True
ba1[1] : False
ba1[2] : True
ba1[3] : False
```

A `BitArray` object can be used like an index[1] as demonstrated in these lines.

```
26:             // Create a BitArray containing true bits
27:             BitArray ba2 = new BitArray(4, true);
28:             Console.WriteLine("ba2");
29:             Console.WriteLine("Length:" + ba2.Length );
30:             Console.WriteLine("Values:");
31:             PrintCollection(ba2);
32:
```

Output:

```
ba2
Length:4
Values:
True,True,True,True,
```

---

1. Apparently a public indexer is implemented within this class. For more information about C# indexers, see Chapter 21.

In this case, a new BitArray object is created with an overloaded constructor which takes in a boolean value too. A BitArray object encapsulating four true bits is created.

```
33:        // Passing in an array of byte values
34:        byte[] myBytes = new byte[4] {1, 2, 3, 4};
35:        BitArray ba3 = new BitArray(myBytes);
36:        Console.WriteLine("ba3");
37:        Console.WriteLine("Length:" + ba3.Length);
38:        Console.WriteLine("Values:");
39:        PrintCollection(ba3);
40:
```

Output:

```
ba3
Length:32
Values:
True,False,False,False,False,False,False,False,
False,True,False,False,False,False,False,False,
True,True,False,False,False,False,False,False,
False,False,True,False,False,False,False,False,
```

A byte takes up eight bits in C#. On line 35, a new BitArray object is created with a byte array containing four byte elements. In all, the BitArray object will have a size of 32 bits. Within the BitArray, the bits are ordered with the least significant bit first. So, decimal 1 is translated into 10000000_2, 2 is translated into 01000000_2 and are saved as bits in the BitArray. Note that the BitArray object does not keep track of the byte boundaries – as far as it is concerned, it simply stores a consecutive meaningless series of 32 bits.

```
41:        // Passing in an array of int values
42:        int[]  myInts  = new int[4] {1, 2, 3, 4};
43:        BitArray ba4 = new BitArray(myInts);
44:        Console.WriteLine("ba4");
45:        Console.WriteLine("Length:" + ba4.Length);
46:        Console.WriteLine("Values:");
47:        PrintCollection(ba4);
48:
```

Output:

```
ba4
Length:128
Values:
True,False,False,False,False,False,False,False,
```

```
False,False,False,False,False,False,False,False,
False,False,False,False,False,False,False,False,
False,False,False,False,False,False,False,False,
False,True,False,False,False,False,False,False,
False,False,False,False,False,False,False,False,
False,False,False,False,False,False,False,False,
False,False,False,False,False,False,False,False,
True,True,False,False,False,False,False,False,
False,False,False,False,False,False,False,False,
False,False,False,False,False,False,False,False,
False,False,False,False,False,False,False,False,
False,False,True,False,False,False,False,False,
False,False,False,False,False,False,False,False,
False,False,False,False,False,False,False,False,
False,False,False,False,False,False,False,False,
```

In line 43, a new `BitArray` instance is created with an `int` array containing four ints. Each `int` is 16 bits long in C#. Hence decimal 1 is translated into 1000000000000000_2 (least significant bit first).

```
49:         // Passing in an array of boolean values
50:         bool[] myBools =
51:           new bool[4] {true, false, true, true};
52:         BitArray ba5 = new BitArray(myBools);
53:         Console.WriteLine("ba5");
54:         Console.WriteLine("Length:" + ba5.Length );
55:         Console.WriteLine("Values:");
56:         PrintCollection(ba5);
57:     }
58:
```

Output:

```
ba5
Length:4
Values:
True,False,True,True,
```

The `BitArray` constructor is also overloaded to take in an array of bools.

```
59:     /* Print out the contents of the BitArray object
60:      * Only 8 elements are printed on each line for
61:      * easy reading.
62:      */
```

```
63:     public static void PrintCollection(IEnumerable bArray){
64:       IEnumerator enumerator = bArray.GetEnumerator();
65:       int i = 0;
66:       while (enumerator.MoveNext()){
67:         if (i>=8){
68:           i = 0;
69:           Console.WriteLine(); // new line
70:         }
71:         i++;
72:         Console.Write(enumerator.Current + ",");
73:       }
74:       Console.WriteLine();
75:   }
76: }
```

19.3 Hashtable

Like a Java's `java.util.Hashtable`, a .NET `Hashtable` is a useful data type which encapsulates key/value pairs.

Objects used as keys in a `Hashtable` must override or rely on the inherited `GetHashCode` and `Equals` methods of `System.Object` because these methods are invoked for matching. Note that the original `Equals` method in `System.Object` returns `true` only if both objects being compared are the same instance created on the heap. Hence, if key equality is simply reference equality, there is no need to override these methods.

The program below demonstrates how `Hashtable` can be used. The output is interspersed with the code to show the outputs of the different sections.

```
 1: using System;
 2: using System.Collections;
 3:
 4: public class TestClass{
 5:   public static void Main(){
 6:     // Using Add
 7:     Hashtable ht = new Hashtable();
 8:     ht.Add("A", "apple");
 9:     ht.Add("D", "durian");
10:     ht.Add("B", "banana");
11:     ht.Add("C", "coconut");
12:     PrintCollection(ht);
13:
```

Output:

```
Key:C Value:coconut
Key:A Value:apple
Key:D Value:durian
Key:B Value:banana
```

The static method `PrintCollection` is defined on line 43 below. It simply prints out all the key/value pairs in the `Hashtable` passed in.

```
14:        // Using Count
15:        Console.WriteLine("Count: " + ht.Count);
16:
```

Output:

```
Count: 4
```

```
17:        // Using ContainsKey
18:        Console.WriteLine(ht.ContainsKey("D"));
19:        Console.WriteLine(ht.ContainsKey("S"));
20:
```

Output:

```
True
False
```

```
21:        // Using ContainsValue
22:        Console.WriteLine(ht.ContainsValue("banana"));
23:        Console.WriteLine(ht.ContainsValue("starfruit"));
24:
```

Output:

```
True
False
```

```
25:        // Using Remove (key)
26:        Console.WriteLine("Removing key B...");
27:        ht.Remove("B");
28:        PrintCollection(ht);
29:
```

Output:

```
Removing key B...
Key:C Value:coconut
```

```
Key:A Value:apple
Key:D Value:durian
```

```
30:       // You can retrieve the keys using property Keys
31:       Console.WriteLine("Looping through Keys...");
32:       foreach (string key in ht.Keys){
33:         Console.WriteLine(key);
34:       }
35:
```

Output:

```
Looping through Keys...
C
A
D
```

```
36:       // You can retrieve the keys using public property
              Values
37:       Console.WriteLine("Looping through Values...");
38:       foreach (string val in ht.Values){
39:         Console.WriteLine(val);
40:       }
41:     }
42:
```

Output:

```
Looping through Values...
coconut
apple
durian
```

```
43:     // Prints out all the key-value pairs in the Hashtable
44:     public static void PrintCollection (Hashtable h){
45:       IDictionaryEnumerator enumerator = h.GetEnumerator();
46:
47:       while ( enumerator.MoveNext() )
48:         Console.WriteLine("Key:" + enumerator.Key +
49:                           " Value:" + enumerator.Value);
50:
51:       Console.WriteLine();
52:     }
53: }
```

19.4 Queue

As the name implies, a Queue encapsulates a standard FIFO abstract data type. Queues are useful for storing objects to be processed in the order that they are received. The three most commonly used methods of a Queue are Peek, Enqueue, and Dequeue. Like an ArrayList, the capacity of a Queue object changes automatically as more objects are inserted.

The program below demonstrates how Queue can be used. The output is interspersed with the code to show the outputs of the different sections.

```
1: using System;
2: using System.Collections;
3:
4: public class TestClass{
5:    public static void Main(){
6:
7:      Queue q = new Queue();
8:
9:      // Using Enqueue
10:      q.Enqueue("A");
11:      q.Enqueue("B");
12:      q.Enqueue("C");
13:      q.Enqueue("D");
14:      q.Enqueue("E");
15:      q.Enqueue("F");
16:      PrintCollection(q);
17:
```

Output:

Queue elements: A,B,C,D,E,F,

The static PrintCollection method defined on line 35 below prints out the elements in the Queue object passed in.

```
18:      // Using Count
19:      Console.WriteLine("Count: " + q.Count);
20:
```

Output:

Count: 6

```
21:      // Using Dequeue
22:      string token = (string)q.Dequeue();
```

```
23:        Console.WriteLine("Dequeued:" + token);
24:        token = (string)q.Dequeue():
25:        Console.WriteLine("Dequeued:" + token);
26:        PrintCollection(q);
27:
```

Output:

```
Dequeued:A
Dequeued:B
Queue elements: C,D,E,F,
```

Notice that the string object A is 'first in' and hence, when dequeued, shall be 'first out'.

```
28:        // Using Peek
29:        token = (string)q.Peek();
30:        Console.WriteLine("Peeked:" + token);
31:        PrintCollection(q);
32:    }
33:
```

Output:

```
Peeked:C
Queue elements: C,D,E,F,
```

Unlike Dequeue, Peek does not remove any element from the Queue object. It simply returns the element at the front of the queue without dequeuing it from the Queue object.

```
34:    // Prints out all elements in the Queue
35:    public static void PrintCollection (Queue q){
36:        IEnumerator enumerator = q.GetEnumerator();
37:        Console.Write("Queue elements: ");
38:
39:        while (enumerator.MoveNext())
40:            Console.Write(enumerator.Current + ",");
41:
42:        Console.WriteLine();
43:    }
44: }
```

19.5 SortedList

Put simply, a SortedList is a Hashtable which is sorted by the keys. Like a Hashtable, it is accessible by both its keys and values. The API documentation describes a SortedList as a hybrid between a Hashtable and an Array. It behaves like a Hashtable when accessed via a key. It behaves like an Array when accessed via its GetByIndex method.

If you do not need to access elements in a SortedList via its indices, then use a Hashtable rather than a SortedList because the sorting has a performance implication, especially if you do not need that functionality.

The program below demonstrates how a SortedList can be used. The output is interspersed with the code to show the outputs of the different sections.

```
1: using System;
2: using System.Collections;
3:
4: public class TestClass{
5:   public static void Main(){
6:
7:     SortedList sl = new SortedList();
8:     sl.Add("A", "apple");
9:     sl.Add("E", "eggplant");
10:     sl.Add("B", "banana");
11:     sl.Add("C", "coconut");
12:     PrintCollection1(sl);
13:
```

Output:

```
Key:A Value:apple
Key:B Value:banana
Key:C Value:coconut
Key:E Value:eggplant
```

Notice that, unlike a Hashtable, the elements in a SortedList are always dynamically sorted by the key every time a new element is inserted.

```
14:     Console.WriteLine
15:       ("Index of key B:" +sl.IndexOfKey("B"));
16:     Console.WriteLine
17:       ("Index of value apple:"
              +sl.IndexOfValue("apple"));
18:
```

Output:

```
Index of key B: 1
Index of value apple: 0
```

The `IndexOfKey` and `IndexOfValue` methods are demonstrated above.

```
19:        sl.Add("D", "durian");
20:        PrintCollection1(sl);
```

Output:

```
Key:A Value:apple
Key:B Value:banana
Key:C Value:coconut
Key:D Value:durian
Key:E Value:eggplant
```

When a new key/value pair is added, the indices of all elements are updated as sorting is performed again.

```
21:    } // end main
22:
23:    // 1st way to do it
24:    public static void PrintCollection1 (SortedList s){
25:        IDictionaryEnumerator enumerator = s.GetEnumerator();
26:        while (enumerator.MoveNext())
27:          Console.WriteLine("Key:"  + enumerator.Key +
28:                            " Value:"+ enumerator.Value);
29:        Console.WriteLine();
30:    }
31:
32:    // 2nd way to do it
33:    public static void PrintCollection2 (SortedList s){
34:        for (int i=0; i<s.Count; i++)
35:          Console.WriteLine("Key:"  + s.GetKey(i) +
36:                            " Value:"+ s.GetByIndex(i));
37:        Console.WriteLine();
38:    }
39: }
```

Both `PrintCollection1` and `PrintCollection2` are functionally identical. Since the elements in a `SortedList` are indexed, you can use the `GetByIndex` and `GetKey` methods to retrieve a value or key by its index respectively (lines 35–36).

A `SortedList` has the following public properties – `Count`, `Keys`, `Values`; and the following methods – `ContainsKey`, `ContainsValue`, `Remove`. These properties and methods are used in exactly the same way as in a `Hashtable` class and are therefore not included in this example again.

19.6 Stack

As the name implies, a `Stack` encapsulates a standard LIFO abstract data type. You use the `Pop` and `Push` methods of the `Stack` class to retrieve and insert elements respectively. Like `Queue`, `Stack` also has a `Peek` method which returns the element that is next to be popped out without actually popping it out.

Calling `Pop()` on an empty `Stack` will result in a `System.InvalidOperationException` exception. To prevent that from happening, you can check the Stack's `Count` public property before invoking `Pop()`.

```
 1: using System;
 2: using System.Collections;
 3:
 4: public class TestClass{
 5:   public static void Main(){
 6:
 7:     Stack s = new Stack();
 8:
 9:     // Using Push
10:     s.Push("A");
11:     s.Push("B");
12:     s.Push("C");
13:     PrintCollection(s);
14:
```

Output:

```
Stack elements: C,B,A,
```

The static `PrintCollection` method defined on line 40 below prints out the elements in the `Stack` object passed in.

```
15:     // Using Count
16:     Console.WriteLine("Count: " + s.Count);
17:
```

Output:

```
Count: 3
```

```
18:     // Using Peek
```

```
19:        string token = (string)s.Peek();
20:        Console.WriteLine("Peeked:" + token);
21:        PrintCollection(s);
22:
```

Output:

```
Peeked:C
Stack elements: C,B,A,
```

```
23:        // Using Pop
24:        token = (string)s.Pop();
25:        Console.WriteLine("Popped:" + token);
26:        PrintCollection(s);
27:
```

Output:

```
Popped:C
Stack elements: B,A,
```

Notice that the last element pushed in (string C) is popped out first.

```
28:        token = (string)s.Pop();
29:        Console.WriteLine("Popped:" + token);
30:        PrintCollection(s);
31:
```

Output:

```
Popped:B
Stack elements: A,
```

```
32:        token = (string)s.Pop();
33:        Console.WriteLine("Popped:" + token);
34:        PrintCollection(s);
35:
```

Output:

```
Popped:A
Stack elements:
```

```
36:        token = (string)s.Pop(); // InvalidOperationException
```

Output (runtime exception):

```
Unhandled Exception: System.InvalidOperationException: Stack
empty at System.Collections.Stack.Pop() at TestClass.Main()
```

When attempting to Pop an empty Stack, an InvalidOperationException will be thrown.

```
37:    }
38:
39:    // Prints out all elements in the Queue
40:    public static void PrintCollection (Stack s){
41:      IEnumerator enumerator = s.GetEnumerator();
42:      Console.Write("Stack elements: ");
43:
44:      while (enumerator.MoveNext())
45:        Console.Write(enumerator.Current + ",");
46:
47:      Console.WriteLine();
48:    }
49: }
```

It is possible to Push onto a Stack a null instead of an object. nulls are often used as placeholders on the Stack to separate consecutive objects.

5

Convenience features

Introduction

The chapters in this part are:

- Chapter 20: C# properties
- Chapter 21: C# indexes
- Chapter 22: Operator overloading
- Chapter 23: User-defined conversions/casts.

Compared to Java, C# has several features that make things more convenient for the developer. Instead of accessor (getter) and mutator (setter) methods, we have C# properties. Besides being a cleaner and more elegant way of implementing getter and setter methods, public properties act and feel exactly like public fields to external parties – without the associated 'it-is-poor-programming-practice-to-make-your-fields-public' stigma.

C# also comes with indexes, operator overloading (a feature of C++ which Java dumped), and user-defined casting operations. These features are not really essential for an OO language and their functionality can be implemented using common methods. Nevertheless, additional convenience features like these add to the power developer's tool box. The downside is that the learning curve is increased a bit.

The first chapter (Chapter 20) is a 'must read' because properties are very commonly employed in C# applications. Tackle the remaining chapters of this part at your own pace.

chapter 20

C# properties

C# properties are convenient alternatives to accessor (getter) and mutator (setter) methods in a class. It is something new and extremely useful. Do not confuse the term 'properties' in C# with the term 'properties' commonly used in OO nomenclature. Here, a property does not refer to a characteristic of a class,[1] although a C# property is still a class member.

What are called instance or static variables in Java, are called instance or static fields in C#. Because fields are often made private members of a class, accessor and mutator methods are written for external parties to retrieve or set their values.[2]

In C#, you can still write accessor and mutator methods to get or set a field's value, but you can also make use of properties. You can think of properties as a more elegant substitute for accessor and mutator methods which you can use to read/write to private fields of a class.[3]

Here is an example of a class with a private field (`MyColor`) together with accessor and mutator methods. It should look familiar:

```
1: using System;
2:
3: public class TestClass{
4:    private string MyColor = "yellow";
5:
6:    // accessor method
```

1. In OO literature, you will often see statements like 'a class contains properties, also known as attributes, which represent characteristics of a class'. properties and attributes in C# have different meanings. You use the term 'fields' or 'field variables' to represent the characteristics of a class.
2. In a good clean implementation (be it in Java or C#, or any other OO programming language), fields should be properly encapsulated in a class by making them private. In the event that their values are to be 'exposed' to the external world, you write accessor methods for them. In fact, your OO lecturers will tell you that none of your fields should be made public, and they are right.
3. I have seen literature referring to properties as 'smart fields'. Properties are not really fields, but behave like fields to external classes – hence that name.

```
 7:     public string GetMyColor(){
 8:        return MyColor;
 9:     }
10:     // mutator method
11:     public void SetMyColor(string newColor){
12:        MyColor = newColor;
13:     }
14:
15:     public static void Main(){
16:        TestClass c = new TestClass();
17:        Console.WriteLine(c.GetMyColor()); // get
18:        c.SetMyColor("blue");              // set
19:        Console.WriteLine(c.GetMyColor()); // get
20:     }
21: }
```

Output:

```
c:\expt>test
yellow
blue
```

20.1 Properties as a replacement for accessor and mutator methods

In C#, instead of writing accessor and mutator methods, you can use a special class member called a property. I have altered the class above to replace the accessor/mutator methods with a public property called Color. This property represents the private field MyColor. Study the code below.

```
 1: using System;
 2:
 3: public class TestClass{
 4:     private string MyColor = "yellow";
 5:
 6:     // property Color
 7:     public string Color{
 8:        get{
 9:           return MyColor;
10:        }
11:        set{
12:           MyColor = value;
```

```
13:      }
14:    }
15:    public static void Main(){
16:       TestClass c = new TestClass();
17:       Console.WriteLine(c.Color); // get
18:       c.Color = "blue";           // set
19:       Console.WriteLine(c.Color); // get
20:    }
21: }
```

Output:

```
c:\expt>test
yellow
blue
```

Notice the special method-like construct called Color (lines 7–14) which is declared public like most accessor/mutator methods. Color contains a 'get section'[4] and a 'set section' which corresponds to the GetMyColor() and SetMyColor() methods which you would normally have written.

When retrieving the value of MyColor, you can simply use the Color property, as in c.Color where c is the variable that refers to the instance with that property (lines 17 and 19). When setting the value of MyColor, just assign c.Color to the new value (line 18). The appropriate sections of code (the get and set sections) will execute.

A note about the value[5] variable used in the set section (on line 12). value is an implicit field (meaning it is not explicitly declared or initialized) that is available for the developer's use in the set section only. value refers to the value that has been assigned by the calling statement (in this example, value is blue because of line 18).

In the example above, I have used the Color property to allow external parties to access and change the private field MyColor. It is usual for C# developers to use the same identifier for the private field and the public property it represents.[6] Of course, the identifiers must have different casings. By convention, if you choose to give the same identifier to a public property and the private field it represents, you can choose to name the private field using camel casing (starting with a lower case letter) and the public property using Pascal casing (starting with an upper case letter). For this example, it is generally acceptable to call the private field myColor, and the public property MyColor.

---

4. Note that 'get' and 'set' are not C# keywords but have special meanings when used in properties.
5. 'Value' is also not a C# keyword.
6. The reason I selected a different identifier for this chapter was to reduce the confusion that might be caused.

It should be obvious that a public property can be used just like a public field outside the class, and that's the cool thing about properties. You maintain absolute control of what you want to happen within the property declaration when the property is assigned a new value, or when a value is obtained via the property. It is unlike a real public field in which there is no way you can control what values are assigned to it.[7]

Another nice about using properties is that, like accessor and mutator methods, you can only have either a get section or a set section. It is not mandatory to have both sections within a property declaration. And this, again, means that, unlike a public field, you can allow external parties to access the value of the property (by providing only a get section), but not change it (don't provide a set section).

20.2 Having only either the get or set section

If `MyColor` only is to be read, and not altered via the `Color` property, you can exclude the set section in the property declaration. When declaring properties, you can exclude either section, but not both.

Let's comment out the set section in the class above:

```
 7:    public string Color{
 8:       get{
 9:         return MyColor;
10:       }
11:    /* set{
12:         MyColor = value;
13:       } */
14:    }
```

Compiling the program gives an error this time because the code in `Main()` still tries to assign a value to the `Color` property (on line 18):

```
C:\expt>csc test.cs
Test.cs(18,5): error CS0200: Property or indexer
'TestClass.Color' cannot be assigned to - it is read only
```

It is also possible to create two or more public properties to access the same private field, although this is usually not done.

---

7. You can perform actions such as checking for valid values in the property's set section before actually assigning the new value to the private field.

20.3 Inheritance of properties

Like other class members, properties can be inherited to subclasses. You can override properties just as you would override other methods. It is possible to just override the get section of a property and inherit the set section, and vice versa.

The example below shows two classes, Parent and Child. Child is the subclass of Parent and inherits both the protected field, MyColor, and the public property, Color.

```
 1: using System;
 2:
 3: public class Parent{
 4:    protected string MyColor = "yellow";
 5:
 6:    // property Color
 7:    public virtual string Color{
 8:      get{
 9:        Console.WriteLine("running GET of Parent");
10:        return MyColor;
11:      }
12:      set{
13:        Console.WriteLine("running SET of Parent");
14:        MyColor = value;
15:      }
16:    }
17: }
18:
19: public class Child:Parent{
20:    public override string Color{
21:      get{
22:        Console.WriteLine("running GET of Child");
23:        return "dark " + MyColor;
24:      }
25:      // the set section will be inherited
26:    }
27: }
28:
29: public class TestMain{
30:    public static void Main(){
31:      Child c = new Child();
32:      Console.WriteLine(c.Color); // get
33:      Console.WriteLine(" -------------- ");
34:      c.Color = "blue";            // set
```

```
35:        Console.WriteLine(" -------------- ");
36:        Console.WriteLine(c.Color); // get
37:    }
38: }
```

Output:

```
C:\expt>test
running GET of Child
dark yellow
--------------
running SET of Parent
--------------
running GET of Child
dark blue
```

Lines 3–17 codes a `Parent` class that contains a public `Color` property, which represents the protected field `MyColor`. This property member contains both the get and set sections, to allow external parties to retrieve and alter the value stored in the private field.

Note that the `virtual` keyword is used to declare this property (line 7) in `Parent`. In C#, you *must* declare a property (and any member of a class) as virtual if you intend to override this property in a subclass. On line 20 in the `Child` class, the `override` keyword tells the compiler that this new property (declared on lines 21–26) is overriding the one in the `Parent` class.

In this example, only the get section of `Color` has been overridden (lines 21–24) in the `Child` class. The set section will be inherited automatically. Conversely, if you implement only the set section of a property in the `Child` class, the get section will be inherited automatically.

Let's examine the output. I have purposely inserted lines 33 and 35 so that we can see which printout is the result of which statement. When statement 32 executes, the get section of the `Color` property *written in* the `Child` class runs. When statement 34 executes, the set section of the `Color` property *inherited by* the `Child` class runs, and alters the value of protected field `Color`, which has been inherited to `Child` too.

chapter 21

C# indexes

I recommend that you complete Chapter 20 before starting on indexes. Indexes are somewhat similar to properties.

Like a C# property, a C# index is a new programming feature embedded into the language to help developers to be more efficient. Indexers enable an instance of a class, which has an array as a field, to be treated like an array itself.

Study the example below.

```
 1: class TestClass{
 2:     // this is the array field
 3:     string[] MyArray = new string[10];
 4:
 5:     // constructor
 6:     public TestClass(){
 7:         for (int i=0; i<10; i++)
 8:             MyArray[i] = "uninitialized";
 9:     }
10:
11:     // here's where the magic works
12:     public string this[int index]{
13:       get{
14:         return MyArray[index];
15:       }
16:       set{
17:         MyArray[index] = value;
18:       }
19:     }
20:
21:     public static void Main(string[] args){
22:
23:         TestClass c = new TestClass();
24:
```

```
25:          // assigning values to MyArray of c
26:          c[2] = "indexers";      // set
27:          c[3] = "are";           // set
28:          c[5] = "convenient";    // set
29:
30:          // extracting values from MyArray
31:          for (int i=0; i<10; i++){
32:              System.Console.WriteLine(i +" "+ c[i]); //get
33:          }
34:      }
35: }
```

Output:

```
C:\expt>test
0 uninitialized
1 uninitialized
2 C#
3 is
4 uninitialized
5 powerful
6 uninitialized
7 uninitialized
8 uninitialized
9 uninitialized
```

As you can see, the indexed class encapsulates a private array which it exposes to the external world via a public indexer. There is a special method in `TestClass` called `this` (lines 12–19), which is declared as `public string this[int index]`. This special method contains get and set sections which execute automatically when the indexer is used (lines 26–28, and 32 respectively). Lines 26–28 set the values in elements 2, 3, and 5 via the indexer, and line 32 gets the values of each array element iteratively for printing out.

In this example, `this` takes an `int` but, like any other method, it can take in anything (but at least one parameter). This indexer method is usually declared as a public method so that external classes can invoke it, but that is not compulsory.

Like properties, you can omit either the set or get section within an indexer declaration (the `this` method) but you cannot omit both. Indexers with only a get section cannot be set via the indexer, and vice versa.

21.1 Overloading indexers

You can have multiple overloaded indexers in the same class to enable access to the private array in other ways. There's a rule though – indexers must take in at least one parameter. Under special circumstances, you may choose to let your indexer take in multiple parameters.

Let's change TestClass a bit.

```
1: class TestClass{
2:      // this is the encapsulated array
3:      string[] MyArray = new string[10];
4:
5:      // constructor
6:      public TestClass(){
7:          for (int i=0; i<10; i++){
8:              MyArray[i] = "uninitialized";
9:          }
10:      }
11:
12:      // here's where the magic works
13:      public string this[int index]{
14:        get{
15:          return MyArray[index];
16:        }
17:        set{
18:          MyArray[index] = value;
19:        }
20:      }
21:
22:      // overloaded indexer method
23:      public int this[string s]{
24:        get{
25:          for (int i=0; i<10; i++){
26:            if (MyArray[i].Equals(s))
27:              return i;
28:          }
29:          return -1;
30:        }
31:      }
```

I have inserted an overloaded indexer into TestClass that takes in a string, and which contains only the get section. What this overloaded indexer does is to check through MyArray for the first occurrence of the string passed in and returns the index value of the first match. The indexer returns –1 if none of the array elements contains a matching string.

Main() is rewritten to try out this new indexer.

```
32:
33:      public static void Main(string[] args){
34:
35:        TestClass c = new TestClass();
36:
37:        // assigning values to MyArray of c
38:        c[2] = "hello";
39:        c[3] = "hello";
40:        c[5] = "hello";
41:
42:        // invoke the overloaded indexer
43:        Console.WriteLine ("The first index which "+
              "contains the string hello is "+c["hello"]);
44:      }
45: }
```

Output:

```
c:\expt>test
This first index which contains hello is 2
```

It seems that the overloaded indexer is working fine.

21.2 Wrong use of indexers

It is possible (but incorrect) to use indexers to retrieve a private field. You should use properties or accessor methods to do that. Indexers only make sense when a class encapsulates an array, and there is an array-like abstraction. Examine this negative example.

```
 1: class TestClass{
 2:    private int MyBirthYear = 1975;
 3:
 4:    public int this[int currentYear]{
 5:      get{
 6:        return currentYear - MyBirthYear;
 7:      }
 8:    }
 9:
10:    public static void Main(string[] args){
11:      TestClass c = new TestClass();
12:      System.Console.WriteLine ("Age is " + c[2002]);
```

```
13:    }
14: }
```

Output:

```
c:\expt>test
Age is 27
```

The program above works but makes use of indexes in a fanciful and unrecommended way. You could have written a getAge() method in TestClass which takes in the current year and returns the difference between the current year and the value stored in the MyBirthYear field. There is no good reason for you to use an indexer in this case.

22

Operator overloading

Operator overloading is a feature of C++, which has (unfortunately or fortunately[1]) been removed from Java. What you can do with operator overloading can be performed with common methods – in fact you define an operator overload using a method itself. Hence, I will not classify operator overloading as an important or essential feature of C#, but rather one which gives good developers more choice and flexibility.

22.1 Explaining operator overloading

In both Java and C#, the binary * operator has always been used to obtain the product of two numerical values, which are the two operands. The code below shows a class which represents a fraction with two `int` fields – numerator and denominator. I have added a constructor which takes in two `int`s to initialize these two fields:

```
 1: class Fraction{
 2:    public int numerator;
 3:    public int denominator;
 4:
 5:    // constructor
 6:    public Fraction (int numerator, int denominator){
 7:      this.numerator = numerator;
 8:      this.denominator = denominator;
 9:    }
10: }
```

1. It is unfortunate because operator overloading is a convenient feature which makes programming more elegant. It is fortunate because since it is not an important feature – you can duplicate operator overloading functionality using normal methods – not including it in Java makes it an easier language to learn.

When you want to perform a fraction multiplication, you can write a static method, called Multiply, which takes in two Fractions and which returns a resultant new Fraction object with the correct values stored in numerator and denominator. We can assume that the Multiply method below is inside the Fraction class.

```
30: public static Fraction Multiply(Fraction f1, Fraction f2){
31:    int newNumerator = f1.numerator * f2.numerator;
32:    int newDenominator = f1.denominator * f2.denominator;
33:    Fraction result =
34:             new Fraction (newNumerator, newDenominator);
35:    return result;
36: }
```

We can also write a Main method to check if our Multiply method works.

```
40: public static void Main(){
41:    Fraction f1 = new Fraction(1,2);
42:    Fraction f2 = new Fraction(3,4);
43:    Fraction r = Fraction.Multiply(f1,f2);
44:    Console.WriteLine(r.numerator + "/" + r.denominator);
45: }
```

Output:

```
c:\expt>test
3/8
```

Everything works fine, but wouldn't it have been neater (and more intuitive) if you could perform the multiplication using the * operator?

This is definitely more intuitive:

```
Fraction r = f1*f2;
```

than this:

```
Fraction r = Fraction.Multiply(f1,f2);
```

You can do that if you overload the * operator. When you do this, you are trying to define different results when you apply the operator to different types of operands. In this case, what you have to do is to write a method containing the multiplication logic like this:

```
public static Fraction operator * (Fraction f1, Fraction f2){
   // logic for Multiplication
}
```

The whole program looks like this.

```
 1: using System;
 2:
 3: class Fraction{
 4:    public int numerator;
 5:    public int denominator;
 6:
 7:    public static Fraction
 8:    operator * (Fraction f1, Fraction f2){
 9:
10:       int newNumerator = f1.numerator * f2.numerator;
11:       int newDenominator = f1. denominator * f2.denominator;
12:       Fraction result =
13:          new Fraction (newNumerator,newDenominator);
14:       return result;
15:    }
16:
17:    public Fraction (int numerator, int denominator){
18:       this.numerator = numerator;
19:       this.denominator = denominator;
20:    }
21:
22:    public static void Main(){
23:       Fraction f1 = new Fraction(1,2);
24:       Fraction f2 = new Fraction(3,4);
25:       Fraction r = f1*f2;
26:       Console.WriteLine(r.numerator + "/" + r.denominator);
27:    }
28: }
```

That's operator overloading! You have overloaded the * operator so that when you supply two operands of type Fraction, it executes a custom-made method, and returns a result.

Lines 7–15 define the overloading method for the * operator. * can now take in two Fraction operands and return a Fraction object.

22.2 Operator overloading proper

After seeing an example, you should have a good idea of what operator overloading is all about. Now, let's go into the specifics. The operator[2] method has to be defined like this:

2. operator is a C# keyword.

```
public static <return_value> operator <operator to overload>
(<operand1>, [<operand2>]);
```

The following lists some rules that need to be followed when overloading an operator.

1 You cannot overload just any C# operator, and you cannot define your own operator. Only the operators shown in Table 22.1 can be overloaded.

TABLE 22.1   Operators that can be overloaded in C#

Category	Operators
Unary operators	+ - ! ~ ++ -- true false
Binary operators	+ - * / % and | ^ << >>
Comparison operators	== != < > <= >=

2 The +=, -=, /=, *=, %=, &=, ^=, \|=, >>=, and <<= assignment operators are automatically overloaded when the corresponding +, -, /, *, %, &, ^, \|, >>, and << operators are overloaded.[3]

   For example, if you overload the * operator, *= will be automatically overloaded. And the following statement assigns the result of f3*f1 to f3:

   ```
   f3 *= f1;
   ```

3 You can pass in only one or two parameters into the operator method, depending on whether you are overloading a unary or binary operator. For example, if you want to overload the unary operator ++, the operator method you need to write can only take in one (and only one) parameter.

4 The first parameter taken into the operator method *must* be of the same type as the class in which the method is defined. The second parameter (if present) can be of any type.

5 Overloaded operators *must* be public and static.

6 If you overload `true` or `false`, the operator method must return either `true` or `false` only. Otherwise, the operator method can return any type, although it commonly returns the class in which it is defined.

   Let's examine the operator method's signature in the `Fraction` example:

   ```
   public static Fraction operator * (Fraction f1, Fraction f2)
   ```

Since the binary * operator is being overloaded, the operator method must take in two parameters (in accordance with rule #3 above). The first parameter must be of type `Fraction` because this method is defined within the `Fraction` class (in accor-

---

3. In C++, the = assignment operator can be overloaded. In C#, you cannot overload = but if you overload a binary operator, the corresponding assignment operator is automatically overloaded. See the example which follows.

dance with rule #4 above). It is not mandatory that the method returns a `Fraction`, nor takes in a `Fraction` as the second parameter. And, of course, this method is declared with the `public` and `static` keywords (rule #5).

22.3 Another example of operator overloading

Just for developers who enjoy dabbling with matrices, here's another full example.[4]

```csharp
 1: using System;
 2:
 3: // class represents a 2 × 2 matrix
 4: class Matrix{
 5:
 6:   // these 4 fields represent the 4 values in the 2 × 2 matrix
 7:   public float TopLeft;
 8:   public float TopRight;
 9:   public float BottomLeft;
10:   public float BottomRight;
11:
12:   // constructor
13:   public Matrix
14:   (float TopLeft, float TopRight, float BottomLeft, float BottomRight){
15:     this.TopLeft = TopLeft;
16:     this.TopRight = TopRight;
17:     this.BottomLeft = BottomLeft;
18:     this.BottomRight = BottomRight;
19:   }
20:
21:   // overrides ToString to show matrix values
22:   public override string ToString (){
23:     return "[" + TopLeft + ", " + TopRight + "]\n"+
24:             "[" + BottomLeft+ ", " + BottomRight+ "]";
25:   }
26:
27:   // overloads + operator to perform matrix addition
28:   public static Matrix operator + (Matrix m1, Matrix m2){
29:     return new Matrix(m1.TopLeft + m2.TopLeft,
30:                       m1.TopRight + m2.TopRight,
31:                       m1.BottomLeft + m2.BottomLeft,
```

4. You can skip this if you have understood the previous example. You need to understand matrix mathematics to appreciate what is going on here. (Time to search for that old high school math textbook!)

```
32:                             m1.BottomRight + m2.BottomRight);
33:     }
34:
35:     // overloads - operator to perform matrix subtraction
36:     public static Matrix operator - (Matrix m1, Matrix m2){
37:       return new Matrix(m1.TopLeft - m2.TopLeft,
38:                         m1.TopRight - m2.TopRight,
39:                         m1.BottomLeft - m2.BottomLeft,
40:                         m1.BottomRight - m2.BottomRight);
41:     }
42:
43:     // overloads * operator to perform product with a real number
44:     public static Matrix operator * (Matrix m1, float realNumber){
45:       return new Matrix(m1.TopLeft * realNumber,
46:                         m1.TopRight * realNumber,
47:                         m1.BottomLeft * realNumber,
48:                         m1.BottomRight * realNumber);
49:     }
50:
51:     // overloads ^ to perform multiplication with another 2 × 2 matrix
52:     public static Matrix operator ^ (Matrix m1, Matrix m2){
53:       return new Matrix
54:         ((m1.TopLeft * m2.TopLeft) + (m1.TopRight * m2.BottomLeft),
55:         (m1.TopLeft * m2.TopRight) + (m1.TopRight * m2.BottomRight),
56:         (m1.BottomLeft * m2.TopLeft) + (m1.BottomRight * m2.BottomLeft),
57:         (m1.BottomLeft * m2.TopRight) + (m1.BottomRight * m2.BottomRight)
58:         );
59:     }
60:
61:     // overloads ! operator to perform matrix inversion.
62:     public static Matrix operator ! (Matrix m1){
63:
64:       float determinant =
65:         (m1.TopLeft * m1.BottomRight) - (m1.TopRight * m1.BottomLeft);
66:
67:       float determinantReciprocal = 1/determinant;
68:
69:       Matrix intermediate = new Matrix
70:         (m1.BottomRight, -m1.TopRight, -m1.BottomLeft, m1.TopLeft);
71:
72:       return (intermediate * determinantReciprocal);
73:     }
74: }
```

```
75:
76:
77: class TestClass{
78:    public static void Main(){
79:
80:      // try out inverse function
81:        Matrix m1 = new Matrix (3,5,1,2);
82:      Console.WriteLine ("m1:\n" + m1);
83:      Console.WriteLine ("m1 inverse:\n" + (!m1));
84:      Console.WriteLine ();
85:
86:      // try out multiplication with a real number
87:        Matrix m2 = new Matrix (1,5,5,1);
88:      Console.WriteLine ("m2:\n" + m2);
89:      Console.WriteLine ("3 multiplied by m2:\n" + (m2*3));
90:    }
91: }
```

Output:

```
c:\expt>test
m1:
[3 , 5]
[1 , 2]
m1 inverse:
[2 , -5]
[-1 , 3]
m2:
[1 , 5]
[5 , 1]
3 multiplied by m2:
[3 , 15]
[15 , 3]
```

chapter 23

User-defined conversions/casts

Here is another C# feature which adds to convenience for C# developers but which can be imitated using normal methods.

A user-defined conversion is a custom-made cast from one class to another. So far, type casting has been performed only if the object being cast is a subclass of the other. User-defined conversions allow you to perform casting of one type into an unrelated type. It also gives you the choice of what you want to do when performing the cast.

Sounds difficult? Study this example first.

```
1: class Inch{
2:    public float InchValue;
3:
4:    public Inch (float value){ // constructor
5:       InchValue = value;
6:    }
7: }
8:
9: class Cm {
10:    public float CmValue;
11:
12:    public Cm (float value){ // constructor
13:       CmValue = value;
14:    }
15: }
```

There are two classes – one to represent inches, and the other to represent centimeters.[1] Of course, since they are not directly related in the class hierarchy, an attempt to explicitly cast an `Inch` object to a `Cm` type will result in a compilation error which

---

1. This is just an example for demonstration purposes. You don't usually write public fields in classes unless there is a *really* good reason.

reads: 'Cannot convert type Inch to Cm'. The same goes for casting a Cm object to an Inch type.

You can write a method in Cm to take in a parameter of type Inch and which returns a Cm object:

```
public static explicit operator Cm (Inch toConvert)
```

You can also write a method to take in a float value and return a Cm object:

```
public static explicit operator Cm (float toConvert)
```

Here is the rewritten class with the two methods added in.

```
 1: class Cm {
 2:    public float CmValue;
 3:
 4:    public Cm (float value){
 5:      CmValue = value;
 6:    }
 7:
 8:    public static explicit operator Cm (float toConvert){
 9:      Cm centi = new Cm (toConvert);
10:      return centi;
11:    }
12:
13:    public static explicit operator Cm (Inch toConvert){
14:      Cm centi = new Cm (toConvert.InchValue * 2.54f);
15:      return centi;
16:    }
17: }
```

With these two methods, you can now cast a float type into a Cm type, or an Inch type to a Cm type! When performing the cast, the special method in lines 8–11 (for a cast from float to Cm) or that in lines 13–16 (for a cast from Inch to Cm) executes.

Examine TestClass, which contains a Main method below:

```
18: class TestClass{
19:    public static void Main(){
20:      Inch inch = new Inch(3);
21:      Cm cm1 = (Cm)inch; // cast an Inch to Cm
22:      Console.WriteLine(cm1.CmValue);
23:
24:      Cm cm2 = (Cm)15.5f; // cast a float to Cm
25:      Console.WriteLine(cm2.CmValue);
26:    }
27: }
```

Output:

```
c:\expt>test
7.62
15.5
```

When line 21 is reached, the conversion method `public static explicit operator Cm (Inch toConvert)` (line 13) is invoked with `inch` being passed in as the method parameter. The conversion method returns a `Cm` object (encapsulating the correct `CmValue` as calculated in that method), which is then assigned to `cm1`.

Similarly, when line 24 is reached the conversion method on line 18 is invoked. This time the method doesn't contain any special business logic, but simply creates a new `Cm` object with `CmValue` assigned the same value as the passed in parameter, and returns the `Cm` object.

So far, it should be quite clear what user-defined casting is about. You write a special method which is automatically invoked when your cast happens.

23.1 The `implicit` and `explicit` keywords

In the above example, you can only perform a cast from `Inch` to `Cm` *explicitly*. That is, if you were to do this:

```
Cm cm1 = inch; // implicit cast
```

instead of this:

```
Cm cm1 = (Cm)inch; // explicit cast
```

You would get a compile-time error which reads: 'Cannot implicitly convert type Inch to Cm'.

It is possible to allow implicit casting by replacing the `explicit` keyword in the conversion method declaration by `implicit`. Instead of:

```
13:    public static explicit operator Cm (Inch toConvert){
```

replacing the `explicit` keyword by `implicit` will enable implicit casting of an `Inch` object to a `Cm` type:

```
13:    public static implicit operator Cm (Inch toConvert){
```

23.2   Syntax of user-defined conversion method declarations

As with operator overloading, you use the `operator` keyword to declare the conversion method. The full syntax for the declaration of the conversion method is:

```
public static <explicit|explicit> operator conv_type_out
(conv_type_in operand)
```

Additional notes

- Besides classes, you can also write conversion methods for structs (see Chapter 26).
- The conversion method *must* be static.
- The conversion method must either return the type for which the conversion is defined, or take that type in as one of the method parameters.

part 6

C#-specific features

Introduction

The chapters in this part are:

- Chapter 24: C# preprocessor directives
- Chapter 25: Using enums
- Chapter 26: C# structures
- Chapter 27: C# attributes
- Chapter 28: Writing custom attributes
- Chapter 29: Writing unsafe codes.

This part covers C# features which are quite specific to C# and not found in Java. Most have been inherited from C++ and make C# a powerful language. Chapters 28 and 29 cover two topics usually classified as 'advanced C#'. It will be a good idea to read Chapter 28 after Chapter 27.

Unlike the core topics covered in Part 4, the Java developer will find the topics here rather foreign. I have illustrated the chapters with lots of code examples so that they can be understood more easily.

24

C# preprocessor directives

If you have ever read C/C++ codes before, you can't have missed those strange looking #define and #include statements found at the beginning of the source codes. These special keywords, which begin with a # sign, are called preprocessor directives.

Preprocessor directives, though part of the source codes, are *not* compiled into IL codes. They are only used by the C# compiler for making certain decisions during compilation. This will become clear as you go through the examples which follow.

Table 24.1 shows the preprocessor directives supported in C#:[1]

24.1 Conditional compilation With #define, #undef, #if and #endif

You use #define to declare a symbol. You can think of a symbol as a variable which is declared but not given a value. These symbols are used only by the C# compiler and have no effect at all on other parts of the source code.

Used in isolation, #define does not make sense but when used with #if and #endif, you can determine if blocks of source code, delimited by #if and #endif, will be included into your final IL codes after compilation. Here is an example:

```
1: #define DEBUG
2:
3: using System;
4:
5: public class TestClass{
6:
```

---

1 C/C++ developers: there have been significant changes to the C/C++ preprocessor directives in C#. Notice that #include is no longer a valid directive and #ifdef has been replaced with #if. #define cannot be used to define constants or write macro functions. #pragma has been also removed.

TABLE 24.1   Valid preprocessor directives in C#

Preprocessor directive	Usage syntax	Comments
`#define`	`#define <symbol>`	Used to define and undefine a symbol
`#undef`	`#undef <symbol>`	
`#if`	`#if <symbol> [operator <symbol>] ...`	Used for conditional compilation
`#else`	`#else`	
`#elif`	`#elif <symbol> [operator <symbol>] ...`	
`#endif`	`#endif`	
`#warning`	`#warning text`	Used to show a warning or error message during compilation
`#error`	`#error text`	
`#region`	`#region name`	Used to mark and unmark a region of code
`#endregion`	`#endregion`	
`#line`[1]	`#line [number ["file_name"] | default]`	Used to modify the compiler's line number and file name output for errors and warnings

1. The `#line` preprocessor directive is seldom used, and will not be discussed in this book.

```
 7:    public static void Main(){
 8: #if DEBUG
 9:       Console.WriteLine("in Main");
10: #endif
11:       Console.WriteLine("running statement");
12:    }
13: }
```

Output:

```
c:\expt>test
in Main
running statement
```

Line 1 #defines the DEBUG symbol. During precompilation parsing, line 9 is included in the IL codes because the #if directive on line 8 is true (since symbol DEBUG has been defined.) The lines in the source file which eventually make it into

IL codes are shown shaded. (Note that the preprocessor directive statements themselves are used only by the compiler, and never included in the final IL codes.)

If you comment off line 1, the output changes:

```
 1: // #define DEBUG - DEBUG is no longer a defined symbol
 2:
 3: using System;
 4:
 5: public class TestClass{
 6:
 7:    public static void Main(){
 8: #if DEBUG
 9:      Console.WriteLine("in Main");
10: #endif
11:      Console.WriteLine("running statement");
12:    }
13: }
```

Output:

```
c:\expt>test
running statement
```

During precompilation parsing, it is determined that #if DEBUG on line 8 is false (since no such symbol has been previously defined with line 1 commented off) and so all the lines between #if DEBUG (line 8) and the next #endif (line 10) are not taken into consideration during compilation. Similarly, the shaded lines are those which eventually make it into IL codes.

The preprocessor directives introduced so far are often used for debugging and versioning purposes, as in the example shown (though other uses are left to your creativity).

Additional notes

- Symbols are case sensitive – by convention, symbols are named using all upper case letters.
- Any #define statement must be made before any type declaration in the source file. You can have multiple #define statements.
- Preprocessor directives do *not* end with semicolons. Each preprocessor directive must start on a new line.
- If you attempt to #define a symbol that has already been #defined, nothing happens.
- If you attempt to #undef a symbol that has not been previously #defined, nothing happens either.

- You can use any identifier for symbol names, including C# keywords and actual identifier names used in the same source code (though this is highly discouraged because it can be confusing).

- #if can be nested, but each #if must have a corresponding #endif directive statement.

Preprocessor directives are read by the compiler from top to bottom regardless of what source codes are in between. You can treat it as if the compiler parses a source file twice: once to check for preprocessor directives and remove all those source codes which should not appear in the final source file; the second parse actually performs the compilation.

24.2 #else and #elif

For more control, you can also use the #else and #elif (else if) directives. The example below should clarify their use. Note that each #if can have zero or more #elif 'blocks', zero or one #else 'block', and must end with a corresponding #endif.

Here is an example demonstrating #else.

```
 1: #define DEBUG
 2: // #define SHOW_ON_CONSOLE
 3:
 4: using System;
 5: using System.Windows.Forms;
 6:
 7: public class TestClass{
 8:
 9:    public static void Main(){
10: #if DEBUG                    // true
11:
12:    #if SHOW_ON_CONSOLE       // false
13:      Console.WriteLine("in Main");
14:    #else
15:      MessageBox.Show("in Main");
16:    #endif // for line 12
17:
18: #endif // for line 10
19:      Console.WriteLine("running statement");
20:    }
21: }
```

```
c:\expt>test
```

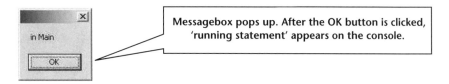

Messagebox pops up. After the OK button is clicked, 'running statement' appears on the console.

```
running statement
```

I have also made use of nested #if directives in this example. You can indent your preprocessor directives too, but use of more than two levels of nesting makes code difficult to read.[2] Lines which eventually make it into IL codes are shown shaded.

In this program, the developer wishes to show debugging statements either on the console or in pop-up message boxes. This can be done by selectively commenting off (or removing) line 2. The statement on line 15 shows the string "in Main" in a pop-up message box.

The #if and #elif directives can take in not just one symbol, but multiple symbols separated by the following operators: !, ==, !=, ||, and &&. So the above example can be rewritten like this, so that we don't have nested #ifs:

```
 1: #define DEBUG
 2: // #define SHOW_ON_CONSOLE
 3:
 4: using System;
 5: using System.Windows.Forms;
 6:
 7: public class TestClass{
 8:
 9:    public static void Main(){
10: #if DEBUG && SHOW_ON_CONSOLE // false
11:     Console.WriteLine("in Main");
12: #elif DEBUG                   // true
13:     MessageBox.Show("in Main");
14: #endif
15:
16:     Console.WriteLine("running statement");
17:   }
18: }
```

2. The last thing you want is to waste time debugging your preprocessor directives to get your source to compile.

The use of #define, #if, #elif, #else and #endif directives to demarcate source codes for compilation is called 'conditional compilation'.

24.3 The /define compiler option and #undef

Instead of defining a symbol using the #define directive, you can define symbols by passing them in as compiler options.[3] If you are using csc.exe, you can pass in defined symbols like this:

```
c:\expt>csc /define:DEBUG,SHOW_ON_CONSOLE test.cs
```

You can use the short form /d: instead of /define:. Symbols to be defined are separated by commas (with no spaces between). Remember that symbols are case sensitive. If your #if directives are expecting the DEBUG symbol, passing in debug (lower case) via the /define option will not satisfy the condition.

You can 'turn off' symbols in the source files by using the #undef directive. You may want to do this if your program execution involves multiple source files, and you want particular symbols to be defined only in certain files. In those source files in which you want the symbols to be undefined, use #undef. Here is an example.

```
 1: #if DEMO
 2:    #undef DEBUG
 3:    #undef SHOW_EASTER_EGGS
 4: #endif
 5:
 6: using System;
 7:
 8: public class TestClass{
 9:
10:    public static void Main(){
11: #if DEBUG
12:       Console.WriteLine("Debugging statements");
13: #endif
14: #if SHOW_EASTER_EGG
15:       Console.WriteLine("Greetings from Geekie");
16: #endif
17:    }
18: }
```

3. This is extremely useful. You would not want to keep commenting and uncommenting your #define directives, although they are usually conveniently located near the top of the source file.

Look at lines 1–4. If DEMO is defined, both symbols DEBUG and SHOW_EASTER_EGGS will be undefined, regardless of whether they were passed in via the /define compiler option. There are probably many other creative uses of #define and #undef. A team leader can include rules about symbols in programming guidelines for his development team.

24.4 #warning and #error

The directives #warning and #error are used to make the compiler display a compiler warning or error message. For warnings, the compiler displays the warning message and then carries on with the compilation. Compilation warnings do not cause compilation to terminate. On the other hand, with errors the compiler displays an error message and terminates the compilation process. Here is an example:

```
 1: using System;
 2:
 3: public class TestClass{
 4:
 5:   public static void Main(){
 6: #warning Main not yet completed
 7:      Console.WriteLine("to be done");
 8:      // insert code here after New Year holidays
 9:      //...
10:   }
11: }
```

Compilation warning:

```
test.cs(6,11): warning CS1030: #warning: 'Main not yet
completed'
```

Output:

```
c:\expt>test
to be done
```

If line 6 is replaced by:

```
 6: #error Main not yet completed
```

a compilation error is produced, and no EXE file is created:

```
c:\expt>csc test.cs
test.cs(6,8): error CS1029: #error: 'Main not yet
completed'
```

#warnings and #errors are useful for absent minded developers dealing with lots of code simultaneously, and who need some helpful self-imposed reminders.

Note that you can place #warnings and #errors between #if and #endif 'blocks' so that a compilation warning or error appears only when certain symbols are defined.

24.5 #region and #endregion

You can mark arbitrary sections of your code using region names using the #region and #endregion directives. These directives are totally ignored by most compilers but may be useful for C# IDEs (such as VS .NET), which may use regions defined this way for special display purposes.

An IDE may want to demarcate a source file into several regions and insert these region directives 'behind the scenes'. When the source is displayed within the IDE, these directives are usually not displayed, but used internally by the IDE.

25

Using enums

Java developers may be new to this keyword, though C/C++ users will find it very familiar. Enums are used frequently because it is a very convenient way to represent shared constants.

An enumeration is a collection of int elements. However, unlike other collections or arrays, enums are usually used to assign arbitrary int values to a series of strings, so that they can be used like constants. For example:

```
 1:  using System;
 2:
 3:  public class TestClass{
 4:    enum Month
 5:      {Jan,Feb,Mar,Apr,May,Jun,Jul,Aug,Sep,Oct,Nov,Dec};
 6:
 7:    public static void Main(){
 8:      Console.WriteLine(Month.Jan);
 9:      Console.WriteLine(Month.Oct);
10:      Console.WriteLine((int)Month.Jan);
11:      Console.WriteLine((int)Month.Oct);
12:    }
13:  }
```

Output:

```
c:\expt>test
Jan
Oct
0
9
```

In TestClass, an enum is created consisting of 12 int elements. By default, the first element in the enum will be assigned the value of 0, the second element the value of 1, and so forth. So when `Month.Jan` is cast into an int and printed out, 0 is displayed.[1]

25.1 Specifying different `int` values for enum elements

Although numbering starts from 0 by default, if you have a good reason for assigning each element in the enum a different int value, you can specify counting to start from any other value:

```
enum Month
{Jan=1,Feb,Mar,Apr,May,Jun,Jul,Aug,Sep,Oct,Nov,Dec};
```

In this case, `Month.Jan` will be 1, `Month.Feb` will be 2 and `Month.Dec` will be 12.

In fact, you can specify numbering for each int element in an enum, as this example shows:[2]

```
 1:   using System;
 2:
 3:   public class TestClass{
 4:     enum Month {
 5:       Jan=12,
 6:       Feb=5,
 7:       Mar=3,
 8:       Apr, // 4
 9:       May, // 5
10:       Jun=9,
11:       Jul, // 10
12:       Aug, // 11
13:       Sep, // 12
14:       Oct, // 13
15:       Nov=4,
16:       Dec // 5
17:     };
18:
19:     public static void Main(){
20:       Console.WriteLine("Jan: "+(int)Month.Jan);
21:       Console.WriteLine("Feb: "+(int)Month.Feb);
22:       Console.WriteLine("Mar: "+(int)Month.Mar);
23:       Console.WriteLine("Apr: "+(int)Month.Apr);
```

1. Enums are seldom printed out in numeric form though. They are very commonly used to give a meaningful name to otherwise meaningless integer values used for classes or methods to communicate.
2. There had better be a good reason for doing this!

```
24:        Console.WriteLine("May: "+(int)Month.May);
25:        Console.WriteLine("Jun: "+(int)Month.Jun);
26:        Console.WriteLine("Jul.  +(int)Month.Jul);
27:        Console.WriteLine("Aug: "+(int)Month.Aug);
28:        Console.WriteLine("Sep: "+(int)Month.Sep);
29:        Console.WriteLine("Oct: "+(int)Month.Oct);
30:        Console.WriteLine("Nov: "+(int)Month.Nov);
31:        Console.WriteLine("Dec: "+(int)Month.Dec);
32:    }
33: }
```

Output:

```
c:\expt>test
Jan: 12
Feb: 5
Mar: 3
Apr: 4
May: 5
Jun: 9
Jul: 10
Aug: 11
Sep: 12
Oct: 13
Nov: 4
Dec: 5
```

Examine lines 10–14. Since `Month.Jun` is assigned the value of 9, the next `int` element (`Month.Jul`) will be automatically assigned the next larger `int` value because an explicit value hasn't been given to it. Note that you can have enum elements sharing identical `int` values (in this case, both `Month.Nov` and `Month.Apr` have 4 as their values).

Your enumeration can be assigned accessibility protection too:

```
public enum Month
{Jan=1,Feb,Mar,Apr,May,Jun,Jul,Aug,Sep,Oct,Nov,Dec};
```

makes the `Month` enum available to any other class.

Enums are useful for comparing return values from methods without really bothering about what its underlying `int` value is. For example:

```
1:  using System;
2:
3:  public class TestClass{
```

```
 4:    enum Months
 5:       {Jan,Feb,Mar,Apr,May,Jun,Jul,Aug,Sep,Oct,Nov,Dec};
 6:
 7:    public static void Main(){
 8:       TestClass tc = new TestClass();
 9:       if (tc.DoSomething() == Months.Feb){
10:          // other codes
11:       }
12:    }
13:
14:    Months DoSomething (){
15:       return Months.Feb;
16:    }
17: }
```

This is usually accomplished by using final variables in Java. But enums gives a more elegant and convenient way to do this.

26

C# structures

Structs (structures) in the C language were used very commonly long before OO programming became popular.[1] They are used to group together multiple primitive data types to create a new data type (or data structure). Today, OO classes have taken over much of the functionality of structs, but they are still relevant in C# because careful use of structs can improve the performance of a program significantly.[2]

If you are not familiar with structs at all, just think of them as being very similar to classes. Simplistically speaking, structs can be viewed as classes with certain limitations. I shall start with a brief example involving structs so that you can see the similarity between structs and classes. The quickest way to learn about structs if you already know about classes is to highlight their differences – I will do that after the example. This chapter concludes with an important discussion on the circumstances whereby you would prefer to use a struct rather than a class.

26.1 First look at structs

You will be surprised how much structs *appear* to be like classes at first sight.

A struct is declared in the code below to represent a person's name. This is done using the `struct` keyword.

```
1: using System;
2:
3: struct Name {
4:     private string FirstName;
5:     private string LastName;
6:
```

---

1. Structs in C# are slightly different from structs in C++ (and significantly different from the original structs in C). So even if you are familiar with C/C++, it is not recommended to skip this chapter.
2. I have to note too, that poor use of structs can also decrease performance. For this reason, I think section 26.3 is an important read.

```
 7:    public string GetName(){
 8:       return FirstName + " " + LastName;
 9:    }
10:
11:    // accessors and mutators
12:    public string GetFirstName(){
13:       return FirstName;
14:    }
15:    public void SetFirstName(string newFirstName){
16:       FirstName = newFirstName;
17:    }
18:    public string GetLastName(){
19:       return LastName;
20:    }
21:    public void SetLastName(string newLastName){
22:       LastName = newLastName;
23:    }
24: }
```

That's the Name struct. Now you can instantiate and use it.

```
25: class TestClass{
26:    public static void Main(){
27:       Name n = new Name();
28:       n.SetFirstName("Charlie");
29:       n.SetLastName("Brown");
30:       Console.WriteLine(n.GetName());
31:    }
32: }
```

Output:

```
c:\expt>test
Charlie Brown
```

On line 27, a new instance of the Name struct is created. On lines 28–30 its methods are invoked.[3]

Like classes:

- structs can contain both function members[4] and data members[5] – they can be static or non-static;

3. In this example, public accessor and mutator methods are used to access the private fields. Structs can also contain public properties instead.
4. Function members are indexers, constructors, operators, properties, and any method. There is one exception here – a struct cannot have a destructor.
5. Data members are read-only variables, constants, events, and fields.

- structs can be declared with the following accessibility modifiers – `public`, protected, `internal`, and `private` with the same effect as classes;
- structs can be hidden using the new modifier;
- structs can implement one or more interfaces (though they cannot extend another class or another struct) – to make the `Name` struct implement the `MyInterface` interface, just declare the struct like this:

```
struct Name:MyInterface{
    ...
}
```

26.2 Differences between a struct and a class

Despite their apparent similarity, there are several differences between a struct and a class – and you cannot use structs as if they are identical to classes. Five major differences are discussed below.

26.2.1 Value type versus reference type

The most important distinction is that a class is a reference type, while a struct is a value type.[6]

A reference type variable stores the address of an object. It is possible to have multiple reference type variables referring (or pointing) to the same object in memory, so that any operations on one of the variables will affect the same shared object.

A class is a reference type:

```
 1: using System;
 2:
 3: class Book {
 4:     public string Title;
 5:     public float Price;
 6: }
 7:
 8: class TestClass{
 9:     public static void Main(){
10:
11:         Book b1 = new Book();
12:         b1.Title = "Romeo and Juliet";
13:
14:         Book b2 = b1;
```

6. A brief recap of reference and value types follows for convenience. See Chapter 9 for a fuller explanation.

```
15:        b2.Title = "Julius Caesar";
16:
17:        Console.WriteLine(b1.Title);
18:    }
19: }
```

Output:

```
Julius Caesar
```

On line 14, the address where the Book object is stored is assigned to b2, so that both reference type variables, b1 and b2, refer to the same Book object. The expressions b1.Title and b2.Title refer to the same Title field of the shared Book object. Throughout the whole program, only one Book object is created.

A value type variable, on the other hand, stores the actual value of the type instead of an address. It is, of course, possible for two value type variables to store the same value, but changing the value of one will not affect the other.

Changing line 3 of the code above from:

```
3: class Book {
```

to

```
3: struct Book {
```

will result in a totally different output:

```
Romeo and Juliet
```

What's the reason for the different output? In this case, Book is a struct instead of a class, and a struct is a value type. When assigning a value type variable to another value type variable, a copy of the value is created. Hence on line 14, when b1 is assigned to b2, a copy of the Book struct is created and assigned to value type variable b2. When b2's Title field is changed to "Julius Caesar", b1's Title field is not affected (b1.Title remains as "Romeo and Juliet").

It is important to understand that structs are value types and not reference types like classes because of this significant implication. This is shown in Figure 26.1.

26.2.2 Inheritance

Unlike classes, structs cannot be inherited from. A struct:

● is automatically a direct subclass of System.ValueType. You cannot specify that a struct be a subclass of any class (even System.ValueType, since that is the default). ValueType is a direct subclass of System.Object.

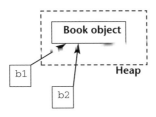 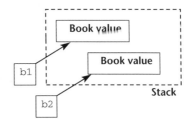

- Book **is a class**
- b1 **and** b2 **are both reference type variables**

- Book **is a struct**
- b1 **and** b2 **are both value type variables**

FIGURE 26.1   A representation of how memory looks after the assignment on line 14 if Book is a class (left), and if Book is a struct (right).

- is implicitly sealed[7] but cannot be declared with the sealed modifier. (Hence, you cannot inherit from a struct.)
- cannot contain abstract methods[8] and cannot be declared with the abstract modifier.
- cannot contain members that are declared as protected or protected internal.[9]

Nevertheless, a struct can implement interfaces. Since structs cannot have any abstract methods, all abstract methods in the interfaces implemented must be coded in the struct. The following program shows an example of a struct implementing an interface.

```
 1: using System;
 2:
 3: interface SolidShape{
 4:     float CalculateSurfaceArea();
 5:     float CalculateVolume();
 6: }
 7:
 8: struct Cube:SolidShape {
 9:     public float Side;
10:
11:     public float CalculateVolume(){
```

7. A sealed class in C# is a final class in Java nomenclature. You cannot subclass a sealed class.
8. It makes complete sense that a sealed class cannot contain abstract methods. Hence if you view a struct as sealed, it too cannot contain abstract methods.
9. A protected member does not make sense in a struct, simply because structs cannot be inherited from.

```
12:      return Side*Side*Side;
13:   }
14:
15:   public float CalculateSurfaceArea(){
16:      return 6*Side*Side;
17:   }
18: }
19:
20: class TestClass{
21:   public static void Main(){
22:      Cube c = new Cube();
23:      c.Side = 2f;
24:      Console.WriteLine(c.CalculateSurfaceArea());
25:   }
26: }
```

Output:

```
c:\expt>test
24
```

26.2.3   Default constructor

A struct implicitly has a default constructor.[10] For classes, a default constructor is provided only when no constructor is explicitly coded. In the case of structs, the default constructor is always provided regardless of whether other overloaded constructors are coded or not.

What this default constructor does in a struct is set all the struct's field values to their default values (`null` for reference types or 0 for numeric types). Interestingly, you *cannot* override the implicit default constructor provided in a struct, though you can have other overloaded constructors which take in other parameters.

All a struct's fields *must* be initialized before the constructor completes. Study the following example.

```
1: using System;
2:
3: struct Book {
4:    public string Title;
5:    public float Price;
6:
7:    public Book (string newTitle, float newPrice){
```

---

10. A default constructor is one which takes in no parameters. It is also known as a parameterless constructor.

```
 8:        Title = newTitle;
 9:        Price = newPrice;
10:    }
11• }
12:
13: class TestClass{
14:    public static void Main(string []args){
15:
16:        Book b1 = new Book();
17:        Console.WriteLine("Title is " + b1.Title);
18:        Console.WriteLine("Price is " + b1.Price);
19:    }
20: }
```

Output:

```
Title is
Price is 0
```

Lines 7–10 code an overloaded constructor for the Book struct which takes in a string and a float. On line 16, a new struct is created.[11] In this case, the default constructor is invoked,[12] which initializes the fields Title and Price to null and 0 respectively. When printed out (line 17–18), the value of the Title and Price fields are null and 0 respectively.

Changing line 16 from:

```
16:        Book b1 = new Book();
```

to:

```
16:        Book b1 = new Book("Macbeth",10.30f);
```

will result in a different output:

```
Title is Macbeth
Price is 10.3
```

This proves that the overloaded constructor which was written has executed.

However, consider the case if line 9 is removed so that the Price field is not initialized in the overloaded constructor which takes in a string and a float.

---

11. Remember that unlike a class, a struct – being a value type – is created on the stack, rather than the heap. No new object is created although the new operator is used here.
12. The default constructor is not coded but always provided free-of-charge even if you explicitly provide another constructor (you cannot override the default constructor in a struct anyway).

```
7:    public Book (string newTitle, float newPrice){
8:      Title = newTitle;
9:      // Price = newPrice;
10:   }
```

Compilation error:

```
Test.cs(7,10): error CS0171: Field 'Book.Price' must be fully
assigned before control leaves the constructor
```

Compilation isn't successful because a constructor has been written which does not initialize all the struct's fields before returning. You must ensure that *all* fields of a struct are explicitly initialized before the constructor ends. For classes, all fields will be automatically initialized to their default values regardless of which constructor runs. For structs, field initialization must be explicitly performed by the constructor which runs.

Attempting to alter the overloaded constructor so that it calls the default constructor first (which initializes every field to default values) by using the base keyword does not work. The following change to line 7 results in a compilation error which explains why:

```
7:    public Book (string NewTitle, float newPrice):base(){
```

Compilation error:

```
test.cs(7,10): error CS0522: 'Book.Book(string,float)': structs
cannot call base class constructors
```

It seems that you have to initialize all your fields manually in every overloaded constructor you provide since you cannot invoke the default constructor to do that using the base keyword.

26.2.4 Using a struct without the new keyword

So far, you have used the new keyword to create a new struct value. Declaring a class type variable such as the following (assuming MyClass is a class type):

```
MyClass mc;
```

does not actually create an object on the heap.

On the other hand, when a struct type variable is declared, the declaration actually allocates space for the whole struct on the stack. However, note that on variable declaration only, the struct's fields are not initialized and that implies that you cannot access any field's value yet. Study the example below.

```
1: using System;
2:
```

```
 3: struct Book {
 4:    public string Title;
 5:    public float Price;
 6: }
 7:
 8: class MainClass{
 9:    public static void Main(string []args){
10:
11:        Book b1; // Stack space allocated
12:        b1.Title = "Macbeth";
13:        b1.Price = 7.35f;
14:        Console.WriteLine("Title is " + b1.Title);
15:    }
16: }
```

Output:

```
Title is Macbeth
```

Note that the declaration statement on line 11 itself does not initialize the struct's fields. If you comment away lines 12–13 but keep line 14, a compilation error occurs:

```
11:        Book b1;
12:        // b1.Title = "Macbeth";
13:        // b1.Price = 7.35f;
14:        Console.WriteLine("Title is " + b1.Title);
15:    }
16: }
```

Compilation error:

```
test.cs(14,44): error CS0170: Use of possibly unassigned field
'Title'
```

You need to explicitly assign values to the fields you are going to access. When you assign a value to one field, other fields are *not* automatically initialized.

This works:

```
11:        Book b1;
12:        b1.Title = "Macbeth";
13:        // b1.Price = 7.35f;
14:        Console.WriteLine("Title is " + b1.Title);
15:    }
16: }
```

but with a compilation warning:

```
Test.cs(5,16): warning CS0649: Field 'Book.Price' is never
assigned to, and will always have its default value 0
```

Output:

```
Title is Macbeth
```

However, attempting to access Price without initializing it results in a compilation error:

```
11:     Book b1;
12:     b1.Title = "Macbeth";
13:     // b1.Price = 7.35f;
14:     Console.WriteLine("Price is " + b1.Price);
15:   }
16: }
```

Compilation error:

```
test.cs(14,44): error CS0170: Use of possibly unassigned
field 'Price'
```

Just remember that a struct's field can only be accessed after it has been initialized – and the default constructor initializes all fields to their default values. If you declare a struct without using the new keyword, the default constructor is not invoked and you will have to manually initialize each field before you can use it. So much for complex rules!

26.2.5 Field initializers

If Book is declared as a class like this:

```
3: class Book{
4:    public string Title = "Othello";
5:    public float Price = 9.73f;
6: }
```

the bold parts of lines 4–5 are called the variable initializers or field initializers.

For classes, field initializers are legal.[13] Structs, however, do not allow field initializers. If line 3 is changed to:

```
3: struct Book{
```

13. Some developers would argue that field initialization is an activity that should be performed in a constructor.

The following compilation error appears:

```
test.cs(4,17): error CS0573: 'Book.Title': cannot have instance
field initializers in structs
test.cs(5,16): error CS0573: 'Book.Price': cannot have instance
field initializers in structs
```

26.2.6   Summary of differences

Table 26.1 shows a summary of the points discussed above.

TABLE 26.1   Differences between struct and class

Feature	C# class	C# struct
Type	Reference	Value
Inheritance	Allowed	Not allowed (implicitly subclassed from System.ValueType) – can implement interfaces though
Declaration	Declaration itself does not create an object, or reserve memory space	Declaration reserves space on stack for whole struct even if the new keyword is not used
Default constructor	Provided implicitly only if no constructor is explicitly coded	Always provided implicitly and cannot be overridden – default constructor initializes all fields to their default values
Fields	Instance (non-static) or class (static) fields are automatically assigned a default value if not explicitly assigned	If the default constructor is not invoked, you have to ensure that each field is manually assigned a value before accessing it
Field initializers	Allowed	Not allowed
Destructor	Allowed	Not allowed

26.3   Why use a struct?

Even if you have never heard of structs before reading this chapter, the chances are that you have already used them quite a bit. Simple (or primitive) types in C# are implemented as structs internally.[14]

You should choose to use a struct rather than a class for performance reasons. If you are writing a class that:

14. Your sbyte, short, int, long, byte, ushort, uint, ulong, float, double, decimal, char, and bool types are all internally implemented as structs.

- represents a small data structure with few data members,[15] *and*
- does not require the use of inheritance, *and*
- it is convenient for it to be a value type instead of a reference type,

you might want to consider implementing it as a struct instead.

26.3.1 Performance implications

Being a value type, a struct is created on the stack rather than on the heap. Operations involving structs generally perform faster for this reason. It is often superfluous to implement a simple and small data structure as a class. One thing which a developer scrutinizing code for optimization should do is search for classes that would be better implemented as structs.

However, because a struct is a value type, an assignment results in the whole struct's value being copied over. If you have a huge struct containing many members, a simple assignment operation may be inefficient since the whole struct is being duplicated. If implemented as a class instead, an assignment is as simple as setting the second reference variable to point to the same object (which is already on the heap anyway).

Consider both sides before deciding if you want a struct or a class.

---

15. Examples of simple data structures better implemented as structs than classes include a complex number (with only two fields – a real part and an imaginary part), a point of the coordinate system (with only two fields – an x value, and a y value), or a key/value pair (with only two fields – a key and a value).

chapter 27

C# attributes

C# attributes[1,2] are a new feature with no equivalent in Java.[3] Put simply, C# attributes are comment-like tags enclosed in square brackets used to label or mark a class, interface, assembly, method, event, field, delegate, or method parameter in codes. Attributes enable these entities in source codes to be tagged with additional declarative information. These tags can be 'read' during runtime using C#'s built-in support for reflection.

You can also think of an attribute as a language construct that decorates a class entity[4] with additional information which can be used by the CLR (standard attributes) or your own codes (custom attributes).

Attributes is not an easy topic to understand, and writing custom attributes can be very complex. I shall start by looking at an example, and then move on to explain what is happening. After giving you a general grasp of the idea, I shall then discuss several standard predefined attributes you can use. Writing your own custom attributes will be covered in the next chapter.

---

1. Do not be confused over the use of the term 'attribute'. In OO terminology (and also commonly in Java) the terms 'attribute', 'field', and 'property' are often used interchangeably to mean a class's field. In C#, 'fields' and 'properties' refer to different class members, and 'attributes' are special constructs used to tag (or label) classes, interfaces, or class members.
2. If you have ever done any COM+ programming before, you might have used a less refined form of attributes too. COM attributes, like 'transaction_required' or 'queueable', are added to a COM component's IDL to provide transaction support or MSMQ functionality. In .NET, attributes are coded within the source code itself, instead of in a separate IDL file.
3. The nearest Java feature to C# attributes is marker interfaces. Marker interfaces are interfaces which do not contain any members, and are only used during runtime to determine if a particular object is of this interface type. The most famous marker interfaces in Java are probably `java.lang.Serializable` and `java.lang.Cloneable`. However, as you will see, comparing marker interfaces with C# attributes is like comparing a Californian Redwood with a bean sprout.
4. I use the term 'class entity' in this chapter (and the next) to refer to classes, methods, interfaces, method parameters, fields, properties, indexes, delegates, events, and method parameters which can be marked by an attribute. The 'marked' entity is known as the attribute target.

27.1 First look at attributes

Let's look at a first example of attributes. In the code fragment below, each method is tagged with an `Author` attribute:[5]

```
 1:   // MyClass.cs
 2:   using System;
 3:
 4:   public class MyClass{
 5:
 6:     [Author("Mok","21 Dec 02")]
 7:     public void DoSomething(){
 8:       // some code
 9:     }
10:
11:     [Author("Mindy","22 Dec 02")]
12:     public void DoSomethingElse(){
13:       // some code
14:     }
15:
16:     [Author("Abigail","27 Nov 02")]
17:     public void DoNothing(){
18:       // some code
19:     }
20:   }
```

Parameters passed into the attribure instance

Attribute specification

I use the term 'attribute specification' to describe the attribute tags used in the source code.

In this example, it may be that several developers are doing concurrent development work on the same class. They have been instructed by the team leader to update the `Author` attribute to reflect the name of the developer who last made a change to each method, and the date the change was made. In this case, the `Author` attribute takes in two string parameters – a name and a date (both as strings).

During compilation, these attribute values are actually stored as metadata in the resultant .NET assembly file. These values can be obtained during runtime by another .NET application via reflection. In this case, the other application can dynamically load the `MyClass` assembly into memory and use C#'s reflection API to extract the attributes and their values for each method – and display them in a text file. For the example here, this text file can be used as some kind of interim documentation for the source code.

5. Another way to put it is that the three methods are the targets of the `[Author]` attribute.

We shall revisit the Author attribute again.

After looking at the coded example, I hope you have got the idea that attributes are tags in the source codes which provide additional information, and which is stored in the assembly together with the IL codes (attribute information is not stored in the IL codes, but in the assembly file together with the IL codes they describe). This information can be used during runtime via reflection in any creative manner. Not only can attributes be used to describe methods, they can also be applied to classes, interfaces, assemblies, method parameters, and other entities. Here is an example of how a *class* is tagged with a class attribute called Version.

```
1:   [Version("1.1")]
2:   public class ClassA{
3:      // codes
4:   }
5:
6:   [Version("1.0")]
7:   public class ClassB{
8:      // codes
9:   }
```

Having seen attributes at work, let's carry on with our introductory discussion.

There are two types of attributes – see Figure 27.1:

- Custom attributes. These are attributes written and used by yourself. They will be covered in Chapter 28.
- Standard attributes. These are attributes built into the .NET framework. Standard attributes[6] are predefined, and recognized by the C# compiler or CLR.

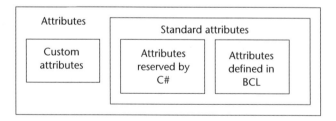

FIGURE 27.1   C# attributes can be classified into custom or standard attributes. Standard attributes can be further subdivided into two subgroups.

6. Standard attributes have also been called 'intrinsic attributes' or 'predefined attributes' in some books.

Standard attributes can be further subdivided into two groups:

● Attributes reserved by the C# language itself. There are only three of these – [Obsolete], [AttributeUsage], and [Conditional]. These attributes are recognized by the C# compiler, and documented in the C# language specification.

● Attributes built into the .NET framework. These are attributes coded by Microsoft engineers when writing the .NET BCLs. Examples include the [WebMethod] and [DllImport] attributes.

Use of an attribute is not all magic – you require a corresponding *attribute class* to be written. In the case of [Author] and [Version], as you have seen, there have to be corresponding attribute classes called AuthorAttribute and VersionAttribute coded somewhere, and which the compiler must be able to find during compilation.

The remainder of this chapter will discuss some important standard attributes and show how to use them. Writing custom attributes is a difficult topic in itself – it has the entire next chapter dedicated to it.

27.2 Standard attributes

Most of the time you will be using a standard attribute provided by the .NET framework. Standard attributes are 'picked up' and interpreted by the C# compiler to have special meanings. Unlike custom attributes, you do not need to write a special attribute class to use them. They have either been coded – and are part of the .NET BCLs – or are implicitly understood by the C# compiler.

I will examine two of the three standard attributes reserved by C# first – Obsolete and Conditional. The third reserved attribute, AttributeUsage, is a bit special and is discussed in Chapter 28.

27.2.1 The Obsolete attribute

This attribute is used to mark types and type members that should no longer be used.[7] You can use this attribute on classes, structures, and members such as delegates, methods, constructors, properties, fields, and events. Here is an example of how the Obsolete attribute can be used.

```
1:   using System;
2:
3:   public class ClassB{
4:
```

7. Such members are described as 'deprecated' in Java terminology.

```
 5:    [Obsolete()]
 6:    private int MyInteger;
 7:
 8:    public static void Main (){
 9:      ClassA a = new ClassA();
10:    }
11:
12:    public int PerformOp (int i){
13:      MyInteger = i;
14:      return i*2;
15:    }
16: }
17:
18: [Obsolete("There are problems with this class")]
19: public class ClassA{
20:   // codes
21: }
```

Compiler warning:

```
c:\expt>csc test.cs
test.cs(9,5): warning CS0618: 'ClassA' is obsolete: 'There are
problems with this class'
test.cs(9,20): warning CS0618: 'ClassA' is obsolete: 'There are
problems with this class'
test.cs(13,5): warning CS0612: 'ClassB.MyInteger' is obsolete
```

In the example above, I have tagged ClassA (on line 18) and field MyInteger (on line 5) as obsolete using the [Obsolete] attribute specification. During compilation, warning messages inform you about that. If you are using csc.exe, note that the compilation warning messages appear only when there are attempts to use the entities tagged as Obsolete. (If you comment out line 9, the obsolete warning for ClassA will not appear because ClassA is never used).

Another observation is that you can pass into the Obsolete attribute specification either nothing (line 5) or a string (line 18). If nothing is passed in, a default warning is shown. If a string is passed in, the string is shown as the warning message. In fact, the Obsolete attribute can take in an additional boolean parameter:

```
[Obsolete ("My message", true)]
```

The boolean parameter is the error parameter. If true is passed in, a compilation error is created instead of a warning.

Remember the attribute class needed to write our own custom attributes I mentioned briefly? Just keep in mind that the possible parameters an attribute specification can take in is determined by the different overloaded constructors written in this attribute class. For `Obsolete`, you can imagine that the `ObsoleteAttribute` class has three overloaded constructors – one which takes in nothing, one which takes in a string, and one which takes in a string and a boolean parameter. I will revisit this idea in writing our custom attribute classes.

27.2.2 The `Conditional` attribute

This section assumes that you understand preprocessor directives and conditional compilation (see Chapter 24) but skipping this section will not affect your understanding of the remaining material in this chapter.

The `Conditional` attribute can be used instead of the `#if`, `#elif`, and `#else` preprocessor directives for conditional compilation. By tagging a method as `Conditional`, that method may or may not be included in the resultant IL codes, depending on whether a particular symbol has been defined. Study the example below:

```
 1:  #define DEBUG
 2:  using System;
 3:  using System.Diagnostics;
 4:
 5:  public class TestClass{
 6:
 7:    public static void Main (){
 8:      PerformOp();
 9:      Console.WriteLine("Finishing Main");
10:    }
11:
12:    [Conditional("DEBUG")]
13:    public static void PerformOp (){
14:      Console.WriteLine("Running PerformOp");
15:    }
16:  }
```

Output:

```
c:\expt>test
Running PerformOp
Finishing Main
```

Line 3 has to be included so that the `Conditional` attribute class can be found by the compiler.

Notice that the DEBUG symbol is `#defined` on line 1. The `PerformOp` method (lines 13–15) has been tagged with the `Conditional` attribute specification, which takes in a string as parameter (line 12). In this case, the DEBUG symbol is passed into the `Conditional` attribute specification. What line 12 effectively says, is if the `DEBUG` symbol is defined, compile the `PerformOp` method normally. Otherwise, do not compile the `PerformOp` method – or any other statements in the code that invoke the `PerformOp` method (such as line 8) – into IL codes.

The output shows that `PerformOp()` has been invoked, as expected, in `Main()`. Let's comment off line 1, so that the `DEBUG` symbol is not defined.

```
 1:   // #define DEBUG
 2:   using System;
 3:   using System.Diagnostics;
 4:
 5:   public class TestClass{
 6:
 7:     public static void Main (){
 8:         PerformOp();
 9:         Console.WriteLine("Finishing Main");
10:     }
11:
12:     [Conditional("DEBUG")]
13:     public static void PerformOp (){
14:         Console.WriteLine("Running PerformOp");
15:     }
16:   }
```

Output:

```
c:\expt>test
Finishing Main
```

In this case, the whole `PerformOp` method (lines 13–15) is being ignored, together with any invocations of `PerformOp` (line 8) during compilation. The shaded lines are the lines which eventually make it into IL codes, and the new output reflects exactly that.

`Conditional` can only take in a single string, and can only be applied to methods. You cannot use it to tag classes, fields, and other class entities. There are some other special rules concerning its use:

● Methods tagged as `Conditional` must return `void`. Otherwise it would be very difficult for the compiler to ignore all method invocations, especially if it is part of other C# expressions!

● Methods tagged as `Conditional` must not be declared with the `override` modifier,[8] though it may be declared with the `virtual` modifier. This does not mean that overriding methods cannot be `Conditional` (see next rule).

8. In C# (unlike Java), all class members that are to be overridden in subclasses must be declared with the `virtual` modifier, and members in a subclass that are overriding a member of the same identifier in its superclass must be declared with the `override` modifier. See section 7.10.

TABLE 27.1   Standard attributes

Standard attribute	Description
Serializable	Used to tag components which are to be serialized
DllImport	Used to specify the DLL location that contains the definition for an extern method.[1]
StructLayout	Used to specify the layout (in memory) of the fields of a struct – this attribute can only be applied to structs and classes
WebMethod	Used to tag methods which are to be exposed as XML web services
CLSCompliantAttribute	Used to tag assemblies, modules, types, and class members as compliant with the CLS, or not

1. An extern method is one which is declared but not implemented locally. The implementation for an extern method is usually found in some legacy COM DLLs. The DllImport attribute tags a method as being defined in some external DLL.

- When virtual methods, which are marked as Conditional, are overridden in subclasses, that overriding method will automatically become Conditional too. However, you cannot explicitly tag that overriding method with the Conditional attribute specification, since it is already implicitly so.[9]

Not following these rules will simply result in a compilation error.

27.2.3   Other standard attributes

Table 27.1 gives a brief description of other standard attributes in the .NET framework. There are *many* others not listed.

In the code fragment below, the [Serializable] attribute is applied to the class MyClass. This tells the compiler to make the class serializable:

```
[Serializable]
public class MyClass {
   // codes here
}
```

I shall discuss how to write custom attributes in the next chapter.

9. In the next chapter, where I shall discuss more about the parameters of AttributeUsage, you will see that the Conditional attribute's behavior is what is called 'inherited'.

28

Writing custom attributes

It is recommended that you read and understand Chapter 27 before tackling this chapter.

Custom attributes are attributes which you write and use in your own creative way. However, unlike standard attributes, there is no way you can create custom attributes which can affect how your code compiles (i.e. attributes which are recognizable by the C# compiler) or that may be automatically interpreted by the CLR. Instead, custom attributes are only useful when you use reflection code to interpret and respond to them during runtime.

28.1 An attribute class

Using a custom attribute involves writing an attribute class first. Let's examine an example of a custom attribute class called `AuthorAttribute`:[1]

```
1: // AttributeClass.cs
2: using System;
3:
4: [AttributeUsage(AttributeTargets.Method)]
5: public class AuthorAttribute:Attribute{
6:
7:    public string AuthorName;
8:    public string LastEditDate;
9:
```

1. You will have noticed that I have deliberately made my class fields public. This is, of course, lousy programming practice. The reason is that my reflection codes need to access these fields in a later example. What I should have done, in accordance with good programming practice, is to make these fields private and 'expose' them using public properties. But, for now, I do not wish to complicate issues, especially for those who have not yet read Chapter 20. I will have to bring in properties eventually, in section 28.4.1, but for now, just bear with my public fields.

```
10:    // constructor
11:    public AuthorAttribute(string authorName, String
                                    lastEditDate){
12:       this.AuthorName = authorName;
13:       this.LastEditDate = lastEditDate;
14:    }
15: }
```

The first thing to realize is that an attribute class must be a direct or indirect subclass of System.Attribute (line 5). Interestingly, you might notice that the class itself is tagged with an [AttributeUsage] attribute specification. [AttributeUsage] is a special standard attribute recognized by the C# compiler. It is used to provide more information about the attribute class you are writing.

[AttributeUsage(AttributeTargets.**Method**)] on line 4 means that this AuthorAttribute attribute can only be used on methods. Tagging a class, event, delegate, or any other class entity with [AuthorAttribute] will cause a compilation error. If you want your attribute to be used for any class entity, replace line 4 with:

```
[AttributeUsage(AttributeTargets.All)]
```

Lines 11–14 define the constructor for AuthorAttribute. The constructor takes in two strings – the author's name, and the last edited date (as a string). This is the way the attribute is to be used in MyClass.cs (section 27.1):

```
[AuthorAttribute("Name", "23 Dec 02")]
```

What the attribute specification above actually does is create an instance of the AuthorAttribute class and pass in the strings "Name" and "23 Dec 02" into the constructor, which in turn initializes fields AuthorName and LastEditDate to these values passed in. You can write other overloaded constructors for your attribute class, as long as the attribute specification matches any one of them.

Since custom attributes are only useful if you want to retrieve their values during runtime via C#'s reflection API, here is another class which does just that.

```
1: // Test.cs
2: using System;
3: using System.Reflection;
4:
5: class TestClass{
6:    public static void Main(){
7:
```

```
 8:        Type type = typeof(MyClass);
 9:        object []methods = type.GetMethods();
10.
11:        foreach(MethodInfo method in methods){
12:          object []attributes =
                           method.GetCustomAttributes(true);
13:
14:        Attribute attr;
15:
16:        for (int i=0; i<attributes.Length; i++){
17:          attr = (Attribute)attributes[i];
18:          if (attr is AuthorAttribute){
19:            AuthorAttribute author = (AuthorAttribute)attr;
20:            Console.Write("method name: " + method.Name);
21:            Console.WriteLine
22:                (", Written by: " + author.AuthorName);
23:          }
24:        }
25:
26:      } // end foreach
27:    } // end Main
28: }
```

You should be able to work out what is happening in Main() since the reflection method names are quite intuitive. See Chapter 16 for more information on reflection.

When TestClass executes, line 8 will assign the Type of the MyClass class to local variable type. Line 9 uses reflection to obtain the methods (encapsulated as an array of MethodInfo object) of the MyClass type dynamically.

For each MethodInfo object, the custom attributes applied to the method are obtained (again through reflection) (on line 12) into an array of Attribute objects. Each method may be associated with more than one attribute. If the method's attribute matches AuthorAttribute, a cast is performed (line 19), and the method's name together with the corresponding Author attribute's AuthorName field are printed out (lines 20–22).

We need to compile all three classes (Test.cs, AttributeClass.cs, and MyClass.cs in section 27.1). If you are using csc.exe and have coded the classes in three separate source files, this is the way to do it:

```
c:\expt>csc AttributeClass.cs MyClass.cs Test.cs
```

This command will produce a single `Test.exe` assembly containing all the codes in the three files.[2]

Here is the output when `Test.exe` is executed:

```
c:\expt>test
method name: DoSomething, Written by: Mok
method name: DoSomethingElse, Written by: Mindy
method name: DoNothing, Written by: Abigail
```

You have dynamically searched for methods tagged with the `Author` attribute in a .NET assembly, and retrieved the value stored in the public field `AuthorName` of each `Author` attribute instance. All this is done during runtime via reflection.

28.2 Another custom attribute example

Let's complicate things a bit more by writing another custom attribute – this time for a class only. Let's modify `AttributeClass.cs` to include two more attribute classes called `StatusOfClassAttribute` and `BuggyAttribute`:

- `StatusOfClassAttribute` shall be a class-only attribute (you can only use it to tag a class, not a method nor any other class entity). This attribute will be used to denote if the class is completed, or still under development.

- `BuggyAttribute` shall be a method-only attribute used by a team leader to tag poorly written methods from sleep-deprived developers. `BuggyAttribute` doesn't contain any fields within the attribute class.

Here's the new `AttributeClass.cs`:

```
1: // AttributeClass.cs
2: using System;
3: // ----------------------------------------------------
4: [AttributeUsage(AttributeTargets.All)]
```

2. If you compile multiple C# source files like this, the default assembly name will be the same as the class which contains the `Main()` method. In this case, since only `Test.cs` contains a class with a `Main()` method, the resultant assembly file is `Test.exe`. In order to change the default assembly name, use the `/out` option of the compiler. If you compile like this: `csc /out:ultimate.exe AttributeClass.cs MyClass.cs Test.cs`, you will get `ultimate.exe` instead of `Test.exe`. Of the list of source files to compile, only one of them should contain a `Main()` method. It becomes ambiguous to the compiler if more than one source file contains a class which has a `Main()` method. In such cases, you have to explicitly tell the compiler which `Main()` should be the entry point by using the `/main` option. Assuming that both `MyClass.cs` and `Test.cs` have their own `Main()` methods, you can do this: `csc /main:Test AttributeClass.cs MyClass.cs Test.cs` to specify that the `Main()` of the `Test` class is the entry point when the assembly runs.

```
 5: public class AuthorAttribute:Attribute{
 6:
 7:    public string AuthorName;
 8:    public string LastEditDate;
 9:
10:    // constructor
11:    public AuthorAttribute(string authorName, string
                              lastEditDate){
12:      this.AuthorName = authorName;
13:      this.LastEditDate = lastEditDate;
14:    }
15: }
16: // -----------------------------------------------
17: [AttributeUsage(AttributeTargets.Class)]
18: public class StatusOfClassAttribute:Attribute{
19:
20:    public string Status;
21:
22:    // constructor
23:    public StatusOfClassAttribute(string status){
24:      this.Status = status;
25:    }
26: }
27: // -----------------------------------------------
28: [AttributeUsage(AttributeTargets.Method)]
29: public class BuggyAttribute:Attribute{
30: }
```

Let's change MyClass.cs by applying the two new custom attributes.

```
 1: // MyClass.cs
 2: using System;
 3:
 4: [StatusOfClass ("developmental")]
 5: public class MyClass{
 6:
 7:    [Author("Mok","25 Nov 02")]
 8:    public void DoSomething(){
 9:      // some code
10:    }
11:
12:    [Author("Mindy","25 Nov 02")]
13:    public void DoSomethingElse(){
```

```
14:       // some code
15:    }
16:
17:    [Buggy]
18:    [Author("Abigail","27 Nov 02")]
19:    public void DoNothing(){
20:       // some code
21:    }
22: }
```

Note that the DoNothing method (lines 19–21) has been marked using two different attribute specifications. This is perfectly legal. It also doesn't matter if you swap lines 17 and 18.

Test.cs is altered to show the status of the class and only those methods marked as buggy:

```
 1: // Test.cs
 2: using System;
 3: using System.Reflection;
 4:
 5: class TestClass{
 6:   public static void Main(){
 7:
 8:     Type type = typeof(MyClass);
 9:
10:     // show all class attributes for this class
11:     StatusOfClassAttribute statusAttr;
12:     Object []classAttr = type.GetCustomAttributes(true);
13:     for (int i=0; i<classAttr.Length; i++){
14:       statusAttr = (StatusOfClassAttribute)classAttr[i];
15:       Console.WriteLine("class status: " + statusAttr.Status);
16:     }
17:
18:     // show methods marked with BuggyAttribute
19:     object []methods = type.GetMethods();
20:     Attribute methAttr;
21:     Console.WriteLine("These are the buggy methods:");
22:
23:     foreach(MethodInfo method in methods){
24:       object []methAttrArr = method.GetCustomAttributes(true);
```

```
25:
26:          for (int i=0; i< methAttrArr.Length; i++){
27:             methAttr = (Attribute) methAttrArr [i];
28:             if (methAttr is BuggyAttribute){
29:                BuggyAttribute buggy = (BuggyAttribute)methAttr;
30:                Console.WriteLine(method.Name);
31:             }
32:          }
33:
34:       } // end foreach
35:    } // end Main
36: }
```

Output:

```
c:\expt>test
class status: development
These are the buggy methods:
DoNothing
```

28.3 Naming attribute classes and attribute specifications

By convention, attribute class names are post-pended with 'Attribute' (we have named our attribute classes Author**Attribute**, StatusOfClass**Attribute**, and Buggy**Attribute**). This is not compulsory, but it is conventional and highly recommended.

You might have realized that when using the three attributes as attribute specifications in MyClass.cs, I used the shortcut Author instead of AuthorAttribute, and Buggy instead of BuggyAttribute. The C# compiler automatically searches for the AuthorAttribute class when it encounters 'Author' in an attribute specification.[3]

You can replace the [Author] attribute tag in attribute specifications with [AuthorAttribute] with no consequences. C# gives you this flexibility.

This code:

```
6:    [Author("Mok","21 Dec 02")]
7:    public void DoSomething(){
```

3. It is possible to write two separate attribute classes – one by the name of AuthorAttribute, and the other called Author. In such cases, ambiguity will arise when 'Author' is used in attribute specifications. There will be a compilation error in such cases. Nevertheless, you shouldn't be writing attribute classes with such confusing names. Stick to naming all your custom attribute classes Something*Attribute*.

```
8:     // some code
9:   }
```

and this:

```
6:   [AuthorAttribute("Mok","21 Dec 02")]
7:   public void DoSomething(){
8:     // some code
9:   }
```

are therefore equivalent.

28.4 Custom attributes in depth

The following sections are intended for advanced developers who want to fully unleash the powers of custom attribute classes.

28.4.1 Named and positional parameters

Attribute classes can have named and positional parameters. So far, you have only written positional parameters which correspond to the parameters of a constructor in the attribute class. Figure 28.1 shows the attribute class with two overloaded constructors, hence allowing the Author attribute specification to be structured in either way as shown. No other attribute specification format is allowed. Something like [Author()] will give a compilation error because there is no corresponding constructor in the AuthorAttribute class which does not take in any parameter.

If the attribute class has public fields or public properties,[4] it is possible to use named parameters in the attribute specification. A named parameter looks like an assignment expression. In the following attribute specification:

```
[Author("Mok", "21 Dec 02", AuthorId=999)]
```

AuthorId is the named parameter and "Mok" and "21 Dec 02" are the positional parameters. If you look at the attribute specification, there shouldn't be any difficulty differentiating a named parameter from a positional one! (Named parameters have this =<value> thing, such as =999 for the AuthorId parameter.)

What this means is that during instantiation of the attribute class:

● a constructor in the AuthorAttribute class which takes in two strings is searched for and executed;

4. See Chapter 20. A property is a special C# class member that is often used in place of accessor and mutator methods for a private field.

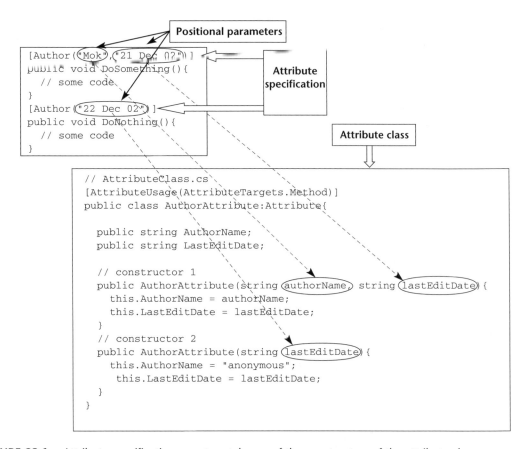

FIGURE 28.1   Attribute specifications must match one of the constructors of the attribute class.

- a public field or public property in the `AuthorAttribute` class by the name of `AuthorId` is searched for, and assigned the value of `999`.

If such a constructor cannot be found, or if the attribute class does not have a public field or property with a matching identifier, a compilation error occurs.

In the attribute class in Figure 28.2 I have inserted an additional public property `AuthorId` (which controls access to private field `authorId`) for demonstration purposes.

You can have multiple named parameters, separated by commas, in the same attribute specification as long as there are matching public fields or properties. This is shown in Figure 28.2. In this case, the attribute specification has one positional parameter, and two named parameters (which matches the public field `AuthorName` and public property `AuthorId`). The constructor which is invoked is constructor 2.

Figure 28.3 shows another example of using the `Author` attribute. In this there are two positional parameters and one named parameter (which corresponds to the public field `AuthorId`). Constructor 1 is invoked instead of constructor 2 in this case.

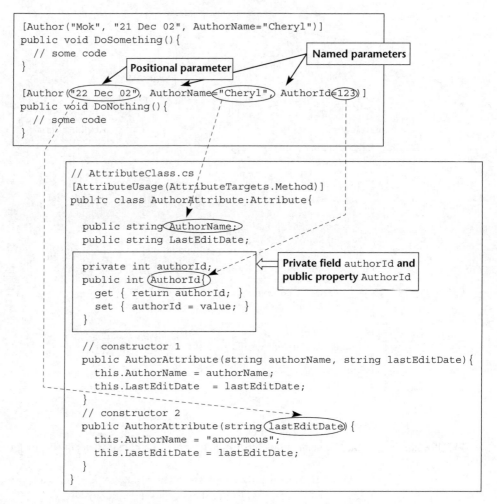

FIGURE 28.2 Named parameters must match existing public fields or properties, while positional parameters must match one of the constructors.

Before moving to the next section, there are two more points to make about named parameters.

- If you have multiple named parameters, their order does not matter.

```
[Author("22 Dec 02", AuthorName="Cheryl", AuthorId=123)]
```

and

```
[Author("22 Dec 02", AuthorId=123, AuthorName="Cheryl")]
```

are equivalent.

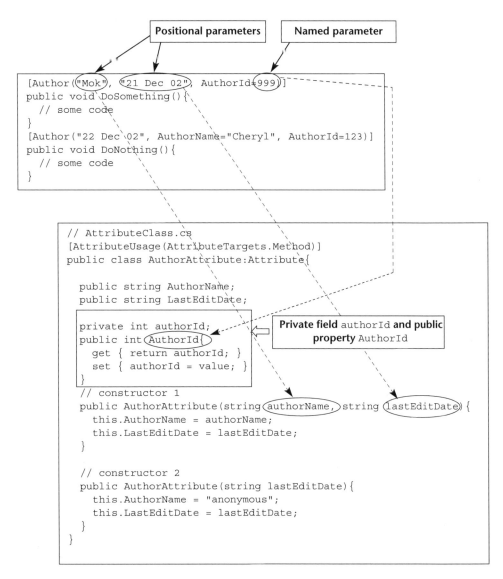

FIGURE 28.3   A final example showing how named and positional parameters correspond to public fields/properties and constructors, respectively, in the attribute class.

● All positional parameters must come before any named parameter. This attribute specification:

```
[Author(AuthorName="Cheryl", AuthorId=123, "22 Dec 02")]
```

causes a compilation error because of a violation of this rule.

There is one other important rule concerning attribute parameters, be they named or positional – the types of an attribute parameter must be:

- `object`
- `System.Type`
- an enum type
- any of the following simple types: `bool`, `byte`, `char`, `double`, `float`, `int`, `long`, `short`, `string` or
- a 1-dimensional array of any of the above mentioned types.

28.5 The `AttributeUsage` attribute

It's about time we examined the `AttributeUsage` attribute in greater detail. After all, `AttributeUsage` is the special attribute you apply to all your attribute classes so that the C# compiler knows how you want your attribute to work.

A class that is tagged with `AttributeUsage` must be a subclass of `System.Attribute`, or else a compilation error will occur. The `AttributeUsage` attribute specification can take in three parameters – one positional (and hence mandatory) and two named ones:

- `AttributeTarget` – an `int` to indicate which types and class entities this attribute class can be applied to (this parameter is mandatory[5]);
- `AllowMultiple` – a boolean public property of the `AttributeUsage` class (optional; default = `false`);
- `Inherited` – a boolean public property of the `AttributeUsage` class (optional; default = `false`).

Details of each of these follows.

28.5.1 `AttributeTarget` parameter

You need to provide a value for this positional parameter. You can use the `AttributeTargets` enum to pass in an `int` value to the `AttributeTarget` parameter.

You can pass in any of the following enum elements:

- `AttributeTargets.All`
- `AttributeTargets.Assembly`
- `AttributeTargets.Class`
- `AttributeTargets.Constructor`
- `AttributeTargets.Delegate`

---

5. Take it that the `AttributeUsageAttribute` class itself has only one constructor which takes in an `int` as a parameter.

- AttributeTargets.Enum
- AttributeTargets.Event
- AttributeTargets.Field
- AttributeTargets.Interface
- AttributeTargets.Method
- AttributeTargets.Module
- AttributeTargets.Parameter
- AttributeTargets.Property
- AttributeTargets.ReturnValue
- AttributeTargets.Struct

Passing in AttributeTargets.All into this parameter will make this attribute class applicable to all the types and class members listed. Passing in AttributeTargets.Field, for example, will restrict this attribute to tagging fields only. Figure 28.4 shows some examples.

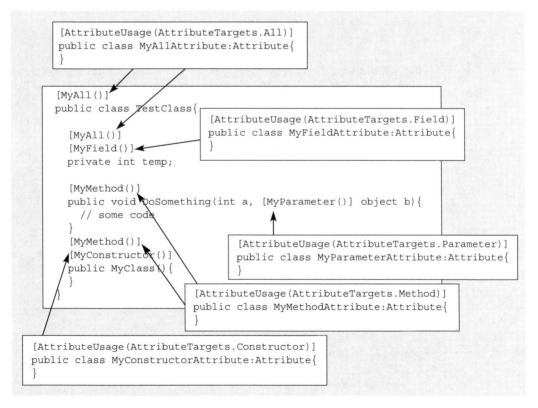

FIGURE 28.4   Examples of how different attribute classes are used. Each attribute class is given a default constructor since none is coded.

You can use the bitwise OR operator (|) to create your own combinations:

```
[AttributeUsage(AttributeTargets.Method|AttributeTargets.Class)]
public class MyMethodAttribute:Attribute{
}
```

The code fragment above defines an attribute class that can be applied to either methods or classes.

28.5.2 AllowMultiple parameter

This is an optional named parameter. If AllowMultiple is set to true, this attribute becomes a multi-use attribute. Otherwise, it becomes a single-use attribute. The default value of the AllowMultiple property is false.

   The code fragment below creates an attribute class that can be applied to methods only, and which is a multi-use attribute:

```
[AttributeUsage(AttributeTargets.Method, AllowMultiple=true)]
public class MyMethodAttribute:Attribute{
}
```

Just what are multi-use and single-use attributes? Attributes can be classified as single-use or multi-use. A single-use attribute is one which can be applied only once to a particular type or class entity. For example, if [Author] is a single-use attribute which is to be tagged to methods, the following will cause a compilation error:

```
[Author("Mok","21 Dec 02")]
[Author("Mandy","22 Dec 02")]
public void DoSomething(){
  // some code
}
```

A single-use attribute can only be applied *once* to the same type or class entity. A multi-use attribute, on the other hand, can be applied an unlimited number of times. If [Author] is a multi-use attribute, the above code fragment will work fine and each attribute specification will correspond to a distinct attribute instance of the AuthorAttribute class.

   It does not matter which attribute specification appears first. Functionally there is no difference between the code fragment above and this:

```
[Author("Mandy","22 Dec 02")]
[Author("Mok","21 Dec 02")]
public void DoSomething(){
```

```
  // some code
}
```

Another way to use two [Author] attributes on the same method is this:

```
[Author("Mok","21 Dec 02"),Author("Mandy","22 Dec 02")]
public void DoSomething(){
  // some code
}
```

This code fragment is equivalent to the previous one, and creates two distinct instances of the AuthorAttribute class.

28.5.3 Inherited parameter

This is an optional named parameter. If Inherited is set to true, this attribute, when applied to a type or class entity, will be automatically inherited to subtypes and overridden class entities.

The code fragment below creates an attribute class that can be applied to methods only, and which is inheritable:

```
3: [AttributeUsage(AttributeTargets.Method,Inherited=true)]
4: public class MyMethodAttribute:Attribute{
5: }
```

MyMethodAttribute is applied to the DoSomething method in the Parent class:

```
 7: class Parent{
 8:    [MyMethod()]
 9:    public virtual void DoSomething(){
10:    }
11: }
12: class Child:Parent{
13:    public override void DoSomething(){
14:    }
15: }
```

Since MyMethodAttribute is inheritable, the DoSomething() method in the Child class also inherits the attribute implicitly. And here's the proof:

```
1: using System;
2: using System.Reflection;
3:
4: [AttributeUsage(AttributeTargets.Method,Inherited=true)]
```

```
5: public class MyMethodAttribute:Attribute{
6: }
7: // ---------------------------------------------------
8: class Parent{
9:    [MyMethod()]
10:   public virtual void DoSomething(){
11:   }
12: }
13: class Child:Parent{
14:   public override void DoSomething(){
15:   }
16: }
17: // ---------------------------------------------------
18: class TestClass{
19:
20:   public static void Main(){
21:
22:     Type type = typeof(Child);
23:
24:     object []methods = type.GetMethods();
25:     Attribute methAttr;
26:     Console.WriteLine("These are the marked methods:");
27:
28:     // print all methods which are marked with MyMethod attribute
29:     foreach(MethodInfo method in methods){
30:       object []methAttrArr = method.GetCustomAttributes(true);
31:
32:       for (int i=0; i<methAttrArr.Length; i++){
33:         methAttr = (Attribute) methAttrArr[i];
34:         if (methAttr is MyMethodAttribute){
35:           MyMethodAttribute buggy = (MyMethodAttribute)methAttr;
36:           Console.WriteLine(method.Name);
37:         }
38:       }
39:     } // end foreach
40:
41:   } // end Main
42: }
43:
```

Output:

```
c:\expt>test
These are the marked methods:
DoSomething
```

Note that we are reflecting on the Child class, not the Parent class (line 22). From the output, it would seem as if DoSomething() of Child has had the MyMethodAttribute applied.

Let's change line 4 to:

```
4: [AttributeUsage(AttributeTargets.Method,Inherited=false)]
```

The output changes:

```
c:\expt>test
These are the marked methods:
```

No method in Child has been determined as tagged by MyMethodAttribute. Child's DoSomething() is no longer considered tagged because the attribute is not inherited.

29

Writing unsafe codes

When the makers of Java were deciding what to remove and retain from C++,[1] they made a huge improvement by getting rid of all pointer operations. One very important concept, which all C/C++ developers must learn early in their familiarization with that language, is pointer operations and manipulation. Pointer operations give the C/C++ developer much programming power – you can obtain the actual address of each variable, and manipulate the values stored at any address you choose. Though important, many C/C++ developers can't do pointer operations well, and the use of pointers caused many bugs in C/C++ programs. When people say that Java is an easy language to learn, one significant reason is be that Java does not allow the developer to deal with memory addresses and the values stored there directly. Everything is shielded – you get to store values at memory locations without being able to manipulate the low-level details.

Removing pointer operations not only helped Java become a simpler (but still effective) language, but indirectly saved millions of man hours which would have been spent on debugging code to do with pointer operations. Nevertheless, the removal of pointers is an engineering compromise. Without pointer operations, there are some things which a Java program can never do. Java developers can never write codes that access memory locations directly.

This chapter starts with an academic comparison of Java and C#/.NET in the areas of performance optimization, direct memory manipulation, and limitations. This is followed by a primer on pointer operations specially written for Java developers who have no background in C or C++.[2] How C# can be used to write unsafe codes (codes involving pointers) is then slowly introduced with appropriate examples.

29.1 Definitions

With so many new terms flying about, it is appropriate to clear the air before moving on. Table 29.1 defines some terms which will be needed in the discussion that follows.

1. Java is an offspring of two main languages, C/C++ and SmallTalk.
2. Or for those who were once acquainted with pointers but need some oiling.

TABLE 29.1 Definitions of managed versus unmanaged, and safe versus unsafe codes

Term	Meaning
Managed codes	Codes which run within the confines of the .NET CLR. Managed codes are first compiled into IL codes, then executed on-the-fly by the CLR. All your C# codes are managed – you cannot write unmanaged codes using C#.
Unmanaged codes	Codes which do not run in the CLR, and are totally independent of it. Unmanaged codes will be native codes written for a specific operating system. Examples include legacy DLL files which run on top of the Win32 API directly.
Safe codes	Managed codes which have type safety and security embedded within. All the C# codes you have seen up to now are considered safe codes.
Unsafe codes	Managed codes which involve 'unsafe' operations, such as pointer operations which access memory directly. Unsafe codes must be marked by the `unsafe` modifier. Unsafe codes are seldom written by most application developers, unless they need the power provided by pointer operations. It is not possible to write unsafe codes in most .NET languages. C# and C++ allow you to write unsafe codes, while VB .NET and J# do not have such a feature.

One important thing to understand is that both safe and unsafe codes are considered to be managed codes. Despite the use of pointer variables and other 'unsafe' stuff, unsafe codes still run within the confines of the .NET CLR (see Figure 29.1).

C# has three special keywords for writing unsafe codes only: `sizeof`, `stackalloc`, and `fixed`. Both the `fixed` and `sizeof` keywords will be covered in this chapter, but `stackalloc` is outside the scope of this book.

29.2 Comparing Java and C#/.NET

I shall start by discussing the limitations of Java in general. You can skip to the next section if academic comparisons do not interest you.

I hope that the issues brought up in this section will show what you cannot accomplish in Java because of the absence of pointer operations, and also what you can do in C# because of the ability to perform pointer operations.

Java has three significant limitations.[3]

● Coding beyond the JVM is impossible. You cannot write very low-level codes below the JVM layer. For example, you cannot write codes that interact with the underlying operating system's API using pure Java. The JVM checks for errors at runtime and prevents overwriting memory outside the allocated buffers.

3. You can perform some of the listed operations via JNI. However, JNI is not a pure-Java solution.

- Direct memory manipulation is not possible. You cannot write codes that deal with memory directly. And that completely eliminates Java as a programming language suitable for writing codes which interact with memory mapped devices, such as device drivers. It is impossible in Java to write to element n+1, when an array has been set up to have only n elements.

- Operating system-specific features are not supported for portability. You cannot write codes for specific operating systems. And that means there is no way a pure Java program can make use of, say, the Windows registry. This is a trade-off for portability, and portability is one of the core tenets of the Java language.

    How does C#/ .NET compare with Java in the points discussed above?

- Coding beyond the .NET runtime is still not possible using C#. Like the way Java byte codes run within the JVM, .NET IL codes run within the .NET CLR. However, with C# it is possible to write unsafe codes. Unsafe codes are those which involve pointer operations, and are to be differentiated from unmanaged codes.[4]

- Direct memory manipulation is possible in unsafe codes. You can perform pointer operations in unsafe codes. Pointer operations allow you to write codes that interact with memory directly. Theoretically, C# can be used to write low-level programs, such as those that deal with memory-mapped devices. With C#'s unsafe codes, you can write to element n+1, when an array has been set up to have only n elements.

- Windows-specific features are supported in .NET BCL. Despite claims that the .NET framework is portable to other operating systems, the .NET BCL actually contain code and functionality specific to Windows. It is probably possible to port a large part of the .NET framework to another platform, but I can almost certainly say that only the simplest .NET programs will be portable without requiring code-level changes of some kind or other.

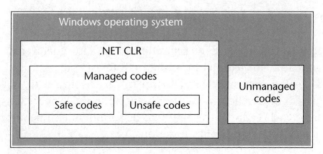

FIGURE 29.1   Managed codes run within the confines of the CLR, while unmanaged codes do not.

4. Unmanaged codes are codes which run *outside* the boundaries of the .NET CLR, and you cannot write unmanaged codes using C#. Unsafe codes, however, allow you to invoke legacy and native (unmanaged) codes which are running outside the CLR. An example will be an unsafe statement in C# which invokes a method of the Windows API, or some method in a legacy Windows DLL written in Visual C++ 6.0. With pure Java, you can also interact with native codes running outside the JVM via JNI.

29.2.1   Writing real time applications

One issue that is haunting Java is the suitability of this language for writing real time applications.[5] Most real time applications are still written in C[6] and assembly language. Java isn't really suitable for real time applications for two main reasons.

- Code optimization via direct memory access is impossible. If you can perform pointer operations, you can tweak your code for the best performance. A good example is the manipulation of codes so that time-critical operations are performed on the stack instead of the heap. You can't do that in Java.

- Java's performance depends a lot on the JVM. With the advent of very efficient JVMs,[7] it seems that speed is no longer as damning a factor. Nonetheless, the uncontrollable behavior of the JVM leaves much to be desired. The JVM is just like a wild beast – there is no way you can tell it when to perform a garbage collection sweep, and when not to. Critical real time systems cannot tolerate such unpredictable behavior, especially when each garbage collection sweep may temporarily stall the whole application for a few milliseconds.

C#, with its ability to write unsafe codes, seems to have solved these two problems partially.

- Code optimization via direct memory access is possible. You can write pointer operations in unsafe C#. With pointer operations, a good developer can write highly optimized code for specific purposes. You are talking about real pure power here – the power to retrieve anything from any memory location, and the power to set the value stored in any memory location. Of course, good code optimization via direct memory access is still a very difficult task requiring lots of careful planning, a cool clear mind, and experience, but the point is that this is possible with C# and .NET.

- The .NET runtime is a little more controllable. At least, there are methods in the .NET BCL which C# codes can call to force a garbage collection. Other than that, IL codes are also 'controlled' by the .NET CLR.

Although it still has to be seen if C# will ever become popular with real time engineers,[8] it is one step nearer than Java to solving optimization and performance problems.

Not all .NET languages allow you to write unsafe codes. You can do so with C#

---

5. Currently, we have the Real Time Specification produced by the JCP, and an alternative (non-complementary) specification for real time applications released by an independent group called the J-Consortium.
6. Even C++ may not be suitable in strict real time systems because of the overheads of object-oriented features embedded in the language.
7. Java JIT compilers and other high performing JVMs such as Sun's HotSpot Engine.
8. My guess is that C and assembly will still remain the all-time favorites for real time teams.

and C++, but not with J# and VB .NET. Unsafe codes are tagged with the `unsafe` modifier, as you will see later. Codes involving direct memory access and pointer operations are considered unsafe, and must be specifically tagged with this modifier to prevent accidental use.

Of course, you should be especially careful when writing unsafe codes because, like C/C++, you can crash a system or cause strange runtime results by writing garbage to random areas in memory. You have to be extremely careful about not corrupting other memory locations with random data.

29.2.2 Why write unsafe codes?

Unsafe codes can perform pointer operations, read beyond an array boundary, and read/write directly to arbitrary memory locations. There are several scenarios in which you will need to write unsafe codes.

● To communicate with a memory-mapped device or write very low-level codes such as device drivers.

● To write highly optimized performance-critical codes. Unlike safe codes, unsafe codes are not scrutinized by the .NET CLR for security and type safety. Under normal circumstances, the CLR performs runtime checking, such as whether you are trying to access an out-of-bounds index of an array. Such checks cut down on bugs, but have a performance overhead.

● To interoperate with legacy codes (probably written in C or C++). Such legacy codes may contain methods/functions that take in pointers. Many existing DLLs written in C or C++ require pointer types to be passed into their methods. You can only invoke these legacy methods with unsafe codes. Many methods of the Windows API also take in strange pointer types, or return pointer types. Although the rich .NET BCL should abstract almost everything you would possibly want to do with the Windows operating system, you can still interact with the Windows API directly via unsafe codes if desired.

29.3 Introducing pointers

There are three types in C#: value type, reference type, and the pointer type. Value types and reference types have been thoroughly covered in Chapter 9. Pointer types are only used in unsafe codes.

You will realize that pointer types are, in fact, very similar to reference types with two main differences. Like a pointer type, a reference type does not store the actual object or the values stored in the fields of an object, rather it stores an address to the actual object on the heap.

However, with a reference type you are unable to retrieve the actual address of the object it is referencing. C# shields you from all these low-level issues. You can retrieve the address of an object pointed to by a pointer type though. The second difference is that a reference type is tracked by the garbage collector, but a pointer type is not. The garbage collector is totally ignorant of the existence of pointers, and the data they point to.

There are other differences between these two types:

- pointer types do not inherit from System.Object – you cannot cast a pointer type to System.Object
- boxing and unboxing do not work on pointers.

Pointer types are not used frequently because, most of the time, reference types are good enough (if you do not need to know the address of an object a reference type variable is referring to). When you need to change the value of any field of the object, all you have to do is to assign the new value via the reference type variable. The address is automatically resolved for you – you don't need, or want, to know whether the object is stored at 0x9999 or 0x8888. When the .NET CLR needs to shift the object to another address in order to optimize memory use, it performs the shift and updates the reference type variable of the new address it should refer to. All this is totally transparent to the developer.

Nevertheless, when there are special circumstances (the same circumstances in which you would want to write unsafe codes) whereby you need to get the actual address of an object in order to manipulate its contents manually, you can do it via pointer types.

Like a reference variable, a pointer variable is one that stores a memory address. The difference is that you can retrieve the address of the object a pointer is referencing (or pointing to, in this case) and do what you want with it.

29.4 Using the unsafe keyword

Probably the first keyword to learn for unsafe programming is unsafe itself. This is used to demarcate a type, member, or code block which contains unsafe codes. The demarcated code region is known as the unsafe context. A compilation error occurs if unsafe codes appear outside an unsafe context.

The unsafe modifier can be applied to a class, struct, interface, delegate, field, method, property, event, indexer, operator, constructor (both instance and static constructors), or destructor. The following code fragments are examples of how the unsafe keyword is used to create an unsafe context.

```
10: public unsafe class UnsafeClass{
11:    // unsafe context with class
12: }

20: public class MyClass{
```

```
21:    public unsafe int* pValue; // unsafe field
22:    public unsafe void MyMethod () {
23:      // unsafe context within method
24:    }
25: }

30: public class MyClass{
31:    public void MyMethod(){
32:       unsafe{ // unsafe block
33:       // unsafe context within arbitrary code block
34:    }
35:    }
36: }
```

The following special keywords can only be used in an unsafe context: `stackalloc`, `fixed`, and `sizeof`. Statements containing pointer declarations and operations must only be written in an unsafe context, or a compilation error occurs.

29.5 Declaring pointers

Here is an example of how a pointer variable of type `int` is declared:

```
int* pInt;
```

or

```
int *pInt;
```

The two statements above are equivalent. A pointer[9] called `pInt`[10] of type `int` is declared. If a pointer stores an address (which is a numeric value), what does its type (`int`) mean? The official term for `int` in this case is the pointer's 'referent type'. The referent type of a pointer tells the compiler what type is expected at the address which it is storing. Here, we know that `pInt` stores the address of an `int`.

It is important to know the referent type of a pointer because when you want to retrieve the `int`'s value from the address stored in `pInt`, the compiler only takes into consideration four bytes from that address.[11] On the other hand, if you have a `double` referent type pointer, the compiler knows that a `double` value is stored at that address and it retrieves eight bytes to determine the value of the `double` instead.

---

9. The term 'pointer' is synonymous with 'pointer variable'. They are used interchangeably in this book and most other literature.
10. It is customary to name pointers with a small p in front.
11. An `int` and a `double` in C# are four and eight bytes wide respectively.

The statement below declares two int pointer variables (*not* an int pointer called pIntA, and an int value variable called pIntB):[12]

```
int *pIntA, pIntB;
```

The * symbol here is used not as a binary multiplication operator, but as a symbol to denote that an int pointer is being declared instead of an int value type.

In C#, pointer referent types can only be unmanaged types. The following statement will result in a compilation error:

```
object* pObj;
```

because object is a managed type.

A pointer can be of type void* too, although such pointers are not very useful.

Why are managed types so called? It is because the .NET CLR is able to relocate managed objects in memory as desired for optimization purposes – hence they are somewhat 'managed'. Table 29.2 shows what a managed type is, as contrasted with their unmanaged counterparts.

The size of a pointer type is system dependent, but the same for all pointer types on a particular system. For example, a pointer of type int*, and another of type char* will take up the same number of bytes to store an address. For most 32-bit systems, the size of a pointer type is four bytes – wide enough to store a 32-bit address.

Like their reference or value cousins, you can apply operators to pointers. Table 29.3 shows the operators which can be applied to pointers in an unsafe context. We shall be covering most of them in the following pages.

TABLE 29.2 Definition of managed and unmanaged types

Managed type	A managed type is a reference type. System.Object (object), System.String (string), and any other user-defined class is a managed type. Managed types and unmanaged types are mutually exclusive.
Unmanaged type	An unmanaged type is any type that isn't a reference type, and does not contain any reference type fields at any level of nesting. Unmanaged types include the following: ● any of the simple types sbyte, byte, short, ushort, int, uint, long, ulong, char, float, double, decimal, bool; ● any enum type; ● any pointer type; ● any user-defined struct type which does not contain any fields which are of managed type.

12. C/C++ developers: C# is different here. In C/C++, this statement will declare an int pointer called pIntA, and a non-pointer 'normal' int variable called pIntB. The statement is similar to int *pIntA, *pIntB; in C/C++.

TABLE 29.3 Operators that can be applied to pointer types

Operator	Description
*	Used for pointer indirection/dereferencing
->	Used to access a member of a struct through a pointer
[ ]	Used to index a pointer
&	Used to obtain the address of a variable
++ --	Used to increment and decrement pointers
+ -	Used to perform pointer arithmetic
== != < > <= =>	Used to compare pointers
stackalloc	Used to allocate memory from the stack
fixed	Used to temporarily fix a variable, so that its address can be obtained without worrying that the garbage collector or .NET runtime will move it

29.6 Using the & address-of operator

The & symbol is used as the binary AND operator when placed between two numbers, or the logical (boolean) AND operator when placed between two boolean values. But when used in unsafe codes, & becomes the 'address-of' operator.

Let's look at the following two statements:

```
10: int myInt = 3;
11: int* pInt = &myInt;
```

&myInt means 'the address of myInt'. What is happening is that the address of this int variable is being assigned to be stored in pointer pInt. Since an address is simply a number, you can do something like this in C#:

```
int* pAny = (int*)0x123456;
```

but statements like the one above are senseless and dangerous unless you are certain of what is stored at 0x123456.

When you create a variable and assign a value to it, the value gets stored at some location in the computer's memory. Each memory location has an address, much like houses along a street have unique addresses. A typical memory map is shown in Figure 29.2.

Figure 29.2 shows a snapshot of what is currently stored in locations 0x9901 to 0x990E. Notice that addresses are usually shown in hexadecimal format, and that a 32-bit machine is used for this example. Each location can store one byte of information.

Address	Value
0x9901	
0x9902	
0x9903	
0x9904	
0x9905	
0x9906	
0x9907	
0x9908	
0x9909	
0x990A	
0x990B	
0x990C	
0x990D	
0x990E	

FIGURE 29.2   Part of the memory map of a construed example.

When the statement int myInt = 3; runs, a section of memory is reserved for storing an int value. An int in C# is a 4-byte-sized numeric value. Assuming the address 0x990A has been selected, the statement would result in the memory map shown in Figure 29.3.

When you declare a pointer with the int* pInt; statement, another location is reserved for pInt. Since this is a 32-bit system, I shall assume that four bytes are

Address	Value
0x9901	
0x9902	
0x9903	
0x9904	
0x9905	
0x9906	
0x9907	
0x9908	
0x9909	
0x990A	
0x990B	3_{10}
0x990C	
0x990D	
0x990E	

myInt { 0x990A–0x990D = 3_{10}

FIGURE 29.3   int variable myInt's value of 3 is stored at 0x990A.

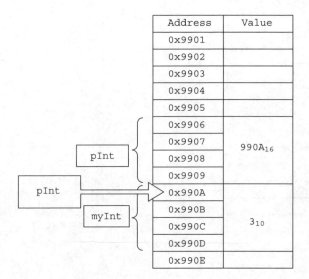

Address	Value
0x9901	
0x9902	
0x9903	
0x9904	
0x9905	
0x9906	
0x9907	$990A_{16}$
0x9908	
0x9909	
0x990A	
0x990B	
0x990C	3_{10}
0x990D	
0x990E	

FIGURE 29.4   Pointer variable pINT is stored at 0x9906. It contains the value 990A – the address of where variable myInt's value is stored.

used to store an address. Hence pInt takes up four bytes of space as well.[13] Let's assume that pInt is allocated the address slot at 0x9906, and since the address of myInt is assigned to it, this results in the new memory snapshot shown in Figure 29.4. pInt is 'pointing' to where myInt's value is stored.

29.7 Using the * Indirection operator

Let's look at the third use of the * symbol in C#. You have seen * used:

- as a binary multiplication operator (e.g. int x = 3*4;);
- to denote a pointer referent type during declaration of a pointer type (e.g. long* pTemp; declares a pointer variable called pTemp of referent type long).

When applied on a single operand in unsafe codes, the * symbol becomes the indirection[14] operator.

The indirection operator is used to obtain the value of the variable to which the pointer points. It can only be applied to a pointer type with the exception of void*. Applying it to a non-pointer type (such as a managed type) or to the void* pointer type results in a compilation error. For example, if pInt is a pointer, *pInt will mean 'the value stored at the address stored in the pointer pInt'.

13. Remember that this is not because its referent type is int. A pointer of type double* will also take up four bytes of space.
14. Indirection is also commonly called 'dereferencing'. These two terms are often used interchangeably in C/C++ literature.

Let's continue our example where we left off:

```
10: int myInt = 3;
11: int* pInt = &myInt;
12: int yourInt = *pInt;
```

In the third statement (line 12), a new int variable is declared and called yourInt, and has assigned to it the value stored at the address location stored in pInt. Now, pInt is storing the address $990A_{16}$. Going over to that address retrieves the value stored there (which is 3). Since pInt is of referent type int, it is supposed to store the address of an int, and that tells the compiler to retrieve only four bytes from 0x990A.

The statement on line 12 results in the memory map shown in Figure 29.5.

The expression *pInt means:

- get the value stored in pInt (=0x990A);
- go to that address;
- get the value stored at this address. The number of bytes to consider in determining the value depends on the referent type of pInt. (Since pInt is of type int*, only four bytes will be taken from 0x990A to 0x990D)
- return this value (which is 3).

Having gone through both the indirection pointer and address-of operator, it's time to see a full example. Study the following program.

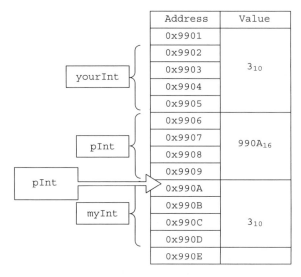

FIGURE 29.5   The final memory map.

```
 1: using System;
 2:
 3: public class TestClass{
 4:
 5:   public unsafe static void Main(){
 6:     double d1 = 3.45;
 7:     double* pD = &d1;
 8:     double d2 = *pD;
 9:
10:     Console.WriteLine("d1 :"+ d1);
11:     Console.WriteLine("&d1 :"+ (int)&d1);
12:
13:     Console.WriteLine("pD :"+(int)pD);
14:     Console.WriteLine("&pD :"+(int)&pD);
15:
16:     Console.WriteLine("d2 :"+ d2);
17:     Console.WriteLine("&d2 :"+ (int)&d2);
18:   }
19: }
```

Value stored in d1: 3.45

Address of d1:1243312

Value stored in pD:1243312

Address of pD: 1243320

Value stored in d2: 3.45

Address of d2: 1243328

If you are using csc.exe, you must compile any source file containing unsafe codes with the /unsafe flag:

    c:\expt>csc /unsafe test.cs

Output:[15]

```
C:\expt>test
d1   :3.45
&d1 :1243312
pD   :1243312
&pD :1243320
d2   :3.45
&d2 :1243328
```

Here is another example. This time, a pointer is declared to a user-defined struct called Temp.

```
 1: using System;
 2:
 3: public class TestClass{
 4:
```

15. The output may vary depending on the actual address allocated to the variables by your .NET runtime.

```
 5:    public struct Temp{                    Unmanaged struct type
 6:       public int a;
 7.       public int b;
 8:    }
 9:
10:    public unsafe static void Main(){
11:       Temp t1 = new Temp();
12:       t1.a = 1;
13:       t1.b = 1;
14:
15:       Console.WriteLine("t1.a : " + t1.a); // 1
16:
17:       Temp* pTemp = &t1;
18:       Temp t2 = *pTemp;
19:
20:       t2.a = 9;
21:       Console.WriteLine("t1.a : " + t1.a); // 1
22:       Console.WriteLine("t2.a : " + t2.a); // 9
23:
24:       int* pA = &t1.a;
25:       int myInt = *pA;
26:       Console.WriteLine("myInt: " + myInt); // 1
27:    }
28: }
```

Output:

```
c:\expt>test
t1.a : 1
t1.a : 1
t2.a : 9
myInt: 1
```

Note that the statement on line 18 makes a copy of t1, so that t1 and t2 are stored at unique addresses. Changing t2.a (line 20) will not affect t1.a.

On line 24, a new int pointer is created which stores the address of t1's int field a. This is perfectly legal.

Remember that a struct containing a managed type is no longer considered an unmanaged type itself. In the code fragment below, NonPointerStruct is no longer considered to be unmanaged because it contains a AnotherStruct field. AnotherStruct contains a reference to object, a managed type. An unmanaged struct may not contain any reference to any managed type at any level of nesting.

```
10: public struct NonPointerStruct {
11:     int a;
12:     int b;
13:     AnotherStruct another;
14: }
15:
16: public struct AnotherStruct {
17:     object o;
18: }
19:
20: public unsafe static void Main(){
21:     NonPointerStruct* pNps;
22: }
```

Managed struct types

Field of managed type

Compilation error:

```
c:\expt>csc /unsafe test.cs
test.cs(21,20): error CS0208: Cannot take the address or
size of a variable of a managed type
('TestClass.NonPointerStruct')
```

29.8 Passing pointers to methods

Let's put together what we have learnt so far, and take a look at a general example of how pointers are passed between methods.

Examine this program:

```
 1: using System;
 2:
 3: class TestClass{
 4:
 5:     static unsafe void PerformOp (int* pX){
 6:         *pX = 99;
 7:     }
 8:
 9:     public static unsafe void Main(){
10:         int a = 1;
11:         Console.WriteLine("a was :" + a);
12:         PerformOp (&a);
13:         Console.WriteLine("a is :" + a);
14:     }
15: }
```

Method takes in a parameter of type int*, a pointer

Uses indirection to change the int value stored at the address in pX

Invoke method by passing in the address of an int variable.

Output:

```
c:\expt>test
a was :1
a is :99
```

In the example above, the PerformOp method (lines 5–7) is marked with the unsafe modifier. It takes in a pointer to an int, dereferences the pointer to obtain the address where the int is stored, and stores the value 99 there.

Main has to be marked as unsafe too because it uses the indirection operator to get the address of local int variable a. The output shows that local variable a has been altered by PerformOp.

29.9 Using the –> member access operator

Examine the program below.

```
 1: using System;
 2:
 3: public class TestClass{
 4:
 5:    public struct Temp{
 6:       public int a;
 7:       public int b;
 8:       public void SaySomething(){
 9:          Console.WriteLine("hi!");
10:       }
11:    }
12:
13:    public unsafe static void Main(){
14:       Temp temp = new Temp();
15:       Temp* pTemp = &temp;
16:
17:       // invoke method of temp by indirection
18:       (*pTemp).SaySomething();
19:
20:       // access field of temp by indirection
21:       Console.WriteLine((*pTemp).a);
22:    }
23: }
```

Output:

```
c:\expt>
hi!
0
```

Line 18 invokes a method and line 21 retrieves the value of a field indirectly by applying the indirection operator on the pTemp pointer. C# has a simpler syntax to access a member. Instead of:

```
(*pTemp).SaySomething();
```

it uses the -> operator like this:

```
pTemp->SaySomething();
```

Similarly, the following two expressions are equivalent:

```
(*pTemp).a
pTemp->a
```

The operand on the left of the -> operator must be a pointer type (except void*), and the operand on the right must refer to an accessible member that matches the pointer's referent type.

The -> operator does not add new functionality to unsafe coding, it simply serves to simplify the syntax of potentially intimidating codes. This operator can only be used in an unsafe context.

29.10   Using the `sizeof` operator

This operator returns the number of bytes (also known as the size) occupied by a variable of a given type. You can only use the sizeof operator in an unsafe context marked with the unsafe keyword. The operand to sizeof must be one of the unmanaged types.

An example of sizeof's use is shown below. Remember to compile with the /unsafe option if you are using csc.exe.

```
1: using System;
2:
3: class MyClass{
4:
5:     public static void Main(){
6:         unsafe{
```

```
 7:            Console.WriteLine(sizeof(int));
 8:            Console.WriteLine(sizeof(double));
 9:            Console.WriteLine(sizeof(MyStruct));
10:        }
11:    }
12: }
13:
14: struct MyStruct {
15:    int i;
16:    double d;
17: }
```

Output:

```
c:\expt>test
4
8
16
```

The output shows that the int and double type take up four and eight bytes respectively (which correspond to the information in Table 9.2). It also shows that user-defined struct type MyStruct takes up 16 bytes.

29.11 Pointer casting

You can cast pointer types. Casting has to be done explicitly since pointer types are not related by a common class hierarchy. The only exception to this rule is a cast from any pointer type to void* – this can be done implicitly.

Here is an example of casting an int pointer to a long pointer type:

```
 1: using System;
 2:
 3: public class TestClass{
 4:
 5:    public unsafe static void Main(){
 6:        int myInt = 3;
 7:        int* pInt = &myInt;
 8:        long* pLong = (long*) pInt;
 9:
10:        long myLong = *pLong;
11:        Console.WriteLine(myLong);
12:    }
13: }
```

Output:[16]

```
c:\expt>test
8727635315138756611
```

This is a nonsensical output. Line 8 performs a pointer type cast. Casting pointers does not change the value stored in a pointer (remember that all pointers take up the same number of bytes in a particular operating system, regardless of its referent type). This implies that pLong and pInt store the same value (an address of myInt). The difference is that because of the pointer's referent type, a long* pointer will attempt to retrieve eight bytes from the address it stores when dereferenced, while an int* pointer will attempt to retrieve only four bytes from the same address and make sense out of it.

On line 10, myLong is assigned eight bytes stored at the address it contains. The first four bytes will encode the value 3, but it is not certain what the next four bytes contain. When the eight bytes are interpreted together as a long value, it is not surprising that a long value is produced which doesn't make sense.

You do not usually perform pointer type casting unless you know what you are doing, and are very sure of the address boundaries you use to store values. Pointer casting from a referent type of wider range to one of a narrower range might be useful, such as in the scenario where you are interested in only the first four (more significant) bytes of a 8-byte long value.

29.12   Pointer arithmetic

You can perform pointer arithmetic in an unsafe context. Let's discuss the + and − binary operators when applied to pointers.

Adding a number n to a pointer will increment it by (n*y), where y is the size of the pointer's referent type in number of bytes. For example, if you are dealing with double pointers, adding 3 to the pointer will increase its value by 24 since the double type takes up eight bytes of space.

Study the example below:

```
1: using System;
2:
3: public class TestClass{
4:
5:    public unsafe static void Main(){
6:       int a = 100;
7:       int b = 101;
```

---

16. Output will vary.

```
 8:        int c = 102;
 9:        int d = 103;
10:
11:        Console.WriteLine("Addr of a :"+(int)&a);
12:        Console.WriteLine("Addr of b :"+(int)&b);
13:        Console.WriteLine("Addr of c :"+(int)&c);
14:        Console.WriteLine("Addr of d :"+(int)&d);
15:        Console.WriteLine(""); // newline
16:
17:        int* pInt = &d;
18:        Console.WriteLine("pInt is pointing to :"+(int)pInt);
19:        Console.WriteLine("value stored there:"+(int)*pInt);
20:        Console.WriteLine(""); // newline
21:
22:        pInt += 1;
23:        Console.WriteLine("pInt is pointing to :"+(int)pInt);
24:        Console.WriteLine("value stored there:"+(int)*pInt);
25:        Console.WriteLine(""); // newline
26:
27:        pInt += 1;
28:        Console.WriteLine("pInt is pointing to :"+(int)pInt);
29:        Console.WriteLine("value stored there:"+(int)*pInt);
30:        Console.WriteLine(""); // newline
31:
32:        pInt += 1;
33:        Console.WriteLine("pInt is pointing to :"+(int)pInt);
34:        Console.WriteLine("value stored there:"+(int)*pInt);
35:   }
36: }
```

Output:

```
c:\expt>test
Addr of a :1243332
Addr of b :1243328
Addr of c :1243324
Addr of d :1243320

pInt is pointing to :1243320
value stored there:103

pInt is pointing to :1243324
value stored there:102
```

```
pInt is pointing to :1243328
value stored there:101

pInt is pointing to :1243332
value stored there:100
```

The memory map after line 14 is executed is shown in Figure 29.6.

On line 17, pInt is assigned the address of d (124320_{10}). When 1 is added to it (on line 22), instead of becoming 124321, pInt's new value becomes 124324 – and that's where c is storing its int value. You should be able to work out the logic behind the rest of the output based on this knowledge.

From this, it can be concluded that pointer additions and subtractions take place in 'chunks' of number of bytes depending on the pointer's referent type. You can also use the ++, – , +=, and –= operators to move pointers about. Note that you can easily move your pointer 'out of bounds' to any desired address. Remember that resetting the value stored at random addresses results in unpredictable effects, especially if the value stored there is eventually used for other operations.

You can 'deduct' a pointer from another of the same type using the binary subtraction operator –. For example, if both pIntA and pIntB are pointers of type int*, the following statement is valid:

```
long difference = pIntA - pIntB;
```

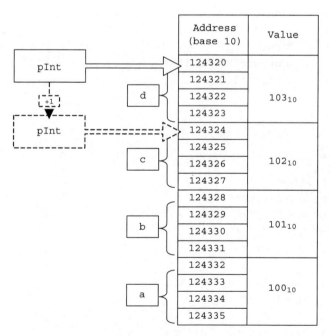

FIGURE 29.6 The result of pointer arithmetic.

However the difference between two pointers does not give the number of bytes in between the two addresses they store. It gives the number of bytes divided by the size of their referent type (in number of bytes). The difference operation always returns a `long` result. In the statement above, `(pIntA-pIntB)` will return the actual 'distance' between the two addresses they store, divided by 4 (the size of an `int`). You can only perform a difference between two pointers of the same type.

Here is an example:

```
 1: using System;
 2:
 3: public class TestClass{
 4:
 5:    public unsafe static void Main(){
 6:        int a = 100;
 7:        int b = 101;
 8:        int c = 102;
 9:        int d = 103;
10:
11:        Console.WriteLine("Addr of a :"+(int)&a);
12:        Console.WriteLine("Addr of b :"+(int)&b);
13:        Console.WriteLine("Addr of c :"+(int)&c);
14:        Console.WriteLine("Addr of d :"+(int)&d);
15:
16:        int* pIntA = &a;
17:        int* pIntB = &b;
18:        int* pIntC = &c;
19:        int* pIntD = &d;
20:
21:        Console.WriteLine(pIntA-pIntB); // 1
22:        Console.WriteLine(pIntA-pIntC); // 2
23:        Console.WriteLine(pIntA-pIntD); // 3
24:    }
25: }
```

Output:

```
c:\expt>test
Addr of a :1243332
Addr of b :1243328
Addr of c :1243324
Addr of d :1243320
1
2
3
```

29.13   Using the `fixed` keyword

You have seen that pointer types can only be unmanaged types. You can have a pointer of a struct type as long as this struct does not contain any field with a managed type. It is illegal to declare a pointer of a class type because a class is a managed type.

For managed types, the garbage collector is free to shift the actual location of managed objects in memory as the runtime desires. This is usually done for optimizing memory use. As far as the developer or application user is concerned, it doesn't really matter where a particular managed object is stored, as long as the variable referencing that object is updated accordingly with the new address if a shift occurs. The garbage collection is unaware of any pointers, and where they point to.

Here comes the problem. Assume that you have a class containing an int field. It is perfectly alright to declare an int pointer and pass to it the address of this int field, as long as these statements are in an unsafe context. Because the field is part of the object, won't there be a problem when the garbage collector decides to move the object – which is considered to be managed data? Won't that result in the pointer pointing to an invalid address, which probably contains values that are part of another object which was recently shifted over?

I have altered the program listed in section 29.8 by pulling out the variable a from within Main() so that it is now an instance field instead of a local variable (line 5 below) – the reason for doing this will be explained later. This results in a compilation error.

```
 1: using System;
 2:
 3: class TestClass{
 4:
 5:    int a = 1; // field
 6:
 7:    static unsafe void PerformOp (int* pX){
 8:       *pX = 99;
 9:    }
10:
11:    public static unsafe void Main(){
12:
13:       TestClass tc = new TestClass();
14:       Console.WriteLine("a was :" + tc.a);
15:
16:       PerformOp (&tc.a); // or PerformOp(tc->a);
17:
18:       Console.WriteLine("a is :" + tc.a);
19:    }
```

```
20: }
```

Compilation error:

```
c:\expt>csc /unsafe test.cs
test.cs(16,16): error CS0212: You can only take the address of
unfixed expression inside of a fixed statement initializer
```

For the above code scenario, Main passes the address of instance field a to PerformOp (line 16). Imagine a garbage collection sweep being performed immediately after this statement, and before the first line in PerformOp actually executes. What happens if this garbage collection activity decides to relocate the object tc? If this happens, when the first line of PerformOp executes it sets the value stored at a's *previous* memory address to 99! This might or might not be disastrous depending on luck, but the point is that the outcome will be non-deterministic. And that is why the compiler gives a compilation error.

What is needed is some way of telling the .NET runtime not to relocate a particular managed object on the memory map, because you might have a pointer pointing to it – this is where the fixed keyword comes in useful. It is used to fix a movable variable so that its address remains constant for the duration of the statement.

The fixed keyword is used like this:

```
fixed (type* ptr = expr) {
  // embedded statement
}
```

where type is void or any unmanaged type, ptr is a pointer name, and expr is an expression that is implicitly convertible to type*. The embedded statement is a block of code or a single executable statement. (Curly brackets are optional if there is only one embedded statement.) When the embedded statement(s) is being executed, the .NET runtime guarantees that it will not relocate expr.

Assuming that MyChar is an instance field, and DoSomething is a method that takes in a char pointer, here is an example of how fixed can be used:

```
fixed (char* pChar = &MyChar)
  DoSomething(pChar);
```

In this case, for as long as DoSomething() is executing, the address of MyChar will not be changed, and it is alright for DoSomething() to contain codes that rely on this fact.

Local variables in an unsafe method are automatically fixed, so that the garbage collector never relocates them. Non-local fields will have to be specifically declared with fixed to prevent relocation. [17]

Let's alter the program above so that you are assured of consistent results. This

17. This is the reason why I made a a field variable instead of a local variable in the code example on page 398. If a remains a local variable, there is no need for it to be fixed.

time there is no compilation error.

```
 1: using System;
 2:
 3: class TestClass{
 4:
 5:    int a = 1; // field
 6:
 7:    static unsafe void PerformOp (int* pX){
 8:      *pX = 99;
 9:    }
10:
11:    public static unsafe void Main(){
12:
13:       TestClass tc = new TestClass();
14:       Console.WriteLine("a was :" + tc.a);
15:
16:       fixed(int* p = &(tc.a))
17:         PerformOp (p);
18:
19:       Console.WriteLine("a is :" + tc.a);
20:    }
21: }
```

Output:

```
c:\expt>test
a was :1
a is :99
```

In this case, when `PerformOp` is invoked (on line 17), the .NET runtime will not relocate `tc.a`, and the value of 99 will be assigned to the address intended (on line 8).

Things may become inefficient when an object is fixed, since the garbage collector and the .NET runtime cannot move it around in memory to optimize it. Fixed objects may hence lead to memory fragmentation[18] – a good rule of the thumb is to fix objects only when necessary.

29.14 A further example

To finish this chapter, here is another example of how you can access beyond the boundaries of an array[19] in unsafe codes. Study this program carefully – it should be

18. Memory fragmentation is somewhat similar to disk fragmentation, except that it now happens to bytes in memory instead of to clusters on a disk.
19. This is impossible in Java or safe C# codes, but could be done easily in C and C++ where array boundaries are not checked for the developer.

self-explanatory.

```
 1: using System;
 2:
 3: class TestClass{
 4:
 5:    static string name = "c sharp";
 6:
 7:    unsafe static void PerformOp(char* p) {
 8:       int i;
 9:
10:       // will print out 'c sharp' (7 characters)
11:       for (i=0; p[i]!='\0'; i++)
12:          Console.Write(p[i]);
13:
14:       // will print out 13 more characters which
15:       // are beyond the array boundaries.
16:       for (int j=i; j<20; j++)
17:          Console.Write(p[j]);
18:    }
19:
20:    unsafe static void Main() {
21:       fixed (char* p = name)
22:          PerformOp(p);
23:    }
24: }
```

Output:[20]

c sharp ??   A

20. Output may differ depending on what is stored beyond your array's allocated space.

part 7

Appendices

Keywords in C#

Keywords are reserved and cannot be used as identifiers. If you really want to choose a C# keyword as an identifier name, prefix it with a @.[1] For example, @new is a legal identifier but new is not.

Table A.1 shows the list of C# keywords, and the chapters in which they are described in this book. Of all the C# keywords, only extern and stackalloc are beyond the scope of this book.

TABLE A.1 C# keywords

Keyword	Comments	Chapter
abstract	Modifier – used to declare a class or class member as abstract	6
as	Operator – a convenient combination of the typeof and is operators	10
base	Used to invoke a constructor in the super(base)class	7
bool	Simple type	9
break	Looping	11
byte	Simple type	9
case	Decision – used together with switch	11
catch	Exception handling	13
char	Simple type	9
checked	Exception handling	13
class	Type – used to declare a class type	6
const	Modifier – used to declare a field as constant	8
continue	Looping	11
decimal	Simple type	9
default	Decision – used together with switch and case	11
delegate	Modifier – used to declare a delegate type	14

(*Continued*)

---

1. Highly discouraged by myself – there are lots of other words you can choose for your identifiers.

TABLE A.1　Continued

Keyword	Comments	Chapter
do	Looping	11
double	Simple type	9
else	Decision – used together with `if`	11
enum	Type – used to declare an enum type	25
event	Modifier – used to declare an event instance	15
explicit	Modifier – used to user-defined casts/conversions to declare that a user-defined cast is to be explicit	23
extern	Modifier – to declare that a method implementation is in some external library	–
false	Value for boolean	9
finally	Exception handling	13
fixed	Used to mark a block of codes in a class which contains members which has pointer variables referencing them	29
float	Simple type	9
for	Looping	11
foreach	Looping	11
goto	Looping	11
if	Decision making	11
implicit	Modifier – used to user-defined casts/conversions to declare that a user-defined cast is to be implicit	23
in	Looping – used only together with `foreach`	11
int	Simple type	8
interface	Type – used to declare an interface type	6
internal	Access modifier	8
is	Operator – used to check if an object is of a particular type	6
lock	Marks a code block as a critical section	17
long	Simple type	9
namespace	Used to define a namespace	5
new	Used to create a new object or struct – also used in name overriding	6/7/26
null	Literal for reference types	6
object	Alias for `System.Object`	6
operator	Modifier – used to declare a method for operator overloading	22
out	Used to pass parameters by reference in methods	7
override	Modifier – to declare a method as overriding a virtual one in a superclass	7
params	Type – used to pass in a variable number of method parameters	7
private	Access modifier	8

(Continued)

TABLE A.1 Continued

Keyword	Comments	Chapter
protected	Access modifier	8
public	Access modifier	8
readonly	Modifier – used to declare a field as read-only	8
ref	Used to pass parameters by reference in methods	7
return	To return from a method call	7
sbyte	Simple type	9
sealed	Modifier – used to declare a class which cannot be subclassed, or method which cannot be overridden	6/7
short	Simple type	9
sizeof	Operator – returns the size of a struct (including simple types) in number of bytes	10
stackalloc	Used in unsafe coding to allocate space on the stack manually	–
static	Modifier – used to declare a class member as static	8/9
string	Alias for `System.String`	9
struct	Type – used to declare a structure type	26
switch	Decision making	11
this	Represents the current object	6
throw	Exception handling	13
true	Value for boolean	9
try	Exception handling	13
typeof	Operator – to return a `System.Type` instance representing the type of an object	10
uint	Simple type	9
ulong	Simple type	9
unchecked	Exception handling	13
unsafe	Modifier – used to mark unsafe methods, classes, structs, class members, and an arbitrary block of code which contains pointer operations	29
ushort	Simple type	9
using	Used to import a namespace	5
virtual	Modifier – to declare a method as overridable in a subclass	7
volatile	Modifier – used to declare volatile fields	8
void	Return type for a method	7
while	Looping	11

appendix **B**

Comparing Java and C# keywords

Table B.1 shows the closest matching C# equivalents to the 49 Java keywords.

TABLE B.1   C# equivalents to Java keywords

Java keyword	Closest C# equivalent	Comments
abstract	abstract	
assert[3]	–	Use the Debug.Assert static method in C# instead
boolean	bool	
break	break	
byte	sbyte	An sbyte is a signed 8-bit numeric simple type, while byte is an unsigned 8-bit numeric simple type in C# – Java's primitive types are all signed
case	case	
catch	catch	
char	char	
class	class	
const*	const	This keyword is reserved in Java, but not used – in C#, const is used to declare a constant
continue	continue	
default	default	
do	do	
double	double	
else	else	
extends	–	In C#, : is used to denote class inheritance instead of using the extends keyword
native	extern	

(Continued)

TABLE B.1 Continued

Java keyword	Closest C# equivalent	Comments
final	const/readonly	Java final variables are similar to C# constants and read-only variables, though there are differences between the latter two
finally	finally	
float	float	
for	for	
goto[1]	goto	Java's goto keyword has no functionality although it is reserved – C#'s goto keyword can be used to 'jump' to a labeled statement
if	if	
implements	–	In C#, : is used to denote interface implementation instead of using the implements keyword
import	using	
instanceof	is	
int	int	
interface	interface	
long	long	
native	extern	
new	new	
package	namespace	
private	private	
protected	protected	
public	public	
return	return	
short	short	
static	static	
strictfp[2]	–	
super	base	
switch	switch	
synchronized	lock	
this	this	
throw	throw	

(Continued)

TABLE B.1 Continued

Java keyword	Closest C# equivalent	Comments
throws	–	All exceptions in C# are unchecked – unchecked exceptions are automatically propagated backwards to the calling method if not handled without the need to specify the throws clause in the method prototype
transient	–	
try	try	
void	void	
volatile	volatile	
while	while	

1. reserved but not used in Java
2. added into the Java language in Java 2
3. added into the Java language in Java 2 SDK 1.4

C# coding conventions

C# coding conventions and guidelines are very different from Java's and take some getting used to if you have been a 100% Java developer so far.[1]

This appendix lists and compares the standard coding conventions of both languages. Bear in mind that conventions and guidelines (unlike specifications) are not mandatory, and can be extended or modified to suit a development team's culture and preferences. Nevertheless, it is highly recommended that you stick to a common convention so that your codes are much more readable outside your

TABLE C.1 Common casings/notations used in programming

Name	Description	Example
Pascal casing	The first letter of each word is capitalized and the first letter of each word in the string also starts with a capital letter – no underscores are used to separate words	`ShowWarningMessage` `GetColor`
Camel casing	The first letter of each word is not capitalized but each word in the string starts with a capital letter – no underscores are used to separate words	`showWarningMessage` `getColor`
All upper case	Every letter in the string is capitalized – to improve readability, it is common to separate words in the string with an underscore	`SHOW_WARNING _MESSAGE` `GETCOLOR`
Hungarian notation	Variable names are prefixed with letters that represent the data type	`String sMessage` `char cLetter`

1. C++ developers should also take note of the new set of guidelines. Even within the C++ community, significant but different naming and casing conventions have sprung up. For example, Windows C++ developers usually prefix strings with `psz` or `lpsz`, but Unix C++ developers do not. Some C++ developers also use the Hungarian notation (which is popular in VB programs) but some do not. It would be nice if all C# developers adopted an 'international' convention as documented in the C# Language Specification.

project team. Adherence to common practices and guidelines is also good practice in software professionalism.

Table C.1 gives some common notations/casing.

C.1   General naming conventions

The casing conventions for C# are shown in Table C.2

TABLE C.2   Casing conventions for C#

Category	Casing
Local variables	Camel casing
Parameters passed into methods (considered local variables)	Camel casing
All other identifiers (names of namespaces, classes, interfaces, all class members)	Pascal casing

This implies that your method and field names should use Pascal casing, like your classes. In C#, camel casing should be reserved only for local variables.[2]

Table C.3 lists some common suffixes and prefixes that should be used in C#.

Additional notes

● Hungarian notation is to be avoided, even for method parameters.

TABLE C.3   Special naming requirements for naming C# members

Category	Naming comments
Attributes	Suffix with `Attribute`
Exceptions	Suffix with `Exception`
Events	Suffix with `Event`
Event arguments	Suffix with `EventArgs`
Event handler delegate	Suffix with `EventHandler`
Interfaces	Prefix with `I`
Pointer variables	Prefix with `p`

2. This is very different from Java's naming conventions. Java advocates that all class and interface identifiers should use Pascal casing, and all other identifiers use camel casing. C# says that all identifiers should use Pascal casing, except for local variables which should use camel casing.

- All upper case casing is to be avoided, even for constants. Use Pascal casing for constants.[3]

- The only occasion when all upper case casing can be considered is when the whole name is an abbreviation. For example, instead of choosing `Windows.Forms.UserInterface` as a namespace, you can use `Windows.Forms.UI` since 'UI' is universally accepted as an abbreviation for user interface.

- All other commonsense guidelines apply. For example, you should select meaningful names for identifiers and use abbreviations sparingly (or avoid them altogether).[4]

C.2 Naming C# events

Delegate names which are to be used for declaring events (event handlers) should end with `EventHandler` to differentiate them from other delegates. If your event handler takes in the standard reference to sender/event source and event argument object parameters, use the variable names `sender` and `e`. For example:

```
delegate void MouseEventHandler(object sender, MouseEvent e);
```

Event argument class names should end with `EventArgs`. For example:

```
public class MyEventArgs: EventArgs{...}
```

C.3 Naming C# enums

Use Pascal casing for both enum identifiers and enum value names. For example:

```
enum Day {Monday, Tuesday, Wednesday, Thursday, Friday,
Saturday, Sunday};
```

It is *not* recommended to add `Enum` after the enum identifier. In the case above, `Day` would be more appropriate than `DayEnum`.

Enum names should be singular – `Day` is preferable to `Days` (it is obvious that an enum type will represent multiple items).

---

3. I have noticed that some constants in sample C# codes in the MSDN documentation and VS.NET help files are being named using all upper case casing. However, it is clearly noted in the C# Language Specification itself about constants using the Pascal notation. As I have mentioned, conventions and guidelines are flexible, but I would recommend following the official language specification.
4. Commonsense guidelines are not listed here because people without commonsense won't make developers.

C.4 Naming C# interfaces

Interface identifiers should start with an 'I'. For example, ISerializable is preferable to Serializable as an interface name. Do not separate the 'I' from the remaining characters with an underscore – ISerializable is preferable to I_Serializable.

Unlike class identifiers (which should be noun phrases), interface identifiers can be either noun phrases or adjectives (phrases describing behavior). Examples of suitable adjectives include IFormatable and ISerializable.

It is okay to name interface/class pairs (a class that is meant to implement an interface) so that their names differ only by the 'I' suffix, especially if a noun phrase has been selected for the interface name. For example, the IComponent interface is expected to be implemented by the Component class.

C.5 Naming C# properties

If you choose to use the same name for a public or protected property which 'represents' a private field in a C# class, they should be differentiated by capitalization. The public/protected property name should use Pascal casing, while the private field should use camel casing. Here is an example:

```
 1:   private string name; // private field name
 2:
 3:   public string Name{ // property Name
 4:     get{
 5:       return name;
 6:     }
 7:     set {
 8:       name = value;
 9:     }
10:   }
```

C.6 Naming namespaces

Like Java package names, C# namespaces should be unique so that the chance of another development team somewhere across the globe choosing an identical name is extremely small.

While Java recommends that you name your Java packages using your company's allocated domain name on the world wide web, Microsoft recommends that you name your C# namespaces like this:

```
<CompanyName>.<TechnologyName>
```

For example, a class written by Addison-Wesley's technical department can be placed into the `AddisonWesley.TechDept` namespace. `TechDept` can be further divided into multiple namespaces based on the project title.

Additional notes

- Use plural nouns where appropriate. For example, `AddisonWesley.TechDept.SharedUtilities` is preferable to `AddisonWesley.TechDept.SharedUtility`.

- Avoid giving a class the same name as a namespace. If you already have a `SharedUtility` namespace, try not to have a class of that name.

- In the same way that you should avoid putting your Java classes into the `java.lang` package, you should also avoid using the `System` namespace for your own classes, even though nothing prevents you from doing so. Other namespace identifiers to avoid include words like `Collections`, `Forms`, and `UI`.

C.7 Language interoperability issues

Unlike Java's single language platform, C# is just one of the many languages targeted at the .NET platform. There is a possibility that your C# modules will need to interoperate with modules written in other .NET languages. Hence, you should be careful to avoid using keywords in other *major* .NET languages[5] as identifiers (especially public class members which are visible to other .NET modules).

Since C# is case sensitive, it is also possible for a class to expose more than one *public* member of the same name but with different capitalization.[6] The situation may be disastrous if VB .NET codes are trying to access these identically named public members, since VB .NET is *not* a case sensitive language.

J# keywords are similar to Java keywords.

Table C.4 lists all the VB .NET keywords.

---

5. Since anyone can write a new .NET language and compiler with selected keywords, it is impossible to ensure totally that your identifiers will not clash with any new .NET languages that are yet to be released. It is probably wise to take note of the keywords in VB .NET and J# since these are the other two .NET languages which will be used widely.

6. Doing something like this that may lead to confusion is always bad programming practice, regardless of whether your module is to interoperate with other modules or not.

TABLE C.4 VB .NET keywords

Alias	Ansi	As	Assembly
Auto	ByRef	ByVal	Case
Default	DirectCast	Each	Else
ElseIf	End	Error	Explicit
False	For	Friend	Handles
In	Is	Lib	Loop
Me	Module	MustInherit	MustOverride
MyBase	MyClass	New	Next
Nothing	notInheritable	NotOverridable	Off
On	Option	Optional	Overloads
Overridable	Overrides	ParamArray	Preserve
Private	Protected	Public	ReadOnly
Resume	Shadows	Shared	Static
Step	Then	To	True
TypeOf	Unicode	Until	When
While	WithEvents	WriteOnly	

D

XML documentation

Java simplified code documentation by introducing the special `/** */` Javadoc comments and providing the `javadoc.exe` tool. C# also provides a mechanism for developers to document their code using a special comment syntax.

There are two ways to insert document comments in C# codes – the second syntax should be familiar to Java developers:[1]

- single line document comment `/// doc comments here`
- delimited document comment `/** doc comments here */`

While Javadoc parses the document comments to form HTML files, C#'s documentation generator creates an XML file. You can view the generated XML document with any XML file reader (Microsoft Internet Explorer is quite rudimentary but useable).

In C#, your XML comments must be well-formed.[2] While `javadoc.exe` tolerates non-well-formed HTML tags, the C# documentation generator will complain when it encounters non-well-formed documentation comments in your source codes.

In the spirit of XML, developers are free to invent and define their own documentation tags for their own project team. The C# Language Specification lists a set of recommended documentation tags, which is shown in Table D.1.[3]

The 'verified' column in the table shows if the tag is verified by the documentation generator. For verified tags, any verification problem (for example, you specified an exception type which cannot be resolved, or a method parameter that does not exist) will be shown as warnings or errors by the documentation generator.

---

1. Unfortunately, if you are using `csc.exe` as the documentation generator, the delimited document comments are not recognized by it. Use the single line document comment instead.
2. Well-formed XML documents must obey basic XML constraints. If a document is not well-formed, it is not an XML document. Basic XML constraints include rules such as only one root element, elements properly nested, attribute values quoted, every start tag with a corresponding end tag, and case sensitivity.
3. I would suggest sticking closely to the recommended tags. You can invent your own in the unlikely event that the recommended tags do not meet your requirements.

TABLE D.1   Description of recommended documentation tags

Recommended tag	Applies to	Description	Verified
`<c>`	All	Used to delimit short code fragments in your documentation	
`<code>`	All	Similar to `<c>` except that it is used if one or more lines of code are to be marked	
`<example>`	All	Used to provide an example of how a method or member of your class can be used	
`<exception>`	Method	Used to list an exception a method can throw (use the `cref` attribute of this tag to specify the exception type that will be thrown by this method) – one method can have multiple `<exception>` tags	✓
`<list>`	All	Used to create a (numbered or bulleted) list of items or a table	
`<para>`	All	Used inside other tags as a paragraph start – similar to the HTML `<p>` tag	
`<param>`	Method	Used for describing a method's parameter; use this tag for methods, constructors and destructors. Similar to Javadoc's `@param` tag – you can have multiple `<param>` tags for each method, one for each parameter	✓
`<paramref>`	Method	Used to show that a word is a method parameter – the documentation generator verifies that this parameter exist for this method	✓
`<permission>`	Member	Used to indicate the accessibility of a member – the documentation generator verifies that the member specified by the `cref` attribute exists	✓
`<remarks>`	Type	Used to describe a type – to describe a member of a type, use the `<summary>` tag instead	
`<returns>`	Method	Used to describe the return value of a method – similar to Javadoc's `@return` tag	
`<see>`	All	Used for specifying a link (cross reference) in your comments to another member – use the `cref` attribute to indicate the name of the member you want to link to; similar to Javadoc's `@see` tag	✓
`<seealso>`	All	Used for generating an entry in the 'See also' section	✓
`<summary>`	Member	Used to describe a member – to describe a type, use the `<remarks>` tag instead	✓
`<value>`	Property	Used to describe a C# property	

Table D.2 gives the syntax of each recommended tag.

TABLE D.2   XML syntax of recommended documentation tags

Recommended tag	Syntax and example

`<c>`	*Syntax:*
	`<c>text to be set like code</c>`
	
	Example:
	`Use the static methods in the <c>Utility</c> class if necessary.`

`<code>`	*Syntax:*
	`<code>source code or program output</code>`
	
	Example:
	`This is the way to use this method:`
	`<code>`
	`  MyClass m = new MyClass();`
	`  m.DoThis();`
	`</code>`

`<example>`	*Syntax:*
	`<example>description</example>`
	
	Example:
	`<example>The following shows an example of how to use this method:`
	`<code>`
	`  MyClass m = new MyClass();`
	`  m.DoThis();`
	`</code>`
	`</example>`

`<exception>`	*Verification:*
	The documentation generator will verify if this exception exists.
	
	Syntax:
	`<exception cref="name of exception">description of when this exception will be thrown</exception>`
	
	Example:
	`<exception cref= "FileNotFoundException">`
	`If indicated file cannot be found.`
	`</exception>`

(Continued)

TABLE D.2   Continued

Recommended tag	Syntax and example

`<list>`	*Syntax:*
	`<list type="bullet"|"number"|"table">`
	  `<listheader>`
	    `<term>term</term>`
	    `<description>description</description>`
	  `</listheader>`
	  `<item>`
	    `<term>term</term>`
	    `<description>description</description>`
	  `</item>`
	`...`
	  `<item>`
	    `<term>term</term>`
	    `<description>description</description>`
	  `</item>`
	`</list>`
	
	Example (a numbered list without a header):
	`<list type="number">`
	  `<item>`
	  `<description>Point 1</description>`
	  `</item>`
	  `<item>`
	  `<description>Point 2</description>`
	  `</item>`
	  `<item>`
	  `<description>Point 3</description>`
	  `</item>`
	`</list>`

`<para>`	*Syntax:*
	`<para>contents</para>`
	
	Example:
	`<example>There are two scenarios whereby this method can be used:`
	`<para>When an instance of this class is shared by more than one thread concurrently running.</para>`
	`<para>When there seems to be synchronization problems.</para>`
	`</example>`

(*Continued*)

TABLE D.2 Continued

Recommended tag	Syntax and example

`<param>`	*Syntax:*
	`<param name="name">description</param>`
	
	Example:
	`<param name="currPwd">Current password</param>`
	`<param name="newPwd">New password</param>`

`<paramref>`	*Verification:*
	The documentation generator verifies that this parameter exists for this method.
	
	Syntax:
	`<paramref name="name"/>`
	
	Example:
	`<summary>`
	`Pass into <paramref="currPwd"/> the user's current password.`
	`</summary>`
	`<param name="currPwd">Current password</param>`

`<permission>`	*Verification:*
	The documentation generator verifies that the member specified by the `cref` attribute exists.
	
	Syntax:
	`<permission cref="member">description`
	`</permission>`

`<remarks>`	*Syntax:*
	`<remarks>description</remarks>`
	
	Example:
	`<remarks>The <c>Vehicle</c> interface contains the abstract methods that must be implemented by any <c>Car</c> class.</remarks>`

`<returns>`	*Syntax:*
	`<returns>description</returns>`
	
	Example:
	`<returns>A <c>float</c> value indicating the calculation results.</returns>`

`<see>`	*Verification:* The document generator verifies that the member specified in the `cref` attribute exists.

(*Continued*)

TABLE D.2 Continued

Recommended tag	Syntax and example

	Syntax:
	`<see cref="member"/>`
	
	Example (`DoThat` is another method in the same class):
	`<see cref="DoThat"/>`

`<seealso>`	*Verification:*
	The document generator verifies that the member specified in the `cref` attribute exists.
	
	Syntax:
	`<seealso cref="member"/>`
	
	Example (`DoThat` is another method in the same class):
	`<seealso cref="DoThat"/>`

`<summary>`	*Syntax:*
	`<summary>description</summary>`
	
	Example:
	`<summary>This method is called to return a random <c>int</c> between 1 and 10.</summary>`

`<value>`	*Syntax:*
	`<value>description</value>`
	
	Example:
	`<value>Represents the number of objects this collection currently contains.</value>`

A full example is shown below. It shows a `Car` class containing a single constructor, two private fields called `maxSpeed` and `currSpeed` (for maximum and current speeds respectively) accessible via two public properties, `MaxSpeed` and `CurrSpeed`. `Car` contains two public methods – `Accelerate` and `Decelerate` – which alter `currSpeed`'s value.

```
1: using System;
2:
3: /// <summary>
4: ///     This class is usually subclassed to more specialized
5: ///     car types. Known subclasses include <c>Toyota</c> and
6: ///     <c>Nissan</c>.
7: /// </summary>
```

```
 8:
 9: class Car{
10:
11:    private int maxSpeed;
12:    private int currSpeed;
13:
14:    public Car (int maxSpeed){
15:       this.maxSpeed = maxSpeed;
16:    }
17:
18:    ///    <remarks>
19:    ///       Invoke this method to increase the current speed
20:    ///       by a <paramref name="factor"/>. The current speed
21:    ///       will never go beyond the car's maximum speed. So,
22:    ///       if this method is invoked when the sum of
23:    ///       <paramref name="factor"/> and the current speed is
24:    ///       greater than the maximum speed, the current speed will
25:    ///       be set to the maximum speed only.
26:    ///    </remarks>
27:    ///
28:    ///    <param>
29:    ///       <c>factor</c>
30:    ///       Factor you want to increase the current speed by
31:    ///    </param>
32:    ///
33:    ///    <see cref="Decelerate">
34:    ///       Use <c>Decelerate</c> to decrease the current
35:    ///       speed by a factor.
36:    ///    </see>
37:    ///
38:    ///    <returns>
39:    ///       An <c>int</c> which is the current speed.
40:    ///    </returns>
41:
42:    public int Accelerate(int factor){
43:       CurrSpeed += factor;
44:       if (currSpeed>maxSpeed)
45:          currSpeed = maxSpeed;
```

```
46:        return CurrSpeed;
47:    }
48:
49:    ///   <remarks>
50:    ///       Invoke this method to decrease the current speed
51:    ///       by a <paramref name="factor"/>. The current speed
52:    ///       will never go below zero. If this method is invoked
53:    ///       with the difference between the current speed and
54:    ///       <paramref name="factor"/> less than zero, a
55:    ///       <c>InvalidSpeedAssignmentException</c> will be
56:    ///       thrown.
57:    ///   </remarks>
58:    ///
59:    ///   <param>
60:    ///      <c>factor</c>
61:    ///       Factor you want to decrease the current speed by.
62:    ///   </param>
63:    ///
64:    ///   <exception cref="InvalidSpeedAssignmentException">
65:    ///       This exception is thrown if an attempt is made to
66:    ///       decrease the current speed to a negative value.
67:    ///   </exception>
68:    ///
69:    ///   <see cref="Accelerate">
70:    ///       Use <c>Accelerate</c> to increase the current
71:    ///       speed by a factor.
72:    ///   </see>
73:    ///
74:    ///   <returns>
75:    ///       An <c>int</c> which is the current speed.
76:    ///   </returns>
77:
78:    public int Decelerate(int factor){
79:      currSpeed -= factor;
80:      if (currSpeed<0)
81:        throw new InvalidSpeedAssignmentException();
82:      return currSpeed;
83:    }
```

```
 84:
 85:    /// <value>
 86:    ///    The maximum speed of this car. <c>MaxSpeed</c> is a
 87:    ///    get-only property.
 88:    /// </value>
 89:
 90:    public int MaxSpeed{
 91:      get {
 92:        return maxSpeed;
 93:      }
 94:    }
 95:
 96:    /// <remarks>
 97:    ///    <c>CurrSpeed</c> cannot be higher than
 98:    ///    <c>MaxSpeed</c>. If you set <c>CurrSpeed</c> to a
 99:    ///    value higher than <c>MaxSpeed</c>,<c>CurrSpeed</c>
100:    ///    will be automatically set to <c>MaxSpeed</c>.
101:    /// </remarks>
102:    ///
103:    /// <value>
104:    ///    The current speed of this car. <c>CurrSpeed</c>
105:    ///    is a get-set property.
106:    /// </value>
107:
108:    public int CurrSpeed{
109:      get {
110:        return currSpeed;
111:      }
112:      set {
113:        if (value>maxSpeed)
114:          currSpeed = maxSpeed;
115:        else
116:          currSpeed = value;
117:      }
118:    }
119: }
120:
121: class InvalidSpeedAssignmentException
122:        :ApplicationException{
123: }
```

If you are using csc.exe, it comes with a fully fledged documentation generator. Use the /doc option to generate the XML documentation of a source file:

```
c:\expt>csc /doc:TestClass.xml TestClass.cs
```

In this case, because my class does not contain a Main method, and is meant to be compiled into a DLL assembly, I compiled using the /target:library option too:

```
c:\expt>csc /doc:TestClass.xml /t:library TestClass.cs
```

On successful compilation, I get TestClass.dll and TestClass.xml.

Part of the XML document generated from the above source file is shown in an Internet Explorer window in Figure D.1

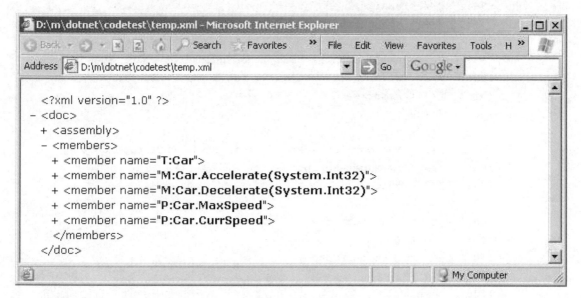

FIGURE D.1   Showing a high-level view of the XML documentation generated.

Notice that additional tags such as <assembly> have been inserted for you. Each member name attribute is given a value prefixed by a letter – T is for type, M for method, P for property, F for field, E for event, and N for namespace.

Let's 'expand' out the Decelerate method. This is shown in Figure D.2.

Other tools are needed to convert the XML documentation file into something more presentation friendly. If you are using VS .NET then under the Tools menu select Build Comment Web Pages, and the corresponding HTML pages will be created for you. csc.exe cannot do that for you.

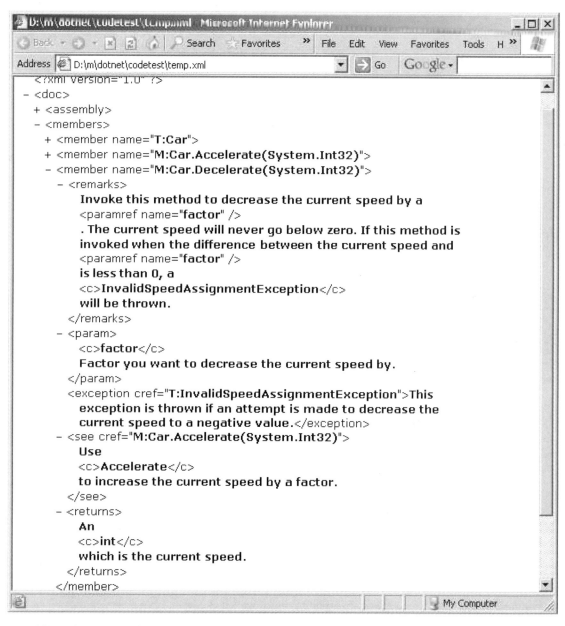

FIGURE D.2   XML documentation generated.

appendix E

C# command line tools

TABLE E.1 C# command line tools

Tool	Description
adepends.exe	Assembly dependency list
al.exe	Assembly linking utility
cordbg.exe	Runtime debugger
csc.exe	C# compiler
dbgurt.exe	GUI debugger
gacutil.exe	Global assembly cache utility
ilasm.exe	MSIL assembler
ildasm.exe	MSIL disassembler
instalutil.exe	Installer utility
nmake.exe	Make utility
peverify.exe	Portable executable verifier
regasm.exe	Registry assembly tool
regsvcs.exe	Register services utility
sn.exe	Shared name utility
soapsuds.exe	SoapSuds utility
tlbexp.exe	Type library exporter
tlbimp.exe	Type library importer
webserviceutil.exe	Web service utility
wincv.exe	Windows class viewer
windes.exe	Windows designer
xsd.exe	XML schema definition tool

There are several useful command line tools which come as part of .NET SDK. They are listed in Table E.1 together with a brief description of what they are used for. You can execute them from the special VS .NET command prompt (not the usual cmd or command shell) accessible via START→Program→Microsoft Visual Studio .NET→Visual Studio .NET Tools→Visual Studio .NET Command Prompt.

For detailed information, including command switches, execute the tool with the /? switch (for example, to find out more about ildasm, type ildasm/? at the command line.)

About .NET assemblies

This appendix contains an introductory description of .NET assemblies and explains how to use some options of `csc.exe`.

F.1 What is an assembly?

'Assembly' is a new term coined in .NET to represent a collection of software modules or components. An assembly is a file with a `.dll` or `.exe` file extension. A DLL assembly contains library classes and is not executable (much like a Java class without a `main` method), while an EXE assembly is executable (like a Java class with a `main` method).

You may have heard of the word 'module'. An assembly can consist of one or more modules. A module is an MSIL file that does not have an assembly manifest. Multiple modules can then be merged into a single assembly. A module file ends with the `.netmodule` extension.

You use your .NET compilers (such as your C# compiler) to generate assembly and module files from your .NET language source codes.

Despite the `.exe` extension, executable assemblies are not the same as ordinary Win32 EXE files. Assemblies contain IL code with associated metadata (the metadata describes the IL codes within). Each assembly has one special metadata file called the manifest, which describes the contents of the assembly as a whole.

If you try to run a .NET assembly under Win32 without the .NET framework installed, you will get a message box popping out informing you of a missing DLL file that is required for the execution of that assembly.

A .NET assembly contains a Win32 PE header – this enables the Win32 environment to run the first part of it like a normal Win32 executable. What happens is that this header references an important method in a DLL file which is part of the .NET framework. This method then interprets the remaining parts of the assembly (which is IL code) and executes them. Win32 cannot understand IL code, but is at least able to run the PE header to invoke the correct method of the .NET framework.

The assembly's manifest contains the following information about the assembly:

- Assembly name – the assembly name is a text string.
- Version number – each assembly has a 4-part version number; a typical version number would look like 3.4.1.9 (where 3 is the major version number, 4 is the minor version number, 1 is the revision number, and 9 is the build number).
- (optional) Shared name (sn) and signed assembly hash.
- Actual files containing IL codes or other resources.
- Referenced assemblies – external assemblies that are referenced from the current assembly.
- Types.
- Security permissions.
- Custom attributes – custom attributes are stored here for quicker access during reflection.
- Product information – company name and other copyright stuff.

F.2 Shared assemblies and the GAC

.NET assemblies can be categorized into two groups:

- shared – common libraries which are used by more than one .NET application;
- stand-alone – assemblies used by only one particular .NET application.

The global assembly cache (GAC) is where global shared assemblies are placed. Treat it like a normal folder (or directory) in a shared server from which client machines can retrieve shared assemblies in a distributed environment. You can view the contents of your local machine's GAC using Windows Explorer (go to `c:\winnt\assembly` – if `c:\winnt` is where your Windows operating system is installed).

The assembly cache viewer[1] is installed together with the .NET framework. When you view your GAC using Windows Explorer, the assembly cache viewer kicks in automatically and, instead of the usual file attributes, you will see columns pertaining to assemblies such as type, version, and public key token – see Figure F.1.

There is a useful command line tool called `gacutil.exe` that you can use to perform tasks such as:

- store an assembly to the GAC (use the `-i` option);
- remove an assembly from the GAC (use the `-u` option);
- list the contents of the GAC (use the `-l` option).[2]

---

1. The assembly cache viewer is actually the file `shfusion.dll`.
2. It is probably preferable and friendlier to view the GAC contents using Windows Explorer rather than `gacutil`.

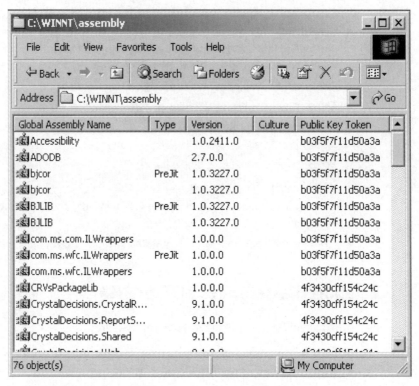

FIGURE F.1   Viewing the GAC using Windows Explorer.

F.3   What is DLL hell?

Probably unheard of in the Java world, 'DLL hell' is a common problem faced by COM developers. A DLL can be treated like a library component which contains methods to be used by other DLL or EXE files. In the COM world, you can have many unrelated programs calling methods from the same shared DLL file. Now, the rule is that you can update a DLL by releasing a newer version of the DLL with the same name. That means that your new DLL file must contain the same method signatures as the older one so that they can still be invoked by current applications using that shared DLL. You can change the encapsulated logic within the existing methods, or add in new methods, but the old method signatures must remain intact if existing applications are not to be broken.

In the COM days, DLLs could not be versioned – you might have been able to deduce the relative newness of a DLL by examining its date, but that was it. When a new version of `MySharedLibrary.dll` was to be rolled out, you usually replaced the existing one on your local PC with the newer file. Theoretically speaking, existing applications dependent on version 1 should not break, but the truth is that many problems arose due to incompatibility. What's worse is that some installation programs simply overrode shared DLLs in the system folder without bothering to check if the date of the existing DLL was newer than the one being installed (this will definitely break newer applications using the newer version of the shared DLL previously installed).[3]

This scenario is popularly known as 'DLL hell' in the Microsoft world.

And that's also why Microsoft has designed .NET assemblies to be versionable. Shared assemblies of different versions sharing the same name can exist in the same folder. Furthermore, applications using these shared assemblies are tied to specific versions of the assemblies. So, in the .NET world you can have version 1 and version 2 of the `MySharedLibrary.dll` shared assembly existing in the same folder on the same server. They have the same name but different version numbers recorded in their manifest file. So, `MyApplication1.exe`, which uses version 1 of `MySharedLibrary.dll`, will continue to use that version even when some installer puts version 2 of `MySharedLibrary.dll` into the system. The additional hard disk space required to store multiple versions of a .NET assembly is relatively small and definitely worth the trouble caused by DLL hell of COM times.

Another improvement of .NET assemblies over traditional COM DLLs is the inclusion of a hash code in the manifest. The assembly will work only if the .NET runtime has verified that the assembly hasn't been altered. An alteration will produce a new hash code which mismatches the one recorded in the assembly's manifest.

F.4 Creating DLL assemblies using `csc.exe`

If you are using `csc.exe`, you will need to know how to reference classes coded in other assemblies using the `/reference` option.

Let's say you have two classes, called `MyClass1` and `MyClass2`, in separate source files.[4] `MyClass1` creates a new instance of `MyClass2` in its `Main` method.

```
1: // MyClass1.cs
2: public class MyClass1{
3:   public static void Main(){
4:     MyClass2 mc2 = new MyClass2();
5:     System.Console.WriteLine(mc2.Add(3,4));
6:   }
7: }
```

3. Of course, such brutal installation programs can only be written by lousy programmers. But, alas, the world is full of lousy programmers.

4. Of course, you can put them into the same source file and no referring will be required. But I am trying to show how you can reference something coded in another source file (which will eventually be compiled into a separate assembly).

```
1: // MyClass2.cs - in separate source file
2: public class MyClass2{
3:    public int Add (int a, int b){
4:       return a + b;
5:    }
6: }
```

You need to compile `MyClass2.cs` into a DLL assembly. It cannot be an EXE assembly since it doesn't contain a `Main` method, and hence isn't 'executable'.

Use the `/target:library`[5] option to compile `MyClass2.cs` into `MyClass2.dll`:

```
c:\expt>csc /target:library MyClass2.cs
```

When you compile `MyClass1.cs`, make sure you reference `MyClass2.dll` like this:

```
c:\expt>csc /reference:MyClass2.dll MyClass1.cs
```

Try compiling without the `/reference:MyClass2.dll` switch and the compiler will complain that `MyClass2` is an unknown symbol.

You can reference multiple DLLs when compiling a single C# source file by separating them with commas:

```
/reference:MyClass2.dll,MyClass3.dll,MyClass4.dll.
```

You can also combine multiple source files into a single DLL assembly. The following command will compile both source files and put the resultant IL codes into a single DLL assembly called `MyClass2.dll`:

```
c:\expt>csc /target:library MyClass2.cs MyClass3.cs
```

F.5 Compiling to modules

Instead of compiling your source file into an assembly, you can also compile it into a module (`.netmodule` file). You can compile a C# source file into a module using the `/target:module` option. The following commands will generate `Class1.netmodule` and `Class2.netmodule` from their respective source files:

```
c:\expt>csc /target:module Class1.cs
c:\expt>csc /target:module Class2.cs
```

5. You can use `/t` instead of `/target`. `/t` is a shortcut.

To link both modules into a single DLL assembly, you can do this:

```
c:\expt>al /out:Class3.dll Class1.netmodule Class2.netmodule
```

AL.exe (Assembly Linker[6]) is a tool which generates a file with an assembly manifest from one or more files that are either modules or resource files.

F.6 Referencing an external module during compilation of an assembly

You have seen how to use the /reference:AssemblyName.dll option of csc.exe to reference an assembly. What happens if the method or class you want to use is not in an assembly, but in a module instead? You cannot reference a module which is not in the same assembly, but you can *add* that module in the new assembly you are generating during compilation.

Here's an example. It will compile MyMath.cs into a module instead of an assembly.

```
1: // MyMath.cs
2: public class MyMath{
3:    public static int Triple(int a){
4:      return a*3;
5:    }
6: }
```

The following command generates MyMath.netmodule:

```
c:\expt>csc /target:module MyMath.cs
```

Another class, MyClass.cs, invokes the static method in MyMath:

```
1: // MyClass.cs
2: public class MyClass{
3:    public static void Main(){
4:      System.Console.WriteLine(MyMath.Triple(1));
5:    }
6: }
```

As expected, during a normal compilation, you get a compiler error.

```
c:\expt>csc MyClass.cs
```

6. Also known as the Assembly Generation Tool in Microsoft documentation.

```
MyClass.cs(4,30): error CS0246: The type or namespace name
'MyMath' could not be found (are you missing a using directive
or an assembly reference?)
```

If you try to use the /reference flag to reference a module, it still doesn't work:

```
c:\expt>csc /reference:MyMath.netmodule MyClass.cs
error CS1509: Referenced file 'C:\expt\MyMath.netmodule' is not
an assembly; use '/addmodule' option instead
```

Use the /addmodule option to include the module into your class during compilation:

```
c:\expt>csc /addmodule:MyMath.netmodule MyClass.cs
```

Compilation should work, and MyClass.exe runs.

Note that the codes in MyMath.netmodule are not really physically inserted into MyClass.exe but rather referenced as an external resource. If you delete MyMath.netmodule, MyClass.exe will no longer be able to execute.

You can use the /addmodule option together with the /target:library flag to generate a DLL assembly instead of an EXE assembly.

Abbreviations used in this book

Abbreviations and acronyms figure prominently in computer literature. Rather than define them on first use (and then have difficulty finding a definition again) all those used in this book are defined in Table G.1.

TABLE G.1   Abbreviations used in this book

ADO .NET	ActiveX Data Objects .NET
API	Application Programming Interface
ASP	Active Server Pages
BCL	Base Class Library
CCW	COM Callable Wrapper
CF	(.NET) Compact Framework
CIL	Common Intermediate Language
CLI	Common Language Infrastructure
CLR	Common Language Runtime
CLS	Common Language Specification
COM	Component Object Model
CORBA	Common Object Request Broker Architecture
CTS	Common Type System
DCOM	Distributed COM
DLL	Dynamic Link Library
DNA	Distributed interNetwork Architecture
ECMA	European Computer Manufacturer's Association
EJB	Enterprise JavaBean
FIFO	First in, First out
GAC	Global Assembly Cache
GDI+	Graphical Device Interface+
GUI	Graphical User Interface
IDE	Integrated Development Environment
IDL	Interface Definition Language
IIOP	Internet Inter-ORB Protocol
IIS	Internet Information Server

(Continued)

TABLE G.1 Continued

IL	Intermediate Language
I/O	Input/Output
J2EE	Java 2 platform, Enterprise Edition
J2ME	Java 2 platform, Micro Edition
JAXP	Java API for XML Processing
JCP	Java Community Process
JCW	Java Callable Wrapper
JDBC	Java Database Connectivity
JDK	Java Development Kit
JIT	Just-in-time
JLCA	Java Language Conversion Assistant
JMS	Java Messaging Service
JNI	Java Native Interface
JRE	Java Runtime Environment
JRMP	Java Remote Method Protocol
JSP	JavaServer Pages
JUMP	Java User Migration Path
JVM	Java Virtual Machine
LIFO	Last in, First out
MFC	Microsoft Foundation Classes
MSIL	Microsoft Intermediate Language
MSMQ	Microsoft Message Queue
MTS	Microsoft Transaction Server
OO	Object-oriented
PDA	Personal Digital Assistant
PE	Portable Executable
RMI	Remote Method Invocation
SDE	Smart Device Extension
SDK	Software Development Kit
SOAP	Simple Object Access Protocol
SSI	Single Sign-In
UCS	Universal Character Set
UDDI	Universal Description, Discovery and Integration
UML	Unified Modeling Language
UNC	Universal Naming Convention
URL	Uniform Resource Locator
UTF	UCS Transformation Format
VB .NET	Visual Basic .NET
VB 6	Visual Basic 6
VS .NET	Visual Studio .NET
WSDL	Web Services Description Language
XML	Extensible Markup Language

index